D1124558

Organizing Through Division and Exclusion

China's Hukou System

FEI-LING WANG

Organizing Through Division and Exclusion

China's Hukou System

STANFORD UNIVERSITY PRESS 2005

Stanford, California

Stanford University Press
Stanford, California
© 2005 by the Board of Trustees of the
Leland Stanford Junior University

Library of Congress Cataloging-in-Publication Data

Wang, Fei-Ling.
    Organizing through division and exclusion : China's *hukou*
system / Fei-Ling Wang.
        p. cm.
    Includes bibliographical references and index.
    ISBN 0-8047-5039-4 (alk. paper)
    1. Social institutions—China. 2. Recording and
registration—China. 3. Economic development-China.
4. China-Social conditions—2000–. I. Title.
HN733.5.W3623 2005
306'.0951—dc22   2004014568

Printed in the United States of America
Original Printing 2005
Last figure below indicates year of this printing:
14   13   12   11   10   09   08   07   06   05

Typeset at Stanford University Press in 10/13 Sabon

TO YAN, YVONNE, AND JUSTIN

Acknowledgments

As a member of the last group of urban youth "sent down" to the countryside, I experienced at first hand the ubiquity and power of the *hukou* (household registration) system as a teenager in China. My academic interest in the subject, however, started to develop later, when I was studying political economy and development issues at the University of Pennsylvania in the late 1980s and early 1990s. Writing my Ph.D. dissertation and thereafter books on China's modernization and labor allocation offered me a chance to begin collecting materials on the *hukou* system. For the early construction of the conceptual and analytical framework used in this book, I am personally indebted to my teachers and advisors at Penn: Thomas Callaghy, Francine Frankel, Avery Goldstein, Joanne Gowa, and Friedrich Kratochwil.

I have enjoyed wonderful support from my colleagues and students at Georgia Institute of Technology ever since I began working on the *hukou* system in the mid-1990s. I want especially to thank William Long for his specific help. The Sam Nunn School of International Affairs has provided me leave time and valuable logistic support.

My numerous field research trips and my writing of this book have had the benefit of financial support from the Georgia Tech Foundation, the Board of Regents of the University System of Georgia, the Georgia Tech Center for International Business Education and Research, the Coca-Cola Foundation, the East Asian Institute of the National University of Singapore, the Francis Wood Wilson Foundation, the Chinese Economist Society, and the Renmin University of China.

It is impossible to write a book on the *hukou* system without the help of many friends and anonymous interviewees in China. The following people deserve special recognition: Duan Huaqia, Li Canli, Li Feihu, Li Wei, Wang Feihong, Wang Shuobai, and Zhang Nan of Anhui; Li Lei, Li Qiang, Li Qiusheng, Ma Fuyun, Qin Saiyu, Ren Qimin, Song Xinning, Zhang Xiaojin, Xie Zheping, Zhang Yan, and Zhang Yaowu of Beijing; Li Xing, Yang Weihong, and Zhao Chengping of Chongqing; Chen Yongjun and Zeng Huaiquan of Fujian; Bai Li, Chen Ping, Lin Hong, Tang Jinping, Wang Junshi, and Yao Shujie of Guangdong; Fang Zhuangzhi and Li Ang of Hubei; Liu Minquan, Sun Hui, and Wang Guanying of Jiangsu; Yan Xiaochuan of Liaoning; Cai Cuihong, Chen Xiaodan, Guo Henchui, Guo Lin, Miao Qiuchen, Sha Hailin, Sheng Fumin, Sun Qi, Zhang Liming, and Zhang Wangyao of Shanghai; Chen Yuan, Ge Bin, and Li Changan of Shangxi; Liu Yonghao and Shi Jian of Sichuan; Tai Lingjuan of Tianjin; Lu Zaihua and Bao Desheng of Xinjiang; Shi Benzhi and Zhang Guangping of Yunnan; and Zhao Qianqian of Zhejiang.

Danielle Caminha, Jose Filho, Andriana Sampaio, and Tatiana Souza showed me Brazil and especially its *favelas*. Lily Chorei, Philix Gerald, and Eswaran Sridharen helped me to observe the caste system in India. Heona Loshakova, Andrei Muchnik, Maria Rubanovskaya, and Suchova Valentina guided me in Russia. Bao Wen-lee, Chang Ya-ting, Maggy Chien, Kawai Ayako, Kobayashi Azusa, Mun Yun-Jun, Paik Hak-Soon, Shinko Takahashi, and Wu Sou-chang assisted me in seeing the urban and rural lives in Japan, Korea, and Taiwan.

The late Robert Warren Barnett (1915–97) personally encouraged my work on the *hukou* system. Mary Axford, Kirk Bowman, Tiejun Cheng, Zhiyuan Cui, Usha Nair-Reichert, Elspeth Thomson, and Aselia Urmanbetova helped with my research. Thomas Bernstein, Keith Forster, Xiaobo Lu, Ian Malcolm, Suzanne Ogden, Dorothy Sollinger, and John Wong read and commented on parts of the manuscript. Andrea Littman, Austin Long, and Yvonne Wang edited the chapters. The external readers of the manuscript provided thorough and very valuable comments. Muriel Bell, Carmen Borbón-Wu, John Feneron, and copyeditor Paul Psoinos at Stanford University Press finally made this book possible. Any remaining errors, needless to say, are all mine.

Finally, as always, I am extraordinarily lucky and deeply grateful to have the love, patience, understanding, and support of my family.

F.L.W.

Marietta, Georgia

Contents

Tables and Figures

Tables

Figures

Preface

Let us consider this scenario. You are a citizen in your own country. Like the majority of the population (74 percent in 2000),[1] you were born in a village to a registered agricultural family. Like most of the people in the village, you learned only some basic work skills through the minimal education available and affordable before growing up. You could no longer make a decent living in your home village because of the increasing scarcity of land, water, and capital,[2] and the rising life expectations powered by movies and especially television.[3] You learned that there was a different, prosperous, and far superior world in the cities not too far away, and you endured all the hardships to get there—only to find that you were no longer exactly in your own country and your citizenship was clearly incomplete.[4]

You cannot vote in the cities, regardless of how long you have lived there. You cannot apply for most of the jobs there—the good jobs often explicitly require a permanent local residency that can be had only by grant of the authorities.[5] Without a permanent local residency, you and your children cannot go to local public schools for the compulsory state-subsidized education and cannot take part in the easier college entrance exam and admission process in the city. You cannot enjoy a host of urban benefits and subsidies in medical care, housing, job training, and social welfare programs, nor even public library access and phone services. You may be jobless, but you are not even counted as unemployed by the government, and thus you are completely outside the relief and assistance programs.[6] Once you quit the only jobs—usually dirty, heavy, exhausting, low-paying jobs—that you could find in the cities,[7] or the jobs more easily found in the so-called special professions and industries,[8] you soon lose your temporary residence permit and are subject to fines, detention, and forced deportation for further stay.[9] You are openly looked down upon by your countrymen who have local urban residency. You can never expect to marry one of those privileged urbanites unless you are rich or else attractive and lucky.[10]

To legally acquire permanent local residency in an urban center as someone from the countryside, you must be wealthy enough to invest or spend at least a few dozen times your annual income or educated with at least an undergraduate degree, and you must have available to you an in-migrant quota slot (nationally set at a very low 0.2 percent of the total rural population annually in 2000).[11] Otherwise, you must be a sports star or a national hero. Only if you are able to show your assets and your talents by elevating yourself through such narrow governmentally defined channels can you acquire transitional urban legal residence and become an elite urban resident within a few years. Indeed, virtually all the country's political, military, economic, cultural, and social leaders are urban residents.

Perhaps you will feel a strange consolation seeing other newcomers, even people from other cities who are officially categorized as urban residents, also treated as second-class citizens in your particular city. You may try to complain, or you may even want to find out how many others share your grievances and your desire to do something about the discrimination that you encounter: then you will quickly be put on a secret list of targeted people (*zhongdian renkou*) and be watched by an army of police, local residents, and informants both professional and amateur, all using an increasingly sophisticated surveillance technology . . .

Is this scenario realistic in the twenty-first century? you may wonder. Yes, it is. It is actual daily life in the People's Republic of China (PRC), the most populous nation in the world, under the PRC's *hukou* or *huji* (household or residential registration) system. The *hukou* system profoundly shapes the life chances of 1.3 billion Chinese people by registering, segmenting, and dividing them in their various regions, especially along the urban-rural fault line. Interregional migration and population mobility are controlled and regulated; people's rights and opportunities differ according to where they are registered; yet the interregional borders are open to travelers, and a centralized political authority nationally enforces laws and regulations and redistributes some income. The Chinese people are thus organized through a peculiar, profound division that mimics a truncated Westphalia international system based on citizenship: people are treated differently in accordance with where their legal residency is, and the change and relocation of any citizen's legal residency must be approved by the government.

This book is about China's *hukou* system, especially the PRC's version of it. The PRC *hukou* system, as a qualitatively different sequel to the imperial versions of China's *hukou* system, is a unique form of institutional exclusion that divides and organizes the largest nation on earth according to officially differentiated and registered families and locations. It is a proven and traditional mechanism of Chinese statecraft ensuring political stability and social control under an authoritarian regime. It has contributed significantly to rapid but uneven economic growth and technological sophistication, acting as a leading cause of China's peculiar socioeconomic stratification and characteristics, a key factor shaping China's institutional framework and future, and a major source of China's injustice, inequality, and irrationality.

This book has seven chapters. Chapter 1, a general introduction, proposes a theory of institutional exclusion and examines specifically the inevitability, typology, and implications of institutional exclusion. It also provides an overview of China's *hukou* system, and especially the PRC version of it, as a Type 3 institutional exclusion (based on *where one is*), summarizes the main arguments and findings of the book, and discusses the methodology and terminology of this study and issues remaining for further ones.

Chapter 2 traces the origin of China's *hukou* system, outlines the evolution of the imperial *hukou* system before the mid-twentieth century, and describes the rationale and development of the PRC *hukou* system. It reports on the adaptation of the PRC *hukou* system in the reform era and explains the deep legitimacy of the *hukou* system in contemporary China.

Chapter 3 explores the PRC *hukou* system in depth. It describes and examines the operational mechanisms of the *hukou* system in detail and presents the key registration forms and the data available on the PRC *hukou* system, as well as field observations of its administration.

Chapter 4 describes the institutional and policy role of the PRC *hukou* system by exploring its two leading functions: the internal migration regulations and the focused management of targeted segments of the population. It examines the principles and methods of internal migration restrictions, reports on the *zhongdian renkou* (targeted people) management scheme, and outlines recent adaptive measures regarding these two functions.

Chapter 5 describes the profound impact of the PRC *hukou* system on Chinese politics, economic development, and social life. It reveals the unique *hukou*-based horizontal stratification or spatial hierarchy in the PRC and analyzes the impact, both positive and negative, that the *hukou* system has had on China's economic development. It also presents a case study of the impact of the PRC *hukou* system by examining China's college entrance examination and admission system.

Chapter 6 attempts a comparative analysis of institutional exclusion in general and the *hukou* system in particular. It briefly reports on *hukou*-like residential registration, identification, and internal migration control systems in other parts of the world. It specifically examines and compares the cases of India and Brazil in some detail and assesses the *hukou* system and the general nature and functions of institutional exclusion.

Chapter 7 reports the latest ideas and actions regarding the reform of the PRC *hukou* system in the 2000s and offers some concluding remarks about the system's future.

A Postscript

Four months after my article on the *hukou* system was published (*China Quarterly*, March 2004) and four days after I learned that the proof pages of this book were ready for me to read, on July 25, 2004, on my way back from directing Georgia Tech's Summer Program in China, I was suddenly detained by the Chinese State Security (SS) police in Shanghai. They held me secretly for two weeks and then deported me to punish me for my "bad attitude" and my "non-cooperation."

A major cause of my ordeal, as I learned from my interrogators, was my work on China's *hukou* system. The SS police either had been attentively following my work in English or had had the assistance of informers who know my work. Their strong hatred towards my work on the *hukou* system was very apparent. As a key issue of their questioning, the SS police insisted that I must have had "insiders in the Chinese government" giving me "state secrets." Apparently, they did not read my work carefully or their informers were doing a very poor job.

People pay all kinds of prices for academic explorations and scientific discoveries, and I have had my fair share of that for this book. However, spending time inside the secret jail of the Chinese SS police and fighting them ever since for justice are costs and causes I never planned would be part of my academic exploration of the *hukou* system.

Organizing Through Division and Exclusion

China's Hukou System

CHAPTER ONE

Institutional Exclusion and the Case of China

Humankind is organized and divided at the same time: division and stratification[1] are the sole means whereby nations are organized.[2] How the people are divided and stratified and how they are organized determine the fundamental features of a particular nation's institutional setting, way of life, record of performance and achievement, and standing in international comparison and competition.[3] Hierarchy, inequality, exclusion, and discrimination are some of the inevitable by-products of human organization through division.

China is no exception. As "something akin to a laboratory for social science,"[4] China has organized its people through various divisions for millennia. A key component of China's internal organizational structure today is the *hukou* or *huji* (household or residential registration) system. This book intends to explore the Chinese *hukou* system, especially its current version in the People's Republic of China (PRC), to examine this peculiar way of organizing a people through institutional division and exclusion.

To examine this peculiarly *Chinese hukou* system will require constructing a conceptual framework wherewith to put it under a theoretical microscope. Accordingly the mission of this chapter will be to synthesize existing theories and concepts of human organization and division and to establish analytical guidelines for an exploration of the *hukou* system. I will first discuss the universality of human division and then propose a theory of institutional exclusion, describing four basic types thereof and their various implications. I will argue that, even though the four types are in practice often difficult to rank and ethically impossible to praise, some types of institutional exclusion may be functionally more desirable than others in facilitating economic development and technological so-phistication through, among other ways, an effective circumvention of the so-called Lewis Transition in heavily populated developing nations.

China's *hukou* system, especially the PRC (1949–present) version of it, is viewed in this book as a Type 3 institutional exclusion (based on *where one is*) that has forced so many Chinese to suffer exclusion and discrimi-nation for so long while yet contributing significantly to China's so-ciopolitical stability and economic growth. It is my hope that this study of the *hukou* system may help test hypotheses about institutional exclu-sion and assertions about Chinese political economy and contribute, be-sides, to a theoretical understanding of human organization and division. Naturally, a reader who is interested mainly in the details of China's *hukou* system but not necessarily my theorizing efforts may choose sim-ply to skip the first half of this chapter.

In addition to an analytical and theoretical framework, this chapter provides an overview of China's *hukou* system, summarizes this book's main arguments and findings, and discusses its methodology and termi-nology, as well as issues remaining for further study of the *hukou* system.

Human Organization: The Inevitability of Division and Exclusion

The need for grouping and organizing people is self-evident insofar as the division of labor is the source of the human power allowing civiliza-tion.[5] Furthermore, all resources (including the human), being limited, need to be organized and allocated efficiently. No human organization can be achieved without dividing people into subgroups, necessarily ex-cluding some in the process.

Students of politics, economics, and sociology have attempted to chart and explain various forms of human organization and division from var-ious perspectives. Policy makers and their advisors have tended to focus particularly on the consequences of various systems for managing and modifying these divisions and organizations. Schools of thought have hence been born.[6] Political economists and philosophers from Adam Smith to Émile Durkheim discussed the inevitability and repercussions, primarily human specialization and stratification, of the division of labor as the foundation of society.[7] Later scholars advanced such theses by ap-plying analyses of transaction costs and asset-specificity,[8] or descriptions of education's role in social stratification.[9] In an effort to develop a unified or general sociobiology, thinkers of our own time have attempted to identify the common biological and evolutionary roots of hierarchical social organization with more or less structured and fixed divisions of labor in insect, vertebrate, and human populations.[10]

Vertical stratification—class structure—along the fault lines of property rights and income has been described by the various branches of socialism and acquired its widest recognition in the ideology of Marxism. Vertical stratification based on economic differences—class division—is viewed as the most fundamental division of humankind and the most important organizing principle in any human grouping.[11] Absorbing and modifying Marxist insights, and utilizing sociopsychological findings, a Weberian analysis of social structuration—and especially of its geographically based regionalization and time-specific evolution—can open new horizons for exploring how humans are divided and organized.[12]

Political scientists commonly believe that national boundaries, politically determined by states and separating people into nations, are the most fundamental divides of exclusive human groupings.[13] "Globalization," wrote a group of international organization officials, "is making national citizenship increasingly salient as a social status," endowing those within national boundaries with more or less uniform and equal treatment under the particular citizenship.[14] Among nations, today's citizenship-based socioeconomic stratification, division, and exclusion are perhaps among the most rigid and effective that ever existed in humankind.[15]

Thinkers concerned with what they refer to as the "moral economy" have described different forms of human division and organization with regard to the market economy.[16] Attitudes toward and accommodations of certain inherent or acquired human rights may offer another perspective on the varying patterns of human division and organization.[17] People of greatly divergent backgrounds—members of racist organizations, genocidal murderers, cultural anthropologists, religious fundamentalists, famous scholars—have used religion, culture, language, race, ethnicity, even the vague concept "civilization" itself, to describe groups, divisions, and interactions among human beings within single nations or beyond.[18] Technology and the access to it provide yet another important category in which to view differentiation and linkage among people: here we find a division of enlightened versus uneducated, the so-called digital divide.[19]

Finally, how particular political systems make their decisions—the rule of one, the few, or the many—is frequently cited as the chief differential of human society. A nation is organized politically as one of three kinds—

dictatorship, authoritarian regime, or democracy[20]—featuring different relationships between rulers and ruled, or between the political elite and the masses. The relationship between political democracy and economic growth has hence become a central theme in the study of political economy.[21]

A Theory of Institutional Exclusion

Human organization through division necessarily produces institutional exclusion. Institutional division and exclusion refer to the fundamental fact of any human grouping: people are divided and then organized into hierarchical layers and horizontally coexisting but separated subgroups. By using the word "institutional," I mean to recognize that these divisions and exclusions are not random, ad hoc, or isolated—that, rather, they are stable, consistent, and systematic, and that they are often written into the law of the land and enforced by the state.[22] Institutional exclusion is a concept similar to but broader than the notion of "social exclusion" that has been used in studying poverty, marginalization, polarization, discrimination, dualism, and the breakdown of social cohesion and state capacity.[23] In addition to capturing the negative side of social exclusion, the concept of institutional exclusion also refers to less normative but highly consequential aspects of human division, stratification, and organization. The concept of institutional exclusion is comparable to the neo-Weberian sociologists' notion of "social closure" that describes human stratification systems as based on various fault lines in any society: for example, property, age, gender, ethnicity, skills, or educational credentials.[24]

The universality of institutional divisions is easily seen, whereas institutional exclusion may often be underexposed. In fact, conceptually and empirically, institutional division and institutional exclusion are inseparable: to divide is, by definition, to exclude and to discriminate. These two concepts, therefore, can be used almost interchangeably even though they may be emphasized differently at times. In this book, I will use the concept of institutional exclusion more frequently, both for the sake of brevity and in order to emphasize the nature and functions of institutional division and exclusion.[25]

As Jean-Jacques Rousseau has argued, human beings developed inequalities among themselves as part of their civilized or organized history.[26] Other than in a nuclear family or a very small group that can be dominated by body politic alone, to include everyone and to discriminate against no one remains a noble ideal, in practice impossible in any human society. The issue, then, is not the existence or absence of institutional exclusion; rather, it is the varied types and enforcement mechanisms of institutional exclusion that determine the differing divisions and organizations of people in different nations and at different times.

To theorize institutional exclusion engages the rich literature on citizenship and membership.[27] Indeed, on the most fundamental level, citizenship and membership represent a formal and lasting form of institutional exclusion. All human groupings first identify their members and treat their own more or less equally but others—outsiders or the excluded—very differently. I go further in arguing that within any nation, institutional exclusion necessarily and constantly exists to divide the citizenry along various fault lines. Citizenship represents the most marked, most common institutional exclusion at the international level; yet subnational institutional divisions and exclusions also cut across national borders.

There is always one paramount fault line in our view of any nation that is both divided and organized: the divide between those who are "in," having "access to institutions that provide capacities and resources" as well as information,[28] and those who are "out," excluded from such institutionalized provisions.[29] Although life chances based on the distribution of capacities, resources, and information that enables and improves human life may be affected by many nonuniform but important factors such as genetics, any one human grouping (a nation, in particular) must by definition have some more or less uniform and even centralized way of such distribution to ensure its own cohesion and viability. Unevenly distributed capacities and resources, in turn, ultimately shape the people's sense of ranking and belonging, and hence form the normative social fabric that at once separates and divides everyone while yet linking and organizing them.

Institutionalized divisive and exclusive barriers, or institutional division and exclusion, are among the most fundamental rules, regulations, and behavioral norms and codes defining and constraining people's movements, access rights, and interactions. They are part and parcel of any nation's basic institutional arrangement. Created by legislation or by tradition, existing formally or informally, and enforced primarily by the state, institutional exclusion emerges or is imposed to divide and organize people, to manage and allocate resources, including labor, and to enable political and social control. All economically and politically stratified classes and layers and all culturally and socially separated or differentiated groups and associations are just subunits along this divide of inclusion versus exclusion in varying degrees.

Every sizable human grouping must exclude segments of its population for its polity to function, for its economy to develop, and for its society to be stable. For example, human societies have been long accustomed to the obvious inevitability and necessity of punishing some of their own members through exclusion (imprisonment), discrimination (public humiliation, fines), and even elimination (execution) to maintain law and order. The normative question, therefore, is not how to eliminate institutional exclusions but rather how to minimize the number and the suffering of the excluded. Even in small, supposedly egalitarian societies like the Israeli kibbutzim or tribal lands in Kenya, New Guinea, and Polynesia, equality is often found to be elusive, limited, and fragile, as rules and organization tend to create and maintain inequality and exclusion.[30] While the small citizenry of Athens, for example, achieved a high degree of equity in political participation, economic activities, and social life, a much larger segment of the total population—the slaves—was completely excluded.[31] Today's United States may have achieved a relatively high level of equity for its citizenry with conscientious antidiscrimination efforts of all kinds, yet the differences between the rich and the poor alone, for example, are among the most striking signs of institutional exclusion in human history. The combination of media influence and political power in the United States, both of which are heavily based on wealth, provides the necessary social control and sociopolitical organization via economically based institutional exclusion.

Institutional exclusions have historically developed along different boundaries of human subgroups within any mother grouping (a community, nation, or country) and have evolved over time. These boundaries may be ostensibly natural differences such as skin color, language, or family. Many of the dividing lines, such as national borders, citizenship, membership, legality and criminal punishment, and property ownership, are often man-made and politically enforced by the state.[32] On these varied boundaries, exclusive barriers emerge or are erected to separate people. These exclusive barriers differentiate, limit, reduce, or even eliminate the access of different groups and individuals to economic resources, social opportunities, and political processes. Institutional exclusions thus create unfairness and injustice for the excluded persons and subgroups, yet they perform crucial functions for the whole mother grouping to organize people, prioritize resource distribution, accumulate and invest capital, maintain public order and authority, and legitimize institutional changes. In the light of the basic assumption of economics that all resources are scarce and must be allocated, the inevitability of institutional exclusion is clearly axiomatic.

Primarily determined by its foundation, institutional exclusion in different human groupings and at different times can present itself very differently, producing different sociopolitical and economic consequences. We can easily identify the various institutional exclusions in history that are based on family rankings and lineage (nobles versus commoners; various caste systems), race and ethnicity (various forms of racial and ethnic exclusion and discrimination), citizenship (fellow countrymen versus foreigners), political power (rulers and ruled), legality (law-abiding citizens versus outlaws and criminals), religion (the chosen versus the infidel), economic power (the rich or the haves versus the poor or the have-nots), gender (various forms of sexual discrimination),[33] linguistic and cultural differences (Western versus Eastern, for example), group association (party membership versus nonmembers), personal skills (educated versus uneducated), and locational differences (community members versus outsiders). Some of these differences and dividing lines are factually based, whereas many may be merely perceived or indoctrinated. These fault lines may be thought to be created by nature, as with genetic characteristics, but often they are the creations of political power dependent upon sheer force (as in the case of war or coup d'état) or majority will (as in the case of functional democracy).

In most nations we can find more than one type of institutional exclusion, as few societies are stratified by only one fault line.[34] But in any given nation, institutional exclusion is primarily based on one leading fault line, usually assisted by other types of less important but possibly significant differentiations and separations. Varied preexisting institutions and cultures, divergent political decisions, dissimilar natural endowments, and different stages of economic and technological development have caused different nations to have their own particular types of institutional exclusion at any given time. Different types of institutional exclusion naturally differ in their effectiveness and legitimacy, although they all perform the same three basic functions of dividing people, organizing the society, and prioritizing resource allocation. For example, as economically based institutional exclusion (i.e., exclusion centered in property rights) has become more widely accepted after the end of the Cold War, we see that institutional exclusions based on gender, race, or ethnicity are becoming ever less legitimate and hence ever less effective around the world.

Any nation may manifest different leading institutional exclusions in the different arenas of politics, economy, and social life. In countries like the United States, citizenship and local residency are required for participating in political activities such as elections and government employment, whereas ownership of resources—capital, goods, or skills—is all that is needed for economic transactions. However, economic resources have often been translated into political power, and political power often easily obtains resources, so both are means whereby one person or subgroup can cohesively, effectively, and even simultaneously change his or its overall political and economic position. In social life, although money and political power often cannot overcome divides based on race, language, or religion, the economic divide and the related political differentiation seem to be solidly leading forms of institutional exclusion concerning social stratification in the United States.[35]

Other nations, particularly those with less differentiated domestic organizational structures,[36] may simply employ one main fault line to divide and exclude people in all aspects of life. Their institutional exclusions can be surprisingly simple, based in monolithic divisions. In some countries, social castes have always been very important determining factors for people's life chances in politics, economy, and social life. In countries featuring theocratic regimes, particular religious teachings are the basis on which people are divided, excluded, and discriminated against. In such cases, even the powerful penetrating force of the market is ineffective in shaping people's political rank or social stratification. In China, the *hukou* system serves as the basis for a nationally uniform institutional exclusion with a scope, rigidity, effectiveness, and resilience rarely seen elsewhere.

In short, institutional exclusion, often centered on one leading fault line that is usually assisted by other differences, divides and organizes the people in any given nation. It functions in very important ways to construct and maintain sociopolitical order and stability, to formulate and allocate capital and other economic resources, and thus directly to impact economic development and affect everyone's sense and position of rank and belonging, hence determining social stratification. Various types of institutional exclusion are effective, legitimate, flexible, and persistent in varying degrees. The role of the state is generally crucial to the creation, enforcement, and perpetuation of an institutional exclusion; yet some types of institutional exclusion can function as if autonomously, even contravening political decisions, especially when the state is weak or ineffective. Although a particular nation may have only a single uniform division as its primary institutional exclusion, secondary divides often create complicated subgroupings and exclusive and discriminative barriers, which complement, enhance, and even occasionally replace the main form of institutional exclusion.

A Typology of Institutional Exclusion

Institutional exclusion being necessary and inevitable,[37] its varied effectiveness and consequences in different settings and times stem from the varied bases on which it is built and the different ways in which it is enforced. As a theorizing effort, I hypothesize that there are four major types of institutional exclusion, defined by their different bases. In Type 1, people are divided and excluded because of *who they are* in terms of their racial, ethnic, linguistic, sexual, and religious differences. Under Type 2, people are divided and excluded based on *what they have* regarding their skills and ownership of resources or property. Type 3 allows people to be divided and excluded based on *where they are* in regard to their family associations and their physical location or birthplace. Type 4 divides and excludes people based on *what they have done or do* or their individual work and behavior.[38]

Type 1 institutional exclusion, based on *who one is*, has been very commonly practiced in human history. It includes numerous exclusions and discriminations against racial and ethnic minorities and individuals and groups based on their inherent or inherited characteristics such as age, gender, and family titles. This type of institutional exclusion is easy to maintain because its fault lines are self-evident and thus fairly stable and sustainable. Yet, precisely because of its clear-cut criteria and wholesale nature, having little to do with individual ability and performance, Type 1 institutional exclusion leads to grossly irrational allocation of resources, especially the human resource, and allows enormous waste of human talent. In the era of industrialization, this type of institutional exclusion tends to be economically noncompetitive and inefficient. The economically important slavery system of the United States, for example, had started to run out its string in the South even before the Civil War de-

TABLE I.I

Institutional Exclusion: A Typology

Type	Type 1	Type 2	Type 3	Type 4
Discrimination and exclusion based on	*Who you are*	*What you have*	*Where you are*	*What you do/did*
Example	caste in India	money in U.S.	*hukou* in China	criminal justice systems
Chief enforcer	societal forces	the market	the state	the state
Reliance on the state	can be low	can be low	high	high
Stability	high	low	adjustable	adjustable
Rigidity	high	low	adjustable	adjustable
Current legitimacy	low	high	medium	high
Current effectiveness	low and decentralized	high and increasing	can be high	can be high
Cost of enforcement	low[a]	low	high	high
Leading impact	racial/social biases	economic classes	spatial/regional gaps	job/record biases
Effect on economic development	negative	positive	can be positive	can be positive
Functional/elite democracy	possible	possible	possible	possible
Restriction of internal migration	medium	medium/low	high	medium/low

[a]Contemporarily, it is inexpensive for the societal forces to maintain decentralized a Type 1 institutional exclusion but increasingly costly for the state to maintain it as a centralized national system.

stroyed it.[39] Type 1 institutional exclusion also creates some of the deepest, most rigid, and most painful social injustice and personal damage to the excluded in human history. As a result, resistance to Type 1 institutional exclusion tends to be lasting and powerful. Open and covert rebellions often damage or even destroy this type of institutional exclusion and the whole attached institutional framework. In an era of social progress and global awareness of human rights, Type 1 institutional exclusion is typically and universally criticized, and it is hence costly to maintain as a national system today. The collapse of the apartheid regime in South Africa is a good example. The existence of Type 1 institutional exclusion, however, remains widespread and can be powerful in individual cases, though it is clearly less uniform and is highly informal, even unlawful.

Type 2 institutional exclusion, based on *what one has* or one's economic power and rank, has been perhaps the most common and longest-lasting form of institutional exclusion in human civilization, and it is now perhaps the most uniform, most important form of institutional exclusion in almost all nations. Ostensibly based largely on the results of individuals' or groups' ability and performance in the economy, Type 2 is arguably the most efficient form of institutional exclusion with regard to resource allocation and economic development. It is less rigid than other types of institutional exclusion, apparently relying more on individual differentiation than on wholesale group categorization. Clearly questionable ethically and morally, Type 2 institutional exclusion has indeed often been criticized since the earliest records of civilization. Yet Type 2 institutional exclusion is the most widely accepted form and is perhaps the most easily enforced and the most cheaply maintained, especially after the collapse of the competing socialist or communist systems at the end of the Cold War in the early 1990s. Money sets people apart the world over, in just about every aspect of human life. Money also allows its owners or its handlers or managers to control and rule people and minds, even in so relatively open and democratic nations as the United States.[40]

Type 3 institutional exclusion, based on *where one is* or differences of location and association (usually created by birth and legal registration), is easy to identify and maintain but very rigid and difficult—hence costly—to enforce on a national scale. In essence, Type 3 institutional exclusion tends to divide people into not just two categories—those included and those excluded—but into numerous family-based or clan-based, regionally defined, and mutually exclusive groups. Type 3 institutional exclusion can be less rigid than Type 1, as the dividing lines upon which it is based—family residence and registration—are more flexible than the physical or caste differences supporting Type 1 institutional exclusions. Compared with Type 2, a Type 3 institutional exclusion is less efficient, as it divides people into a multiplicity of subgroups and prevents national labor mobility, and thus creating irrationality and wastefulness in the allocation of human resources. But in those latecomer developing nations, which I will discuss later, a Type 3 institutional exclusion may have a uniquely positive impact on economic development. This type of institutional exclusion is generally insignificant in developed nations, where residential registration is now automatic and family roots or home town address are often irrelevant to one's career and sociopolitical and economic rank.

Type 4 institutional exclusion, based on *what one has done or does*, mostly excludes or discriminates against people based on their past actions or current work and behavior. Outlaws and criminals are the most common examples of those who are institutionally excluded under this type, but job-related social biases and prejudices are also easily observed in almost any society. Type 4 institutional exclusion, generally targeting persons or small groups, is issue-specific and time-specific, and is often the consequence of a person's willing choice, as in the case of convicts. It is highly flexible, dependent upon changeable criminal codes, social tolerance, and police efficiency. It may frequently expand to cover a whole group of people permanently, thus becoming a Type 1 institutional exclusion, as is exemplified in certain professionally defined low-caste families in India or the belittled hereditary handcraft households in ancient China. It may also merge with the fault line between the haves and the have-nots to become a Type 2 institutional exclusion, as is illustrated by discrimination toward workers who have been compelled by poverty to accept work that is thought of as indecent. Type 4 institutional exclusion may be viewed as an offshoot or secondary institutional exclusion, since the idea of what is legal or respectable is primarily derived from the norms of the dominant institutional exclusion of the nation.[41] Although it exists in every nation and can be extremely significant and long-lasting for the excluded, Type 4 institutional exclusion is largely a time-specific consequence of individual choice or action and is not as rigid as the other three types, being thus less important to our conceptual exploration of national institutional exclusions.

The legitimacy and effectiveness of a particular institutional exclusion are linked directly to its foundational type and are affected by how it is created and enforced. All types of institutional exclusion need the political power of the state to emerge and function. Once created or legitimized by a ruler or government, however, different types of institutional exclusion tend to vary in their reliance on state power to continue; yet whether the state involved is stable, effective, and supportive always fundamentally determines the efficacy and strength of any institutional exclusion. Type 1 institutional exclusions may often be meaningfully enforced by societal forces in decentralized, unlawful, or even illegal ways, as is the caste system in today's India. But it is still at the mercy of the state, which, if strong and willing, can effectively dismantle even the oldest racial exclusions. Even such simple exclusionary barriers as are defined and protected by property rights, universally enforced in today's highly legitimized market economy, still rely ultimately on state enforcement. The more complicated types, such as residential registration or criminal sanction clearly require much more direct and forceful action on the part of the state. Force may indeed go a long way in maintaining an unpopular institutional exclusion; in the long run, however, education or indoctrination that helps to legitimize rules and norms is perhaps more important. Moreover, the power of the state as opposed to the society usually is key in determining the longevity and effectiveness of an illegal but societally maintained institutional exclusion.

Let us now examine a few empirical examples illustrating the four types of institutional exclusion as national phenomena. Type 4 institutional exclusion exists in every nation that has any prison population. Such religious fundamentalist regimes as those in Iran or in Afghanistan under the Taliban (1995–2001) are striking examples of national Type 1 institutional exclusion in our own time. The glorious Athenian civilization 2,500 years ago and the unprecedented American superpower today both exhibit institutional exclusion largely based on a Type 2 dividing line. Athens relied on the institutional exclusion of its slaves, who were treated as tools and subhuman property. But Greek slaves could buy their freedom if they had the money.[42] The United States relies mainly on its deep-rooted institutional exclusion of the poor, whose life chances are fundamentally reduced, limited, even annihilated by the dominance of wealth in American politics and social life.[43] China, perhaps the most notable example of Type 3 institutional exclusion, segregates the majority of its population according to administratively determined family origins and legal residence.

Implications of Institutional Exclusion

Institutional division and exclusion are both inevitable and consequential. How an institutional exclusion is built and enforced directly determines its stability and effectiveness, and especially its implications for the nation's political stability, economic growth, social development, and human rights. While it is often hard to distinguish the specific effects of an institutional exclusion from other causal factors, we can still try to analyze the general impact an effective institutional exclusion may have on a given nation's politics, economy, and social life.

The political implications of institutional division and exclusion are easy to see. No government can rule without some institutional exclusion to divide and organize the people. A stable institutional exclusion provides a nation with political and social order through which an effective public authority may be established and exercised. It allows for political rule at minimal administrative cost and for orderly organization of an unevenly developed and diverse nation by a centralized government. It creates segmented and thus manageable minienvironments for institutional experimentation and provides the time, space, and shock-absorbing cushion that ensures gradual but solid growth and legitimization of new institutions and norms.[44]

Institutional exclusion, by definition, creates conditions not particularly conducive to comprehensive democratic politics featuring mass participation in the political process. This is especially true in cases of rigid institutional exclusion based on some inherent and immutable differentiation (e.g., race, ethnicity, gender) of people and groups. The only possible form in which democracy can survive in a nation featuring a rigid institutional exclusion is so-called elite democracy, in which only a small group of people participate in and control the political process while keeping the excluded (e.g., slaves, women, the poor) out of the political arena. We may further hypothesize here that, in view of the inevitable necessity of institutional exclusion in any society, all functional democracies are essentially elite democracies with ruling elite groups of varying sizes and permeability, especially at their beginnings.[45] Conversely, to demand nonexclusive and massive political participation at the very time of creating a democratic regime may be fundamentally impractical and even counterproductive. Stable, lasting, and rigid institutional exclusions usually provide a fertile ground for authoritarianism and even totalitarianism with intervals of rebellions and revolutions. This is especially the case when the excluded become the majority of the population and there is no easy and reliable way to minimize the role of institutional exclusion in politics. Yet a functional and elite democracy may also develop and grow under an effective and even rigid institutional exclusion if other conditions and factors are in place.

Economically, institutional exclusion serves a key role in prioritizing resource allocation and the formulation or accumulation of capital.[46] It enables the state, the ruling elite, or the able citizens to accumulate capital relatively quickly, from the delayed, decreased, or even denied consumption of the excluded.[47] Institutional exclusion, with the implied concentration of decision-making power in the hands of the few haves, may effectively direct investment and the allocation of other resources for the purpose of profit or, in the case of a state-led effort, for certain economic development strategies or other economic policies. It also allows for segregated experiments and a protected trickle-down or spillover process of development through both the forward and the backward linkages of leading industries or sectors. "The equalization of returns to capital and labor solely through the movement of capital will result in the most efficient utilization of resources *given government restrictions on the movement of labor*," although there is always the pure-economics model arguing that "even higher efficiency" of resource utilization is possible if capital and labor are both moving freely.[48] Yet, given the inevitable and varied noneconomic needs served by institutional exclusions in any society, perhaps the empirically optimal efficiency (the so-called Pareto efficiency) in the real world is more desirable and attainable than the merely theoretical optimal efficiency (or maximum efficiency), which only exists in mathematical or econometric models. Therefore, institutional exclusion does not necessarily affect economic growth negatively. On the contrary, institutional exclusion, especially of the right kind, is often indispensable for economic growth. The history of economic development is, and perhaps has to be, colored with sweat, tears, even blood, mainly of those who are institutionally excluded.

Much of the social impact of an institutional exclusion can be inferred from its political and economic effects. Institutional exclusion provides social stability to a large nation, especially at a time of rapid economic development and cultural change. It forms solid groupings and associations beyond family and employment relations, allowing for a sense of continuity. Ethically, however, institutional exclusion produces troubling questions about equity, equal human rights, and the civil rights of the citizens of a nation. Geographically based or horizontal stratification may even harm national unity over the long run. Institutional exclusion naturally segregates the citizens and creates cultural bias against the people or sectors excluded. Furthermore, a society's creativity and ingenuity may be discouraged or even hindered by institutional exclusion, since it reduces people's horizontal and vertical mobility, which usually lead to the efflorescence of new ideas through exchange and competition.

Institutional exclusion, therefore, has a tremendous impact on a nation's politics, economic development, and social life. It is certainly not perfect or morally conscionable, and it may be irrational and inefficient; yet it is both inevitable and necessary. Obviously, not all types of institutional exclusion have the same impact. Some effects, negative in nature, perhaps should be viewed as the necessary organizational cost of a human grouping or a nation. Others may be uniquely positive if the institutional exclusion is founded in the least or lesser of competing evils and is executed well. The following section offers further thoughts on the possible positive impact that an institutional exclusion may have on economic growth and technological sophistication in some nations.

Institutional Exclusion in a Dual Economy:
To Circumvent the Lewis Transition

Institutional exclusion may play a greater role in the economic development of latecomer nations, the so-called dual economies in which there exists a vast supply of low-skilled and unskilled labor from the traditional, agricultural, or backward sector.[49] Development economics models suggest that any nation having a large population, a seemingly endless supply of unskilled labor, and marginal productivity at or near zero is likely to find itself in a dual-economy swamp: massive labor surplus constitutes a key obstacle to meaningful economic take-off.[50] Unless and until industrial jobs with wages above the subsistence level are created in sufficient numbers to absorb enough surplus agricultural labor to turn the overall labor supply from practically unlimited to a normal market-regulated scarcity—a course that requires immense investment, modern technology, and new markets, all of which are in perpetually short supply—a developing nation can expect only economic stagnation and its associated chronic poverty and backwardness. A seemingly unlimited supply of low-skilled and unskilled labor drives wages down to the subsistence level and makes the accumulation of capital difficult but its flight easy, while at the same time creating problems of urban poverty, political tension, and social decay. To absorb surplus labor becomes key to the so-called Lewis Transition, which a dual economy must complete in order to grow out of backwardness and poverty.[51]

W. Arthur Lewis, in his "Economic Development with Unlimited Supplies of Labor" (1954), describes the modern or capitalist sectors as islands in a sea of low-skilled and unskilled labor in developing countries. He discusses how massive supplies of poorly productive labor tend to cause migration and bring down wages in the capitalist sector and what the reasons are for protecting capitalist sectors and countries against unlimited inflow of low-skilled or unskilled labor.[52] How to raise the real wages and thus improve human capital and develop a productive and competitive industrial labor force before completing the long and sociopolitically arduous Lewis Transition (to absorb the traditional or agricultural sector through increased employment generated by urbanization, industrialization, and modernized agriculture), therefore, becomes a fundamental challenge to latecomer developing nations, which by definition lack the capital needed to create large numbers of well-paid industrial jobs.[53] As Lewis puts it, "the central fact of economic development is rapid capital accumulation (including knowledge and skills with capital)."[54]

The Lewis Transition is regarded as a narrow gateway through which heavily populated, heavily rural developing nations must struggle to pass in their efforts for economic development. But, as Lewis himself put it in "Unlimited Labor: Further Note" (1958), because of rapidly advancing technology and a highly competitive international environment of our time, latecomer developing countries or dual economies encounter enormous difficulties in making a Lewis Transition. Hence, "the countries which have surplus labor have never reached" a balance between investment and labor supply in order to move on to the next stage of economic development.[55] Therefore, perpetual economic stagnation and poor technological development, or a problem of underdevelopment, are likely to characterize nations stuck in transition.

Accordingly, a predicament thus arises. To accumulate massive capital quickly and to invest it in order to industrialize the economy becomes key to the development of latecomer nations, which, on the one hand, need quickly to employ a seemingly endless supply of low-skilled or unskilled labor in an era of market economy, modern consumerism, mass mobility, and equal human rights. On the other hand, latecomer nations are usually poor and powerless in the international financial market, where they have access to only a very small share of the world's capital resources. Furthermore, latecomer nations cannot repeat the old strategy of exporting surplus labor like the early industrialized nations in Europe. Indeed, after centuries of colonization and the eventual decolonization of the late twentieth century, massive overseas emigration has become a thing of the past. From China, for example, a nation of 1.3 billion with an estimated 140–240 million surplus laborers, there now emigrate roughly between 100,000 and 180,000 people a year to other countries, and 20 percent of these are so-called illegal immigrants paying between $10,000 and $60,000 each to be smuggled to other countries.[56]

Too many developing nations, indeed, seem to have been held up by this hopeless dual-economy swamp for decades, even indefinitely. The commonly seen free or uncontrolled internal migration of rural and unskilled labor to the cities tends to be enormous, but it is often highly irrational and inefficient.[57] The enormous numbers of new migrant workers in the modern sector (i.e., the cities) commonly end up in crowded slums, earning subsistence wages indefinitely.[58] They also bring down the wages of original urban workers, and often they diminish the profits of investors as well, because pressure increases for more public spending, funded by new taxation. At the same time, farms abandoned by migrants are unlikely to yield any higher income for the remaining villagers. The motivation and energy for economic growth hence are depleted since, as Lewis argued in 1966, *"the possibility of higher individual earnings is the fuel of economic growth."*[59]

A survey of migrating workers in three Chinese cities in 2001 reported that only 18.9 percent of them were migrating because of small per capita acreage of land and not enough income at home in the villages, whereas the majority of them were flowing to the cities simply for the real or imagined lure of urban life.[60] While urbanization, understood as rural-to-urban migration, in the latecomer developing nations of our time may seem to resemble that in the early years of what today are developed nations, the speed of today's internal migration in the developing nations has been much faster, with massive numbers of former peasants flooding almost simultaneously to the cities.[61] These migrants quickly found out that, usually, there is not sufficient or sustainable industrialization to employ them, nor any foreign colonies to which they may emigrate. Consequently, scarce resources of goods and capital needed for industrialization are spent, under the political pressure of the new urban citizens, to handle the endless inflow of low-skilled and unproductive laborers, who often quickly overwhelm the underdeveloped and fragile urban infrastructure, thus significantly damaging and even ruining the environment for investment, invention, and growth in the more advanced parts of the country.

Another leading result of uncontrolled internal (mainly rural-to-urban) migration in a dual economy is the lasting plague of capital flight that has haunted so many developing countries in the era of a globalized international financial market. Once the native capital feels insecure and uncomfortable, perhaps also unprofitable, to stay even in the modernized urban sector, foreign capital naturally tends to become short-term, speculative, and scarce. The chronic hunger for capital and government spending, amplified by the pressure of the growing and organized urban poor, often drives the state into deep international debt, irrational tyranny, simple nongovernance, or all three.[62] A vicious cycle is thus created. In this way, many countries—Venezuela, Brazil, Argentina, and Indonesia, to name just a few—that had great potential and great hopes have indeed fallen inevitably and repeatedly in their struggle to emerge from poverty.

A stable and effective institutional exclusion may provide remedies to a dual economy to allow for an accelerated economic growth and technological development. By excluding surplus laborers from the industrial urban economy and confining them to their home villages, institutional exclusion not only performs its traditional role of capital accumulation but also breaks the dual economy's vicious cycle of diminished income arising in an unlimited supply of cheap labor. At the expense of those excluded—make no mistake about that—a market-oriented industrial sector can achieve a high rate of growth and rapid technological advancement to allow a nation to quickly engage in the world market as a viable competitor. Lewis argued that there must be a 50-percent wage difference between the modern sector and the traditional sector to bring the modern sector "as much labor as it wants, without at the same time attracting much more than it can handle."[63] In reality, because of the rising cost of living and especially education in an era of technological revolution and international competition, this supposedly ideal wage gap tends to be much larger than 50 percent. Consequently, tremendous pushing-and-pulling forces for massive rural-to-urban migration are present. Since the formal urban sector can hardly absorb the flood of unskilled labor, an informal urban sector emerges and develops to breed urban slums, poverty, and a host of sociopolitical problems.[64] The key, therefore, is how to effectively and efficiently maintain and justify this income gap among the same citizenry without drowning the growing modern or urban sector under a sea of unskilled labor. The critical role of an effective, albeit ethically problematic, institutional exclusion is thus apparent.

Well-paid industrial workers and professionals, shielded from the flood of unskilled labor and the urban poor, may form a powerful middle class to create a viable domestic market and to upgrade the quality of life and working skills of the industrial workforce, while a massive amount of surplus labor is still confined to traditional consumption patterns and living in poverty. An effective institutional exclusion, with implied regulation of internal and cross-sector migration, that allows needed talent and labor to move but stabilizes the nonproductive labor for as long as possible also creates a stable sociopolitical order and a relatively orderly and desirable urban environment to attract foreign investors and merchants. This way, modern industries can develop rapidly in the urban or "in" sector, quickly lifting the nation as a whole out of poverty and backwardness. The dual economy continues, but the less developed and the excluded sector will gradually shrink, since the market logic of ceaseless expansion will necessarily bring goods, capital, and technology from the developed "in" sector once it is ready while bringing in the needed labor from the excluded sector in an orderly fashion—the so-called trickle-down and spillover effects.[65]

Indeed, many development economists have long argued for the need to have a balanced, planned, and even controlled economic development to avoid the perpetual economic retardation that many developing nations suffer. To control urbanization has been viewed as a key. Lewis believes that rural-to-urban migration should and can be restricted to prevent the dreadful "excessive mobility of the population" and that the number and size of urban centers should be limited to benefit the whole national economy.[66] To simply rely on a market-driven and spontaneous urbanization to make the Lewis Transition is viewed as undesirable and irrational; hence "more of the rural labor must be kept and absorbed in the rural areas, and the rural-to-urban migration must be curtailed."[67]

A model of economic development assisted by institutional exclusion is by no means ideal or even fair, but realistically it may be the only way for a latecomer nation to accelerate its growth in the information age with a globally integrated financial market, to break the vicious cycle of backwardness, and to avoid being condemned as a permanently slow follower of the developed nations. Institutional exclusion, as long as it is effective and not too costly in terms of sociopolitical stability and national cohesion, will thus allow a developing nation to circumvent its Lewis Transition by temporarily neutralizing the problem of an unlimited supply of unskilled labor. With the right kind of government (such as a so-called hard or strong developmental state)[68] and the right kind of policy, continued adjustment of the institutional exclusion may later facilitate the spillover and trickle-down effects of the developed "in" sector, thereby mitigating and even eradicating the dual-economy problem at a much higher level. That is, with a stable and effective institutional exclusion, a developing nation plagued by a dual economic structure can achieve rapid economic growth and great technological sophistication with sustained gains in real industrial or urban wages and delayed growth of nonagricultural employment, despite the existence of a massive unskilled labor supply.

In a way, the economic impact of an effective institutional exclusion in latecomer nations may be viewed as something similar to the economic impact that the Westphalia international political system has had on the world economy since the end of the Middle Ages. The political division of the sovereign nations, the citizenship-based division of humankind, and the exclusion of foreigners maintained by the regulation and restriction of international migration have contributed indispensably to the development of the modern capitalist market economy that has brought unprecedented economic growth and technological sophistication in the "in" parts of the world, primarily those nations belonging today to the Organization of Economic Cooperation and Development (OECD).[69] The world economy has developed spectacularly in the past few centuries, but an overwhelming majority (80 percent in 2000) of humankind still lives in less developed poor nations, excluded from sharing most of the world's achievements and products. Whereas the developed nations have achieved a per-capita annual income of over $25,000, over half the world's population (3 billion in 2000) lives on an income of less than $3 a day.[70] Today, the uneven distribution of income, resources, information, and opportunities between rich and poor nations, maintained primarily by the politically decided citizenship-based Type 3 (*where one is*) institutional exclusion, is indeed among the greatest that humankind has ever seen.[71]

The down side of institutional exclusion in the economy, however, clearly exists. In theory, there would be massive inefficiency and irrationality in the allocation and utilization of labor resources, because of the incomplete and segmented labor market under an institutional exclusion. Practically, however, such inefficiency and irrationality are largely more projected than real. Another problem is that the economy grows unevenly in different parts and in different communities of the same country. In addition to the common vertical socioeconomic stratification that separates the haves from the have-nots, a horizontal socioeconomic stratification or spatial differentiation develops between the "in" sectors or areas and the excluded ones, creating regional inequalities and disparities in income distribution. And, naturally, the speed of urbanization would tend to be slower than the development of the economy in general and the pace of industrialization in particular. In short, economic development under institutional exclusion means that a dual structure, shrinking so painfully slowly and gradually, continues at the expense of the excluded in the backward sector, which functions as a reservoir for the labor market and exists as a national price paid for economic growth and technological sophistication.

Naturally, not all types of institutional exclusion help the latecomer nations to circumvent the Lewis Transition with equal effectiveness. All institutional exclusions may work to slow down and prevent socioeconomic integration in general and internal migration in particular. But not all of them can sufficiently and cheaply regulate internal migration to allow for a rapid, albeit selected and uneven, economic and technological development in a nation filled with unskilled surplus labor. A major hypothesis of this book is that a stable and effective Type 3 institutional exclusion (based on *where one is*, like the PRC *hukou* system), in addition to the now universal Type 2 form (based on *what one has*), is a perhaps lesser but necessary evil, from which dual economies may well benefit. We will revisit this point later, in Chapters 5 and 6.

Hukou-based Institutional Exclusion in China

Institutional exclusion inevitably exists in China. Today's Chinese institutional exclusion has its peculiarities and is associated with the PRC *hukou zhidu* or *huji zhidu* (household or residential registration system), which was formally adopted nationally in the 1950s.[72] By itself, residential registration is not inherently a form of institutional exclusion and is found in many other nations. (See Chapter 6.) It becomes one when the registered people are treated differently according to the different categories and locations of their registration and when those registered are restricted in their migration between regions. The PRC *hukou* system, therefore, which requires registration of every citizen and controls any change of location and type of registration, provides an ideal foundation upon which to form a Type 3 institutional exclusion (based on *where one is*). It gives every Chinese citizen a geographically defined location and an associated sociopolitical status and identity practically for life. People are treated differently according to their officially registered location and identity in almost every aspect of their lives. This system not only regulates and restricts internal migration in a very unevenly developed nation, but it also treats differently categorized people differently, culminating in its management of *zhongdian renkou* (targeted people).

The *hukou*-based institutional exclusion in China has deep roots in the past that can be traced back centuries, even millennia. (See Chapter 2.) Yet the PRC *hukou* system is qualitatively different from the imperial *hukou* system and the *hukou* system of the Republic of China (ROC), since it reaches an unprecedented level of rigidity, effectiveness, and comprehensiveness in its role and capacity of division and exclusion. The backing of a powerful authoritarian one-party government has been the key to the stability and effectiveness of the PRC *hukou* system in the past half-century. In the 2000s, the *hukou* system still enjoys a strong institutional legitimacy in China,[73] perhaps largely because familial and locational differentiation are more seemingly natural and prevalent than most other human differentiations. Unlike the similar but now disgraced and disintegrated *propiska* (residential permit) system in the former Soviet Union, the PRC *hukou* system is both legal and strong. With only a few reform attempts and limited alterations, the *hukou* system continues to be the backbone of Chinese institutional structure and fundamentally contributes to the seemingly puzzling coexistence of China's rapidly developing market economy and the remarkable stability of the political monopoly maintained by the Chinese Communist Party (CCP).

As "the central institutional mechanism defining the city-countryside relationship and shaping important elements of state-society relations in the People's Republic," the *hukou* system "not only provided the principal basis for establishing identity, citizenship and proof of official status, it was essential for every aspect of daily life."[74] The *hukou* system fundamentally touches and determines the life of every Chinese citizen, since it comprehensively collects data on everyone, identifies and stratifies people and regions, controls population movement, and allocates resources and opportunities.[75] A Chinese scholar concluded that the *hukou* system has been "affixing people's social career, role, personal identity, production and living space; restricting the free migration of people and labor; maintaining and strengthening the dual economic and social structure between the urban and the rural areas."[76]

The PRC *hukou* system requires that every Chinese citizen register with the *hukou* authority (the *hukou* police) at birth. The categories of nonagricultural (urban) or agricultural (rural), legal address and location, and unit affiliation (employment), and a host of personal and family information are documented and verified to become a person's permanent *hukou* record. A person's *hukou* location and categorization or type were determined by his mother's *hukou* location and type rather than his birthplace until 1998, when a child was allowed to inherit the father's or the mother's *hukou* location and categorization. No one can acquire legal permanent residence and the numerous community-based rights, opportunities, benefits, and privileges anywhere other than where his *hukou* is. Only through proper authorization of the government can one change his *hukou* location and especially his *hukou* categorization from the rural type to the urban type. Simple and rigid, the PRC *hukou* system has been enforced stringently for five decades and serves as China's peculiar way of organizing its huge population through institutionally dividing and excluding large segments of the people.

All institutional exclusions encounter resistance from the excluded. The *hukou* system is no exception. But the PRC *hukou* system draws its extraordinary institutional legitimacy, operational effectiveness, and cultural support not only from the power of an authoritarian state but also from the Chinese family or clan structure, regional and community divisions, the tradition of parochial political culture, and the fact that a *hukou* system existed in China for a very long time before the PRC came into being. Since its early days date back to at least the Warring States era, some 2,400 years ago, the *hukou* system has taken various forms and performed in varying degrees its function of population management, taxation, mobilization, and social control during various dynasties and also under the ROC. The size of the population it divides and organizes, the power and rigidity of the system, and its lasting legitimacy certainly make the current PRC *hukou* system one of the best examples of institutional exclusion ever seen.

Consequently, the majority of the Chinese population, the rural residents, have been peacefully excluded under the PRC *hukou* system. The much smaller urban population (only between 14 and 26 percent of the total population) has had decisively much better access to economic and social opportunities, activities, and benefits, and has also dominated Chinese politics. To a lesser extent, urban residents in smaller cities and in less developed regions have also been excluded compared with those living in major urban centers or regions more favored by the government in terms of investment, subsidies, or policy flexibilities.

Functionally, the PRC *hukou* system has been a leading tool for Beijing's control of population and society in two crucial ways: to regulate China's internal migration and to control the politically determined targeted (*zhongdian*) segments of the population. Migration from excluded regions, especially the rural areas, to "in" areas, especially the major urban centers, has been strictly controlled. Thus, a classic case of dual economy and dual society has been developing in China for the past half-century. In practice, not only does a legal rural-urban duality exist in China; there also clearly exists a metropolitan-city-town multi-layer hierarchy in China's unique sociopolitical, economic, and cultural stratification, both vertically and horizontally. Furthermore, the *hukou* system allows the police constantly to monitor and control those persons and groups in the society selected as the most threatening and therefore to consolidate the PRC's sociopolitical order. A quarter of humankind is thus divided, organized, and controlled through an institutional exclusion based on their parents' location and their state-regulated association and identification. This institutional division and exclusion fundamentally determines not only much of the people's rights and benefits but also their and their children's life chances.

As a consequence of Chinese reforms since 1978, the *hukou*-based institutional exclusion has evolved and has been adapting in a number of important ways. Money has eroded some of the old edges of the *hukou* system, while creating new divisions and exclusions in China between the haves and the have-nots. The rich, the powerful, and the talented (the supposed Chinese meritocracy)[77] have now achieved de facto national mobility granted to them by the adaptive measures of the *hukou* system. Controlled, limited, but practical labor mobility has also been developed for low-skilled or even unskilled laborers.[78] At the same time, the PRC *hukou* system has facilitated both regionalism and communitarianism in the Chinese political economy. Many other mechanisms and functions of the system, however, as for example the important management of targeted people, remain basically intact in the early twenty-first century.

Clearly, the PRC *hukou* system poses serious ethical and legal questions that demand creative solutions. The *hukou* system has systematically created barriers against labor mobility—thus limiting the rationalization of a young market economy in the PRC as the serious problem of underemployment continues to devastate the state-owned economy[79]—and perpetuates poverty for the majority of the population living in the rural areas as the surplus and excluded labor.[80] It has legitimized unfair treatment and naked exploitation of the excluded population, again mainly the rural residents. It contributes to the growing regionalization of the Chinese political economy, with profound consequences for Chinese economic development, the capacity of the central government, and even the unity of the Chinese nation. Yet, to Chinese leaders, employing the *hukou* system still appears familiar, important, reliable, effective, and legitimate statecraft. Much of this system has been internalized as part of the Chinese culture and has acquired a high degree of legitimacy, even among the excluded. An adapting *hukou* system is making crucial contributions to China's sociopolitical stability and a segmented but rapid economic growth and technological sophistication in a marketization of the Chinese economy. Because of such important uses and its deeply rooted legitimacy, the *hukou* system, increasingly under scrutiny and criticism now just as are other types of institutional exclusion, is likely to continue while further adapting in the foreseeable future

Main Findings of This Book

The secretive nature of the PRC *hukou* system has hampered academic research on this very important subject. Hence, foreigners "either know very little about the system or hardly understand the system."[81] From 1996 to 2002, the *New York Times*, for example, had only five articles that briefly mentioned the term "*hukou* system" but ninety about college education in China and 920 about Beijing's famous Tiananmen Square.[82] Nonetheless, there has been considerable scholarly effort made in the field.[83] To build upon the existing scholarship, I will in the following chapters first examine China's *hukou* system as an institutional exclusion with deep legitimacy in China, tracing the historical origins of the *hukou* system in the pre-PRC era, and then consider its current operation and function, analyzing the impact, changes, and future prospects of the PRC *hukou* system. A comparative analysis of similar systems in other nations may allow us to address some larger questions about institutional exclusion and China's institutional nature. The main findings of this book can be summarized as follows.

1. The *hukou* system, as a major component of China's institutional framework, has a very long history that dates back many centuries. The PRC version of the *hukou* system is the most comprehensive, rigid, and effective ever in its role and capacity of division and exclusion. It is hence a qualitatively unique sequel to the imperial and ROC *hukou* systems. In the early twenty-first century, the PRC *hukou* system is still a legitimate and effective form of institutional division and exclusion. With accommodations and adaptations, it has survived the reforms undertaken throughout China since the late 1970s. Despite pressures for further changes, the *hukou* system is likely to continue in China for the foreseeable future.

2. The PRC *hukou* system, as a Type 3 institutional exclusion based on location differences (*where one is*), is gradually shifting toward a Type 2 institutional exclusion based on fault lines between haves and have-nots (*what one has*). The rich, the talented or educated, and the powerful now have essentially nationwide mobility under the *hukou* system.

3. Maintained and enforced by the Chinese state through its extensive

police network, under the leadership of the Ministry of Public Security, the PRC *hukou* system seems to enjoy a high degree of social support. With the full backing of an authoritarian state, the *hukou*-based institutional exclusion is not only legal in China but also strongly upheld by social organizations. Many social groups (*hukou* police and urban residents at large) have deeply vested interests in the system and hence strong incentives for preserving it.

4. As detailed in Chapter 5 of this book, the *hukou* system has had a profound impact on Chinese politics, economy, and social life. From among the many effects I will list three major ones here: first, the PRC *hukou* system, especially in its function as social control, has been a cornerstone of the CCP's one-party authoritarian political system. The *hukou* system has constructed a stereoscopic and omnipresent framework of sociopolitical control. Every PRC citizen is politically and socially, if not directly economically, stratified and governed on a near-permanent basis by the government. It is especially difficult, if not impossible, to have any meaningful organized opposition to the CCP under the so-called *zhongdian renkou* (targeted people) management scheme. All these factors explain the seemingly puzzling coexistence of the control and stability of the Chinese government along with rapid economic development and social change in the age of a globalized information revolution.

Second, the PRC *hukou* system has contributed very significantly to the impressive economic growth and development of technological sophistication in China, a typical dual-economy nation featuring massive unskilled and surplus labor,[84] especially in the past two decades of market-oriented economic reform.[85] By the 2000s, Chinese cities, especially the major metropolitan centers, have become fairly well developed without significant urban slums, unlike those in many other developing nations such as Brazil and India. This remarkable circumvention of the Lewis Transition naturally deserves further investigation. This circumvention, however, may be undermined if a changed sociopolitical environment in China abates or even eradicates the *hukou* system's ability to control internal migration.

Third, the PRC *hukou* system has created a unique horizontal socioeconomic stratification or spatial hierarchy in China that ranks different regions and areas. For that reason, inequality and uneven development stubbornly exist in this vast nation. Between cities and rural areas, and between the eastern or coastal and the western or inland regions, China is like a collection of many countries at different levels of development. The long-term impact of regional disparities on the integrity of the Chinese economy and even China's national unity, yet to be fully realized, is likely to be profound.

5. A *hukou* system or the equivalent exists and has served as a form of institutional exclusion, albeit less rigidly and comprehensively, in many nations other than China, including some developed nations. Comparatively speaking, a *hukou*-like Type 3 institutional exclusion or the lack of one appears to have made or reflected substantial differences in political stability and economic development among developing nations ranging from Brazil to India.

Methodology and Terminology

The PRC *hukou* system, far-reaching and important as it has always been, still largely operates in secrecy, with most of its policies, mechanisms, and especially records unknown to the public. The regionalized and secretive operation of the *hukou* system may have effectively minimized criticisms and resistance; it has also immensely hampered scholarly investigations. One major collection of theoretical works on internal migration does not even mention China's *hukou* system and its powerful regulation of internal migration.[86] One sociologist described the difficulty of studying the *hukou* system this way:[87]

> The *hukou* system is omnipresent and omni-pervasive to the Chinese people, but foreigners either know very little about the system or could hardly understand it. The management and data keeping of the *hukou* system are monopolized by the [Chinese] public security and police apparatus, belonging to some sort of state secret. Outsiders have little chance to study the system even if they want to. But the people inside China who really know the system dare not to study it, for the issue is too sensitive. Therefore, so far there has not been a single academic book on the *hukou* system published in or outside China. ... The only few Western academics who have studied China's *hukou* system have not only analyzed the system superficially but also have made many errors.

As other scholars in the field of China studies have felt, existing tools for social-science inquiries often could not be employed effectively in China. It is scarcely feasible, even impossible, for foreign scholars to undertake a large-scale, uniform, and scientific survey study in the PRC, for example.[88] Opinion surveys in the PRC, which started only in the 1990s,

TABLE I.2

China's Hukou System: A Terminology

---

hukou, huji (户口 or 户籍)—household/residential registration and related identification papers (cards/booklets or 户口本).[a] China's *hukou* system has a long history but the qualitatively unique PRC *hukou* system was created in the 1950s.

urbanites, urban residents, urban population, city dwellers—"non-agricultural" *hukou* holders or legally registered permanent residents of the cities. They are not just the people who live in the cities; they may be temporarily working in the rural areas. 26.08 percent of the total population in 2000.

ruralites, rural residents, peasants, rural population, villagers—"agricultural" *hukou* holders or legally registered permanent residents outside the urban areas. May be temporarily working and living in the cities. 73.92 percent of the total population in 2000.[b]

liudong renkou (流动人口)migrant—person who is travelling, moving, or "floating" temporarily outside of where his permanent *hukou* is located. Can be legal (legally registered in the new residence after more than three-day stay and acquiring a *zanzhuzheng* (暂住证) or temporary residential permit after three months) or illegal (stays in one place for more than three days but not registered with the *hukou* police or through a hotel or more than three months without a temporary resident permit). A migrant may live and work in one place for many years but still be considered a temporary *hukou*-holding *liudong renkou* if he cannot get a permanent local *hukou* through *hukou* relocation or permanent migration. The issuance of *zanzhuzheng* and forced repatriation are the main tools to control this type of internal migration.

qianyi renkou (迁移人口)—person who is authorized to migrate to a new place and change the location (and sometimes also the type) of his permanent *hukou* accordingly. It is a one-time and legally permanent internal migration. The urbanization and inmigrant quota (and/or the required "entry conditions or criteria") needed for authorizing and registering newcomers are the main tools to control this type of internal migration. Positive sanctions such as monetary rewards, promotions, and new jobs have been used to encourage people to resettle in certain designated places for policy purposes.[c]

mangliu (盲流)—illegal *liudong renkou* or migrants who have no authorization to relocate *hukou* and are not properly registered as a qualified temporary resident after three-day stay or have no temporary resident permit after three-month stay outside their permanent *hukou* zone.

zhongdian renkou (重点人口)—targeted segments of the population to be specially and focally monitored and controlled by the *hukou* police for the purpose of social control and crime fighting.

---

[a]For an internal discussion in the Ministry of Public Security on the semantics and terminology of *hukou* and *huji*, see Wang Taiyuan 1997, especially 22–28 and 66–73.

[b]MPS 2001, 3.

[c]For the Chinese official definition of the concepts of *qianyi* and *liudong*, see Cai Fan et al. 2000, 80. For an academic discussion of the *liudong renkou* concept, see Wang Jianmin and Hu Qi 1996, 2–9.

have never asked about the *hukou* system or people's reaction to it. Therefore, my study is largely based on library research of published primary and secondary sources and statistical information, my own field observations and interviews, and scholarly journals and newspapers published in and outside China.[89]

Over the years, I have developed for this project a fairly extensive list of interviewees from different parts of China.[90] With the help of numerous Chinese friends, I have acquired a substantial amount of open and internal but unclassified publications and documents about the *hukou* system, its operation, and its implications. My field trips to China have yielded many relevant and interesting anecdotes about the *hukou* system. Although because of limitations of style and space I cannot present most of those often personalized stories in this book, I do utilize them to generate observations and findings.

To study the *hukou* system, one cannot avoid translating and defining a few special terms and phrases. Table 1.2 offers a simple chart explaining a few key terms and concepts.

Remaining Issues

Although I am confident that I have managed to present a fairly complete sketch of China's *hukou* system, especially its distinctive PRC version, and a careful analysis of it with theorizing intentions, there is always room for further work on this very important subject. Very briefly, I believe four issue areas still remain to be further explored: first, to acquire more details of the actual daily operation of the *hukou* system. An in-depth archive and survey study of one or several *hukou* zones over time would serve this purpose—although my personal efforts at this have not been very successful, because much of the *hukou* system is considered off-limits to academic inquiries. One may nevertheless hope that further relaxation and liberalization of Chinese politics and society may allow this line of exploration in the future.

Second, related to the first issue, we need many more precise quantitative measurements of the impact of the *hukou* system. For example, how many ruralites are lined up each year to move to the cities? Where is the longest line? How many people are specified as *zhongdian renkou* (targeted people)? Data needed to answer such questions, as I found out, do exist but still mostly as classified information often dispersed and buried in the complex Chinese bureaucracy.[91]

Third, we need further investigation of how the PRC's peculiar *hukou* system was created and adjusted, and how decisions were made regarding its operation and alterations. On the basis of sporadically published materials, we can now piece together only a very rough picture of the political dynamics behind the *hukou* system, some of which this book reports. But it will require another book, or perhaps a series of books, to explore in full the political evolution of the PRC *hukou* system.

Finally, a more extensive comparative study of institutional exclusion and social control—particularly internal migration patterns and urbanization—may yield valuable theoretical fruits for the study of comparative politics and international political economy. At the very least, we may be more certain in assessing the various types of institutional exclusion and enhancing the descriptive and predictive abilities of this analytical approach. Naturally, observing the fundamentals of quantum physics, particularly Werner Heisenberg's uncertainty principle,[92] the effort to theorize institutional exclusions can hope only to describe the general pattern and probability of organization through division and exclusion in nations rather than to predict the precise action and result for a particular nation at a particular time.

If the globalizing world may be taken as a single human grouping and global employment considered as a whole,[93] a nation-state citizenship-based division of humankind through regulations and restrictions of international migration resembles and may thus exhibit much the same functions and effects as the PRC *hukou* system as a Type 3 (*where one is*) institutional exclusion.[94] If the specter that haunts the world in today's globalization is migration,[95] and national borders continue to be rigid and exclusive,[96] then a key theoretical as well as practical question appears to be what type of institutional division and exclusion the world would best have to divide and organize its six billion (and counting) people.[97] It would be most interesting to see, for example, if China's *hukou* system has any policy relevance and lessons for other countries, including the developed nations that mainly rely on Type 2 (*what one has*) institutional exclusions internally but on citizenship-based Type 3 (*where one is*) institutional exclusion externally.[98] Such an effort, naturally, must have profound policy implications for political and business leaders on the national and international stages.

CHAPTER TWO

The Origin and Evolution of China's *Hukou* System

Various types of institutional exclusion have varying degrees of legitimacy and effectiveness in any given nation. Apart from the power of the enforcer—the state or social organization—that maintains and executes institutional exclusion and the particular fault line on which an exclusion system is based, as discussed in Chapter 1, the history of the exclusion system itself is very important. The human tendency to be path-dependent and the political logic of institutional inertia play a great part in legitimizing and enforcing an institutional exclusion. Furthermore, older institutions tend to be internalized over time and thus form powerful forces of culture and tradition, affecting people's behavior through value construction, habit formation, and conduct constraints. Legal norms, not to mention ethical standards, can often be built on the sheer power of tradition alone. Time, therefore, is of the essence of the development and legitimization of behavior-shaping human institutions, including institutional exclusions.

Currently, the PRC *hukou* (household registration) system divides and organizes the people based on locational and family-membership differentiation as recognized and determined by the state. By regulating internal migration and segmenting the population to manage the people accordingly, the PRC *hukou* system has created a powerful institutional exclusion. The excluded rural and small-town residents form the overwhelming majority of the population in today's China, and it is easy to see the ethical problems of discrimination and inequality that are increasingly magnified by the rapid development of a market economy in an era of globalized information. Yet the *hukou* system still enjoys considerable institutional legitimacy and administrative effectiveness.

A significant explanation for the resilience and effectiveness of the PRC *hukou* system lies in its origin and evolution. Among the oldest, longest-lasting Chinese political institutions, the *hukou* system has been in China for at least twenty-five centuries. Almost all imperial dynasties since the Qin (3d century B.C.) and the Republic of China (ROC) adopted and utilized variations of the *hukou* system, with differing degrees of thoroughness and effectiveness. When the Chinese Communist Party (CCP) came to power in 1949, and especially when it was eager to modernize China for pressing political and international considerations,[1] the *hukou* system was a natural choice for its needs to control the society and plan the economy.

Under the PRC, China's *hukou* system has been comprehensively enforced and greatly rigidified with divisive, exclusive, and discriminative mechanisms, becoming a full-blown nationwide institutional exclusion. The PRC *hukou* system has its distinctive totality, central planning, and Soviet-style ideological coating. But the roots of the system are long and deep in Chinese history, reaching all the way back to the days when the Chinese state and the Chinese nation were formed.

This chapter traces the origin of China's *hukou* system and outlines its evolution. It will also explore and describe the inception and development of the PRC *hukou* system since 1949, showing that the creation and administration of the PRC *hukou* system is inseparable from the CCP political system and the PRC central-planning economy; the PRC *hukou* system is also to a considerable extent a continuation of Chinese political history and organizational structure. The overall continuity of the imperial Chinese political economy in the PRC era has contributed significantly to the legitimacy of *hukou*-based Type 3 (*where one is*) institutional exclusion.

Xiangsui and *Baojia*: The Origins of the *Hukou* System

At the dawn of their long recorded history, the Chinese systematically developed a community-oriented, regionally based organization of families and clans for purposes of taxation and social control, in addition to the common mechanisms of ranked kinship and feudal classes that also existed in many other traditional societies. The Xia Dynasty (21st–16th century B.C.) initiated a population census and household registration.[2] The subsequent Shang Dynasty (16th–11th century B.C.) developed its own record of households.[3] Primitive forms of *hukou*-like institutions were devised in the Western Zhou Dynasty (11th–8th century B.C.).

Zhou rulers charged a *simin* (population managing) ministry based on the well-defined family or clan structure to record household registration annually and verify it triennially as the basis for taxation. A *xiangsui* (districts) system organized families in the cities and the countryside into two hierarchically structured networks.[4] The classic *Zhouli* (Rites of Zhou) describes this early *hukou* system of *xiangsui* thus:[5]

> In the city, five families are organized as a *bi* to be mutually responsible that there are no evildoers; five *bi*s are organized as a *lu*, ... four *lu*s are organized as a *zu*, ... five *zu*s are organized as a *dang*, ... five *dang*s are organized as a *zhou*, ... five *zhou*s are organized as a *xiang*.
>
> In the countryside, five families are organized as a *lin* to be mutually responsible that there are no evildoers, ... five *lin*s are organized as a *li*, ... four *li*s are organized as a *zhan*, ... five *zhan*s are organized as a *bi*, ... five *bi*s are organized as a *xian*, ... five *xian*s are organized as a *sui*.

Politically appointed heads at the *xiang* and *sui* levels would govern the people and manage local affairs, including chiefly tax collection and labor conscription. A major function of this system was to control population migration and exile, since the system would create a situation in which "the exiles have no place to hide, the migrants have no place to go, ... the people have no intention to move, so the officials have no worries about control."[6]

As the intellectual origin of China's *hukou* system, however, the *xiangsui* system is perhaps too perfect a system for a feudal state some three thousand years ago. More than likely, the historical records of this system may actually contain much of the ideals of the authors of the *Zhouli* in the early Han Dynasty (2d–1st century B.C.).[7] Credible evidence of *hukou*-type population registration and migration controls can be found, however, in the *baojia* (mutual responsibility) system, which can be reliably traced to the late Spring and Autumn era in feudal states like the Zheng and the Qi. The prime minister of Qi, Guan Zhong (685–645 B.C.), extensively implemented some of the basic rules of China's *hukou* system, including registering people by where they live and blocking internal migration.[8]

In the middle of the Warring States era (5th–3d centuries B.C.), as part of the reforms launched by Lord Shang Yang, the famous representative of the legalist school, the Qin Kingdom in western China first in 375 B.C. fully adopted a *baojia* system to organize families into units collectively responsible for their activities to the state. The system also achieved the objective of stabilizing and expanding the taxation basis for the Qin court. As expected, the system, accompanied by severe penalties for violators, worked well to make Qin the most powerful of the Warring States. Perhaps ironically, Lord Shang himself tested the remarkable effectiveness of this system with his life when he was refused a hiding place by the organized Qin people during his desperate flight from the new king.[9]

Other warring states soon adopted similar household registration systems for taxation and conscription. When Qin finally unified China in 221 B.C., the *baojia* system was adopted nationally, and the taxation and conscription functions of household registration were enhanced and expanded. Further social-control mechanisms were built into the revised system. Everyone was required to report residence, age, gender, and profession to the authorities. The state verified such information three times a year, and everyone needed official approval to change registration before moving. Illegal migrants were called *wangmin* (fugitives) and subject to prosecution and harsh punishment.[10]

Initially created over two thousand years ago for the purpose of taxation and enhancing imperial rule, China's *hukou* system evolved to become a thoroughly institutionalized and deeply legitimized tradition of Chinese political history.[11] The practical effectiveness of the early *hukou* system, however, is hard to assess.

China's Imperial *Hukou* System: Taxation and Stratification

The dynasty cycles after the Qin characterized Chinese imperial history. These cyclic changes of government brought the rise and fall of the *hukou* system under each dynasty and allowed for certain innovations and adjustments in it. The imperial *hukou* system consistently functioned to allow for taxation, social control, and stratification. It later acquired other important functions like land redistribution.

The Han Dynasty (206 B.C.–A.D. 220) further strengthened the Qin *hukou* system for the same purposes of taxation and conscription. The emperor appointed special *hukou* officials to staff the central, prefecture, and county governments. *Hukou* law became one of the Han Dynasty's nine basic laws, and poll and property taxes were collected on the basis of household registration records. Below the level of county administration, there was a *xiang-ting-li* (town-district-neighborhood) system, featuring local gentry in charge of the *hukou* system at three levels (managing 10,000, 1,000, and 100 households, respectively) and collecting household and poll taxes. Every year, in the fall, every county and prefecture was required to report its people's demographic information to the imperial court, including household income figures, marriage conditions, additions or losses of family members, and everyone's physical features such as height and skin color. People were politically prohibited and socially discouraged from migrating or going into exile at will. Anyone with a legitimate reason for traveling or moving must carry an official *fu* (identification) permit to avoid arrest and imprisonment. Illegal migrants were designated as fugitives, and checkpoint officials who did not inspect *fu* diligently were to be criminally prosecuted.[12]

The Qin and Han *hukou* system was inherited by nearly all subsequent dynasties, with some adjustments and modifications. Some regimes, such as the Wei and the Jin, seeing that large numbers of people were taking refuge in the protection of landholding manors to escape from imperial poll tax, relied on collecting household taxes and suspended the individual poll tax. Their *hukou* system, therefore, mainly recorded information about families, without specific information about the people in the households. The imperial *hukou* system, backed with force including the death penalty, restricted internal migration in order to minimize the numbers of destabilizing *liumin* (migrant people), even in times of natural disasters and famine.[13]

Of course, the administration of such tight population control was often costly, even though much of the burden was shifted to unpaid local gentry.[14] Therefore, in practice, the *hukou* system was enforced to an extent directly correlated with the power of the imperial state, the resources available to the enforcement agencies, and the cost-benefit calculations of local gentry or officials. As a consequence, the *hukou* data collected were often filled with inaccuracies, unintentionally or not. Such a structurally determined inaccuracy, incidentally, has been a prominent feature of Chinese *hukou* systems ever since. The *hukou* laws and regulations were commonly compromised in practice, as there are throughout the history of imperial China countless reports of floaters, migrants, and unrecorded persons who appear to have enjoyed a great degree of internal mobility. Internal migration, largely "invisible in the [official] records," nonetheless took place, as exemplified by the history of the *Hakka* (guest people) and *Pengmin* (shack dwellers).[15] Yet Chinese internal migration in imperial times resulted from a lack or the limit of imperial enforcement more than the absence of *hukou*-based restrictions.[16] China's internal migrants were primarily involuntary, driven either by war, famine, or the brutality of local officials or gentry, or coerced by the imperial court for the purpose of developing uninhabited lands through the practice of *tuntian* (establishing garrisons to be filled by administratively relocated troops and peasants).[17]

After many years of war-driven dislocations and involuntary migrations of the people, the Southern and Northern dynasties (A.D. 420–581) started to register people based exclusively on their current locations, not necessarily their native towns or birthplaces. After their registration, however, families were given a new *hukou* and restricted from moving again. Such a *tuduan* (local determination) policy started to divorce one's *hukou* from birthplace or family origin and made the *hukou* system more an administrative institution than simple clan record keeping. The penalties for hiding from the *hukou* system became rather severe to prevent tax evasion and embezzlement by local officials. The Northern Zhou Dynasty even used the death penalty against those who hid more than five families or ten male laborers from the imperial court.[18] A similar locally determined registration of migrants in their new locations was instituted at the beginning of the Southern Song Dynasty (early 12th century), when massive numbers of people moved to the south, primarily because of war and invasions from northern nomadic regimes.[19]

The Sui and especially the Tang Dynasty (A.D. 581–907) fully incorporated the *hukou* system into the overall imperial political structure. Many of the *hukou* notions and terminology used then are still used in the PRC today. The traditional motive of increasing revenue prompted the Sui government to redefine a household as a paternal family, not including cousins, so as to limit the size of a household and increase income from household taxes. The government then categorized families into different tax brackets with annual adjustments.[20] All households in the same tax bracket or location were assessed the same amount in taxes. Larger families with more male members shouldered a greater burden of labor conscription, which sometimes could be converted into increased tax payments. Prohibition of unauthorized moving and evading registration and measures for more accurate reporting and categorization of households were institutionalized. The Tang continued the Sui policy of detailing every person's physical characteristics in household registration records, and so it became easy to verify the accuracy of the records. Officials used a single national *hukou* form to record the names, ages, genders, and relationships of everyone in a household, including concubines. The completed forms were then duplicated and sealed by the county and prefecture officials, and finally a copy would be sent to the ministers of the imperial court.[21] To ensure the integrity and safety of the *hukou* information, the households were issued *shoushi* (*hukou* booklets); the local governments kept their *hukou* master files (*jizhang*), and the central government maintained a national *hukou* file (*huji*).[22]

The Tang Dynasty, a peak of imperial Chinese civilization, also used the *hukou* system to carry out its *juntian* (equalizing land) policy, thus giving *hukou* a land-based and accordingly great importance to Chinese families in an agrarian economy.[23] Imperial officials, especially at the local level, were evaluated and rewarded on the basis of their work maintaining the *hukou* system. The more households a local official recorded and taxed, the more highly regarded that official would be in the eyes of the emperor.[24] Registered households were required to stay in the same place and report any changes of family size, their own or their neighbors'. The Tang, in theory, allowed peasants to move and migrate. But the migrants could move freely only from places with low tax and conscription rates to places with higher rates. Any moves in the opposite direction had to have official permission. Furthermore, because of concerns about escaped or hidden families and laborers and distrust of local governments, the central imperial court, starting in the reign of Empress Wu Zetian, launched direct registration campaigns called *kuohu* (including the households) to register migrating or floating peasants and send them back to their *hukou* locations so as to resume their tax and conscription obligations to the state.[25]

So sophisticated an imperial *hukou* system for taxation continued for centuries in China with some major technical innovations, three of which remain evident in today's PRC. First, a strict protection of the sensitive *hukou* data: the Song Dynasty (AD 960–1127) developed five different ways to collect *hukou* information and treated *hukou* data as a national secret,[26] much as does the PRC government today. Second, the use of *hukou* booklets: the Ming Dynasty (1368–1644) devised a *hutie* (household card), with serial numbers, that allowed each household keep a copy of its official *hukou* record. This *hutie* can be viewed as the direct ancestor of the *hukoubu* (*hukou* or residence booklet) now in use in the PRC. Finally, China's imperial *hukou* system traditionally categorized and treated people differently. The Ming government, for example, in its *hukou* records called the Yellow Books, updated once every ten years, divided the registered households into various types according to profession.[27] The Ming *hukou* system thus recorded and registered people on the basis of not only where they lived but also what they did.[28]

China's imperial *hukou* system functioned as a quasi-institutional exclusion. In addition to the location-determined population immobility, there always lingered an inherited *hukou* categorization of various noble clans, ordinary people (mainly peasants), and various low-class clans (slaves, floaters, untouchables such as paupers or prostitutes). In the last two dynasties (Ming and Qing), the legally equal ordinary people were categorized into four inherited *hukou* types: military, peasants, merchants, and handicraft workers. They had the same legal status but frequently different and adjustable treatment regarding tax burden and the right to participate in the imperial examinations, as well as the right to move. Several categories of low-class clans were further excluded. The various formal *hukou* classifications of the lower-class clans were formally abolished by the Qing Dynasty (1644–1911) in the eighteenth century, but sociopolitical and economic discrimination against those excluded groups continued until at least the middle of the twentieth.[29] Unlike the current PRC *hukou* system, however, the imperial *hukou* system formally excluded not the majority of the population but mainly the socially undesirable minority or fringe groups.

The economic importance of the imperial *hukou* system started to decline in the late Ming Dynasty (1573) when Prime Minister Zhang Juzheng adopted a new way of collecting the poll tax.[30] The Qing Dynasty's famous *tanding rumu* reform in 1723—fixing poll and household taxes at 1713 levels and replacing them with an acreage tax—severed the traditional links between taxation and the *hukou* system.[31] By 1772, the Qing government stopped registering its people for taxation purposes. The millennia-old *hukou* system lost its tax function but continued in the form of a *baojia* system and became mainly a data-collection and social-control institution.[32] The lifting of poll and household taxes also led to the phenomenal growth (or, perhaps more accurately, the emergence from hiding) of the Chinese population after the late eighteenth century,[33] as the concept of *ding* (males between the ages of 16 and 60) started to lose its often fuzzy official meaning as a tax-accounting unit and began to become a unit for a more accurate head count of male residents.[34]

In practice, the *hukou* system still performed important roles for Qing economic policies such as the famous campaign of moving people from Huguang to fill Sichuan (1683–1796), which moved more than one million male peasants to reclaim fertile lands in the Sichuan Basin that had been devastated by wars and plagues.[35] Emperor Kangxi, for example, explicitly used the *hukou* registration and its expedient manipulation and relaxation to encourage and facilitate the migration and, later, to keep the migrants in their new homes.[36] By 1776, first- and second-generation new migrants already constituted more than 60 percent of the 17 million population in that prosperous province.[37]

The economic role of the imperial *hukou* system subsided further after the mid-nineteenth century, when foreign-induced market-oriented economic activities began to erode the Chinese agrarian economy and started the pushing and pulling mechanisms for the peasants to leave their villages. Under the decaying Manchu regime and the chaotic and divided ROC, the imperial *hukou* system lost much of its role in migration control and taxation. Diminished political and financial incentives for *hukou* management and a vanishing state capacity for social control allowed massive, accelerated internal migrations, primarily toward northwestern and northeastern regions. There was also a significant surge of emigration, primarily to Southeast Asia.[38] In the late Qing Dynasty and the ROC, however, there were sporadic efforts by various rulers and warlords to use the *hukou* system to increase tax revenues. Only the PRC after 1949, in a central-planning economy, managed to nationally restore and greatly enhance the economic function of the *hukou* system, turning it into a full-blown institutional exclusion. Although the PRC does not have poll or household taxes, *hukou*-based institutional exclusion nonetheless allows the government to extract enormous value from the excluded majority of the Chinese people.[39]

Hukou as *Baojia*: A Traditional Means of Social Control

From early on, China's *hukou* system had the important function of controlling the population and maintaining sociopolitical stability. As mentioned earlier, the *baojia* system of collective and mutual responsibility among the households was first devised by the Warring States such as the Qi, and especially under Qin rulers. Sometimes, as for example during the Han Dynasty, the term *baojia* was not used; at other times, the *baojia* system became synonymous with the *hukou* system.[40] A variation of it, the *linbao* (neighbor assurance) system, was fairly well institutionalized by the Tang Dynasty. The Northern Song Dynasty in the eleventh century attempted a comprehensive restoration of a national system of *baojia* through its famous Wang Anshi Reform to control the people and to stabilize its shaky regime.[41] The three layers of *baojia*—*bao*, *dabao*, and *dubao*—organized five to ten, twenty-five to fifty, and 250 to 500 households, respectively. All families in the same *bao* shared a collective responsibility called *lianzhuo*—all were to be punished alike if anyone was found violating the law or migrating illegally.[42]

The subsequent rulers of China, the Yuan, Ming, and Qing dynasties and the ROC governments, all periodically used the Song system with minor changes or technical improvements and varying effectiveness. The Yuan (1271–1368), a Mongol minority regime, registered and treated people differently on the basis of race or ethnicity, profession, and family. Their purpose was to use ethnically based exclusion and discrimination as a powerful means of controlling the Han Chinese ethnic majority.[43]

The national use of the *hukou* system as means of social control, however, was largely a political tradition formed in the last two dynasties of imperial China, the Ming and the Qing. The Ming government ordered all residents of the fortified cities to hang plaques by their doors disclosing their *hukou* information, including native origin, number of household residents, and presence of any live-in guests. The Qing government used a similar open *hukou* declaration. In the early Qing Dynasty, even the Buddhist temples and Daoist shrines had to hang out *hukou* plaques. Every household, temple, and inn must have such a plaque ready for official inspection at any time. Travelers were required to register with innkeepers for official inspections, and innkeepers were liable if such registration was not properly done.[44] Here we see clearly the precedent for mandatory registration of residents and travelers in today's PRC.

Furthermore, the Qing government listed those who had criminal records or who were deemed threatening in separate *hukou* books, the so-called *lingce* (other books), so as to allow local officials to pay them special attention. Only after a certain period of time and after being guaranteed by the local gentry could these people be removed from the special books and put back into the ordinary *hukou* files.[45] This policy is very similar to the PRC's tiered management of *zhongdian renkou* (targeted residents) by the public security agencies, to be examined in detail in Chapter 4.

The *Kuomintang* (KMT) or Nationalist Party government (1927–49) used the *baojia* aspect of the *hukou* system aggressively in its struggle against its domestic enemies, especially the rebellious Chinese Communist Party (CCP). Household registration and the organization of *bao* and *jia* were required to proceed simultaneously. Ten families were organized into a *jia*, and ten *jia*s into a *bao*. The government then appointed officials to the higher levels of township, county, and province to rule the organized people in the *bao*s. People were thus mutually responsible and liable for their activities under this hierarchically organized, geographically defined family-based system.[46] Political and ideological deviance became something that households watched each other for.[47] The CCP later admitted that a tight-knit *baojia* system "performed very importantly" in hurting the communists.[48]

Hukou Laws Prior to the PRC

Today's PRC *hukou* system inherited not only much of the imperial *hukou* system's operational features and mechanisms but also its legal framework and stipulations. The Qing Dynasty in its final years attempted to legalize the imperial *hukou* system with a modern legislature. As part of its 1908 political reform, the Qing started to require a national *hukou* registration for its proposed political elections. A detailed *hukou* law was promulgated only in 1911, however, the year of the dynasty's collapse. The Qing *hukou* law, the first such in modern China, codified the basics of the imperial *hukou* system but interestingly stipulated that the population had freedom of internal migration. Its basic principles, such as mandatory registration and centralized administration and procedural details, "have had strong and lasting impact on the subsequent *hukou* laws in China."[49]

Primarily for social-control purposes and with hopes for a better taxation system and state economic planning, the KMT government further institutionalized the *hukou* system in modern legislation.[50] The Nanjing Government promulgated *Hujifa* (*Hukou* Law) in 1931 (revised in 1934 and 1946), *Detailed Regulations on the Implementation of Hukou Law* in 1934, *Regulations on Hukou Verifications* in 1941, *Regulations on Temporary Resident Registration* in 1942 and 1943, and *Regulations on the Registration of Migrating People* in 1943 (revised in 1946).[51] Like the Qing *hukou* law, the ROC *hukou* laws insisted on people's freedom of internal migration, but they required three years and six months, respectively, for an outsider to change his permanent and temporary local *hukou* status. In those regions where an anticommunist campaign was waged, population movement was especially restricted, and the *baojia* system was used openly. In 1946, the ROC *hukou* laws were simplified and revised with less restriction of internal migration and national resident-identification papers began to be issued. The 1946 ROC *hukou* laws are still largely in use in today's Taiwan.

To a great extent, the CCP directly copied and inherited much of the ROC *hukou* laws and policies on *hukou* registration and verification procedures. The early version of the CCP's *hukou* regulations (before the mid-1950s) also similarly provided for the citizen's right of free internal migration. Before the establishment of the PRC, the CCP established its own *hukou*-like mass mobilization and organization system as early as the 1930s, in its guerrilla bases in Jiangxi Province and later in northern Shangxi Province.[52] The main objective was to safeguard the infant regime and fight the Japanese or the KMT government. Beginning in 1939, the CCP organized people in the areas under its control into a *lianbao* (connected assurance) system, which was actually the aforementioned *baojia* system. Under the administrative villages, which all had a CCP-appointed administration, every five families were put into one *lianbao* group to mutually assure that no one was engaging in any counterrevolutionary activities or receiving outsiders without reporting to the authorities.[53]

When the CCP took over major cities from the Japanese and later from the KMT government, it simply took over the ROC *hukou* system and with it the old KMT *baojia* cadres and *hukou* clerks to update and verify the existing *hukou* records.[54] The CCP started to register the households in such so-called liberated areas even before 1949, first in the northeast, which was the first major urban area under its control.[55] The Administrative Commission of the Northeast—that is, the CCP government in that region—established urban *hukou* files and issued urban *hukou* identification papers in April 1948. On June 25, the Northeastern Public Security Bureau issued *Provisional Measures on Hukou Management*. The CCP in the northeast also, in the tradition of the Qing Dynasty, established special *bingzhong* (category C) *hukou* files listing only *zhongdian renkou* (targeted residents), who were considered threatening to the new regime. Those in category C were hence tightly controlled and closely monitored by the new police force with the help of the CCP-style *baojia* system. All travelers had to show the authorities valid *hukou* papers or an official permit.[56] In 1949, the CCP started to make local regulations governing *hukou* management in metropolitan areas beyond the northeast, covering Shanghai in September and Beijing in November.[57]

The Creation of the PRC *Hukou* System

The chief reason for the PRC to establish its national *hukou* system was its historically proven utility in social control by dividing the people into small segments and then organizing those segments into a centralized hierarchy.[58] It was apparently this political motivation that prompted the CCP to quickly restore the *hukou* system with innovations and enhancements. The big brother Soviet Union, with its Stalinist views on the relationship between the urban industrial workers and the peasants and its *propiska* (resident permit) system, provided the new ideological coating, political rationale, and practical example for the CCP. An instructional manual for PRC *hukou* officials explained in 1994 that the CCP had a "pressing need for a national *hukou* management" in 1949:[59]

> On the one hand, [we] need to find out [hidden] enemies quickly, assist struggles against the enemy, and maintain the revolutionary order through the *hukou* management that controls the information on the population. On the other hand, [we] can provide data to the agencies of the state for their making policies and plans through *hukou* management that controls the population.

Indeed, the CCP quickly used the *hukou* system to single out and control special segments of the population. The PRC *hukou* system thus acquired its institutional exclusionary role right after birth and worked effectively to stabilize the new regime. Between 1949 and 1950, 13,704 enemies and more than 24,000 "questionable persons" were found through *hukou* registration and verification in Beijing, and there were over 61,000 such catches in Jinan.[60] In August 1950, the newly established Ministry of Public Security (MPS) issued its *Provisional Regulation on the Management of Special People*, the first national regulation of the *hukou* system in the PRC. Minister of Public Security Luo Ruiqing concluded in November 1950 at the first PRC public security conference that maintaining *hukou* management "is a major task." A national *hukou* system was decided upon at the conference, to be established first in the cities and nationwide within ten years.

As with many other CCP policy initiatives of the 1950s, the establishment of the *hukou* system was completed well ahead of schedule. The then-powerful influence of the former Soviet Union and the Stalinist version of Leninist ideology played a considerable role in the CCP's devising of the PRC *hukou* system.[61] In 1951, the MPS issued its *Provisional Regulations on Urban Hukou Management*, which stated that the purpose of the PRC *hukou* system was "to maintain social peace and order, safeguard the people's security, and protect their freedom of residence and movement." Even with freedom of migration promised, urban residents were required to have official permission to migrate, and classification of urban households was adopted. The first census of the PRC, in 1953, facilitated the establishment of the urban *hukou* system and created new rural *hukou* files.

By 1955, the State Council ordered local governments to establish a permanent *hukou* system and thus "formally initiated a full-blown *hukou* system on the eve of China's imposed collectivization."[62] The MPS and its local branches were formally given total authority for the management of the *hukou* system in February 1956, after a comprehensive network of public security bureaus and police stations had been established in both rural and urban areas.[63]

At the same time, the PRC established a *tonggou tongxiao* policy (state monopoly of the purchase and marketing of grains)[64] and a guaranteed food ration for all urban residents at a fixed price. The *hukou* system thus acquired a strong role of resource allocation, opportunity prioritizing, and differential treatment by location. Rural and urban residents were thus economically differentiated, with the peasants becoming the institutionally excluded. The significance of *hukou*-based institutional exclusion of the rural population became crystal-clear to everyone after the disastrous Great Leap Forward (1958–61), which made state food rations a lifesaver in a time of national famine.[65] Twenty to thirty million people, almost all from the rural areas, are estimated to have perished.[66]

Finally, the ninety-first meeting of the Standing Committee of the First National People's Congress passed, with Mao Zedong's signature, its *Regulations on Household* (Hukou) *Registration in the People's Republic of China* on January 9, 1958. The PRC *hukou* system, unprecedentedly strong in its institutional exclusion and social control from the very beginning, became law nationwide.

The Evolution of the PRC *Hukou* System

With food rations and the numerous subsidies added later favoring urban residents, the PRC *hukou* system functioned in crucial ways in social stratification, resource allocation, capital formulation, agriculture collectivization, and the division of the urban from the rural.[67] The traditional function of social control was equally extensive and significant. As the disastrous Great Leap Forward was showing every Chinese citizen the importance of the *hukou* system beyond any doubt, the MPS internally issued *Eight Measures for Public Security Management* in 1959, and the CCP promulgated *Ten Measures for Public Security* in 1962, both emphasizing the need for strengthening the role of the *hukou* system in maintaining public security. *Hukou*-based management of *zhongdian renkou* (targeted people) was stressed once again, and management techniques were improved. Starting as a means of social control but quickly evolving into a socioeconomic exclusion as well, the PRC *hukou* system finally became a comprehensive, rigid, national institutional exclusion by the early 1960s. The MPS believes that, by 1965, "our *hukou* system was not only widely established in both urban and rural areas but also basically completed and consolidated."[68]

As reflects the importance of its social-control function, the *hukou* system is officially categorized under the headings "Public Security," "Social Order," and "Public Administration" in PRC legal documents, official statements, and academic writings.[69] It has never been considered a mere issue of internal migration control, resource allocation, or demographics, although the PRC *hukou* system is extremely important in all those areas as well.

A *hukou* system that limits and even eliminates the right of internal migration while creating social injustice and economic inequality in a densely populated but unevenly developed nation can hardly exist without challenges. The *hukou* system has indeed been challenged, even crippled, in the name of revolution twice in the history of the PRC. But each time, the *hukou* system has bounced back and has only become stronger and more rigid. The Great Leap Forward led to widespread disregard of the *hukou* system by state agencies and various state-owned *danwei* (work units) in pursuit of utopian rapid industrialization and urbanization.[70] For a very short period between 1957 and 1959, the Chinese, especially the rural population, had substantial freedom of migration. Massive increases of the urban population pushed the state system of food rations to the edge of collapse and deeply worried the CCP regime about losing social control. The bursting of the Maoist utopian bubble, naturally, led to a forceful reimplementation of the *hukou* system. Beijing was forced to cut its swollen urban population through administrative measures.[71] The CCP coerced many of the twenty-five million new state employees added during the three Great Leap Forward years (some went to the cities before 1957) to return to the countryside in order to reduce the burdens of state provisioning.[72]

By mid-1963, nearly twenty million state employees and some twenty-six to twenty-eight million urban *hukou* holders had been relocated from the cities to their former villages, the economically struggling communes.[73] Chinese industrial labor declined from 16.6 percent of the total labor force in 1958 to only 6 percent in 1965 after this desperate deurbanization.[74] The remaining urban population, therefore, became a truly privileged minority in China for the next three decades and is still heavily subsidized and favored by the state today. It has been only between 12 and 27 percent of the Chinese population from the 1960s to the 2000s.[75] The majority of the Chinese people, in the rural areas, have all been designated "agricultural population," regardless of what they do for a living. Ranging from 73 to 88 percent of the total population, they constitute the institutionally excluded in China under the PRC *hukou* system, economically, politically, socially, and culturally.

The PRC *hukou* system was at least partly smashed at the beginning of the Cultural Revolution (1966–76) by the rebellious Red Guards, particularly the millions of resentful peasants working in the cities with only a temporary urban *hukou*—the so-called *yinong yigong* (peasant worker) employees engineered by Liu Shaoqi in the early 1960s.[76] Many *hukou* records were destroyed, and a massive free movement of the Red Guards took place. Almost all the *yinong yigong* people became permanent urban residents and permanent state employees under the new so-called red regime. The *hukou* system, however, was quickly restored under Zhou Enlai's direct intervention and Mao's military takeover of the nation in 1968–69.[77] The *hukou* system's functions of social control and institutional exclusion were maintained and even further rigidified afterwards.

As the basis for fourteen different sets of policy and regulatory institutions and regimes created by the PRC in the 1950s and improved in the 1960s, 1970s, and 1980s,[78] the *hukou* system gave rise to a rigid, comprehensive institutional duality in China: the rural and the urban. This dual-structure separation of the rural population from the urban was fortified, and the gap between the two in terms of state-subsidized provision of goods and services, political representation, and social opportunities grew continuously in the PRC. For three decades (1960s–1980s), the *hukou* system affixed the workers to their *danwei*s (work units) and communes, respectively, in the cities and the countryside, reduced labor mobility to a minimum, halted China's urbanization, and created deep, comprehensive discrimination against the majority rural residents.

Only a very few narrow bridges existed allowing a ruralite to become an urbanite: getting a college education through politically determined selection (and the highly competitive national college entrance examination after 1977), joining the military and becoming an officer (hence a cadre qualified to have an urban *hukou*), or certain marriage arrangements. Other than by these means, only a very few people were recruited or sent by the state across the boundaries between rural and urban China. The growing gap between the rural and the urban economy led to an increasing disparity between people's living standards in the two Chinas. The income gap between urban and rural residents grew, for example, from 1:2.2 in 1964 (1:2.5 in 1978) to above 1:4 in 1993.[79]

Numerous political campaigns for breaking the barriers between the two sectors failed in the Mao era because of the irreplaceable political utility of *hukou*-based institutional exclusion. More than fifteen million young urbanites, high-school and middle-school graduates, were "sent down" to work and live in the villages, to be reeducated by the peasants, and were forced to give up their privileged urban *hukou* status between 1965 and 1977, creating many tragedies fully comprehensible only to people living under the PRC *hukou* system.[80] The decade-long drama of massive deurbanization still could not relieve the state of its ever-increasing burden of subsidies for the rapidly growing urban population in the general context of chronic stagnation of the central-planning economy. The majority of the sent-down youth, deeply disillusioned about Maoist revolutionary teachings, simply flooded back to the cities to correct the deprivation of their urban birthrights.[81]

By the mid-1980s, China's *hukou* system had reached its historic pinnacle in the PRC's version of it, which was at the peak of its importance, effectiveness, rigidity, and comprehensiveness. The PRC *hukou* system became a classic Type 3 institutional exclusion (based on *where one is*), with all the discriminative colors and contents. Life chances, resources, political power, and social status were all directly affected and even determined by one's *hukou* categorization and location. The urban and rural *hukou* records and household *hukou* booklets, required for all PRC citizens, were all clearly marked either "nonagricultural" or "agricultural"; they were even printed in different colors (urban in black ink, rural in red or green).[82] This intrusive and symbolic use of ink, reflecting the deeply discriminatory nature of the *hukou* system, was not eliminated until nearly twenty years later, in 2000.

The *Hukou* System in the Reform Era: Adaptations and Changes

The profound economic reform of the PRC since 1978 has altered much of China's institutional framework. The PRC *hukou* system has also been deeply affected but has so far largely survived the reform era. This is a testament to the deep legitimacy and resilience of the system. The PRC *hukou* system in the early 2000s, the subject of detailed examination in the rest of this book, while continuing its basic operations and functions, has also undergone significant changes and adaptations. These changes were caused by heated market-oriented economic growth, decentralization of political authority, Deng Xiaoping's experimental strategies of reform, and strong pressures from the swelling ranks of the excluded rural population. Some of the adaptations were initiated by the Chinese government at various levels for the purpose of market-oriented reform or addressing past political injustices. But many of the adaptive measures were actually rectifications by the Chinese state to recognize and accommodate the spontaneous bending of the *hukou* system by millions of Chinese in the form of *liudong renkou* (migrating or floating population) or simply unauthorized internal migration.[83] Rapid economic growth, especially after the 1990s, provided the opportunity for rapid urbanization, forcing the state to adjust the *hukou* system.

The *hukou* system's longtime, much-examined function of resource allocation and subsidization to urbanites has now been reduced and even replaced by advancing market forces as urban rations of food and other subsistence supplies have now either disappeared or become insignificant. The administration of the well-known function of controlling internal migration is now increasingly localized and considerably relaxed. Regional variations, distortions, exceptions, and lapses have hence developed in the *hukou* system in various parts of China, giving rise to increased mobility of the population in general and rural laborers in particular.[84] There has been significant scholarship on the changes of the migration-control function of the *hukou* system in the reform years.[85] The other leading function of the *hukou* system, however, the management of targeted people (*zhongdian renkou*), albeit much less known and hitherto scarcely examined though quite crucial, remains highly centralized, rigid and forceful, and nationally uniform. Changes in the management of targeted people so far are mainly technical and marginal. There actually is a tendency for this function to be improved and enhanced in the early 2000s.

Initially, the agricultural reform (decollectivization) of 1978–82 started to release surplus rural laborers who had previously been administratively confined to the communes.[86] Faced with an increasing number of rural laborers flowing to the cities, the government reacted by setting a rural-to-urban *hukou* permanent-relocation or urbanization quota of no more than 0.15 percent of the total population annually and ordered the nation to strictly enforce it. This quota, later increased to 0.2 percent in the mid-1980s,[87] was still partly in place in the early 2000s, although commonly no longer strictly enforced in small cities and towns by 2004. As reform progresses, the rigid system of migration control quickly encounters increasing pressure to accommodate the labor mobility necessary to any market economy, even in a dually structured rural-versus-urban society. China's politically obstructed urbanization gathered tremendous momentum in the reform era. Spontaneous internal migrations with or without permission spread like wildfire. The PRC *hukou* system had to adapt to continue its mission.

Beijing promulgated a series of regulations and decrees in the 1980s to improve and adjust the PRC *hukou* system. The CCP Central Committee in 1983 issued *On the Issues Related to Enhancing and Reforming Public Security Work*, deeming the *hukou* system the foremost component of public security. As a reflection of the needs generated by economic reform, the State Council published *Notice on the Issue of Peasants Moving to Reside in the Towns* on October 13, 1984. On July 13, 1985, the MPS issued its *Provisional Regulations on the Hukou Management of Temporary Urban Residents*, which authorized a temporary urban-resident permit (*zanzhuzheng* or *zanjuzheng*) for those temporarily migrating with legitimate business or for employment purposes. Significant migration of labor, however temporary it might be legally, thus developed in the reform years, crossing not only regional but also rural-urban barriers. By the early 2000s, the size of the *liudong renkou* (migrant population) was estimated to be between 85 and 120 million, including considerable numbers of illegal *mangliu* (blind floaters) who had neither properly registered with the *hukou* police nor applied for the temporary residential permit or *zanzhuzheng*.[88]

To accommodate increased demands for permanent migration, primarily in the major cities, which are the most desired destination for migrants, a transitional *hukou* was created to allow legal migration of selected groups of people—mainly the rich and the talented or educated—through *hukou* relocations and changes. Nicknamed blue-seal *hukou* because the official seal validating this type of *hukou* registration uses blue ink as opposed to the usual red color, this transitional *hukou* works in roughly the same way as the permanent residency (the so-called green card) that the United States grants to selected foreigners.[89] It allows its holder to have the same rights and status as local *hukou* holders, with the possibility of becoming a permanent local *hukou* holder after five years of qualified residency. The criteria to obtain such a transitional *hukou* are, largely, wealth and education or skills. Self-sponsored applicants must be wealthy and capable of investing, whereas sponsored applicants must have an advanced education and skills that are in great demand or a record of high achievement. By the 2000s, such de facto national mobility for selected groups of people has become a nationwide practice.

The state monopoly on grain purchase and marketing was formally abolished in 1985, and the state-subsidized food rations in the cities started to be phased out in 1987. By the early 1990s, most cities and towns stopped subsidized grain rations for the urban population.[90] Urban housing, jobs, and public facilities became increasingly accessible to outsiders and even rural residents, especially those who had money. The *hukou* system's discriminatory role in resource allocation, however, remains significant in areas like education, especially higher education. (See Chapter 5.) To a slightly lesser extent, state subsidies in housing and other community-defined benefits are still important to the minority of Chinese who have urban *hukou* status. The 1998 *National Housing Reform Plan*, after numerous local experiments, guaranteed every urban family with at least one state employee an apartment fifty to sixty square meters in area, and the state would pay for roughly 80 percent of the already controlled purchase price. This open but onetime state subsidy to urban residents could be as much as 240,000 yuan RMB per household over twenty-five years in the more expensive cities.[91] The newly devised social security system, pension plans, unemployment insurance, medical insurance, and mortgage lending are still available only to local urban *hukou* holders.[92]

As a major technical improvement and standardization of the *hukou* system, the sixth PRC National People's Congress passed *Regulation on Resident's Personal Identification of the People's Republic of China* on September 16, 1985, and the *hukou* police started issuing a personal identification card for every PRC citizen. The *shenfenzheng* (personal ID card) carries a national serial number, personal information, and the *hukou* location of its holder, but without the discriminatory, insulting reference to *hukou* categorization. The regulation formally took effect on September 15, 1989.[93]

After 1998, children could inherit their father's or their mother's *hukou* status, making rural-urban or cross-regional marriages a truly practical means of migration, at least for the next generation.[94] The administration of the *hukou* system in general has fragmented and weakened considerably because of the erosion of the CCP's authority, corruption of the police and officials, political decentralization, and changes in public opinion effected by foreign influence. Both enforcement of *hukou* registration and efforts at verification of *hukou* data have become increasingly constrained by individual rights and legal procedures. At the same time, the *hukou* police have been funded by the central government to computerize data collection and utilization. By the early 2000s, virtually all *hukou* records were electronically stored.

Afraid of losing the highly valuable political usefulness of *hukou*-based institutional exclusion and social control, the Chinese government acted frequently against the general trend of relaxing the *hukou* system during the reform era. In the late 1980s and early 1990s, for example, Beijing curtailed urban employment that was not authorized by the state planning and stopped a variety of unauthorized *nongzhuanfei* practices (changes from agricultural or rural *hukou* to nonagricultural or urban *hukou*) through a recentralization of the *hukou* authority. In December 1988, for example, after a number of softer measures had failed, Beijing bluntly ordered that local governments and state-owned enterprises eliminate more than two million such unplanned or unauthorized employees and sent the majority of them back to rural areas. After October 1989, Beijing imposed a much tougher control on unauthorized changes of *hukou* status by local governments and reduced such changes by over a million cases in two years.[95] Such reactions, however, usually lasted for only a few years and then quietly disappeared.

Apart from the clear and seemingly lasting trend of localization, especially in terms of its administration, the PRC *hukou* system seems to remain deeply legitimized and effective in today's China. At the same time, however, open and in-depth discussions in the PRC on the need and ways to overhaul or fundamentally reform or even abolish the *hukou* system itself have emerged, thanks primarily to the power of the new medium of the Internet. So far, discussions of an overhaul of the *hukou* system have yet to generate any possible momentum to abolish its function of controlling internal migration. The largely secretive scheme of managing targeted people is not even an issue in the public discourse. As I will examine in more detail later (in Chapter 7), reform of the PRC *hukou* system still is a major mission unaccomplished.

Tradition, Acceptance, and Legitimacy

The long history of China's *hukou* system prior to the PRC has contributed tremendously to the deep legitimacy of ethically problematic *hukou*-based institutional exclusion in the twenty-first century. The PRC *hukou* system is still widely accepted not only because of its historical roots and proven political utility for an authoritarian one-party regime, but also because of social and cultural factors that grow out of Chinese history: China has had a honeycomb social structure based on parochial and patrimonial family divisions,[96] dominated by a centralized imperial power coated with a Confucian ideology but having a ruthless Legalist power politics at its core. There has always been a lack of organized political opposition or even a national religion. The Chinese state has traditionally controlled the country's industrial and commercial resources. Divisions and discrepancies between the rural and urban populations in China have been in existence since at least the nineteenth century. All these factors have formed a rich tradition in China that is very conducive for a Type 3 (*where one is*) institutional exclusion to thrive and function.

The "unchanged nature. . . [and] structure" of the Chinese institutional setting, including the *hukou* system and Chinese culture, has had an almost unshakable strength, a "super-stability."[97] *Hukou*-based differentiation and exclusion are not based on such more volatile or often more controversial differences as race, ethnicity, caste, language, religion, skills, profession, gender, or political orientation—although those fault lines do contribute considerably to the overall sociopolitical stratification of the PRC. The *hukou* system has been historically linked to purportedly natural, stable, highly legitimized family structure, community divisions, and physical distance. Kinship cleavages and community boundaries have always been the most stable and important bases for differentiation and grouping in China. The first leader of the CCP, Chen Duxiu, wrote in 1915 that East Asians (mainly Chinese) are family-based whereas Western Europeans are individual-based.[98] A Type 3 institutional exclusion based on family, communal, and regional differences, therefore, appears to be fully natural and legitimate to most Chinese, despite many apparent and lingering moral questions.

In contrast to many other nations, religion and ideology have never been a lasting basis of institutional exclusion in China. As Max Weber noticed long ago, there is not a single dominant religion in the Chinese mind.[99] A peaceful coexistence of the major religions is therefore evident in Chinese history and may still be found in many famous religious shrines today.[100] Thus, the diminishing role of religion and ideology in our time has only a minimal effect on cultural acceptance of *hukou*-based institutional exclusion.[101]

The PRC's *hukou*-based institutional exclusion both reflects and perpetuates the enduring vast socioeconomic differences and disparities among the various regions of China. Mountainous terrain (covering two-thirds of China) and a locally oriented agrarian economy have made regional differences a legacy from the imperial years.[102] Beginning in the last years of the Qing Dynasty, politically created group-based and profession-based differentiations of the population developed as new supplements to the old family-based and community-based divisions. The evolution of industrial enterprises and, later, the *danwei*s (work units) created an additional support to the *hukou* system. These nonkin groupings and units accepted rather than rejected many parochial and patrimonial features of traditional Chinese society. Segmentation under a centralized authoritarian regime continues to be the Chinese way of domestic organization. The *hukou* system hence both represents and supports the organization of the Chinese people through division and exclusion.

The sharp separation of the rural population from urban residents in today's China is the most striking exclusionary or discriminatory aspect and perhaps the most troubling moral problem of the PRC *hukou* system. Yet there appears to be a traditional rationale and a deep cultural acceptance of such a division and duality among the Chinese. Urbanization was never a strong force in China, despite the fact that the history of Chinese urban life can be traced back to the eleventh century B.C.[103] Chinese cities in the imperial era did not produce any true urbanization of the country or an independent urban population. The ancient cities in China sometimes reached very large size,[104] but they were essentially an extension of the agrarian economy and lived on agricultural surplus administratively reallocated through taxation and rent collection. In the mid-nineteenth century, as many as 80 percent of Chinese cities were merely administrative centers, with little urban economic foundation.[105] The urban residents were primarily privileged imperial court officials and the military, a tiny minority of the population. Inequity between urban residents—the ruling class, the affiliated merchants, and the largely temporary servants from rural areas—and the people of the countryside was always legally and culturally accepted.

Once the urban population became sizable and noticeably different from the rural population, as in the heyday of the Tang Dynasty, the emperors made legal distinctions between city dwellers and villagers by registering them separately and preventing any willful migration between the two sectors. Registered urban residents could not participate in land redistribution and were often restricted from owning land in the countryside. To organize the people through dividing them into the rural-urban duality with the *hukou* system is hence not entirely a CCP invention.[106]

The emergence of modern cities in China after the nineteenth century did not erase this culturally accepted rural-urban distinction. On the contrary, the largely colonialist urbanization under foreign influence and even foreign control in the coastal regions prior to the founding of the PRC further enhanced the sense of a necessary differentiation between an industrial and commercial economy in Chinese cities and an agrarian economy in Chinese villages, leading to the formation and consolidation of China's dual economy.[107] The small urban population—only 5.1 percent in 1843, 6 percent in 1883, and 10.6 percent in 1949—had always been considered the wealthy elite or high-income earners of the nation.[108] The PRC *hukou* system, with perhaps the tightest control of internal migration in Chinese history, almost stopped urbanization in the PRC for over two decades. By 2000, nonagricultural *hukou* holders made up only 26.1 percent of the Chinese population (12.3 percent in 1979, 18.7 percent in 1988).[109] This urban minority dominates China politically, economically, and culturally, and often uses its power to maintain and justify the PRC *hukou* system that gives it privilege and a sense of superiority.

Furthermore, the Chinese state has by tradition directly controlled and run a large proportion of the country's industry. By the end of the nineteenth century, the imperial state already employed over one-third of all Chinese modern industrial workers.[110] Later, especially during and after World War II, the ROC government controlled over 45 percent of Chinese industry and an even higher proportion of Chinese industrial workers.[111] Such state control of the urban economy continued in Taiwan and played an important role in the economic development of that island. In

1952, over 57 percent of Taiwan's industrial production was controlled by the KMT party-state, and this state-dominance largely continued till the 1990s.[112]

By the time that the CCP entered the cities as the new ruler of China in 1949, the division between a backward rural sector and a heavily state-dominated but modern urban sector had become a new but widely accepted tradition in China.[113] The then-influential Soviet Union and the Stalinist central-planning system further theoretically justified such a tradition by distinguishing an advanced industrial proletariat from a backward peasantry.[114] The notorious rural-versus-urban division under the PRC *hukou* system was not created by the CCP alone, although the CCP codified and rigidified it. It is a reflection of the development of a dual political economy in modern China. The deterioration of the political fortunes and credibility of the CCP, therefore, so far has had little impact on the legitimacy of *hukou*-based institutional exclusion of the rural population.

A few additional but important characteristics of Chinese political culture have given the *hukou* system a certain humane face and some flexibility, and thus, ironically perhaps, have further strengthened the whole system. Traditionally, Chinese culture favors strongly informal networking or connections (*guanxi*),[115] personal patronage, under-the-table and back-door exchanges, and obedience to those in authority. Face, status, and nominality are crucial. Open contentions among interest groups and loyal opposition are generally exotic foreign ideas in China. The Chinese traditionally have a low opinion of written law and rely heavily on the administrative capacity of the ruler, allowing and tolerating humane circumvention of the *hukou* system in practice.[116] Bribery and connections have become natural companions of the seemingly rigid *hukou* system, giving the few who have the strong will and perhaps also the ability to destroy the system an easy way out short of damaging the whole system.[117] The like was true even in the Mao era, when the state was much more invasive.[118]

Civil society and individual rights are generally absent or fundamentally conditioned by the rulers' often ad hoc permission.[119] As a leading Chinese ethics authority wrote in the official press in 1995:[120]

> The Chinese nation is historically organized upon the fabric of kinship and centered around the family. Thus, cultivating one's character, supporting one's family, and serving one's state become the three levels of [our] ethics. The interest of the state is higher than that of the family and individuals. ... The most fundamental requirements of [Chinese] ethics have been filial piety toward

parents and loyalty to the state. If there is a conflict between the two, one must put loyalty to the state ahead of filial piety toward the parents. For loyalty to the state, one has to endure even the risk of killing his parents.

In 2002, while calling for the rule by law in the PRC, President Jiang Zemin nonetheless also argued for rule by morality and ethics. These morals and ethics, according to the CCP Central Party School's elaboration, appear to be mainly the aforementioned traditional Chinese culture and values.[121] With such ethics and such a cultural tradition, many Chinese are accustomed to living in a permanently divided environment as small groups (families, local communities, units) under one centralized, omnipotent political authority.[122]

The imperial examination system of the past and the college and graduate-school entrance-examination system of today's PRC provide crucial bridges for the capable to overcome the *hukou* barriers through officially sanctioned hard work.[123] Upon reaching a certain level, officials are hardly affected by *hukou*-based institutional exclusion. Money has also given practical mobility to the newly wealthy under the *hukou* system in today's PRC. Since such mobility has widely acquired a high value in a nation where comprehensive institutional exclusion still reigns, the newly rich, the powerful, and the talented who are able to acquire de facto mobility under the PRC *hukou* system have little incentive to genuinely push for abolition of the system on behalf of the excluded poor, powerless, and uneducated.

The adaptive measures of the PRC *hukou* system in the past two decades have further relieved much of the pressure against the *hukou* system through giving the excluded a false sense of citizenship. One survey in three cities of China in 2001 found that a majority (78.5 percent) of excluded peasants working in the cities believed that they were still peasants, even though they had been in the cities for years. A smaller majority (51.9 percent) of these peasants responded that they did not really want to change their rural *hukou* identity. Apart from fatalistic beliefs that they cannot change it anyway or that their roots are in the village, the most important reasons for the seemingly puzzling acceptance of their unfair fate are that it no longer makes much difference whether one is a peasant or not and that one actually enjoys greater freedom as a peasant. Such reasoning is, of course, based largely on ignorance of the extent of *hukou*-based institutional exclusion, but it also reflects the sense of satisfaction of those determined sojourning workers who are now indeed able to make a better living in the urban sectors.[124]

Finally, the administrators of the PRC *hukou* system, especially the police, have a strong microincentive to keep *hukou*-based institutional exclusion alive. The police officers in the PRC are all urban *hukou* holders. In almost all urban and many rural locations, the *hukou* police generate large sums of extrabudgetary income from those seeking favors in regard to *hukou* matters, especially *hukou* relocation. In local public-security bureaus and police stations, such *hukou*-related income (legal fees and simple bribes) constitutes a major source of income often distributed as bonuses for the bureau or station as a whole. In an era when money talks loud in China, *hukou* administrators are predictably interested in maintaining the system in the name of sociopolitical stability, urban security, and public order while in fact intent upon the power and income that it generates.

Conclusion

China's *hukou* system originated some two thousand years ago. The imperial version of it reached a high level of institutionalization, and the ROC established modern *hukou* laws in the early twentieth century before the foundation of the PRC. The CCP established the PRC *hukou* system in the 1950s with an unprecedented degree of totality, divisiveness, exclusiveness, comprehensiveness, and rigidity. Although China's *hukou* system had the intention and function of organizing the people through division and exclusion before the founding of the PRC, it is the PRC *hukou* system that has become a full-blown Type 3 (*where one is*) institutional exclusion

To Chinese rulers, communist or imperial, the *hukou* system has been a familiar, effective, and legitimate device to divide, organize, and rule the population. Much of this system reflects Chinese socioeconomic structure and culture and, in turn, has been deeply internalized as part of Chinese political culture and social norms. The stable institutions of the family or clan and the parochial community structure have served as the *hukou* system's solid foundation. The rural-urban dichotomy and the institution of *danwei* in the PRC political economy have provided additional support and justification. Thus geographically defined, family- and community-based, hierarchically organized *hukou*-based institutional exclusion has become part of officially sanctioned Chinese tradition or character.

In the first PRC constitution of 1954, before the completion of the PRC national *hukou* system in 1958, people were constitutionally guaranteed the right of free migration (*qianxi* or *qianyi*). This right was taken away in the PRC constitution of 1974: *Hukou*-based institutional exclusion finally became constitutional many years after its implementation.[125] In the current PRC constitution of 1982 (amended in 1988, 1998, and 2004), the right of free internal migration is still missing.

Among the countless writings on reform-related ideas, debates, and suggestions published in China in the 1980s and 1990s, only very few mentioned the economic need for labor mobility as the reason for improving the PRC *hukou* system, and almost none have ever questioned the legitimacy or morality of the whole system. The Legal Works Committee of the PRC National People's Congress has published a multivolume series since 1979 with the general title *Fazhi cankao ziliao huibian* (Collections of reference materials on legal rules). As a major internal publication, it collects many controversial viewpoints, even from known anti-CCP dissidents, on nearly every aspect of the PRC. Yet through volume 8 (published in the mid-1990s), there have appeared very few words questioning the legitimacy of the *hukou* system. It is empirically obvious that the bold experiments in the five special economic zones (SEZs) and the Pudong New Area of Shanghai have yet to alter the foundation of the *hukou* system.[126]

Toward the late 1990s, academic and journalistic discussions of the *hukou* system started to emerge, especially of its impacts, first in Hong Kong–based journals and newspapers. Most of their authors, however, lived in the PRC.[127] Professional and scholarly journals such as *Population and Economics*, *Population Research*, *Sociological Studies*, and *Chinese Social Sciences* started to publish essays and articles on the flaws of the PRC *hukou* system and the need for and approaches to reforming it. The tone, however, was largely descriptive and tentative. The depth and coverage of the articles were limited to the economic rationality problems of labor immobility and regional disparity. The remedies offered were largely reformist and within new CCP party lines that had usually first appeared in central documents and various internal journals or official publications.[128]

In the 2000s, one can see in local newspapers and on the Internet increasingly open discussions of the need to reform or even abolish the *hukou* system on grounds of its economic irrationality as well as its ethical problems.[129] But the *hukou* system appears to be politically and culturally safe in China, and its reform is still controlled and limited. Whereas in the small towns and some cities locally required entry conditions are replacing the migration quota, the government in metropolitan areas such as the city of Beijing still asserts the need to maintain the *hukou* system indefinitely.[130] The MPS announced in the fall of 2001 that *hukou* reforms will enhance rather than abolish the PRC *hukou* system.[131]

Historically speaking, for the PRC *hukou* system to be abolished or cease to be an effective institutional exclusion, many great changes have to take place in China's politics, economy, society, and culture. The current PRC *hukou* system comes out of China's long history and draws its power primarily from the CCP's authoritarian regime; yet *hukou*-based institutional exclusion is entirely likely to politically survive even the CCP unless China departs metamorphically from its past.

CHAPTER THREE

The Registrations

Structural and Operational Features of the PRC Hukou System

China's *hukou* (household registration) system has been a lasting mechanism of statecraft in imperial China and in the Republic of China (ROC). Since the 1950s, the version of it articulated by the People's Republic of China (PRC) has been the foundation for a full-blown nationwide institutional exclusion based on the fault line *where one is*. After a half-century of operation and evolution, the PRC *hukou* system now is omnipresent in virtually every corner of the country, dividing and organizing 1.3 billion Chinese people. This chapter describes the status of China's *hukou* system in the early twenty-first century by outlining its structural and operational features in detail.

Like many other important fundamentals of the Chinese institutional fabric, the PRC *hukou* system still largely operates behind the thick curtains of informality and secrecy. Openly published scholarly literature, publications in legal education, and tabloid-style case reportage, while very voluminous in quantity and possibly useful in providing a peek behind the curtain through anecdotes and opinions, are highly superficial and repetitive about the operation of the *hukou* system. From 1983 to 2004, there was only one supposedly authoritative book published openly by a top *hukou* official depicting the *hukou* system, and very few scholarly books discussing the system in the PRC.[1] Empirical observation and fieldwork have allowed the publication of several academic works on various aspects of the PRC *hukou* system, especially its implications outside China.[2] Yet in both the Chinese and the English literature, there is still an absence of any comprehensive account of this system, primarily because of the limited availability of information.

The legal and administrative information about the PRC *hukou* system available to observers outside China is limited to two regulations—the 1958 *Regulation on Household* (Hukou) *Registration* and the 1985 *Regulation on Resident's Personal Identification Card*—and their implementation procedures. Hundreds of ever-changing directives and decrees governing the *hukou* system, issued by various government agencies in Beijing and by the provincial governments, have largely remained classified or designated "For Internal Use Only." Comprehensive narratives and discussions about the *hukou* system, so far, can be found only in Chinese government publications—police handbooks; police academy textbooks, and police training manuals; reports and collections of essays and documents edited by the police—many of these also specifically labeled FOR INTERNAL USE ONLY; FOR CIRCULATION IN LAW-ENFORCEMENT OR PUBLIC-SECURITY AGENCIES ONLY; FOR MPS USE ONLY; or, most straightforward of all, STATE SECRETS.[3]

Furthermore, the national database of *hukou* information (such as the size of the various segments of the *zhongdian renkou* or targeted people) is classified Secret (*mimi*), Critically Secret (*jimi*), or even Top Secret (*juemi*) and can only be partly released after specific approvals.[4] The rationale behind such secrecy, or lack of transparency, is naturally a very interesting issue about Chinese politics in general and about the PRC *hukou* system in particular. As I mentioned in Chapter 2, treating *hukou* data as a national secret has been a Chinese tradition since at least as far back as the Song Dynasty (10–12th century).

To further complicate the situation, the PRC *hukou* system exhibits two features that make it even harder to comprehend: it is universal and highly centralized in its coverage and general principles of operation; yet its administration is localized, with clear regional characteristics. On the one hand, all parts of China—from Shanghai to Tibet, and from prisons to the Zhongnanhai, the Chinese Communist Party (CCP) headquarters—are covered by the same system. The central government nationally makes the general rules and sets the general principles and policies such as migration quotas for the Ministry of Public Security (MPS) to implement. On the other hand, the administration of the *hukou* system is up to local public-security bureaus and police stations, which enforce the system according to local conditions, especially the different decisions of local CCP committees and local governments. Regional variations and distortions hence develop. Experimental modifications and reforms of the system are also commonplace in various localities, although Beijing clearly reserves final authority on *hukou* matters. There have been cases recently of Beijing's issuing orders to reverse localized *hukou* reforms.

During my research on the subject in the past decade, I have had access to substantial open and internal publications that allowed me to portray the PRC *hukou* system with sufficient confidence. In principle, I have refrained from using any classified information in this study.[5] Fieldwork and observations in various parts of China over the years have provided important supplementary information. Accordingly, this chapter and the next are based on a combination of primary document survey, secondary scholarship, media reports (especially information reported in local news media), and field observation and interviews. A nationwide survey and statistical analysis would provide additional information and presumably would increase one's confidence in describing the details of the PRC *hukou* system. But for a foreign-based researcher, any large-scale survey on that system in China or full access to the Chinese national *hukou* database is simply not feasible, if not completely impossible, at this time, and probably also for the foreseeable future.

The PRC *Hukou* System: An Overview

Officially, and mainly internally, the *hukou* system is defined in China as an administrative mechanism for collecting and managing information on citizens' personal identification, kinship, and legal residence as "the necessary foundation of overall population management and social administration."[6] In addition to such administrative tasks as are invariably found in other countries, the PRC *hukou* system has its own unique missions: administrative control of internal migration, management of temporary residents or visitors, and tiered management of *zhongdian renkou* (targeted people).[7]

The basic law governing the operation of the PRC *hukou* system has been the *Regulation on Household* (Hukou) *Registration of the People's Republic of China*, promulgated on January 9, 1958. Twenty-seven years later, on September 6, 1985, Beijing adopted its *Regulation on Resident's Personal Identification Card in the People's Republic of China*. These two regulations and their implementation procedures are the main legal basis for the PRC *hukou* system. The State Council and its ministries and bureaus, especially the MPS, have issued numerous regulations, provisional regulations, directives, decrees, and other documents to substantiate and fine-tuned the *hukou* system. The majority of these state docu-

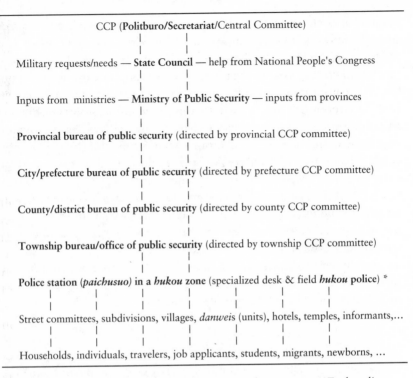

FIG. 3.1. Organizational Chart of the PRC *Hukou* System. (*Each police station [*paichusuo*] constitutes a *hukou* zone where original *hukou* records of all residents [permanent and temporary] in the zone are processed and stored. In the 2000s, most police stations are wired to share their *hukou* records electronically.

ments, estimated to number more than two hundred between 1958 and 1996, have been concerned with ever-changing criteria and mechanisms for the control of internal migration, especially *qianyi* (permanent migration with *hukou* relocation).[8] Local public-security bureaus and police stations are the administrators of the *hukou* system, although many other ministries are involved in its operation. The State Planning Commission, for one, sets the quotas for and monitors cross-regional and especially rural-to-urban migration.

The MPS has been the most active creator of policies governing the operation of the PRC *hukou* system. With the authorization of the central government, provincial and municipal governments have made certain marginal changes and experimental modifications to the *hukou* system in their respective jurisdictions. Despite the fact that the *hukou* system has been so comprehensive, profound, and lasting, the police admit internally, "[the] legal framework of *hukou* management is still very insufficient."[9] In fact, the *hukou* system is largely an administrative device based on very sketchy legal foundations. It is not even mentioned in the PRC constitution or the PRC civil codes. There has been talk in Beijing since the 1980s about creating a PRC *hukou* law to firmly ground this important system in modern legal language. Bills about new *hukou* laws have been proposed by deputies in the National People's Congress since 1992.[10] Yet by late 2004 such a mission is still in its very early stages, with no date in sight for its completion.[11]

Under the PRC *hukou* system, every citizen is legally required to register with the *hukou* authorities and to acquire a *hukou* certification. A police station (*paichusuo*) in the cities or a rural township (*xiangzheng*) constitutes a *hukou* management zone. Full time specialized *hukou* police are in charge of the system, under the supervision of public-security bureaus and local CCP committees.[12] One citizen can have only one permanent *hukou*, at only one *hukou* zone, where he is a permanent resident. The unit of registration is the household, which may be a family (nuclear or extended),[13] a single resident living alone, or a collective household such as a *danwei* (work unit), a dormitory, a military unit, or a religious temple or shrine. The overwhelming majority of the households are families. In 1998, there were a total of 6.35 million *danwei*s and 4.4 million administrative and social organizations in China,[14] but most of them did not register any collective households. Since the start of urban reforms in 1984, the number of people registered in collective households has decreased significantly. In 1999, only 6.6 million people (about 0.5 percent of the total population, down from 33 million or 3 percent in 1986) registered in 836,000 such collective households (about 0.2 percent of all households, down from over a million in 1986).[15]

Anyone who moves out of his *hukou* zone permanently (*qianyi*) must apply for a Migrant *Hukou* Certificate (*hukou qianyi zheng*) from the *hukou* police and then cancel his old *hukou* record and register at his new *hukou* zone. The Migrant *Hukou* Certificate serves as the legal proof of his *hukou* record for a specified period of time (no more than thirty days) until a new permanent *hukou* registration can be made at the migrant's destination. For rural residents resettling in urban areas, one of the following special documents is required in applying for a Migrant *Hukou* Certificate: an employment notice from an urban labor bureau above the county level, or proof of admission to an urban school (which must be a state-accredited professional school, college, or graduate school), or a special *Hukou* Relocation Permit (*hukou zhunqian zheng*) from an urban *hukou* authority. Any migration to a border region must be approved by a public-security bureau at or above the county level.

Military personnel register in the collective household of their military unit. The top CCP and PRC leaders in Beijing generally all have their *hukou* registered in a special police station inside the *Zhongnanhai* compound, and top military leaders tend to have their *hukou* registered nominally at the address of the General Office of the Central Military Commission, located in central Beijing. The Central Military Commission has a special unit to take care of *hukou* registration for top generals who move around, so as to protect the flexibility and secrecy of their assignments. Often military officers can leave their *hukou* in one place while working in another, and their officer identification cards can serve as their only identification documents.[16] Draftees cancel their old *hukou* and restore it upon discharge. Demobilized or retired officers generally are all given an urban *hukou*.

The *hukou* police automatically cancel the *hukou* of convicts and reregister them with the *hukou* police in the area of their incarceration. Upon release, an ex-convict may or may not restore his previous *hukou*. In an anticrime practice frequently used by the government, many urban convicts, especially repeat offenders, are reassigned a new *hukou* in remote towns or rural areas to prevent their moving back to cities upon their release. Those travelling overseas for more than a year must cancel their *hukou* when applying for their passports and may restore their previous *hukou* upon returning permanently.[17]

Anyone living outside his *hukou* zone (except in the same city or county) for more than three days must register with the local *hukou* police. A temporary *hukou* certificate (*zanzhuzheng* or *zanjuzheng*, temporary residential permit) is issued to visitors who stay for more than three months. A temporary *hukou* is good for three to six months (up to a year if needed) and may be renewed by the local *hukou* police for officially accepted reasons.[18] Travelers must register with their innkeepers for inspection by the local police. Violators are subject to fines, arrest, and forced repatriation.

Certain state hires and transfers grant automatic permission for *hukou* relocation. Apart from that, all internal migration is controlled by *hukou* police according to nationally set, regionally adjusted principles. There are four overall principles governing *hukou* relocation and internal migration in the PRC:[19]

1. To strictly control any migration that changes agricultural or rural *hukou* to nonagricultural or urban *hukou*, town *hukou* to city *hukou*, or city *hukou* to metropolitan *hukou* (Beijing, Shanghai, Tianjin, and other major cities).

2. To control migration appropriately from the countryside to suburban areas, from suburban areas to cities, or from small cities to large cities.

3. To allow parallel migrations between or exchanges of *hukou* zones in similar villages, comparable towns, or similarly ranked cities.

4. To encourage dispersal from cities to towns, from large cities to small cities, and from urban areas to the countryside.

Chinese citizens need their *hukou* documentation for education, marriage, passports, travel, employment, business licenses, and even to open an account for a public utility, a fixed telephone line, or cellular telephone service.[20] Couples need to show their *hukou* documentation to acquire their birth quota (*shengyu zhibiao*) so as not to violate the state policy on family planning and birth control.[21] Until the 1990s, many important, heavily state-subsidized economic benefits, such as food rations, were allocated only to urban residents, the nonagricultural *hukou* holders. Subsidized housing, schooling, and health care were generally available only to local *hukou* holders. This changed after 1985, when the PRC started to reform its grain policy. By 1993, nearly five hundred cities or counties had abandoned the grain-ration system, although some major cities restored it in 1994 to guarantee low food prices for urban residents.[22] Market allocation of grain has become the main avenue of food distribution in today's PRC. Since 1998, China has begun replacing its subsidized housing allocation or rental with subsidized housing-purchase plans for its urban residents.[23]

In the early 2000s, urban *hukou* holders still clearly enjoy significant state subsidies in housing, transportation, public utilities, education, and health care.[24] The unsubsidized urban housing market has been generally too expensive for ordinary citizens. Redistribution of income by the local government, in the form of welfare, poverty relief, unemployment insurance, and community cultural activities, generally benefits only local *hukou* holders. Those not holding local *hukou* can send their children to local schools only after making substantial payments for available slots. The children, however, must still return to their permanent *hukou* zones to take college and professional-school entrance examinations, which are usually much more competitive outside the major cities. Incidentally, this requirement is very much in the tradition of the imperial examination system, under which the examinee was required to take the tests in his home town, where his *hukou* was located.

In China, the central and provincial governments pay the bulk of the costs of the nine-year mandatory education for urbanites, but the rural education cost is entirely borne by the much poorer peasants and the cash-strapped local (village and township) governments.[25] Undoubtedly, state-subsidized urban schools offer a much better education. The regional differential in college admissions remains perhaps the most significant state subsidy to the privileged urban population, especially legal residents in major metropolitan centers such as Beijing and Shanghai.[26] Upon graduation from college, students are generally sent back to the urban sector of the province and prefecture, even the county of their original *hukou*. This much-deplored policy is now considerably compromised in a number of ways by various urban governments interested in attracting talent. In the 2000s, college graduates, especially those with much sought-after skills and training, had achieved substantial if only de facto nationwide mobility through such temporary expedients as the blue-seal *hukou* scheme or the increased employment opportunities outside the state sector.

Hukou-based institutional exclusion is especially evident with regard to employment. The PRC records and publishes employment and unemployment data only for the urban population, which has never been as high as 26 percent of the total. The local governments establish unemployment benefits and training programs and create jobs only for local urban *hukou* holders. Furthermore, all employers must record their employees' *hukou* information. Without proper authorization from local labor bureaus, all employers, especially collectives and state-owned enterprises, are generally prohibited from hiring anyone without a local *hukou*, although private employers and foreign investors have been allowed to hire nonlocals since the mid-1990s.[27] Their nonlocal employees, however, still must apply for temporary residential permits before being paid. Beginning in 2001, experimental reform of the *hukou* system in certain localities has relaxed some of these controls and has even allowed outsiders to compete openly for jobs available in designated cities.[28]

Basic Registration

Registration of every citizen is the beginning and foundation of administering the PRC *hukou* system. It is also the sole legal basis of Chinese citizenship, family or kinship identification, and all other individual or family legal rights. The registrations are managed by the *hukou* police in the urban police station (*paichusuo*), sometimes in the newly fashionable police outposts (*jingwuqu*) in some large cities,[29] or by *hukou* officials in the rural township public-security offices. "The basic work of the police station [*paichusuo*]," says an official police manual, is "the *hukou*-based population management, especially the management of temporary or migrant people and targeted [*zhongdian*] people."[30]

Each police station should have one or more *hukou* police doing the desk and office work.[31] For every five hundred to seven hundred households in the jurisdiction of a police station or outpost, there is one nationally mandated full-time *hukou* field police officer (or community police officer, as they were renamed in some cities by the 2000s). Each *hukou* field officer is responsible for getting to know every resident in these households down to the details of their financial status, close friends and main relations, physical features, accent and slang use, and personal characteristics and preferences. The MPS requires a *hukou* police officer to spend at least thirty hours per week in the households of his *hukou* zone.[32] In reality, one *hukou* police officer often has to work on eight hundred to a thousand households. In some rural areas, one officer may be responsible for as many as twenty-five hundred.[33] One model seventeen-year veteran *hukou* police officer was praised for knowing everything about the twenty-one hundred households in his *hukou* zone in Nanchang, the capital city of the underdeveloped Jiangxi Province.[34] In Guangzhou suburbs, one officer on average was in charge of 2,340 people, and one police station with eighty-four officers was in charge of as many as two hundred thousand people (including migrants).[35]

The *hukou* police or *hukou* officials maintain the records of two types of *hukou* registration: permanent *hukou* and temporary *hukou*. A person or family's *hukou* file records seven categories of information: birth, death, personal data, family relations, migration out, migration in, and changes or corrections. Each local *hukou* holder (except for senior officials at or above the level of vice minister and deputy provincial governor, certain VIPs, and active-duty military and police personnel) has a *hukou* dossier, which may be simply a *hukou* information card on file, in the local police station. Individual *hukou* dossiers are available to law-enforcement agencies or other authorized personnel.[36] The *Hukou* Registration Form and its legal copy the *hukou* booklet, kept by the household, and the Migrant *Hukou* Certificate, *Hukou* Relocation Permit, PRC personal identification card, and various authorizing *hukou* seals are produced by the MPS and are nationally uniform. The localities have been authorized to produce their own *hukou*-related documentation such as *hukou* booklets for nonagricultural households that provide their own grain, collective *hukou* booklets, birth registration forms, death registration forms, registration forms for migration within a *hukou* zone and registration forms for migration within a city or county.[37]

Permanent hukou. Permanent *hukou* is the most important registration of the PRC *hukou* system, the basis of *hukou*-based institutional exclusion, social control, political organization, and resource allocation in contemporary China. Permanent *hukou* is the legally recognized location and type of a citizen's *hukou* and is unrelated to actual location and length of residency. A person may actually live outside the zone where his *hukou* is located. Others may live in one area for decades without the local permanent *hukou*. All citizens must be registered within one month of birth or adoption at the local police station to establish a permanent *hukou* record regarding type, location, and family relations.[38] The location and type of one's permanent *hukou* are automatically decided by the permanent *hukou* of the birth mother or the adoptive mother. (After 1998, this could also be determined by the biological or adoptive father's *hukou*.) The *hukou* record as verified and accepted on the permanent *hukou* registration form is the legal basis for issuing the PRC resident identification card (*shenfenzheng*).[39]

Permanent *hukou* can be changed only by the *hukou* authority in the case of permanent internal migration (*qianyi*) for a state-sector job assignment, college or graduate-school enrollment, or specially authorized change of *hukou* such as recategorization of rural residents as urban residents, or for family reunion purposes. The *hukou* booklet is the legal copy of a household's *hukou* record, with each household member's *hukou* registration form as one page of it. It is issued to all households holding urban *hukou* and began to be issued to the rural residents after the mid-1990s. The *hukou* booklet is considered a very important, basic form of identification and an extensively used passage document, so no individual or organization can confiscate it for any reason. Only authorized government agencies can make specific remarks when necessary on the page designated For Remarks Only.[40] In the late 1990s, a new version of the *hukou* booklet, with color photos and anticounterfeiting features, began replacing the old ones. For reasons of convenience and in order to discourage attempts at alteration,[41] a redesigned and expanded personal identification card is being considered to replace the *hukou* booklet in the future as the sole *hukou* identification document for PRC citizens.[42]

In reality, the accuracy of the information registered and the integrity of the *hukou* records are largely a function of the effectiveness and integrity of the local *hukou* police. In the rural areas or small, remote towns, for example, the *hukou* records are sometimes lost, and many people may have two or more *hukou* booklets with different personal information on age, marital status, and family ties.[43] Hidden or unregistered and hence *hukou*-less children (nicknamed "black kids"), born in violation of the authorized birth quota (one child per couple in the urban areas and two children three years apart per couple in the countryside), apparently existed in significant numbers in the rural areas in the 1990s.[44]

Exchange of permanent *hukou* between individuals, with under-the-table monetary compensation, is acceptable and must be finally approved by the *hukou* police at both locations. Sale of permanent or temporary urban *hukou* has been tried, sporadically, by several local governments in the more open areas such as the Pearl River Delta and Sunan (southern Jiangsu Province) to promote rapid urbanization and raise capital. The central government, however, often quickly stopped such measures and penalized the responsible local cadres.[45] Beginning in the late 1980s and widely adopted in the early 1990s, a transitional *hukou*, the so-called blue-seal *hukou*, which is convertible to a permanent local *hukou* in five years if the holder can pass the annual verification, was instituted by most of the major cities to grant a quasi-permanent *hukou* to a select few, usually wealthy and educated newcomers.[46] To control urban population growth, urban *hukou* police generally are allowed a very small new permanent *hukou* quota for newcomers. Such quota limitation is more severe in the major cities.[47] Thus, in places like Beijing, often even properly approved newcomers may wait for months or even years before finally receiving their permanent *hukou* in a particular zone where they have been living and working.[48]

Temporary hukou. A temporary *hukou* is required for those staying or living outside their permanent *hukou* zone for more than three days. According to the *Provisional Regulations on the Management of Temporary Residents in the Urban Areas*, issued by the MPS on July 13, 1985,[49] all temporary residents in a city or township for longer than three days, including tourists and foreigners, must register with local *hukou* authorities.

Temporary *hukou* registration should be done directly in a police sta-

Hukou **type or category**

PERMANENT RESIDENT (*Changzhu renkou*)

Registration Form

Type of household (family, individual, or collective)	Household head (name)	Relationship to household head

---

Name	Gender
Other name	Nationality (one out of 56)
Date of birth year month	day hour minute

Legal guardian (can be two names here)	Place of birth
Guardian relationship	Birth certificate issue date

Residential address
Other address in the same city/county

Family origin (paternal grandfather's address)	Religious belief (can be blank)
Personal ID serial number	ID issue date

Education	Marital status	Military service
Height	Blood type	Profession
Employment		

When, why and from where migrated to this city (county)	year month day
When, why and from where moved to this address	year month day

---

When, why and to where migrated out of this city (county)	year month day
When and why canceled this *hukou*	year month day

Applicant's signature/seal	*Hukou* registration authority's special seal

---

Processor's signature/seal	Registration date

FIG. 3.2 (above and facing page). Registration Form for Permanent Residents (Ministry of Public Security Directive [1995] No. 91, December 19, 1995). The *hukou* police or *hukou* official applies a stamp of "non-agriculture" (urban) or "agriculture" (rural) in red ink to the form. In some major cities, a blue stamp of "non-agriculture (urban)" indicates a transitional and quasi-permanent urban *hukou* status (blue-seal *hukou*). Source: Sun Yao 1994, 58–59, BPT-MPS 2000, 66–84 and MPS-PSMB 2001, 482–500.

Item	Change, Correction	Change date	Applicant's signature/seal	Processor's signature/seal

Remarks

photo 1	photo 2	photo 3

tion within three days of arrival and canceled when the registrant is leaving town. A temporary *hukou* expires automatically in three months if it is not canceled earlier. Parolees must register with the authorities on the day of their arrival, and overseas Chinese staying in the homes of local residents must register within twenty-four hours. Temporary *hukou* registration can also be done indirectly through specially trained and authorized registration clerks when checking in or out at a hotel or guesthouse.[50] By 2001, all hotels and inns with more than fifty beds were required to have computers and scanners directly linked to the local police station to transmit guests' information and photos instantaneously as they check in.[51]

Anyone over age sixteen staying longer than three months must apply for a Temporary Residential Permit (*zanzhuzheng*) as legal proof of temporary *hukou* and the official permit of local residency.[52] Migrants who remain outside their permanent *hukou* zones after three months must have this permit to legally rent housing, work, open a bank account, or receive registered mail, and for other personal identification purposes. The *zanzhuzheng* can be renewed every six to twelve months with proper application from the head of the hosting household, the landlord, or the employer. Temporary workers, investors, and businessmen from outside the town may apply for a similarly devised Guest Residential Permit (*jizhuzheng*), with a longer term. The *zanzhuzheng* and *jizhuzheng* allow their holders longer-term but still temporary local *hukou*. A temporary *hukou* functions like the temporary visas that many nations grant to foreign visitors.

Unlike the more stable blue-seal *hukou*, which resembles the permanent residency (the so-called green card) granted to new immigrants in the United States, temporary *hukou* cannot be changed into permanent *hukou* no matter how long its holder has lived or worked legally in the same city. Temporary *hukou* holders are not considered local residents and are generally restricted from seeking local employment. In the special economic zones (SEZs) and many newly expanded cities along China's coastline, temporary *hukou* holders often far outnumbered the permanently relocated migrants or local *hukou* holders in the 1990s.[53] But a priority of hiring local *hukou* holders first is still clearly mandated by the government there.[54] Even in the remote city of Urumqi, the capital of Xinjiang in the northwest, the city bureau of public security and bureau of labor jointly published an official notice at the train station and the bus terminals proclaiming as follows:[55]

All outsiders who want to work or do business in Urumqi must present personal identification cards and Sojourning Employment Registration Cards issued by the labor authorities in the original *hukou* zones to register at the [only and officially run] Urumqi Labor Market for Outsiders.

All hires of outsiders in the city must be approved by the City Labor Bureau, and the hired must acquire an Outsider Working Permit and then apply for a *zanzhuzheng* [temporary residential permit] from the Bureau of Public Security and a Birth Planning Certificate from the birth-control authorities. No employers or persons can hire outsiders on their own. Violators will be severely punished if caught. Reporting of such illegal hiring is encouraged [two hotline phone numbers are listed].

In reality, different localities have their own regulations about temporary *hukou* registration. Although most of them follow the spirit of Beijing's regulations and directives, there are great variations and significant technical discrepancies in localized implementation procedures. For example, since the three-day preregistration stay limit is increasingly hard to enforce in areas with heavy migrant traffic,[56] some localities (e.g., Fujian Province in 1994, Xiamen in 1998) adopted a new seven-day rule, whereas others (e.g., Daqing in 1996) simply adopted a new ten-day limit.[57] Increasingly in the 2000s, many families do not bother to register their guests for short stays of less than a month. They usually register their guests after weeks, if at all, and often only after being reminded to do so by the *hukou* police, residential association, or street committee. Yet criticism, a nominal penalty such as loss of a star in a Five-Star (or Ten-Star) Household Contest,[58] or a fine is commonly levied against a host family that forgets to do the right thing. All host families are legally responsible and liable for their registered and unregistered guests' deeds. After three days, unregistered outsiders in a city are generally subject to detention and forced repatriation, although they can usually remain by obtaining a make-up registration if they have a local person or family hosting them and a place to stay.

Similarly, the requiring *zanzhuzheng* (temporary residential permit) for a stay of more than three months became increasingly hard to enforce in the 2000s. Many migrants apply for *zanzhuzheng* only when they need one (e.g., for a job application) many months after arrival. Each applicant for *zanzhuzheng* must produce documentation from a local employer, local host, or local landlord, and a character reference from the police in his permanent *hukou* zone. All landlords must bring their prospective tenants to register at the local public-security bureau or police station before renting out houses or rooms. The prospective guests or

Temporary Resident (*Zanzhu renkou*) Registration Form

Original *hukou* type or category   Host/landlord's name

Temporary residential permit serial number   Relationship to host/landlord

Basic information	Name Gender photo Other name Nationality Date of birth year month day Resident Personal ID card serial number Permanent *hukou* address Permanent *hukou* category Education Marital status Profession
Temporary information	Date of arrival Reason of stay Place of stay Current profession Current employment Responsible person Temporary address Temporary residential Temporary residential permit issue date permit expiration date Reason of cancellation Cancellation date Left for where
With persons 15 or younger	Relation Name Gender Date of birth ID card number
Verification by mail	Contacts
remarks	

Filing unit   Processor   Filing date   year   month   day

FIG. 3.3. Registration Form for Temporary Residents (MPS Directive [1996] 3, May 26, 1996). Source: BPT-MPS 2000, 181 and MPS-PSMB 2001, 508–514. "Original *hukou* type or category" = either non-agriculture (urban) or agriculture (rural).

tenants must produce identification papers (including their personal ID cards) issued by their original employers or by the authorities of their permanent *hukou* zones.

People who can afford upscale temporary housing in the so-called star-rated (*xinji*) hotels are often exempted from the temporary *hukou* registration requirement. They have only to check in routinely at the hotel and have their passports or personal identification scanned or copied. Believing that temporary *hukou* holders, many of them *liudong renkou* (migrant people), are highly mobile and prone to committing crimes,[59] the police in many major cities have started to use computer networks to cross-check and monitor them.[60] One internal police study concluded that temporary *hukou* holders, especially unregistered *mangliu* (blind floaters), should be the new focus of China's community police work.[61] In some urban centers like Shanghai, the police have set up outposts on large construction sites to register all migrant workers and check their identification in order to prevent unregistered migrants from living in the workers' quarters.[62]

In practice, many outsiders holding temporary *hukou* are not employed for legitimate or legal jobs. Many urban garbage-recycling workers from rural areas are unlicensed, and as one internal study reported, 66 percent of all prostitutes in China (90 percent in Guangdong, 83 percent in Fujian) are nonlocal residents or floaters, primarily from the countryside.[63] These sojourning workers usually get their temporary *hukou* registrations under an assumed profession and employment, often with a substantial bribe to the *hukou* police. One police-station chief in a large city joyfully described his colleagues' double income from the large number of prostitutes holding temporary *hukou* in his precinct: first the women paid the police for temporary *hukou*; then they paid again in the form of hefty fines once arrested.[64]

At the turn of the twenty-first century, between 100 million and 120 million Chinese, mostly from rural areas and including more than two million school-aged children, were living outside their permanent *hukou* zones. This large migrant population mainly stayed in the cities and towns, which had a total of 327 million permanent or local urban *hukou* holders.[65] Almost every Chinese city and town, and many prosperous villages, had migrant populations, either registered as temporary *hukou* holders or *zanzhuzheng* holders, or else simply unregistered floaters.[66] The size of the migrant population is estimated to reach 300 million by 2015.[67] Only a fraction of the migrants were registered as temporary *hukou* holders applying for the legal *zanzhuzheng*. Many others were registered only as short-term visitors, though many of these frequently stayed longer than the three months allowed.[68] A significant number of the migrants, however, possibly exceeding half even in the better-managed metropolises, were either hiding from or missed by the police and had neither *zanzhuzheng* nor any temporary registration at all.[69]

Temporary *hukou* holders pay local taxes and may have access to local public facilities and sociopolitical activities other than elections or political appointments and other community-based local political and social rights. They have no access to community-defined distribution of benefits such as welfare, housing allocation and subsidies, unemployment relief, and jobs in local collective enterprises such as the township and village enterprises (TVEs) until the local community runs out of local job applicants. They or their children pay additional fees—often ten times the normal fee—to attend local elementary, middle, and high schools upon special approval, usually after intense mobilization of *guanxi* or personal connections. The few but increasingly numerous private schools, however—like Beijing's much-vaunted Xindongfang (New Oriental) Preparatory School, which offers preparation for TOEFL (Test of English as Foreign Language) and for the GRE (Graduate Record Examination)—charge students holding temporary *hukou* the same fee, which is high by Chinese standards.[70] High-school graduates must return to their permanent *hukou* zones to take part in college entrance examinations or state-sponsored employment or training programs.

Cost of basic registration. Permanent *hukou* registration is often a routine formality, normally requiring only a trip to the local police station or *hukou* office. An uncomplicated registration usually takes a few hours to complete. It is similar to the time needed for the *propiska* (registration permit) in the former Soviet Union: some four to twenty hours to prepare the documents and get to the police station, and another three or four hours to register with the police.[71] The cost for the paperwork and the documents issued, which can be as low as 6 Yuan RMB for a simple registration and a new *hukou* booklet, is largely nominal and nationally uniform.[72] Temporary *hukou* registration, however, carries additional fees and is more costly, often complicated, and thus time-consuming.[73] The penalties for not registering properly or for committing fraud include detention, fines, forced repatriation, and public denunciation.

Whereas it is inexpensive and relatively easy for a short-term visitor to register through hotel check-in, to get a *zanzhuzheng* through a sponsoring employer, landlord, or both can be time-consuming and expensive. The difficulty varies in different places, and it may take several trips to a police station to complete the process. The fee for *zanzhuzheng* application also varies in different cities, ranging from 200 to 500 Yuan RMB or more for a six-to-twelve-month renewal, the equivalent of one month's wages for a typical manual laborer.[74] The sponsoring employer is also required to pay other locally determined fees. Sometimes certain local employers, by local police regulations, can sponsor only a short-term *zanzhuzheng* of three to six months, thus effectively increasing the cost to the applicants.[75] Indirect costs such as for connections and bribes vary and can be several times more than the official fee. The Chinese Central Television reported on April 18, 2004, that in the southern cities of Shenzhen and Dongguang, local *hukou* police often charge the *zanzhuzheng* applicant a one-time fee of 155–215.5 Yuan RMB, rather than the 5 Yuan fee stipulated by the law.

As shown in case reports compiled by police and the courts, the local *hukou* police usually issue a citation or warning to those who do not properly register either as permanent local residents or for temporary local *hukou*. Fines stood at 20 to 50 Yuan RMB in the late 1980s and the early 1990s, roughly a quarter to a half of the average monthly wage at that time.[76] Ten years later, for people who counterfeit *hukou* papers or *zanzhuzheng*, who hire an outsider without local *hukou* or local *zanzhuzheng*, or who become involved in other *hukou*-related fraud, the penalties include fines of 500 to 1,000 Yuan RMB, one to three times the related illegal income, and possible imprisonment.[77] Extreme perpetrators of *hukou*-related fraud may be sentenced to prison for twenty years.[78]

The major urban centers in the PRC all have large police forces, usually with a quarter to a third of their staff assigned to managing the *hukou* system. At the end of the 1990s, for example, the city of Beijing had three police per thousand residents, 50 percent more than the average of two per thousand in developed nations. The figure in Shanghai was 2.8 per thousand, in Tianjin 2.3, in Guangzhou 4.0, in Chongqing 3.3, and in the inland city of Lanzhou 2.7.[79] To improve accessibility, the police stations in Shanghai started in 1991 to maintain a twenty-four-hour *hukou* office to receive applications and other *hukou*-related requests.[80] The millions of migrants have clearly increased the workload and created more *hukou*-related jobs for the police, since "the management of temporary *hukou* is usually twice as difficult and costly as the management of permanent *hukou*."[81] In Guangzhou, for example, where there were 2.69 million temporary *hukou* holders in 2000, the police set up a three-layer structure (street, district, and city) to register and manage these outsiders, 14 percent of whom stayed longer than a year. A total of 2,199 teams was created to mange the temporary *hukou* holders and rental houses, and 3,382 full-time *hukou* police were added to register and monitor migrants.[82]

Migration Registrations: Tools of Regulation and Control

In addition to routine basic registration of permanent and temporary *hukou*, the *hukou* police are also in charge of regulating and controlling internal migration through the management of permanent migration or *hukou* relocation.

From the *hukou* system's standpoint, legally permanent internal migration (*qianyi*) in the PRC is defined as involving citizens who move from one *hukou* zone to another and complete *hukou* relocation through registering with *hukou* authorities and thus acquire a new legal address and *hukou* status. It differs from the concept of population movement, which includes legal migration and legal migrants who have yet to complete their *hukou* relocation, as well as people who have left their *hukou* zones without completing *hukou* relocation registrations—the so-called floating people (*liudong renkou*) or more derogatorily, blind floaters (*mangliu*).[83] Registration to relocate permanent *hukou* has two parts: *qianchu* (outmigrant) and *qianru* (inmigrant) registration.

Qianchu (outmigrant) registration. Anyone who moves out of his *hukou* zone must report to the *hukou* police or officials to get a Migrant *Hukou* Certificate (*hukou qianyi zheng*) and cancel his original permanent *hukou*. The Migrant *Hukou* Certificate contains all the information on the permanent *Hukou* Registration Form and specifies the reason and destination of the migration and the effective time of the certificate (maximum 30 days). In 1991, new Migrant *Hukou* Certificates were instituted to prevent abuses and counterfeiting: black for nonagricultural and deep green for agricultural *hukou* holders. In 1995, the current Migrant *Hukou* Certificate was adopted, no longer using two colors to separate agricultural and nonagricultural *hukou* holders symbolically. This certificate is carefully prepared, sealed with at least three stamps, and signed by the processing police officer or official. It has a serial number and two detachable copies for filing purposes. The *hukou* police are instructed to in-

spect carefully the applicant's documentation, mainly his *Hukou* Relocation Permit (*hukou zunqian zheng*), before issuing the Migrant *Hukou*
Certificate, which serves as a transient *hukou* before the holder gets a
new permanent *hukou* through inmigrant registration at the new *hukou*
zone.

Applicants migrating from rural to urban areas—and to a lesser degree
from small cities to major cities, especially Beijing, Shanghai, Tianjin, and
Chongqing, as well as other specially controlled large cities—must fur-
nish proof of employment or admission from labor or education bureaus
at or above the county level. Otherwise, one can apply for a Migrant
Hukou Certificate only with a *Hukou* Relocation Permit from the *hukou*
police of the destination. Only the *hukou* police at or above the level of
the prefecture bureau of public security can issue a Migrant *Hukou* Certificate to a rural resident seeking to move to a city as an applicant for urban *hukou*.

If a *zhongdian* or specifically targeted person is migrating, the *hukou*
police must inform the police in both places to preclude any lapse in managing him internally. For criminal suspects and controlled persons, the
hukou police may delay outmigrant registration so to enable detectives to
finish their investigations. For people migrating abroad, the *hukou* police
must recover the *hukou* booklet and personal identification card. No Migrant *Hukou* Certificate is given to people going abroad, and there
should not be "any *hukou*-related marks on the passport";[84] hence the
PRC *hukou* system never shows up on the radar screens of foreign authorities.

Qianru (inmigrant) registration. Like outmigrant registration, inmigrant registration is a key mechanism for the *hukou* system to control
and manage internal migration in the PRC. Generally the regulations
stipulate that the *hukou* police will register new residents on the basis of
their valid Migrant *Hukou* Certificates and other necessary documentation. In the cities, especially the major ones, people moving from rural areas or smaller cities must have a preissued *Hukou* Relocation Permit.

The *Hukou* Relocation Permit is issued by the *hukou* police at the destination *hukou* zone under authorization by various state or provincial
policies, instructions, and quotas. It must be approved by the *hukou* authority at or above the county level and used as a communication to the
hukou police of the migrant's original *hukou* zone.[85] A *Hukou* Relocation
Permit is good only for a maximum of forty days after issuance.[86]

With the proper Migrant *Hukou* Certificate and *Hukou* Relocation

Permit, the new resident must register within three days (ten days in rural areas) of arrival with the *hukou* police in the new location. After verification, the police of the new *hukou* zone will ask the newcomer fill out the permanent *Hukou* Registration Form and issue him a new *hukou* booklet. All details such as the new address on the new permanent *Hukou* Registration Form and the new *hukou* booklet must be identical with the information on the *Hukou* Relocation Permit and other papers. If the migration is within the same city, then the original permanent *Hukou* Registration Form can be used for the new *hukou* zone. The authorized migrant's *hukou* dossiers and files will be sent by the police to his new *hukou* zone within one month, shipped through the *jiyao tongxin* (classified mailing) system as required by regulations.[87] Sometimes in practice, migrants are observed to simply carry their *hukou* dossiers in an officially sealed envelope.

Even with all required documentation in hand, however, a migrant does not automatically complete inmigrant registration as a permanent *hukou* holder at the new *hukou* zone. Local *hukou* police have the authority to delay or even reject applications for inmigrant registration on grounds of improper documentation or local quota limits. In the major cities, migrants anxious to complete their inmigrant registration and thus to acquire a new permanent local *hukou* commonly use connections and bribes to move to the top of the waiting list. Even those who have all the necessary documents in a city whose inmigrant quota is available may still want to pay off the *hukou* police to ensure a smooth process.

The inevitable corruption related to migrant registration has increased since the early 1990s. Many *hukou* police report that migrant payoffs have become important *chuangshou* (created or additional revenue, often shared with colleagues in the same station or office) for maintaining a decent standard of living.[88] Judging by the numbers of internal migrants, both *qingyi renkou* (people of permanent migration or *hukou* relocation) and *liudong renkou* (temporary migrants or floating population),[89] such additional revenue has been quite significant and thus has provided *hukou* officials and police with profoundly vested interests in keeping the *hukou* system.[90]

Cost of migrant registration. Although there are nationally and regionally published standards for Migrant *Hukou* Certificate, *Hukou* Relocation Permit, and both outmigrant and inmigrant registrations fees,[91] the actual cost of migrant registration is highly case-specific and usually many times more expensive. Stories are common about migrants with all the necessary papers still having to pay thousands of Yuan RMB to complete their registration. Moreover, some major cities require almost all newcomers to pay a onetime urban construction or urban expansion fee, which can be as high as 50,000 Yuan RMB, equivalent to several years' average urban wages.[92]

Until the mid-1990s, it was common to require five or six supporting letters, a dozen or more official seals, more than ten steps of approval, and several years' effort before a migrant could complete his registration and relocate his *hukou*.[93] A decentralization of authorities governing *hukou* relocation in the mid-1990s helped considerably to streamline the process. In the early 2000s, migrant registration became much simpler, and the MPS asked police stations if at all possible to stay open twenty-four hours a day and to complete migrant registrations within a month of the migrant's arrival.[94] Yet it is in fact very rare for an ordinary citizen to be able to complete the migrant registration with just two or three trips to the police station. Good connections (*guanxi*) are always very helpful.

Other Hukou-related Actions

In addition to the all-important basic *hukou* and migrant registrations, the PRC *hukou* system is charged with the collection of other important information about the citizens. Birth, death, and marriage are routinely monitored by *hukou* police and officials. The PRC government relies on *hukou* records as its legal source for information about population changes and for purposes of criminal investigation. Changes and corrections are made to *hukou* files when a household changes its address in the same *hukou* zone, merges with another household, or divides into several new households. *Hukou* police are responsible for changing the permanent or temporary *hukou* records and booklets, and for the computerization of the *hukou* system that started in the major cities in 1992.[95] By the end of 2001, more than thirty thousand police stations had computerized their *hukou* files; 1,180 cities and counties had joined regional computer networks for sharing 1.07 billion people's *hukou* files (about 83 percent of the total population), and 250 cities had joined a single *hukou* computer network to allow instantaneous verification of *hukou* information covering 650 million people (about half the total population) nationwide.[96]

In the major cities and some sensitive areas such as transportation hubs and border regions, routine or ad hoc *hukou* information verification campaigns (*cha hukou* or *hukou jiancha*) can be launched at the discretion of local public-security bureaus under instruction from local CCP committees. Occasionally, grand *hukou* verification and inspection (*hukou da jiancha*) may take place nationwide. During these campaigns, police, street-committee members, and local government officials will visit literally every household and hotel room unannounced—sometimes in the middle of the night—to check the accuracy of the *hukou* records, to record any changes, to make corrections, and to catch unregistered and illegal migrants. For example, in August 2000, prior to the fifth national census on November 1, major cities like Beijing launched *hukou* information verification campaigns manned by more than seventy thousand officials and police.[97] Most police and public-security officials whom this author interviewed in the early 2000s seemed to believe that such surprise visits were powerful tools in fighting crime.[98] Unannounced *hukou* inspection, according to police reports and detectives' accounts published in China, is indeed an excellent excuse very frequently used by the police detectives to have a convenient visit to and even a quick search of people's residences without waiting for a search warrant or unduly alerting potential suspects.

The availability of upscale hotels and private housing on the open market in the cities and the intention of meeting international standards (*yu shijie jiegui*) have substantially reduced the frequency and intrusiveness of these inspections and verifications since the late 1990s. In a major effort to quell foreign criticism and create a tourist-friendly environment, after 1997 the Chinese local governments, beginning in Shanghai, changed local regulations in order to end surprise *hukou* inspections of hotels rated three-star or above by the PRC State Tourism Bureau (usually qualified to receive foreign visitors). Many Chinese citizens have started to demand court authorization papers before allowing *hukou* police or officials to enter their houses or apartments, since on-the-spot *hukou* inspection or verification remains the public-security bureau's administrative action and usually not one mandated by the law or court order. But if any illegal or inappropriate behavior (unregistered rental, undocumented migrants, unmarried couple spending the night in a hotel room, etc.) is discovered, police have all necessary legal support for prosecution or settlement upon payment of fines. In the name of creating a friendly environment for businesses and tourism in the early 2000s, local governments commonly grant many hotels, entertainment facilities, and even companies and factories exemption from routine or unannounced *hukou* verification.[99]

Conclusion

This chapter has reported the structural and operational features of the PRC *hukou* system in the early 2000s. The *hukou* system, as far-reaching and as important as it has always been, is still largely operating in secrecy, with most of its policies and mechanisms unknown to the public. Through various *hukou* registrations, the Chinese government collects extensive information on all Chinese citizens and monitors and regulates their movements. Thus the *hukou* system allows Beijing to rule and organize the population by dividing them into segments bounded and controlled by individual *hukou* location. The powerful regulation and control of internal migration by the *hukou* system in particular has provided the foundation for a stable Type 3 institutional exclusion (based on *where one is*) in the PRC.

In the past two decades, the strains and forces generated by economic reform have had a significant impact upon the *hukou* system's operation. Especially in its implementation, the system has become less rigid as it now strives to accommodate population mobility and the needs of the labor market.[100] Localized experimentation on and distortions of the *hukou* system are common and obvious. Yet in the main, the system's functions and implications remain remarkably stable and significant in China, as we will see.

CHAPTER FOUR

The PRC *Hukou* System in Action

Division, Exclusion, and Control

Two important functions make the PRC *hukou* (household registration) system an extensive and powerful institutional exclusion in China: its institutionalized regulation of internal migration and its focused social control of specified or targeted segments of the population (*zhongdian renkou*).

Thorough and rigid, the PRC *hukou* system divides China into an urban-rural duality with the latter as the institutionally excluded. It regulates and restricts internal migration, especially rural-to-urban migration, in a very unevenly endowed and developed nation. It organizes the Chinese into a clearly defined and carefully maintained sociopolitical hierarchy according to where one's *hukou* is located: metropolitan centers, large cities, medium-sized cities, small cities, towns, suburban villages, countryside, and remote or backward regions. Economically, the *hukou* system hierarchically orders China's uneven distribution of opportunity and resources among the population.

Two decades of reform and opening in the PRC since 1978 have considerably reduced the direct subsidies that the state gives to its urban residents. A market economy and the government's adaptive measures have also created flexibility, leading to a visibly increased internal migration and significant compromises of *hukou*-based discrimination. Yet the *hukou* system's fundamental role of institutional exclusion in the PRC remains considerable in the early 2000s. The *hukou* system continues to largely predetermine life chances on the basis of where and to whom one is born.

Inheriting the tested and traditional role of *baojia* (mutual responsibility), the PRC's *hukou* system performs a highly valued political function of social control. Its detailed, comprehensive data collection, restricted population mobility, daily monitoring of all residents, and focused management of *zhongdian* (targeted) people have continued to support China's sociopolitical stability during an era of vast, rapid change in almost every aspect of economy, politics, and society.

This chapter will outline these two functions of the *hukou* system, discussing the official internal principles, policies, and mechanisms for regulating internal migration and for social control, especially in the management of so-called targeted people.

History and Principles of Regulating Internal Migration

For observers, perhaps the most striking features of the PRC *hukou* system have been its rural-urban dual structure and its related control of internal migration. Some have explored this institutional peculiarity of the PRC from the analytical perspectives of citizenship, labor mobility, social justice, and urbanization.[1] In a very Chinese way, this significant and enduring institutional exclusion is based on only a few sentences in the basic law of the PRC *hukou* system, the *Regulation on Household* (Hukou) *Registration of the People's Republic of China* of 1958:[2]

> ARTICLE 10: Citizens migrating out of a *hukou* zone: the citizen or household head applies for outmigrant registration to the *hukou* agencies and claims migration documents; the original *hukou* is canceled.
>
> Citizens migrating from the countryside to cities must have proof of employment from urban labor agencies, proof of admission from schools, or proof of inmigrant permission from urban *hukou* registration agencies.

Article 16 further stipulates:

> Citizens leaving the permanent place of residence for personal reasons and living temporarily elsewhere for longer than three months must apply for extension [of temporary residence] or migration; those with no reason to extend and not qualified to relocate should return to their permanent place of residence.

This additional requirement for rural-to-urban migration later developed into a legal Great Wall separating the majority of the Chinese in the countryside from the minority in the cities, institutionally creating the most striking community-based, family-defined, and geographically founded legal exclusion in modern history. Chinese citizens have thus become divided into two segments: agricultural and nonagricultural *hukou* holders.[3] To a lesser extent, there is also a legal separation between the metropolitan centers and smaller cities and between cities and townships.

There was a short period of free migration between 1949 and 1957, when early versions of the PRC *hukou* system were mainly designed for government purposes of social control. In 1950, Beijing directed its *hukou* system to guarantee the freedom of migration. In 1951, and again in 1954, various registrations under the *hukou* system were codified, but without any specifics on migrating from rural to urban areas.[4] Even though a chronic shortage of supplies in the cities started to appear almost immediately after the urban economy became socialized and rural areas collectivized in 1956–57, the Chinese Communist Party (CCP) did not fully realize that its planned economy simply could not provide the increased urban subsidies that urbanization required. Nonetheless, after 1953, the importance of dissuading peasants from migrating into the cities was mentioned almost annually in CCP central documents.[5] The 1958 *Regulation on Household Registration* gave the *hukou* system its urban-rural duality, but this legal separation was not actively enforced until the early 1960s. The need to control internal migration, especially migration from villages to cities, became painfully clear as Mao's Great Leap Forward (1958–61) resulted in economic collapse of a magnitude rarely seen in human history.

Ever since the beginning of the 1960s, the PRC has restricted migration from the countryside to the cities by controlling changes of agricultural to nonagricultural *hukou*. The motivation for this role of the *hukou* system has been political and economic necessity. Politically, the CCP has felt its inability to develop China's largely agrarian economy and fulfill its burning political ambitions. To search for a solution in the traditions of the past was only natural. The centuries-old *hukou* system hence became a new lifeline for the CCP's political regime, social control, and economic planning. Economically, the dire need for capital under a centrally planned economy smashed the hopes of the rural population for a better life associated with rapid urbanization. Squeezing the generally uneducated, unorganized peasantry became Beijing's chief means of quickly accumulating capital. Inefficient, stagnant, and mismanaged, Beijing simply could not sustain the politically crucial ration system in the cities if the urban population kept growing. The *hukou* system was an almost perfect way to extract resources from the countryside while preventing the peasants from sharing the fruits of urban development.

Between these two Chinas—the urban minority and the rural majority—the sole, narrow bridge is state-approved change of *hukou*. Within
each of the two Chinas, the cities and villages (or communes, until the
end of the 1970s) were also kept apart from one another by *hukou* relocation control. Internal migration until the mid-1980s was primarily initiated by the state. Over 43 million urban residents were forcibly "sent
down" to the countryside while several million peasants were allowed to
become nonagricultural *hukou* holders through state employment, military service, or admission to college.[6] The *hukou* system was so resilient
that even the chaotic Cultural Revolution in the years 1966–76 barely
scratched it.[7] The previously constitutional stipulation of citizens' right of
freedom of migration, however nominal it might have been to begin with,
was finally removed from the PRC constitution in 1974, and it is still
missing in the current PRC constitution.

Since the 1980s, decollectivization has dislodged many formerly fixed
rural laborers and created pushing and pulling forces driving many rural
hukou holders to work and even live in cities and towns. However, their
hukou types are still strictly controlled as agricultural, so the rural-urban
institutional exclusion continues despite the fact that many of the excluded have now crossed this divide spontaneously. They are on temporary *hukou* (*zanzhuzheng*, temporary residential permits) and thus do not
have the full citizenship or membership of local communities as do local
urban *hukou* holders. These new urban residents with agricultural
hukou, just like those still living in the villages, cannot access exclusively
urban, heavily subsidized housing, education, and other benefits. Jobs in
the state sector, including in the government itself, state-subsidized training, and unemployment insurance are off-limits to urban-resident agricultural *hukou* holders.[8] The smaller numbers of migrants with urban *hukou*, fewer than 20 percent of the total migrant population in China in
the late 1990s, are generally treated like rural migrants when outside
their own *hukou* zones.[9]

Under the PRC, rural *hukou* holders can obtain nonagricultural *hukou*
in several government-designated ways. One way is through promotion
as a state cadre above a certain rank, usually *kezhang* (section chief) or
xiangzhang (township head). Other ways include becoming a military officer at or above the rank of platoon leader, acquiring an accredited college degree, or winning a national or international medal in sports or
other competitions. Beyond these, only limited quotas of *hukou* relocation under certain policy-dictated programs are available to peasants.

Each year the government allows a very small number of agricultural *hukou* holders to change their status to nonagricultural.[10] (Since 1980, that limit has ranged between 0.2 percent and 0.5 percent of the total agricultural population.) On that basis, each locality develops an annual quota of *nongzhuanfei* (agricultural *hukou* changed to nonagricultural), to be observed by the *hukou* police. The *hukou* police are instructed nationwide that "other than allowed for by the state planning and migration policies, no rural resident can move into urban areas, especially the large cities, without approval."[11] Stringent control based on quotas of rural migrants was only partly and gradually eliminated at the level of small cities and towns and in a few selected large cities in 2001–4, being replaced with restrictions based on locally defined entry conditions.[12]

Principles of migration regulation. The PRC State Council approved on August 14, 1964, and reaffirmed on November 8, 1977, the Ministry of Public Security's *Rules on Handling* Hukou *Relocation*. These internal rules have been the foundation for managing the rural-urban institutional exclusion in China. Various agencies of the PRC central government from 1958 to 1988 issued more than two hundred policies and decrees—most of them never publicly released—regulating internal migration, especially of the rural-to-urban sort.[13] Several dozen more policies were added in the 1990s.[14] In the early 2000s, Beijing has a four-part guideline for *hukou* changes and internal migration:[15]

> *Chongyan kongzhi* [strict control]: *Hukou* relocation from rural to urban areas (including forestry and mining zones) or from other cities to Beijing, Shanghai, and Tianjin [municipalities directly under the central government] must be controlled as restrictively as possible.
> *Shidang kongzhi* [appropriate control]: *Hukou* relocation from township to city; from small city to large city; from ordinary village to outskirts of city or township, state-run farm, village specialized in vegetable growing, or cash crop–growing area should be controlled appropriately.
> *Buyu kongzhi* [no control]: *Hukou* relocation from city or township to village; from city to township; from large city to small city; and between similar cities, between similar townships, or between similar villages, with proper reasons (such as marriage), should be approved.
> *Guli liudong* [encourage migration]: *Hukou* relocation by college graduates and professionals from city or township to village, from interior to border regions, or from areas or units with plenty of technical talent to places lacking such talent should be encouraged by various means.

In 2000, an internal *hukou* police manual candidly described the purpose of *hukou* relocation control as:[16]

[We should] encourage the dispersal of the population. [We should] make it harder to migrate to major cities, easier to small cities; harder to migrate to cities or townships, easier to villages; harder to migrate to the southeast, easier to the northwest; harder to migrate to economically developed areas, easier to old revolutionary bases [usually in remote and mountainous areas], [ethnic] minority regions, border regions, and poor areas. ... [We should] make it easier for high-quality people to relocate, harder for low-quality people; easier for professionals to relocate, harder for general labor; ... [We should] work especially to *prevent national blind floating of low-quality people.*

These current principles are indeed very blunt, albeit still only internally stated, about the nature of *hukou*-based institutional exclusion of the rural population, the residents of small cities and backward areas, and people of purportedly low quality and low skills. As with the control of internal migration before the reform era, these principles are motivated by the same political concerns and aimed at serving Beijing's economic policies and development strategies without shouldering the burden of providing for peasants sojourning in the cities.[17] The current principles, however, appear to be somewhat less manipulative and more stable than before.[18] Beyond these principles, there are over two dozen government and military agencies in Beijing and numerous local government agencies that regulate *hukou* relocation. A considerable decentralization of policy making with regard to *hukou* relocation has provided the PRC *hukou* system with a much-needed flexibility and room for experiment but has also created problems of equality and uniformity of law, and much chaos besides.[19]

Hukou Relocation: Ways and Characteristics

On the basis of various internal documents, the internal assessment reports on the *hukou* system and studies of its operation, and field observations in several locations, I have been able to piece together a general picture of the main characteristics and means of *hukou* relocation control in the PRC.

Permanent relocation through state employment and military service. Apart from increasingly rare state hiring of rural residents as permanent employees, there have remained two realistic ways of permanently changing *hukou* status from agricultural to nonagricultural: passing the entrance examination of a college, graduate school or designated professional school, or else becoming an officer in the People's Liberation Army

(PLA). College graduates and retired or demobilized PLA officers are guaranteed an urban *hukou*. Practically, in the most restricted cities—mainly Beijing, Shanghai, Tianjin, Chongqing, and special economic zones (SEZs) like Shenzhen—the local *hukou* authority may actually veto new inmigrant applications, citing quota limits. Local labor bureaus or other agencies may appeal to the central government in Beijing on behalf of rejected applicants. There have been reports that even an order from the Central Military Commission may not immediately secure urban *hukou* for decorated military officers in a highly controlled city like Beijing.

Because of the existence of local *hukou* quotas in the most controlled cities, many newcomers may have to be temporary *hukou* holders, waiting a long time to get their permanent local *hukou*. In Beijing, because of the frequent promotion of local cadres to the central government, *hukou* control is a very difficult job for the local government, and 90 percent of those who are promoted to Beijing manage to keep their families there even when they later are reassigned to other places. Thus the CCP ruled that "other than in exceptional cases, leading cadres assigned to jobs in Beijing should not bring their own secretaries, chauffeurs, or servants," and all family members of the cadres assigned jobs elsewhere must move out of Beijing.[20] Of course, such requirements are often ignored if the cadres are ranked high enough. Usually the families of senior cadres who have left Beijing manage to stay on there.

Mobility for the powerful. All retired state employees, especially the old cadres, may resettle in their home towns or live with relatives in a different location. The higher their preretirement rank, the easier and faster their acquiring a new *hukou* in a desired location. Those senior cadres (*gaogan*, cadres above the level of prefecture head or bureau chief) and their immediate family members can practically choose any city to live in after leaving office—other than Beijing.[21] A Beijing *hukou* is readily available at any time to party and state leaders at or above the level of CCP Central Committee secretary, state councilor, vice premier, National People's Congress vice chairman, or commander of a military region, and to their extended families down to the third generation.

Mobility for the wealthy. In a new and largely localized reform initiative, a new road to permanent *hukou* relocation for the wealthy emerged in the mid-1990s. As Chinese capitalism has quickly emerged in the PRC, so have property owners, industrialists, rich merchants, top salary earners, and wealthy people with incomes from legitimate or questionable sources.[22] They naturally need and demand mobility under the *hukou* system, and they have been quickly getting it.

High-paid workers and especially self-employed businessmen from rural areas or from other cities may now acquire a transitional urban *hukou* in the cities where they live (the blue-seal *hukou*, so called because the *hukou* police apply a blue stamp to the *hukou* form and booklet instead of the regular red one). But in order to qualify they must meet stringent conditions, such as being healthy, making a large job-creating investment, being sponsored by a large local employer annually paying local corporate income taxes of at least one million Yuan RMB, or purchasing commercial housing at a locally set higher-than-normal price in a designated area.[23]

Transitional urban *hukou*, much like permanent residency (the so-called green card) in the United States and still subject to the national and local annual quotas, may allow its holder to enjoy almost all the rights and benefits of local residents,[24] and to apply for permanent local *hukou* after a certain period, usually five years.[25] The transitional urban *hukou* regulations are generally local (provincial or metropolitan) policies that are not yet nationally uniform, although in 1998 the central government legitimized them in principle.[26] The associated requirements thus vary in different locations.[27] Beijing still retains the authority to strike down any similar but inappropriate local initiatives.[28] Eventual conversion to permanent urban *hukou* is subject to the usual *hukou* registrations described in Chapter 3 and to quota availability. By 2004, many cities, in the latest effort to reform the *hukou* system, had authorized an automatic conversion of the blue-seal *hukou*.

Mobility for the educated or talented. A graduate of any state-accredited college, graduate school, or designated professional school is guaranteed urban *hukou* upon graduation in the place where his state-assigned job is, without being subject to migration quotas. If the graduate refuses the assigned state job or finds a job on his own, his urban *hukou* will be automatically relocated to where his original *hukou* was. If the original *hukou* was rural, his new urban *hukou* will be relocated to the city or the county seat nearest to his home village, subject to migration quotas. The most attractive cities like Beijing and Shanghai routinely keep the top 20 to 30 percent of local college graduates originally from outside by luring them with the local urban *hukou*.[29] Expelled or dropout college students must be relocated to their home town or village without an urban *hukou* guarantee.[30] Indeed, this way, both the Chinese virtuocracy and meritocracy have been granted privileges of mobility beyond the *hukou* system's confines. [31]

Beginning in the late 1980s, those with postgraduate degrees have been given more mobility. Holders of the doctorate in any field, for example, are now by national regulation allowed to relocate their *hukou* to any city of their choice, with or without local employment or family acceptance. They and their immediate family members can choose to live in any city or town and are not subject to local *hukou* quotas.[32] A master's degree can also allow its holder to take advantage of various local policies that offer preference and flexibility in *hukou* registration and relocation. Some localities have made policies attracting people who have won major national or international awards, such as an Olympic medal, by granting them up to three local urban *hukou* (for a couple and child).[33] In consequence, there has been a clear internal brain drain in China, with the highly educated or talented flocking to desirable metropolitan areas even when relocation necessitates abandoning their profession or specialty or accepting an undesirable job.[34] This highly prized mobility and other privileges attached to degrees and academic titles and ranks have also led to the widespread occurrence of academic corruption which has sometimes made degrees, titles, and academic repute directly purchasable in Chinese universities and academic communities.[35]

PLA relocation rights. Discharged military draftees must return to their original *hukou* zones. Draftees from rural areas who have earned decorations at or above the second degree (*erdeng gong*) should be offered state jobs, hence urban *hukou*. Active-duty volunteer soldiers, after a certain term of service, may be offered state jobs and thus urban *hukou*.[36] Military officers who have served for more than fifteen years, are over thirty-five years old, and have a rank higher than deputy battalion commander (usually captain or major) may have their families living with them in the same barracks. Air-force pilots and naval ship-based officers are exempt from rank and seniority restrictions.[37] With the approval of a division commander or officer of higher rank, such *hukou* relocation is usually not subject to local inmigrant quotas, unless the barracks are located in highly restricted cities such as Beijing or Shanghai. Retired officers can move back to the urban section of their home town. Senior officers (above division commander or the rank of senior colonel) are treated similarly as those senior cadres mentioned before: after leaving the service they and their immediate family can choose practically any city to live in, other than Beijing.[38]

Relocation through marriage. A rural *hukou* holder married to an urban *hukou* holder generally cannot change his or her *hukou* status. Rare exceptions, which usually take a very long time and much effort, can be made if the rural spouse or the urban spouse has no other family members or relatives taking care of him or her during long-term illness or disability. This kind of relocation is subject to quota in the desired *hukou* zone and generally has a low priority. Basically the same rules apply to the rural parents of urban *hukou* holders. Often, such rural spouse or rural parents simply get a *zanzhuzheng* (temporary residential permit) and live in the urban area while working or awaiting eventual change of *hukou* status in the indefinite future.

As a major reform in 1998, the children of a rural-urban or cross-regional couple now are no longer required to inherit the mother's *hukou* type and location. A child may now settle in the place of the father's or the mother's *hukou*.[39] This reform took away effective *hukou* relocation control and reduced one important barrier in China's internal migration, since traditionally and culturally a rural-urban marriage usually takes place between an urban male and a rural female, and rarely the contrary. Marriage, it seems, now has become a more meaningful way for *hukou* relocation, at least for the next generation. Hence in one central district of Beijing, for example, cross-regional marriages suddenly jumped from 11 percent in 1998 to 22 percent in 1999.[40]

Policy favors and adjustments. Since the late 1990s, the rural spouse of the following types of state employee has been allowed change her *hukou* status from agricultural to nonagricultural: specified science and technology cadres (scientists and engineers) with certain ranks (e.g., a Ph.D. or professor); excavation workers in the coal mines, hardship workers in the Third Front areas (state-owned enterprises moved from major cities to remote or more backward areas in the past), correctional officers (prison managers), and veterans with extraordinary or first-degree disabilities. *Hukou* relocation of this kind generally reflects changeable policies of the CCP and the military at any given time. Applicants for such *hukou* relocation usually still have to wait for the available quota in a specific *hukou* zone, although they should have a higher priority than ordinary cases of relocation through marriage. In the People's War on SARS (severe acute respiratory syndrome) in 2003, as a desperate measure, the city of Beijing offered immediate local *hukou* to recruit much-needed medical students from the provinces.[41]

Corrections of past "mistakes." All past sent-down or purged cadres and other former urban *hukou* holders, once their cases have been reversed and they have been exonerated, can regain urban *hukou* immediately without being subject to available *hukou* quotas. All retired old cadres (cadres who joined the CCP or the PLA before 1949), if they still hold rural *hukou,* can change that to the urban type at once without being subject to local migration quotas.

Special cases. For certain special urban residents, the government now allows migration between urban areas without a specific state order. Their *hukou* relocation, mostly still subject to the destination *hukou* zone's inmigrant quota, is now basically automatic. Retired state cadres and employees, children of those who were sent to work on the Tibetan Plateau, and children of traveling workers such as sailors and geographical surveyors may apply to move to cities where their relatives live.[42]

For religious clerics, the *hukou* police register each temple, monastery, church, mosque, or shrine as a collective household. After approval and acceptance by legally registered and accredited religious organizations,[43] clerics, priests, nuns, or monks from rural areas can be granted nonagricultural or urban *hukou* at their places of residence or work as a full-time cleric away from their home towns. Upon leaving their religious organizations or returning to secular life, however, clerics must revert to their original *hukou* type and location. Traveling preachers must apply for temporary *hukou* in places away from their home temples.[44]

Hukou *changes through land development.* Peasants whose land has been taken over by the state for urbanization and economic development may be given local urban *hukou* only when the whole township's land is used up, with approval by the provincial government. Otherwise, the local government shall rely on the township and the new enterprises on the land to hire qualified landless peasants. The local urban *hukou* quota applies. In many new development areas, the land-losing peasant may have to wait a very long time to get a new job or a new urban *hukou*. This has created major problems for local PRC officials. One CCP chief in Pudong of Shanghai estimated that he spent nearly 80 percent of his time dealing with such unfulfilled demands and was even personally detained once in a county-government office by angry landless peasants.[45]

Incomplete or temporary relocation. A rural *hukou* holder or an outland urban *hukou* holder can apply, for a fee each time, for a renewable temporary *hukou* (*zanzhuzheng*) in a city where he lives and works. A temporary *hukou* or residential permit can be good for three to six months or longer.[46] A job, a landlord's sponsorship, a crime-free record, and a PRC personal identification card issued by the authorities of the permanent *hukou* zone are required. Most migrant workers in the construction and domestic-care industries in major cities like Beijing and Shanghai hold temporary *hukou*, which allows legal residence and employment but not full local rights or access to local benefits. It generally could not be converted to permanent local *hukou* until 2001, when the small cities and towns began to allow qualified migrant workers to apply for permanent local *hukou*. In the early 2000s, people living and working in major cities without local *hukou* or valid temporary *hukou* are still subject to arrest, fines, and forced deportation.[47] Police in Shanghai, for example, annually detain and repatriate over ten thousand *hukou*-less floating people.[48]

A special class of temporary urban residence has been the revival of the *yigong yinong* (peasant worker) system initiated by Liu Shaoqi in the early 1960s. Certain rural *hukou* holders may be hired by state employers to work in hard or heavy jobs such as underground excavation or hazardous cleaning. Since 1980, the rotating peasant workers have been allowed to contract for three to ten years of such employment, then go back to their villages upon fulfilling their commitments. During the period of their employment, their *hukou* remain agricultural, but their employers are responsible for providing them grain, job subsidies and bonuses, and other supplies at the state-subsidized price.[49] They cannot participate, however, in subsidized housing allocations or other local social welfare plans. Their children have to pay extra in order to attend the subsidized local urban schools and cannot take college entrance examinations in the local urban location. As a consequence, now almost all the state-owned enterprises have hired substantial numbers of such cheap and easy-to-manage peasant workers to do the heavy and dirty jobs, while having the serious problem of underemployment of the regular state employees with urban *hukou*.[50]

Gradually, the regulations about the length and the nature of temporary *hukou* are becoming more relaxed. A rural *hukou* holder who can arrange a permanent residence, have a business, or work for urban employers on a long-term basis may change his rural *hukou* to a permanent town (*jizheng* or *jianzhizheng*) *hukou*. The towns, about 19,780 in 2000, are generally urban areas smaller than the 2,109 county seats and much smaller than the 662 cities.[51] New town *hukou* holders may live in designated towns or move between similar towns like ordinary urban *hukou* holders, but cannot take advantage of state-subsidized supplies of grain or other essentials, and they are still subject to rules governing rural *hukou* holders when applying for *hukou* in cities at or above the county-seat level. Their nonimmediate family members must keep their agricultural *hukou*.[52] Since 2001, in a new round of *hukou* reforms, town *hukou* holders have been allowed to change to regular urban *hukou* at the level of small cities and towns provided that they have held stable jobs and permanent residence for at least two years.

These incomplete, temporary, or limited *hukou* relocations are clearly the state's compromise between maintaining the existing PRC *hukou* system and allowing controlled urbanization at the level of small cities and towns. They are designed to divert and control the massive surplus of rural laborers who began inevitably flooding the privileged urban areas for jobs and better lives once the communes were disbanded and agricultural productivity increased. As a result, there has been tremendous growth of small towns in the PRC in the past two decades. In many cases, some formerly rural villages and townships just simply converted themselves to *jianzhizheng* (established towns) for better social status. Gradually, as grain-related state subsidies decrease and even disappear, holders of incomplete or temporary urban *hukou* have begun to blend in with original urban *hukou* holders in towns and small cities.

Hukou relocation as a legal weapon. A released inmate may be given local *hukou* where his new employment is, usually at the very same labor camp. These tend to be located in sparsely populated western provinces such as Gangsu, Qinghai, and Xinjiang. If the inmate is originally from an urban area, his new *hukou* will again be urban. A released convict may request *hukou* relocation to his original city, town, or village, provided that his family agrees to receive him or there is a job for him, and the police at his home *hukou* zone approve.

It is not unusual to observe a PRC court adding an additional penalty to certain sentences: banning convicts' *hukou* relocation back to their home cities, towns, or villages. Upon release, they will be required to have a local *hukou* in the city, town, or village nearest their labor camp or prison, usually in a less developed, harsh, sparsely populated area. First-time offenders may or may not be allowed to regain their old urban *hukou*. Repeat offenders or those who attempt escape "must not regain the *hukou* they had from major and medium cities."[53] This rule, however, applies only to convicts from large and medium-sized cities, those having more than three hundred thousand urban *hukou* holders. Those compelled to remain near their prisons may regain their original urban *hukou* if they can prove satisfactory rehabilitation after three years.[54] Over the decades, such forced permanent resettlement has created new townships and villages in western China.

Overseas Chinese. Chinese from Hong Kong and Macao may apply for permanent urban *hukou* in any city in which they wish to live permanently, subject to approval of the *hukou* authorities at or above the city level. People from Taiwan may also do so, subject to approval from the CCP's Central United Front Department, the Ministry of Public Security (MPS), and the provincial government. New settlers from Hong Kong, Macao, and Taiwan are generally all given urban *hukou*. Overseas Chinese must be preapproved by the PRC Office of Overseas Chinese Affairs before they can apply for permanent local *hukou*. Preferential treatment is given to those who were state-employed professionals of the PRC before they left China. Foreign nationals of Chinese ancestry who are deemed experts in science and technology may apply for urban *hukou* once they complete the process of naturalization to become Chinese citizens. Since there are currently many *hukou* applications from overseas Chinese in the former Soviet Union, Mongolia, and North Korea, "their applications must be handled more restrictively."[55]

Distortion, stability, resistance. In reality, different localities in the PRC can and often do have their own practices and policies regarding *hukou* relocation. Many of these are ad hoc and undocumented. There are cases of local leaders' bending Beijing policies and regulations, especially in the name of local CCP committees. Cases of *hukou*-related corruption or distortion are sometimes reported in the Chinese media as part of the overall corruption of the Chinese bureaucracy.[56] But generally the government's control of *hukou*-relocation appears to be less subject to the eroding forces of corruption and local corporatist resistance (*duice*) to Beijing than many other areas, such as the PRC's industrial policies or even its taxation system.

The reasons for that relatively high effectiveness and stability of the control of *hukou*-relocation may lie in the strong political and social legitimacy that the PRC *hukou* system still enjoys, the relatively simple and uniform mechanisms of that system, the newly devised and localized accommodating measures such as the blue-seal *hukou*, and the strict enforcement of quotas by public-security agencies. When money can legitimately buy urban *hukou*, the incentive is reduced for the rich to bribe the *hukou* police.

There are still almost daily occurrences of harassment, arrest, and deportation of unregistered or unauthorized migrants in many Chinese cities in the 2000s. The police often physically mistreat *hukou*-less floating people and confiscate their personal belongings.[57] A somewhat surprising finding has been that, despite the clear rise of individualism and a sense of human rights in the PRC in the past decade, culminating in the landmark amendment of the PRC constitution in March 2004 to guarantee citizens' human rights, most people, including excluded rural residents, seem to view the control of *hukou*-relocation as a necessary and legitimate means of ensuring order and stability. Through the early 2000s there has been very little public discourse on the discriminatory aspects of the *hukou* system or the human-rights abuses associated with its implementation, except for some overseas Chinese electronic bulletin boards and Web postings.[58] Most people interviewed in private tend to believe that the control of *hukou*-relocation is a necessary evil. Even internal police studies have found that only a small minority questions the control of *hukou*-relocation and suggests eventual restoration of the freedom of migration.[59]

Passive or individual resistance or challenge to the control of *hukou*-relocation, however, is clearly widespread. Open criticism, even just in words, is often quickly suppressed, with harsh penalties.[60] For those who oppose the system with their feet, the Ministry of Civil Affairs and the police have set up repatriation centers and stations in almost all medium-sized and large cities to handle the repatriation of unregistered migrants.[61] But repatriation from hot spots (highly attractive places) such as Beijing and special economic zones like Shenzhen, despite its high cost's being borne by the government, has been a losing battle, as many of the repatriated often simply float back right away.[62]

As a consequence of spontaneous acts and political decentralization, *nongzhuanfei* (agricultural *hukou* changed to nonagricultural) or legal urbanization has developed rapidly in the decades after 1980. Over 40 million agricultural *hukou* holders became urban *hukou* holders in the 1980s in addition to government plans, creating heavy burdens on the state. The State Council responded by issuing its *Notice on Strictly Controlling the Overgrowth of* Nongzhuanfei on October 31, 1989. Numerous other decrees for controlling *nongzhuanfei* were issued by the State Council, the MPS, and other ministries in the 1990s, including one on August 2, 1994, reaffirming the 1988 prohibition of the sale of urban *hukou* to rural *hukou* holders.[63] Consequently, growth of *nongzhuanfei* slowed in the first half of the 1990s. It is officially estimated that in 1992 there were about a million fewer cases of *nongzhuanfei* than in 1989.[64] Toward the end of the 1990s, however, *nongzhuanfei* picked up steam, and in the early 2000s, after a two-year experiment in selected localities, Beijing authorized small cities and towns to eliminate inmigrant quotas and grant local urban *hukou* to all rural residents who satisfy locally determined entry conditions.[65] Some medium-sized and even large cities (such as Shijiazhuan in Hebei Province, Ningbo in Zhejiang Province, and Guangzhou in Guangdong Province) also relaxed their migration controls, allowing qualified rural residents to apply for local urban *hukou* unconstrained by quota.[66]

Tiered Management of Targeted Persons: Social and Political Control

The all-important social-control function of the PRC *hukou* system is primarily carried out by the *hukou* police in public-security bureaus and police stations throughout the country. The typical police station (*paichusuo*) in charge of a *hukou* zone has one or more *hukou* police, some of them full-time desk officers in charge of *hukou* registration, filing, research, and other related tasks. For every five hundred to seven hundred households in a police precinct (or up to two thousand households in some areas), there is one nationally mandated full-time *hukou* police field officer responsible for getting to know each and every member of these households. *Hukou* field police often work as plainclothes detectives in the neighborhoods to collect, verify, and update *hukou* information in the name of managing the *hukou* system and safeguarding political order, social stability, and public security.

Nationally, there are currently over three hundred thousand *hukou* police field officers working in the PRC. They are to collect and update information in eight categories on each and every resident in the precinct: the basic information on the *hukou* form and booklet, current behavior including political attitude and activities, family and personal financial status and standard of living, personal friends and relations including love relations, physical features including body size and shape, accent and slang use, personal character and hobbies, daily associations, and other consequential past activities.[67] In addition to the state-paid police officers, who are all urban *hukou* holders (even when they work in the rural areas), each police station usually has a large number of police assistants. The police assistants are not state employees and are hired by police stations from the local communities; hence they can be rural *hukou* holders. They are paid by the station and the local government, usually the township or district.[68]

The social-control function of the *hukou* system relies heavily on so-called public-security activists such as street-committee or residential-committee members and so-called eyes and ears of public security (*zhian ermu*)—secret informants cultivated by the *hukou* police to collect, verify, and update information on every resident in the neighborhood.[69] According to official regulations, each urban *hukou* zone usually has at least one street or residential committee under the supervision of the local government and police station. Each committee typically has between a hundred and six hundred households, organized into residential groups; each group normally has fifteen to forty households.[70] A typical street committee in Beijing, for example, has full-time salaried cadres (73.5 percent of them actually live outside the community) and part-time cadres (mostly mobilized retirees) earning half the pay of the full-timers.[71]

Informants are generally not salaried, although rewards in the form of benefits, favors, or even cash are very common, usually paid for with temporary *hukou* registration fees or administrative appropriations.[72] Many informants tend to serve ad hoc, although I have found in field interviews that most *hukou* police in each *hukou* zone do have long-term reliable informants. This well-knit *hukou*-based sociopolitical-control network is indeed, at least in its design, an ideal way for the authoritarian CCP to safely rule the massive 1.3 billion population in a vast and rapidly changing land, this People's Democratic Dictatorship, as the regime officially categorizes itself.

However, even the much more centralized and much less diversified China of the Mao Zedong era (1949–76) could not fully implement *hukou*-based totalitarian control. The PRC *hukou* police realized that they could not simply keep track of all residents all the time in all the *hukou* zones long before the present reform era (1980s–), which has featured impressive advances of the market economy and openness to the outside world, political decentralization and social relaxation, increased population mobility, deep and extensive political cynicism among the citizens, regional differentiation and diversification, and widespread corruption of PRC officials, including the police. To restore an old-fashioned *baojia* (mutual responsibility) system among households would also be extremely difficult and unrealistic. Once again, the solution lies in the past. Sociopolitical control under the PRC *hukou* system, therefore, inherited and developed a highly effective but clearly discriminatory traditional feature in its practice: the tiered, focused management of the so-called *zhongdian* (focal, specified, targeted) segments of the population.

Modeled after the Qing Dynasty's *hukou* practice of other or special records (*lingce*, described in Chapter 2) and begun in 1949 in order to control a vast population quickly and effectively while consolidating a new regime, the PRC *hukou* system has featured tiered or layered (*fencengci*) population management, allowing the state to segment and control the population. Instead of collecting information on and monitoring all residents equally, the *hukou* police are required to develop a focused approach allowing them to concentrate on and control *zhongdian renkou* (targeted people).

The MPS periodically and secretly informs the *hukou* police nationwide on who should be targeted and requires them to monitor such persons more or less uniformly. For the rest of the general population, the *hukou* police in different localities determine their own focus, depending largely on the police resources available. For example, in a major city like Beijing, the *hukou* police now are required to know only two of the aforementioned eight categories of information for the general population, basic information and current behavior. But the *hukou* police are expected to update the information on targeted people in all eight categories and to supply other information on demand besides.[73] Essentially, such a *hukou* operation is a group-based sociopolitical-control system that singles out the segments of the population designated as bad, threatening, or targeted and treats them differently—a bona fide discriminatory and exclusionary institution of social control.

According to the mid-1990s internal MPS definition, "tiered population management is, depending on whether or how much they threaten public order and national security, to categorize all residents above the age of fourteen into different tiers and manage them accordingly." The purpose of tiered population management is "to better protect the good people and restrict the bad."[74]

The Evolution of the Blacklist

In the *Draft of the Provisional Regulations on the Management of Special Residents*, issued by the MPS on August 12, 1950, five types of people were listed as special residents to be closely monitored and controlled: bandits, spies, local tyrants, cadres of reactionary parties and groups, and leaders of reactionary superstitious sects and secret societies. Detailed measures were ordered to be devised, and police could do pretty much anything, including daily eavesdropping on special residents almost without regard for their legal rights or personal privacy. With such a mission, the young PRC *hukou* system proved to be very effective in the CCP's struggles against enemies. These special residents usually became the main targets of numerous political campaigns. In Beijing alone, the *hukou* police made 12.5 percent of all arrests during the Movement of Suppressing Counterrevolutionaries (1950–52) and 74.5 percent of all arrests during the subsequent Campaign of Eliminating Counterrevolutionaries based on the files of special residents.[75]

The name "special residents" changed in September 1953 to *zhongdian renkou* (targeted people), and the list became longer with new additions: unrepentant family members of counterrevolutionaries, landlords in exile, and suspicious people from Hong Kong, Macao, Taiwan, and imperialist countries. The MPS issued its *Provisional Regulations on the Management Work of* Zhongdian Renkou in March 1956 and a revision in 1957; both remain internal directives only.

The mid-1950s list of targeted people included the addition of the broad categories of those suspected of counterrevolutionary activities and their family members and close relatives, persons suspected of all sorts of illegal activities, and those considered simply bad people or class enemies. This list contributed to and was also shaped by the increasingly fierce power struggles and heated political campaigns that culminated in the chaotic Cultural Revolution (1966–76). The list of targeted people was clearly political in nature, consisting mainly of political dissidents, Mao's critics, or subversive suspects—enemies of the CCP, broadly and arbitrarily defined. In 2000 the MPS itself admitted that during the Mao era the list of targeted people was too political, quite off base, and too large, and that it damaged the whole tiered-management operation by rendering it unpopular and inefficient.[76]

The reform era demanded a new definition of targeted people. The management of targeted persons generally relaxed beginning with the famous reform of college entrance examinations and admissions in fall 1977, when all Chinese youth not incarcerated were able to take the examination and enter college if they passed. Background checking of college applicants, based on *hukou* files and *danwei* (work unit) dossiers, was reduced to mere formality, including basic information in *hukou* forms and booklets. The management of targeted persons became depoliticized in December 1980, when the MPS revised and reissued the pertinent provisional regulation. The new list included four reclassified residential types with or without permanent local *hukou*: those suspected of counterrevolutionary activities, those suspected of other criminal activities, those posing a threat to public order, and suspicious ex-convicts. In order to address the rising rate of juvenile crime, the minimum age of the targeted people was lowered from sixteen to fourteen. Several old categories of class enemies were dropped. The management of targeted persons became increasingly institutionalized over the next two decades with increased emphasis on monitoring and controlling common criminals and disruptive behavior, and with increasing albeit still fundamentally inadequate awareness of law and individual rights.

On March 21, 1985, the MPS finally codified the management of targeted people, which had been provisional for over three decades, by issuing an internal directive titled *Regulation on* Zhongdian Renkou *Management Work*. A revised version was reissued on May 25, 1998. That regulation, still classified and still in effect, now serves as the legal foundation redirecting and refining the mission of the management of targeted people and, in legal language, has redefined the list of targeted people. According to the new revisions, both permanent residents and temporary *hukou* holders can be listed as targeted people.

The 1985 regulation on the management of targeted people lists six categories and fifteen types of residents as subject to targeted focus and special monitoring. "More realistic" as it was, so long a list still "has the problem of insufficient focus."[77] As yet another reform measure, on April 24, 1989, shortly before the Tiananmen Tragedy of June 4th, the Third Bureau of the MPS issued its *Opinion on Solving Certain Issues in Reforming Urban Public-Security-Station Work*, which proposed a four-tiered management. The whole population in a *hukou* zone above age fourteen was divided into four tiers, with the first three the same as the old targeted residents and the fourth the general population. The provinces could make their own criteria for tiers two and three and address their management accordingly. This new, more focused approach, claimed the *hukou* police interviewed, significantly improved the effectiveness of *hukou*-based population control.[78]

The first tier, based on the nationally established criteria, includes dangerous people who pose major threats to public and national security. It is subject to police monitoring and rapid actions such as preventive detention and intervention. A common practice is to develop informants in the neighborhood of the listed people and to coordinate with the security officials of the listed people's working unit (*danwei*) to have around-the-clock nonstop monitoring.

The second tier includes generally controlled residents, including persons suspected of common crimes such as racketeering, stealing, and smuggling, and frequent gamblers. The police should develop secret monitoring networks and cultivate helping or educational relationships between listed persons and approved educators or helpers, who are usually CCP members living in the community.[79]

The third tier includes residents on the monitoring screen, including ex-convicts released less than three years ago, jobless or uneducated migrants, and other suspicious residents. The police may rely on residential committees or similar organizations to monitor and control this tier.

The fourth tier is the general population, for whom only basic required *hukou* information should be collected and updated. In some places, *hukou* police are still expected to focus on a special group of this tier, the 14-to-35-year-olds, for possible additions to the first three tiers.

After the political scare and social upheavals in 1989, Beijing tightened its control of targeted people on November 30, 1991, by issuing its *Notice on Strengthening Zhongdian Renkou Management*, which once again established a long list of specified and targeted segments of the population by extending it to include six categories and twenty-three types of residents. A major change was to include several new types of those suspected of common crimes. Indeed, common crime increased significantly during the reform era. Before the 1980s, at most 550,000 criminal cases were processed and investigated annually; by the early 1990s, Chinese police were handling over 2.3 million criminal cases every year.[80]

Finally, on May 25, 1998, the MPS reissued the 1985 *Regulations on Zhongdian Renkou Management*. The accompanying *Notice* added some new types—cult or sect believers, those who sabotage ethnic solidarity, those who sabotage socialist market economic order—while dropping some general types of suspicious resident.

Furthermore, by 2000, *hukou* police manuals began to require the police to be discreet and to respect the legal rights and confidentiality of specially monitored targeted people.[81] As evidence of progress and new norms of litigation in Chinese society,[82] the legally and ethically questionable management of targeted people now is operated in designed secrecy. The names of and the information collected about targeted residents must be treated as state secrets, classified information.[83] Even the concept *zhongdian renkou* is now treated as an internal term, any use or discussion of which outside the police system is strictly prohibited.[84] Though still uniformly implemented across the nation, the secrecy and low legality of the scheme are nonetheless affecting its enforcement. Local police report internally that it has become harder for them to manage targeted people because they cannot cite any public law or regulation to mobilize the community for assistance and cooperation in an era when increasing numbers of urban residents are becoming aware of their legal rights.[85]

Targeted People in the 2000s

Currently, the PRC list of targeted people consists of five categories and twenty types of residents. (See Table 4.1.) Since, statistically, migrant workers from other cities and especially from rural areas have been responsible for most crime in Chinese cities since the 1980s,[86] temporary *hukou* holders and no-permit floaters are a commonly targeted group not included in the written regulations. The *hukou* police are instructed to have complete up-to-date information on those people, openly and secretly monitor them as closely as possible, and review their cases, educate them as necessary, and detain them at the first sign of any trouble. Often, especially during periodical national or regional *yanda* (harsh or strong anticrime strike) or *saohei* (sweeping organized crime) campaigns, targeted people, together with undocumented floating people, may be preventively detained and interrogated without evidence of criminal activity.[87] However, operational procedures, means of collecting information, and names and files of targeted people in a *hukou* zone are classified and available only to law-enforcement agencies.

In the early 2000s, the Chinese government mandates that beyond the nationally required regular *hukou* files and investigations each *hukou* zone must keep and update listings of these five categories of targeted people based on daily and extensive investigations, archives, and information collected from the *zhian ermu* (ears and eyes of public security— i.e., informants). Field police officers are assigned individual responsibility for managing targeted residents.

In practice, a police station's leadership determines the particular people targeted based on information collected through the population census, police informants' tips, police case files, *hukou* files, circulars from other public-security agencies, and reports from special industries (e.g.,

TABLE 4.1

The Zhongdian Renkou (Targeted People) in the PRC

Category One

Residents suspected of threatening national security.

1. People suspected of being subversive activists, separatists, traitors, and defectors.
2. People suspected of being part of riots, mob, uprising, or other destabilizing and/or sabotaging activities.
3. People suspected of developing, joining, and communicating with hostile organizations that destabilize and threaten national security and stability.
4. People suspected of joining cults, sects, and gangs or using religion for illegal or criminal activities.
5. People suspected of engaging in propaganda and agitation to sabotage ethnic solidarity and/or resist state laws.
6. People suspected of spying or collecting, searching for, purchasing, or illegally providing state secrets or intelligence.
7. People suspected of having other activities that are threats to national security.

Category Two

Residents suspected of serious criminal activities.

1. People suspected of having violated citizens' physical and personal rights through activities such as murder, rape, bodily injury, and trafficking of women and children.
2. People suspected of having violated public and private property rights through activities such as robbery, stealing, and fraud.
3. People suspected of having violated public security through activities such as arson, bombing, poison, and illegal manufacturing, sale, transport, storing, or stealing of firearms, ammunition, and explosives.
4. People suspected of trafficking, sale, transport, and production of narcotics.
5. People suspected of being involved in domestic and foreign underground societies or gangs.
6. People suspected of having sabotaged monetary order through activities such as counterfeiting of currency, national treasury bonds, and other securities or sale/purchasing of counterfeits.
7. People suspected of having engaged in financial fraud such as illegal fund raising and lending, or fraud involving financial documents, credit letters, insurance, and credit cards.
8. People suspected of having often organized gambling activities.
9. People suspected of having organized, hosted, and pimped for prostitution activities.
10. People suspected of other serious criminal activities.

Category Three

Residents who, due to intensification of various conflicts, have shown early tendencies toward violent revenge, making trouble, and other violent acts.

Category Four

Residents who were ex-convicts due to "purposeful crimes" and released within the last five years.

Category Five

Narcotics users.

nightclubs, massage parlors, and video-game arcades).[88] In some areas, police obviously use quotas in establishing lists of targeted people.[89] Internal police reports reveal that one police station secretly listed and monitored two hundred targeted persons.[90] One relatively large police station located in central Tianjin with thirty-nine full-time police, twelve of them *hukou* police, had 35,784 residents, 34,626 of these holding local urban *hukou*, and listed 247 targeted people in 1998: 6 in category 1, 30 in category 2, 205 in category 3, 1 in category 4, and 5 in category 5.[91]

Being listed does not always mean being effectively monitored or controlled. In a medium-sized city of 1.1 million people, there were 22,046 residents listed by the police as targeted people in 1998. About 12 percent of them, however, were found to be unmonitored and uncontrolled because of increased population mobility.[92] Internal police studies concluded that by the late 1990s a common major problem in managing targeted persons was that many were listed but simply missing from police view and control. The changed social environment in China, which has led to increasing distaste for secret dossiers, informants, persecution by association and suspicion, and general intolerance, is viewed by the police as a leading cause for widespread relaxation of the management of targeted people.[93]

The supervising public-security bureau at or above the county or city level must approve changes to the list of targeted persons, whether adding or dropping people. For listings in Category 1, an even higher authority, the public-security bureau at or above the prefectural level must approve any changes. All verified information about targeted people becomes permanent record in police dossiers and can be forwarded to another *hukou* zone if a listed person is allowed to relocate. The *hukou* police are required to cooperate with other agencies of public security to share and utilize the files of targeted people in a timely and aggressive manner. In one city, police reported that nearly 40 percent of criminal cases were solved based on information provided by the targeted-people management program.[94] The even more secretive police work of political investigation, including counterespionage operations by the MPS and the Ministry of State Security, appears frequently to utilize the assistance of the targeted-persons management program.[95] Unverified information, however, is to stay in the police station of the *hukou* zone for its internal use only. Statistical information about the management of targeted people must be reported to the MPS for addition to a national database classified as critical state secrets.[96]

Zhongdian Renkou (Listing or Dropping) Approval Form

Name	Gender	Date of birth	Education
Nickname(s)	Birth place	Physical features	
Employer and job/title		Current address	
Main family members			
Biographic sketch			
Reasons for listing/dropping			
Control/educating personnel name(s)		Job/relation	Employer
Processor's view			
Superior's comments			
Reference			

Filing unit   Processor   Filing date   year month day

FIG. 4.1. Approval Form for Targeted People (adopted March 12, 1985). *Zhongdian Renkou* (Listing or Dropping) Approval Form.

People targeted in different tiers or categories of the list are generally unaware of where exactly they belong on it, although finding out one's listing from the local *hukou* police or their informants is often possible through friends, relatives, or connections (*guanxi*). People differently categorized on a list of targeted persons may be treated differently in significant ways concerning their economic, political, and social lives in and even outside their local communities. Certain people, such as the managers and workers in so-called special industries and suspicious hotel guests,[97] may be put on de facto or informal lists of targeted people and treated accordingly to control and prevent crime, especially organized crimes.[98]

In the 1990s and 2000s, Chinese police fought often very violent Muslim separatist groups in Xinjiang. *Hukou*-based social control proved to be an effective tool even in that remote region, where many non-Han ethnic groups live.[99] Between 1999 and 2002, in the CCP's national campaign against the Falungong sect throughout the country, all known active Falungong members in major cities such as Beijing and Shanghai were put on the local list of targeted people and closely monitored and educated by the police. During major holidays, they were often advised not to go out by police stationed right at their doors. A repentant statement by an inactive Falungong member usually would reduce police surveillance and gradually remove him from the list.[100]

Conclusion

This chapter has reported on two leading functions of the PRC *hukou* system: a highly institutionalized exclusion and division based on tight restriction of internal migration, especially migration from rural to urban areas; and a firm sociopolitical control through tiered management of *zhongdian renkou* or targeted segments of the population.

After two decades of the PRC's economic reform and opening to the outside world, the *hukou* system's functions of institutional exclusion and social control have undergone some adaptation. Rigid exclusion of those residing in the countryside and in small cities has developed measures to allow for varying degrees of de facto mobility for the rich, the educated, and the talented, as well as for needed manual laborers. The new mobility privileges for the rich and the talented, in addition to the mobility previously mainly enjoyed by officials, apparently work to construct a new elite and mobile class in the PRC and help the continuation of the *hukou* system as a politically highly valuable institutional exclusion that also serves socioeconomic purposes. In 2001, migration quotas in the small cities and towns began to be replaced by locally set entry conditions that still nonetheless function as an effective tool for the Chinese government to regulate and restrict rural-to-urban migration, with perhaps increased local control and variations, increasingly based on the new fault line between haves and have-nots.

The tight social control under the *hukou* system has shown few signs of relaxation, although its administration has been somewhat rationalized in the direction of fighting crime and increased awareness of law and individual legal rights. Still largely operating in secrecy, the social-control function of the *hukou* system is expected to continue as a pillar of the PRC's unparalleled organization of the largest nation on earth. In late 2001, when rural-to-urban migration quotas were partly eliminated in the PRC, one MPS senior official called for further reducing the undue burden of the *hukou* system by getting rid of its economic and education functions so as to enhance the *hukou* system and restore its original main mission of population management and social control.[101] Indeed, the police called for a further enhancement of the targeted-people management program in their battle against separatist terrorism in western China, especially in Xinjiang.[102] In the late 1990s and early 2000s, *hukou*-based sociopolitical control worked effectively for national control and suppression of the banned semireligious meditation group Falungong, which dared to openly and politically challenge the CCP.[103]

CHAPTER FIVE

The Impact of the PRC *Hukou* System

The PRC *hukou* system institutionally divides and organizes the Chinese people. Inevitably, it extensively and powerfully affects almost every aspect of the Chinese society and way of life. To fully appreciate the significance of the *hukou* system, however, is not easy, even though many, especially those who have lived under the system, can vividly and endlessly attest its mighty presence. The main difficulty is twofold: the PRC *hukou* system is now still a semisecret and increasingly localized operation that offers little room for a systematic study of its impact. Data needed for ascertaining causal relations are often incomplete, hidden, or simply nonexistent. Furthermore, the *hukou* system tends to generate multifaceted, sometimes even contradictory and conflicting effects on China's politics, economy, and social life. Assessing the role of the *hukou* system often requires normative weighing of those effects, which may lead to the undesirable appearance of opinionated statements rather than scientific discoveries.

Nonetheless, one cannot understand the *hukou* system without at least making an effort to evaluate its meaning and consequences. As a continuation of my effort to investigate China's *hukou* system and to theorize the study of it, this chapter attempts to describe the impact of the PRC *hukou* system, as a Type 3 (*where one is*) institutional exclusion, on China's politics, economy, and social life. I will try to outline the main effects of the *hukou* system and depict the inherent conflicts in the system. While the system may have contributed significantly to China's sociopolitical stability, it creates an environment that is conducive to the perpetuation of an authoritarian regime, albeit still leaving some room for a possible elite democracy to develop.

The examination of the complicated economic impact of the *hukou* system requires three sections. I will argue that the *hukou* system has allowed the PRC to circumvent the Lewis Transition and hence to enjoy rapid economic growth and technological sophistication in a dual economy with the existence of massive surplus labor. Yet I will also report that the *hukou* system has created tremendous irrationalities, imbalances, and waste in the Chinese economy and barriers to further development of the Chinese market. In the absence of systematic and complete data, and given the multifaceted complexity of China's economic development, my preliminary inquiry into the economic impact of the PRC *hukou* system does not aim at a clear-cut one-word assessment of whether the system is good or bad for the Chinese economy.

Finally, as my case study on China's college admissions must illustrate, the PRC *hukou* system has created clear horizontal stratification, regional gaps, and personal discrimination that not only directly challenge social justice and equity but also potentially call China's political cohesion and national unity into question.

The Hukou System and Chinese Politics: Stability, Authoritarianism, and Elite Class

The political impact of an institutional exclusion, as I discussed in Chapter 1, may be summarized as follows. Institutional exclusion allows for orderly organization of an unevenly developed and diverse nation by a centralized government. It creates segmented and hence manageable minienvironments for institutional experiments and provides time, space, and shock-absorbing cushion for the gradual growth and legitimation of new institutions and norms. It is usually a fertile ground for authoritarianism and even totalitarianism, although a functional elite democracy may develop.

The PRC *hukou* system has contributed to a stable political order featuring a centralized authoritarian regime under the one-party rule of the Chinese Communist Party (CCP). More specifically, it has allowed Beijing to organize and rule the massive Chinese population with considerable effectiveness and ease, in spite of a great many internal and external challenges and disturbances. At a time when a governance crisis is seen coming in the PRC,[1] the *hukou* system may have become especially crucial to the stability and even survival of the CCP's political power. But all these political values and achievements have come at the expense of the political rights of the Chinese majority who are institutionally excluded, politically unrepresented, and hence utterly powerless.

The *hukou* system has enabled a political structure in the PRC that is completely dominated by the urban residents, who have never been more than 26 percent of the total population. In the mid-1990s, over 10 percent of urban *hukou* holders were CCP members, whereas less than 2 percent of ruralites were among the estimated fifty million party members.[2] Ever since the 1960s, virtually all of the PRC's political leaders, cadres inside the CCP at and above the township level, and government officials and clerks down to the level of township director are all privileged urban *hukou* holders.[3] Except for a few symbolic rural *hukou* holders (almost all newly rich business people) who are deputies and even standing-committee members of local people's congresses and even the National People's Congress (NPC), the majority of the Chinese, the excluded rural residents, have virtually no representation in Beijing or at provincial or prefectural levels of the Chinese political hierarchy.

Only at the township and to a lesser extent the county level can one see rural *hukou* holders in political office, in the form of the so-called *pinyong* (hired) cadres and police assistants. *Pinyong* cadres are basically clerks hired by the government on a contractual basis to staff local governments below the county level.[4] Appointment of *pinyong* cadres is for a fixed term, and when not renewed they are required to return to their previous localities and lose their pay and other benefits, generally with a lump sum severance pay or pension.[5] Those rural residents hired lose their temporary urban *hukou* as well.[6]

All China's military officers (on active duty or retired) at or above the platoon-leader level (usually second lieutenant) hold or are guaranteed urban *hukou*. All police officers are urban *hukou* holders, except police assistants working in the rural areas. All the highly educated (with a college degree or higher) are guaranteed urban *hukou*. All permanent state employees hold urban *hukou*. Urban *hukou* holders, a minority as they have always been, thus comprise China's undisputed elite and privileged in every regard. That leaves the uneducated or poorly educated and powerless ruralites, who have always been China's majority of 87 percent (in the 1960s–70s) to 74 percent (in 2000), to be excluded second-class citizens labeled with an agricultural *hukou* or rural status that can be changed only with state approval.

Political elections in the PRC have also clearly discriminated against the rural population. For the election of people's deputies to the NPC,

TABLE 5.1

People's Deputies of the Ninth NPC (1998–2003)

Total number of NPC deputies	2,984[a]
Average representation	One per every 400,000 people
"Election Districts"	35[b]
Minimum Deputies from each District	15[c]
Minimum Deputies for each of the 56 nationalities	1[d]
Guaranteed seats for the PLA	270[e]
Remaining seats allocated by population	
Urban	One per every 200,000 people
Rural	One per every 800,000 people[f]

SOURCES: Information based on author's interviews with NPC senior officials in 2001.
NOTE: Over 70 percent of the deputies were CCP members and about 20 percent were women in 2001.
[a]The PRC Constitution sets the limit of People's Deputies at 3,000.
[b]The 32 provinces, regions, and metropolises, plus the military, Hong Kong, and Macao.
[c]Macao (with a population of only 300,000) has 15 deputies in the NPC.
[d]The smallest recognized minority nationality in China has about 3,000 people and one deputy in the NPC.
[e]The military (with three million people) has many deputies because it has "many highly ranked units at or even above the provincial level."
[f]This seems to be the only way in which rural *hukou* holders may become people's deputies. But many of those elected as rural representatives are actually urban *hukou* holding cadres.

China's nominal lawmaking institution and the constitutionally designated highest organ of political power in the country, the rules insure that the majority of the Chinese, the rural population, are only fractionally represented. By law, each rural deputy to the NPC represents many more voters (eight times as many in 1952–95 and four times as many after 1995) than an urban deputy.[7]

Instead of allocating seats according to the population size of each administrative unit, PRC election districts are drawn based on a combination of *danwei*s (work units) and population size,[8] thus being subject to official manipulation. As a result, from 1949 to 1995 urban residents, never more than 24 percent of the total population, elected twice as many People's Deputies to the NPC as the rural population. Only in 1995, in a major political and legal reform, was the rural population, nearly 80 percent of the nation, for the first time allowed to elect the same number of People's Deputies as the urban residents.[9] Many of the people's deputies elected from rural areas turned out to be variously ranked officials with urban *hukou*. In the early 2000s, the allocation of seats in the NPC is grossly biased against the rural population.

Similar data about delegates to the much more powerful CCP National Congress are unavailable, and the composition of the CCP Central Committee (CCPCC) is less transparent, but informed sources told this author that the situation there is even more biased against residents from rural and smaller, less developed urban areas. In the past four CCPCCs, for example, no member has been reported as genuinely holding rural *hukou*.

The PRC's *hukou*-based institutional exclusion hence segments the people into the privileged and the excluded while allowing the privileged urban minority to solidly control the excluded majority and to politically maintain their institutional exclusion. A stable but undemocratic political order and a centralized administrative effectiveness are achieved at the expense of the rights of the Chinese majority and the rationality of an open and representative political process. The rural majority, although poor and rigidly excluded, is unlikely to cause serious political instability, since this family-based agrarian population is much less concentrated, much less group-conscious, much less organized, and much less informed than the urban population.[10] *Hukou*-based institutional exclusion relies on the political power of the authoritarian CCP-PRC state and, in turn, supports that nondemocratic regime. With the *hukou* system functioning to shape China's political structure, a Chinese democracy, if possible at all, is likely to be only an elite democracy at best. In other words, the CCP's one-party monopoly on political power in China now rests heavily, with perhaps an increased dependency after two decades of economic reform, on the PRC *hukou* system.

The Hukou System and the Chinese Economy: Rapid Growth in a Sea of Unskilled Labor

As Chapter 1 suggested, institutional exclusion has different economic impacts in different nations. In general, institutional exclusion enables capital accumulation and investment and the allocation of other resources for purposes of economic developmental strategy, economic policy, or simply for maximum profit. But it strips the excluded of consumption and participation in the economy and shapes a segregated development that may or may not gradually spill over the whole economy. For latecomer developing nations besieged by a dual economy internally and global control of migration abroad, institutional exclusion, in addition to the common Type 2 (based on *what one has*), may be a major factor in the nontraditional model of economic growth.[11] In a dual economy where there is a nearly unlimited supply of low-skilled or unskilled labor, capital needs to be formed quickly and invested productively in the "in" areas and sectors, at the expense of the excluded. Institutional exclusion thus provides the possibility of a nation's circumventing the difficult and precarious Lewis Transition and achieving rapid growth and technological sophistication, albeit in a very uneven way that sacrifices the excluded. Naturally, institutional exclusions that are not of Type 2 generate economic problems including low efficiency of labor resources because of low labor and social mobility, uneven development, vertically and horizontally uneven distribution of income, and usually a slow urbanization that tends to perpetuate a dual economy.

The economic impact of the PRC *hukou* system is profound, extensive, and complex. On the one hand, the *hukou* system has directly and significantly contributed to impressive economic growth and technological advancement in China. On the other hand, the *hukou* system has perpetuated the duality of the Chinese economy and the economic irrationalities and inefficiency associated with low labor mobility. I will examine the positive impact that the PRC *hukou* system has generated for the Chinese economy in this section and discuss the problems that it has contributed to in the next two sections. I will endeavor to weigh the system's various economic impacts; yet, in the absence of complete data (which are beyond a foreign-based scholar's reach), it will be necessary to avoid any sweeping verdict about its economic role.

The PRC *hukou* system has fostered rapid economic growth and significant technological sophistication in a nation that has the world's largest unskilled labor force and one of the world's lowest per-capita resource and capital endowments.[12] Like other developing nations with nearly unlimited supplies of unskilled labor, China faces the narrow, arduous, precarious Lewis Transition. In the late 1990s, China had nearly five hundred million rural laborers (people aged 16–55), about 150–240 million of whom were estimated to be the so-called surplus labor, with the rural population still growing by more than ten million every year.[13] Moreover, only about 5 percent of rural laborers had any professional training or industrial skills by the early 2000s.[14] A normal Lewis Transition model of development would take too long and inevitably become impractical and unacceptable.[15] With *hukou*-based institutional exclusion, however, the PRC so far appears to have circumvented if not replaced the Lewis Transition. Instead of being impeded by a seemingly endless process of absorbing hundreds of millions of unskilled rural laborers before achieving economic take-off and eradicating dreaded poverty and backwardness, the Chinese economy has sustained a high rate of growth (8–9 percent annually) for more than two decades,[16] a duration and scale rarely seen and more than twice the average growth rate of other developing countries, basically bypassing this process while perpetuating its economic duality.

The exclusive and discriminatory nature of the PRC *hukou* system enables easy and fast capital accumulation in the urban sector and in the hands of the state (gradually the new, so-called Red Capitalists too), through naked massive extraction of value from the excluded rural population, and to a lesser extent from the smaller cities as well.[17] It also allows for easy prioritization of resource allocation in education and social development in the "in" areas and sectors, modernizing them quickly and well ahead of the rest of the country. Together, these efforts provide the basis for a state-led or guided economic development strategy to proceed.[18] A prosperous, protected, and privileged "in" urban China is also effective in reducing capital flight, a common occurrence that has plagued so many developing nations.

Such positive functions of the PRC *hukou* system have been especially obvious since the early 1980s, when the market was finally introduced to replace the failed central-planning system as the main economic institution in China. It takes the right kind of politics (a developmental commitment) and economic institution (the market system and norms) for *hukou*-based institutional exclusion to function positively for a rapid economic development in the sea of unskilled labor. Conversely, the positive potential of the *hukou* system could not be well realized in a nonmarket economy, as was the PRC's before the 1980s. A combination of Type 3 (based on *where one is*) and Type 2 (based on *what one has*) institutional exclusions appears to be an effective way to circumvent the Lewis Transition.

Circumventing the Lewis Transition. The PRC *hukou* system creates an artificial environment in which the unskilled labor has been administratively, cheaply, yet effectively excluded rather than genuinely but exorbitantly absorbed. Despite low and diminished income in the agricultural sector, the *hukou* system contributes immensely to the stable retention of millions of surplus rural laborers,[19] assisted by the widespread family-based but highly labor-holding agrarian moral economy in the countryside.[20] The excluded rural sector functions as an artificial reservoir to endlessly supply fresh workers or store surplus labor, conditioned by the ups and downs of the urban sector.[21] The Chinese socioeconomic duality is thus stabilized, even when a market economy is rapidly advancing. The drag effect commonly seen in large developing nations of a dual economy on economic and technological progress in the modern or urban sector is hence minimized and controlled. China's economic development, therefore, was able to maintain high-speed growth in a stable dual economy for many years. It is the constant and continued sacrifice of the excluded majority in the Chinese villages that makes the Chinese economic miracle possible.

Under the PRC *hukou* system, selective regulation of internal migration provides the talented or educated and the rich a de facto cross-regional and cross-sector mobility so that skilled labor can achieve quasi-national circulation and allocation. Regulated and restricted rural-to-urban migration also allows for a limited but steady supply of low-skilled but very hard-working labor that can be forced to work long hours with minimum pay and protection. The *liudong* (migrant) rural laborers are highly mobile and responsive to market demands for cheap labor. They create only temporary, minimal burdens for the cities and usually have no means of raising their own demands for benefits, promotion, job security, or asserting their right to get the promised pay.[22] Lacking organization and even a stable legal status, the migrant ruralites working in the cities have been politically powerless and generally peaceful as a group,[23] much like first-generation immigrants in developed nations such as the United States. The wealth they create has indeed been a major source of growth of the Chinese economy in the past two decades.[24]

As a consequence, the Chinese urban economy, especially in the metropolitan centers and state-designated special economic zones (SEZs: Shenzhen, Zhuhai, Hainan, Shantou, and Xiamen), has experienced spectacular development since the early 1980s. Capital-intensive and technology-intensive industries have achieved considerable scale and sophistication in a short period of time. More remarkable, this has taken place in a nation that still has between 150 million and 240 million unemployed, underemployed, or surplus laborers. The cities of Shanghai and Beijing, for example, have now achieved a per-capita GDP equivalent to that of some European nations and the general technology and cultural sophistication of world-class metropolises. The first step of Deng Xiaoping's development strategy of letting some people and some places get rich first and then pulling and pushing the whole nation into common prosperity was indeed well carried out in the Chinese cities, especially those in eastern and coastal China.[25] *Hukou*-based institutional exclusion provided the basis for urban-first rapid growth in a sea of unskilled and surplus labor. Indeed, as one econometric study of Chinese rural-to-urban migration concluded, uncontrolled migration would not have benefited China's impressive economic growth in the cities.[26] Of course, whether the second step of this strategy, common prosperity, can take place extensively and quickly enough in China remains to be seen. It appears that the entire success or eventual failure of this two-step development model rests heavily on the future role of the PRC *hukou* system.

Focuses, communities, experiments. The *hukou* system allows the PRC to utilize its limited resources of capital and talent to pursue state-of-the-art technology in selected sectors and industries. For example, Chinese achievements in space technology, culminating in the manned space flight of *Shenzhou* (Divine Vessel) V in October 2003, and nuclear technology were made much easier with *hukou*-based institutional exclusion, social control, and resultant state extraction and allocation of resources. *Hukou*-based institutional exclusion hence contributed to the unusually rapid development of the Chinese economy in geographically designated areas and chosen industrial sectors. Focused efforts have transformed China from a near autarky economy to the sixth largest trader (with increasing technology exports) and the second largest recipient of foreign direct investment in the world in less than twenty years. As a result, China's foreign currency reserve ballooned from $10 billion in 1990 to over $380 billion in 2003, second only to Japan's, making China now a significant new player on the international financial market.[27]

Manipulation or creative use of the *hukou* system is seen by some Chinese scholars as an effective way to relocate people for the purpose of environmental protection.[28] It is also important to the PRC's segmented and gradualist approach to economic reform and experimentation since the late 1970s. China's decollectivization (1978–82),[29] scheme of special economic zones and open cities, and numerous other reform steps were all taken with the help of the *hukou* system. Controlled labor allocation in China provides the government with the means to distribute human resources and the economy with protected zones in which high salaries can exist to draw talent and nourish new commercial demands as well as entrepreneurship to facilitate the growth of the new market economy. At the same time, controlled labor mobility under the *hukou* system helps to ensure that the fast-developing urban centers have a continuous supply of cheap, able, willing labor with only minimal problems of massive relocation from rural areas. The PRC's slower urbanization, about half the average speed in developing nations after World War II but roughly comparable to that before 1900 in what are today's developed nations,[30] may indeed hold an important explanation for China's sociopolitical stability and economic success.

Hukou-based institutional exclusion and discrimination also allowed certain better-endowed or better-managed rural communities (townships and even villages) to develop rapidly and raise living standards for their legal permanent residents while shielding themselves from the sea of unskilled labor. Outsiders are clearly excluded in the countryside as many villages have tied local benefits and rights openly to local *hukou* status since the early 1990s. In the early 2000s, migrants working in the rural areas outside their home villages experience just as rigid and as comprehensive an exclusion and discrimination as those working in the cities.[31]

In a phenomenon described as "community-based labor markets,"[32] many rural communities have indeed made great progress in economic growth, technological development, and standard of living while excluding the large number of outside workers from participating in community-based sharing of wealth. A good example of such segmented rural development can be seen in a socialist and even Maoist economic model in Henan Province, in the Nanjie Administrative Village of Lingying County.[33] Through massive and rapid development of rural industries (township and village enterprises) and trade, Nanjie has achieved a high level of prosperity collectively for its 3,130 residents, about two thousand of whom are employed. The local legal residents all enjoy a high level of welfare provided by the redistribution of profits (estimated to be 80,000 Yuan RMB for housing and furnishing per household in 1995 alone) created by the collective enterprises (with a whopping 1.2 billion Yuan output in 1996). The majority (over 10,000 in 1996) of a total of 12,000 workers employed in village enterprises came from other villages and counties or provinces. Having no local Nanjie *hukou*, they could make only meager wages (less than 250 Yuan per month) and could not enjoy most of the fruits of the economic success of the community.[34]

Countering capital flight. Another economic effect of the PRC *hukou* system is equally important, even critical, in the era of increasing globalization: helping to minimize the capital flight that has plagued so many developing nations. The artificially maintained tranquility, safety, and profitability in the urban centers, at the expense of the excluded rural majority under the *hukou* system, have made Chinese cities highly attractive for nationally accumulated capital to stay and for significant foreign investment to pour in. Consistently since the mid-1990s, China has been the second largest recipient of foreign direct investment (FDI) every year, next after only the United States.[35] By 2003, China attracted over $446 billion FDI, or more than half of all FDI in developing countries.[36] Most of this massive foreign capital went to China's "in" urban sector.

Despite Beijing's tight control of a closed domestic capital market, China nonetheless started to have its own capital-flight problem in the late 1980s. A decade later, by the end of the twentieth century, even the official media started to report that China had the fourth largest capital flight in the world, behind the well-known victims of capital flight Venezuela, Mexico, and Argentina. In 1998 alone, at least $35 billion of capital illegally flowed out of China.[37] It is no exaggeration to argue that, without *hukou*-based institutional exclusion, Chinese cities would be much less attractive to native and foreign investors, and China might indeed quickly have developed a so-called Latin Americanization or, worse, become another Indonesia.[38]

As conceptually sketched in Chapter 1, the economic impact of effective *hukou*-based institutional exclusion in China may be viewed as similar to that of the Westphalia international political system on the world economy since the end of the Middle Ages. Under the Westphalia system, there is a political division of the sovereign nations, a citizenship-based division of humankind, and an exclusion of foreigners maintained by the regulation and restriction of international migration. These may have indispensably contributed to the development of the modern capitalist market economy that has brought unprecedented economic growth and technological sophistication in the "in" parts of the world, primarily the nations that today form the Organization of Economic Cooperation and Development (OECD). The world economy has developed spectacularly in the past few centuries, but in the 2000s, 80 percent of humankind still lives in the less developed nations, excluded from most of the world's achievements.[39] China's prosperous urban centers in its eastern and coastal regions, compared with the country as a whole, may be functionally viewed as roughly equivalent to the OECD nations in comparison with the world. A key difference, however, is that the citizenship-based institutional divide between the OECD nations and the rest of the world is much more rigidly defined and forceful, hence more effectively enforced than the *hukou* barriers that separate the urbanites in Shanghai and Beijing from the ruralites in the inland Chinese provinces. Furthermore, a central government in Beijing that regulates the *hukou* system and provides some cross-regional resource reallocation may have made the *hukou* system more humane and more tolerable to the excluded than the Westphalia system.

Slow Urbanization and a Stable Dual Economy

A leading negative consequence of the PRC's *hukou*-based institutional exclusion has been, not surprisingly, a relatively small and slow urbanization in China.[40] "Affected by the strict *hukou* management and the policy restricting rural-to-urban migration," concluded one Chinese scholar, "our urbanization has always fallen behind our industrialization and developed slowly ... [hence] hundreds of millions of peasants who should have been in the cities are still kept away."[41] China's urbanization has been small and very slow ever since the mid-nineteenth century, compared with the world urbanization rate.[42] Under the PRC, China's urbanization stagnated for about two decades under Mao Zedong. During the reform era, China's urbanization has been significantly slower than its economic growth and industrialization rate, even though the adaptive measures and the practical relaxation of the *hukou* system have accelerated urbanization since the late 1980s.

By 2000, China's urbanization was still only less than 30 percent, whereas countries in the same range of per-capita GDP ($500–$730 by standard method or $2,000–$3,800 by purchasing-power-parity method) had an urbanization of 42.5–50 percent.[43] Although by some indicators China's economic development in the late 1990s was at the level that the United States attained from the 1950s through the 1970s, China's urbanization was comparable to that in the United States only in the 1880s and 1890s.[44] As a result, on the one hand the United States and other developed countries treated China largely as an industrialized nation during its arduous entry into the World Trade Organization (WTO) between 1987 and 2001. On the other hand, the overwhelming majority (74 percent) of China's population is still institutionally characterized as rural residents, even though they do not all live in the countryside and work in the agricultural sector.

As a direct consequence of slow urbanization, China perpetuates a stable dual economy featuring a rural majority of the population and a stable, large, ever-increasing rural-urban disparity of income and resource distribution. The living standards and cultures of the separate urban and rural sectors have become greatly incommensurate in recent decades. Officially, the urban and rural incomes were disparate by a factor of about 2.2 in 1964, 2.6 in 1978, 2.7 in 1995, and 2.8 in 2000. Semiofficially, the urban-rural income gap was estimated to stand at a factor of about 4.0 in 1993.[45] Including indirect income in the form of state subsidies, the gap stood at a staggering 5.0–6.0 by 2001.[46] Furthermore, while per-

TABLE 5.2

Urbanization in China

(urbanites as % of population)

Period	China's urbanization	World urbanization
Pre-PRC: Small and slow urbanization		
1843	5.1	5.0
1893	6.0	
1949	7.7	28.7 (1950)
PRC–Mao Era: Stagnation		
1953	12.0	
1961	16.1[a]	33.9 (1960)
1965	14.0[a]	
1976	13.0[a]	
PRC–Reform Era: Rapid urbanization		
1978	12.9	39.3 (1980)
1988	18.7[a]	45.0
2000	26.1 (or 33.8)[a,b]	46.5 (1999)[c]
Eastern/coastal China	41.9	
Rest of China	16.1	

SOURCES: Ma Xia 1994, 232–241; MPS 2001, 3–5; UNDP 2001, 157.

[a]"Non-agricultural" *hukou* holders or permanent urban residents, not just the PRC official term of "urban population." Chinese government statistics often misleadingly count the total population under a "city" government's administration, including the peasants living in the villages, as "urban population," which was about 45 percent in 2000.

[b]Although the *hukou* system institutionally excludes and discriminates against the "agricultural" *hukou* holders in the PRC, functionally speaking, the agricultural *hukou* holders who work and live in the cities under temporary *hukou* or no *hukou* at all (the "floating people"), estimated to be nearly 100 million by 2000 (Solinger 1999, 15–23; Solinger 2001; and Wu Xiaoping 2001, 146), could be considered *quasi* urban residents. That would bring the Chinese urbanization rate from 26.1 percent to 33.8 percent.

[c]The average urbanization rate for developing nations in 1999 was 38.9 percent.

capita income for urbanites grew at 8.5 percent annually between 1999 and 2001, rural per-capita income increased barely 2 percent each year.[47]

Per capita government spending on social welfare for urban residents in the 1990s was some thirty times greater than in rural areas.[48] In 2000, Zhejiang Province, one of the three administrative units (along with Shanghai and Guangdong) that have experimented with a uniform social-welfare program called "minimum living-standard protection," guaranteed poor urban *hukou* holders a minimum living standard of 240 RMB each per month while assuring poor holders of rural *hukou* only 67 RMB.[49]

A rigid and stable dual economy based on the exclusion of the rural population has systematically and artificially suppressed the rural Chinese market and may have severely limited the growth potential for the Chinese economy as a whole, which needs domestic demand to increase continually. Nationally, per-capita consumer spending in the cities is 3.5

TABLE 5.3

Income and Consumer Market: Rural vs. Urban

	1978	1985	1990	1995	1998	1999	2000
Per capita income (RMB)							
Urban	343	748	1,523	4,288	5,458	5,889	6,317
Rural	134	398	686	1,578	2,162	2,210	2,253
Per capita consumer spending (RMB)							
Urban		673	1,278	3,538	n.a.	4,616	4,998
Rural		195	375	859	n.a.	1,144	1,287
Per capita spending on clothing (RMB)							
Urban		479	528	521	481	482	501
Rural		31	45	90	98	92	96
Per capita spending on education and entertainment (RMB)							
Urban		313	375	448	499	567	628
Rural		12	31	102	159	168	187
Durable goods per 100 households							
Color TV set							
Urban		89.8	93.5	100.5	105.4	111.6	117
Rural		0.8	4.7	16.9	32.6	38.2	48.7
Washing machine							
Urban		88.9	90.1	89.1	90.6	91.4	90.5
Rural		1.9	9.1	16.8	22.8	24.3	28.6
Air conditioning							
Urban		8.1	11.6	16.3	20.0	24.5	30.8
Rural		—n e g l i g i b l e —					1.3
Camera							
Urban		30.6	32.1	33.6	36.2	38.1	38.4
Rural		—	—	1.4	2.2	2.7	3.1
Refrigerator							
Urban		66.2	69.7	72.9	76.1	77.7	80.1
Rural		0.1	1.2	5.1	9.3	10.6	12.3
Personal computer							
Urban		—	—	—	—	5.9	9.7
Rural		—n e g l i g i b l e —					

SOURCE: SSB 2000, 312–42. SSB 2001, 303–30.

times as great as in the rural areas. The consumer market in PRC cities is now fairly saturated for durable goods such as color TV sets, washing machines, and refrigerators, whereas the rural consumer-goods market has been small and has developed slowly over the past fifteen years. The rural residents, more than two-thirds of the total population, consume less than one-third of the goods and services produced in the PRC.[50] Raising the purchasing power of the rural Chinese majority would likely provide the Chinese economy a great push in the years ahead.

In addition to perpetuating a dual economy and retarding the rural consumer market, the *hukou* system has created significant irrationalities in labor allocation and utilization. The young labor market is fundamentally controlled by the *hukou* system, especially the massive pool of low-skilled or unskilled workers. A two-tier, well-segregated labor market for local urban *hukou* holders and outsiders exists in Chinese cities, leading to inequalities and inefficiencies within the same locality.[51] There is often an oversupply of educated and skilled labor, especially professionals, in the major urban centers while a chronic shortage of such labor plagues the small cities, remote regions, and especially the rural areas. In order to continue living in the desirable urban centers to which they are socially accustomed, many of the highly educated have abandoned their acquired expertise and skills to take whatever jobs they can get, thus wasting tremendous educational resources.[52] In almost every Chinese city, there are hundreds of thousands of surplus laborers, usually former state employees with urban *hukou*, who could not find or are not willing to take jobs outside their *hukou* zones, while millions more rural workers are floating among the cities looking for any work at all.

A Regionally Uneven Development and Spatial Inequality

As the high price of *hukou*-confined rapid growth, China has had a very uneven economic development across all regions. A group of influential Chinese scholars concluded that "there are three main disparities in contemporary Chinese society: the disparities between the peasants and the industrial workers, between the urban and rural areas, and among the regions."[53] The PRC *hukou* system is fundamentally responsible for all three. Other than the first two disparities described earlier in this chapter, very consequentially, *hukou*-based institutional exclusion has directly contributed to a grossly unequal income distribution across regions in particular and an uneven economy in general.[54] In addition to the chronic and enlarging income and spending gaps between rural and urban residents delineated in Table 5.3, there is a clearly visible regional gap of per-capita income in China. In fact, the government in the late 1990s officially divided the country into three regions: the developed region of the twelve eastern and coastal provinces and metropolises, the less developed region of the nine central provinces, and the undeveloped region of the remaining nine western provinces.[55]

Despite official efforts for a more balanced development, including the latest Grand Development of the West campaign, the gap of investment, growth and technology levels between eastern China and central and western China and among the provinces has continued to grow.[56] The major urban centers continue to get the lion's share of investment and government spending. Six provinces or metropolises in eastern China received 54 percent of all Chinese research and development funding in 1994; the eighteen provinces in central and western China got only 35.9 percent.[57] In 1990, Beijing had the highest per-capita government spending at 633 Yuan RMB, about 2.7 times the lowest, 106 Yuan in Henan Province, only a couple of hundred miles away. In 1996, Shanghai had the highest per-capita government spending of 2,348 Yuan, 8.45 times the lowest, 278 Yuan, still in Henan Province.[58] In 1998, per-capita investment in the three metropolises Shanghai, Beijing, and Tianjin was 7.3, 5, and 3.1 times higher, respectively, than the national average, while the like in Guizhou Province was only 33 percent of the national average.[59] Not surprisingly, foreign investment has had a very uneven concentration. By 1998, 88 percent of foreign direct investment was in eastern and coastal China, and five provinces in this region received over 63 percent of China's total foreign direct investment.[60]

The ten provincial units in the eastern and coastal regions ranked as the top ten fastest-growing areas, while the growth rate of ten central and western provinces was declining in the 1990s.[61] The share of the eastern region (36.7 percent of the total population, 10.7 percent of territory, but 60.1 percent of all urban *hukou* holders) in the Chinese GDP rose from 52.3 percent in 1980 to 60.1 percent in 1993 and 67.98 percent in 2000. At the same time, the share of the west (25.2 percent of the total population) declined from 16.5 percent to 13.1 percent. Among the hundred most prosperous counties in 1993, 91 were located in the east, whereas there were nine in the central region and the western provinces had none. Ninety percent of the 592 poor counties were in the west.[62] By the late 1990s, 90 percent of an estimated 12 million urban residents living in absolute poverty were in the cities and towns in the western and central regions.[63]

At the end of the 1990s, per-capita annual GDP in Shanghai was over twenty-eight thousand Yuan RMB, twelve times higher than in Guizhou Province (merely 2,323 Yuan).[64] The average annual urban wage in the eastern coastal provinces was 2,702 Yuan, 35 percent (up from 29.2 percent in 1994) higher than in the central and western areas. The average annual wage in the same period in the coastal province of Guangdong

TABLE 5.4

Per Capita Income Gap by Regions and the Rural-Urban Divide, 2000

Regions	% of population urban	rural	HDI rank[a]	Urban (RMB)	% of average	Rural (RMB)	% of average	rural/ urban income
National average	100	100	—	6,137	100	2,253	100	0.37
4 Metropolises	9.3	7.0		9,170	149	3,929	174	0.43
Shanghai	3.2	0.2	1	11,802	192	5,596	248	0.47
Beijing	2.3	3.8	2	10,416	170	4,605	204	0.44
Tianjin	1.6	0.4	3	8,165	133	3,622	161	0.44
Chongqing	2.2	2.6	—	6,297	103	1,892	84	0.30
Eastern/coastal	49.3	35.9		6,594	107	2,913	129	0.44
Guangdong	10.4	4.9	4	9,854	161	6,355	282	0.65
Zhejiang	5.0	3.0	5	9,334	152	4,254	189	0.46
Fujian	3.1	2.5	8	7,486	122	3,231	143	0.43
Jiangsu	6.7	5.4	6	6,842	112	3,595	160	0.53
Shangdong	7.5	7.0	9	6,521	106	2,659	118	0.41
Hebei	3.8	6.2	12	5,686	93	2,479	110	0.44
Liaoning	5.0	2.4	7	5,389	88	2,356	105	0.44
Hainan	0.7	0.6	11	5,416	88	2,182	97	0.40
Helongjiang	4.1	2.2	10	4,946	81	2,148	95	0.43
Jilin	3.0	1.7	13	4,829	79	2,023	90	0.42
Western/interior	41.4	57.1		5,510	90	1,772	79	0.32
Tibet	0.1	0.3	30	7,477	122	1,331	59	0.18
Yunan	2.2	0.4	26	6,370	104	1,479	66	0.23
Hunan	4.2	5.6	20	6,261	102	2,197	98	0.35
Sichuan	4.9	7.6	21	5,926	97	1,904	85	0.32
Guangxi	2.8	4.0	18	5,882	96	1,865	83	0.33
Xinjiang	1.4	1.6	15	5,687	93	1,618	72	0.29
Hubei	5.3	4.5	17	5,542	90	2,269	101	0.41
Anhui	3.6	5.4	19	5,332	87	1,935	86	0.36
Qinghai	0.4	0.4	28	5,197	85	1,491	66	0.29
Inner Mongolia	2.2	1.7	22	5,151	84	2,038	91	0.40
Shangxi	2.5	3.0	25	5,149	84	1,444	64	0.28
Guizhou	1.8	3.3	29	5,137	84	1,374	61	0.27
Jiangxi	2.5	2.5	23	5,130	84	2,135	95	0.42
Gansu	1.3	2.4	27	4,944	81	1,429	63	0.29
Ningxia	0.4	0.5	24	4,948	81	1,724	77	0.35
Henan	4.7	8.8	16	4,784	78	1,986	88	0.42
Shanxi	2.5	2.7	14	4,745	77	1,906	85	0.40

SOURCES: SSB 2001, 101, 310–11 and 324–25. (The data on income collected by the PRC government may report a smaller than actual Gini Index due to the difficulty in calculating household income figures. See Bramall 2001, 689–705.)

[a]Based on HDI (human development index) calculation for 1995. UNDP 1999 (*The China Human Development Report*), 13 and 58. China's world rank based on HDI was number 87 out of 162 nations in 2001 (UNDP 2001, 154–57).

was twice that in neighboring Jiangxi Province (3,595 vs. 1,713 Yuan).[65] It is estimated that the east-west annual income gap grew from 48 percent in 1986 to 52 percent in 1991 (2,283 Yuan in the east and 1,095 in the west).[66] In 2000, urban *hukou* holders' highest per-capita annual income was 11,802 Yuan (in Shanghai); the lowest was only 4,745 (in Shanxi). Rural *hukou* holders' highest per-capita annual income was 5,596 Yuan (again in Shanghai), and the lowest was only 1,331 (in Tibet: Table 5.4). By 2001, the highest per-capita urban income was 4.8 times greater in eastern than in western China.[67] Some cities' average income of urban *hukou* holders was six to seven times higher than others'.[68]

Several interesting findings flow from Table 5.4: First, we see that urban residents enjoy a much higher income level than rural residents in every administrative unit across the country. Rural residents on average make only a third of urban income, and some actually earn less than 20 percent. The impetus for the ruralites to flow to the cities appears to be strong and lasting. Simultaneously, for the urbanites, the need to keep *hukou*-based migration restriction in place also appears to be imperative.

Second, the four metropolises clearly enjoy higher than average urban (149 percent) and rural (174 percent) income, with perhaps the exception of the rural population in Chongqing's largely mountainous rural area. Both urban and rural residents in eastern and coastal China have a higher than average per-capita income (107 percent and 129 percent, respectively), whereas the western and interior regions, with the majority of the Chinese population, have a significantly lower than average income in the cities and in the rural areas (90 percent and 79 percent, respectively). The force driving people to move from the west to the east and from smaller cities to major cities for economic betterment is apparent.

Third, the income gap between urban and rural residents in eastern and coastal China is significantly smaller than in the rest of the country. In places like Shanghai (5,596 Yuan RMB), Beijing (4,605), Guangdong (6,355), and Zhejiang (4,253), we see rural per-capita annual income actually matching or even higher than per-capita income of urban residents in many other provinces. This finding is well supported by field observations in rural areas in the Pearl River Delta, Zhejiang, and southern Jiangsu Province. This fact provided Beijing with the possibility of a faster urbanization in those regions, especially through rapid and convenient administrative conversion of villages into towns and towns into small cities.

Finally, the dual economy of the PRC is more evident in the poorest and most remote regions of China. The urban population enjoys an income higher than the national average in places like Tibet and Yunnan, whereas the local rural residents have the lowest income in the country. This reflects internal colonization over the past four decades in the form of state-directed relocation of urban populations for industrialization—the so-called Third Front development in the 1960s and 1970s, and the Grand Development of the West since the 1990s—and military deployments into these regions.[69] Often Beijing would encourage state employees (all urban *hukou* holders) to work in harsh regions like Tibet by paying them substantially more than in their original cities.

By comparison, the United States, a country of comparable size, also naturally has regional income gaps. In 2002, the highest per-capita annual income was $42,706, in Connecticut, 138 percent of the national average; the lowest was $21,654, in Mississippi, 72 percent of the national average.[70] The regional income gap in the United States appears to be significantly smaller than that in the PRC, the more so if we consider the sharp divide between the Chinese rural and urban incomes. To accept the reality of regional disparity legally and politically, the PRC has set dif-

TABLE 5.5

Legal Minimum Wages in Selected Areas of the PRC
(mid-1990s)

Place	RMB/month	Region
Shenzhen SEZ	420	East
Zhuhai SEZ	380	East
Guangzhou	320	East
Xiamen SEZ	280	East
Shanghai	220	East
Fuzhou	225	East
Beijing	210	East
Zhejiang Province	200	East
Hefei	198	Central
Wuhu	180	Central
Nanchang	170	Central
Huaibei	165	Central
Zhengzhou	163	Central
(Other Henan cities)	129	Central
Deyang	141	Central
Jingzai	135	Central

SOURCES: *Beijing Ribao* (Beijing Daily), Dec. 2, 1994, 1; *Xinmin wanbao* (Xinmin evening news), Shanghai, Mar. 3, 1995, 3; *Xinan wanbao* (Xinan evening news), Hefei, June 6, 1995, 1; and Fan Ping 1996, 68.

TABLE 5.6

*Amount of Welfare Pay in Selected Areas
of the PRC (mid-1990s)*

Regions/Places	RMB/month	Type
Shanghai City	135–180	Metropolis
Tianjin	127–152	Metropolis
Guangzhou City	160	Metropolis
Beijing City	120	Metropolis
Qingdao City	96–120	Metropolis
Helongjiang Province		
Provincial capital	75	Large city
Medium size city	70	Medium city
County seats	65	Small city
Township	60	Town
Jilin Province		
Provincial capital	70	Large city
Medium size city	65	Medium city
County seats	60	Small city
Township	55	Town
Henan Province		
Provincial capital	50	Large city
Medium size city	45	Medium city
County seats	40	Small city
Township	35	Town
Hubei Province		
Provincial capital	90–120	Large city
Prefecture city	80	Medium city
County seats	70	Small city

SOURCE: Fan Ping 1996, 68–69. Only the local urban *hukou* holders who are officially recognized as below the poverty line can apply for this pay.

ferent pay scales for state employees in the different regions ever since the mid-1950s.[71] By the 1990s, the government-mandated minimum wage in the PRC also varied drastically across regions, separated by the *hukou* system and other community barriers (Table 5.5). The state's urban poverty-relief scheme also varied across regions (Table 5.6).

Not only does there exist in China a huge income gap between urban and rural residents and between the eastern and coastal areas and the interior regions, but also the price of state-allocated resources is significantly different across the *hukou*-divided sectors and layers of Chinese society. In 2001, for example, China's state-monopoly power companies charged residents in the prosperous urban centers of Shanghai and Beijing only 0.5 Yuan RMB per kilowatt. But they charged the residents of other large and medium-sized cities about 0.78 Yuan per kilowatt, county towns 45 percent more, and rural areas still another 50 percent higher.[72]

This regional gap in income and standard of living, associated with and compounded by the regional investment and development gap, imposes increasing pressure on the PRC *hukou* system by creating voluntary, spontaneous, massive, lasting migrations to the richer regions and forcing the *hukou* system to make adaptive changes. Furthermore, the regional gap is contributing to the rise of regionalism and regional protectionism that have already become major destabilizing factors in Chinese politics in the early 2000s.[73] Regional differentiation in production costs, especially labor costs, may lead to a segmented Chinese market.[74] A legal fragmentation seems to have emerged, facilitating local protectionism and agency protectionism to pervert and hinder reforms and development of the Chinese legal system.[75] In response, Beijing has issued numerous decrees to tear down economic barriers erected by local corporatist and protectionist activity.[76] The central government's political stability and power and even the unity of the nation may be at stake.[77] In many ways, the Chinese economy is not just a dual economy of rural and urban sectors but more a collection of several regional economies that are at various stages of development, with hugely different degrees of economic prosperity, separated chiefly by the PRC *hukou* system.

The Hukou System and Chinese Social Life: Horizontal Stratification

Institutional exclusion may provide social stability and continuity to a large nation, especially in a time of rapid economic development and social and cultural change. It forms solid groupings and associations beyond family and employment relations. Ethically, however, institutional exclusion produces troubling questions about the equity and equality of the human and civil rights of citizens of the same nation. A slow urbanization naturally segregates the citizens and creates cultural biases against the excluded rural population. Furthermore, institutional exclusion discourages and even hinders the development of creativity and ingenuity that often accompany people's horizontal and vertical mobility in a society. The PRC's *hukou*-based institutional exclusion and social control have deep, extensive, lasting social consequences naturally related to its aforementioned political and economic impact. Chinese culture, social stratification, and social norms and values have all developed regional characteristics as well as a rural-versus-urban differentiation.[78]

As in other developing nations, vertical economic stratification has developed very rapidly in China. The government estimates that an increasingly small group of upper-income earners are now controlling a staggeringly large portion of China's wealth: in 1990, about 10 percent of the Chinese owned 40 percent of the total bank deposits; by 2000, 1 percent of depositors (or 5 percent of the total population) owned 40 percent of the total bank deposits, and 20 percent of the depositors, mainly urban *hukou* holders, owned 80 percent of the total bank deposits, which is still the main form of savings and investment in China.[79] The aggregate national Gini index (a measurement of income equality) was a staggering 0.45 by 2001 (0.397 in 1999; a Gini index of 0 means perfect equal distribution of income and 1 means perfect inequality), already at the red-alert level,[80] although the perhaps more accurate and applicable urban and rural Gini indexes, separately calculated for the urban and rural residents, were both around the much more tolerable figure of 0.32 (0.33 for urban residents and 0.295 for rural residents in 1999).[81] Naturally, a social stratification in both rural and urban communities has significantly developed vertically along the fault line of haves versus have-nots. One survey study in the city of Wuhan, for example, showed that more than 90 percent of urban residents interviewed used property rights and wealth as the chief criteria distinguishing people in their city.[82]

In contrast to many other countries, the increasingly serious inequality of income distribution appears in China not only vertically but also horizontally or geographically.[83] Social stratification in the PRC, therefore, is not only vertical, as in all other nations, but also rigidly spatial and horizontal, based on the administratively defined geographical location of the people under the *hukou* system. A horizontal stratification has hence deeply colored Chinese society and culture.

In the early 2000s, the PRC has about 1.3 billion people living in twenty-three provinces, four province-level regions, and four province-level metropolises. These thirty-one administrative units have a total of 675 cities,[84] with about 350 million urban residents or nonagricultural *hukou* holders, 26.1 percent of the total population. These cities are administratively ranked at four levels: municipal or provincial (4), deputy-provincial (SEZs or separately planning cities, 15), prefectural (229), and county (427).[85] Of China's cities, 5 have over 4 million urban residents, 8 have 2 to 4 million, 25 have 1 to 2 million, 43 have one-half to one million, 461 have 100 to 500 thousand, and 133 have fewer than a hundred thousand urban residents. In addition, there are between 1,683 and 1,718 county towns or county seats with a total of 92.3 million urban residents.[86] Beyond that, China has 7,622 city-administered towns and 12,158 county-administered townships that have a combined 135.9 million urban residents.[87] Cities at different levels enjoy different authorities and state subsidies in socioeconomic development and *hukou* administration.[88]

Generally, a city at or above the deputy-provincial level is considered to be among the elite metropolises, subject to the tightest migration control. Cities that have over a million urban residents are considered to be large cities; those with five hundred thousand, medium-sized cities. Together, these three types of cities constitute China's cultural and socioeconomic centers, the most desirable places to live. The remaining small cities and towns are urban areas of lower social rank, but these clearly are still ranked higher socially and culturally by the people than the rural areas. The reform era has somewhat blurred the boundaries between some urban areas (especially the small cities and towns) and prosperous villages in suburban regions like the Pearl River Delta and the Lower Yangtze River Delta. Therefore, many small cities and towns located in the remote interior or less developed regions of the PRC are often considered socially less desirable than some prosperous, better-located suburban or rural areas.

Using the information in Table 5.7, we can depict a peculiar social stratification in the PRC in the early 2000s (Table 5.8). In addition to the vertical social stratification based on income and political power seen in every community, every nation, and every ethnic and racial group in multiethnic countries, China has acquired a strong horizontal or geographical socioeconomic stratification of its population based on the PRC *hukou* system. Such a social division is a result and, in turn, a cause of the grossly uneven distribution of political power and economic resources and opportunities based on people's *hukou* type and location. For a socialist PRC, the existence of such a complicated, comprehensive, rigid, highly entrenched social stratification, created and maintained by the people's government, is indeed one of the great ironies in human history. The findings of a study on regional demographic features and the direction and volume of internal migration in China nicely fit the pattern of such a horizontal stratification.[89] Even the newly emerging "class relations and class consciousness" in China now "center upon place, power, and particularism."[90]

Dividing China's provincial-level administrative units into four regions, one recent study found great inequality in education and educa-

TABLE 5.7

Social Stratification by Hukou Location

Location	No.	Urban residents (millions) (% of total population)	Desirability	Migration control
Metropolises[a]	12	13.7 (1.1%)	Elite	
Eastern/coastal China	11	13.0 (1%)	Highest	Tightest
Rest of China	1	0.7 (0.008%)	Highest	Tightest
Provincial capitals[b]	27	46.2 (3.6%)	Elite	
Eastern/coastal China	10	25.5 (2%)	Very High	Very tight
Rest of China	17	20.7 (1.6%)	High	Very tight
Large cities[c]	20	19.6 (1.6%)	Elite	
Eastern/coastal China	17	16.5 (1.3%)	Very high	Very tight
Rest of China	3	3.1 (0.02%)	High	Tight
Medium cities[d]	141	61.2 (4.8%)	Second tier	
Eastern/coastal China	68	29.5 (2.3%)	Very high	Tight
Rest of China	73	31.7 (2.5%)	High	Tight
Small cities	478	70.4 (5.6%)	Second tier	
Eastern/coastal China	267	39.3 (3.1%)	High	Medium
Rest of China	211	31.1 (2.5%)	Medium	Minimal
County-seat towns	1,683	92.3 (7.3%)	Third tier	
Eastern/coastal China	483	26.5 (2.1%)	High	Controlled
Rest of China	1,200	65.8 (5.2%)	Medium	Minimal
Towns	19,780	135.9 (10.9%)	Third tier	
Eastern/coastal China	9,844	68.6 (5.5%)	High	Controlled
Rest of China	9,966	67.3 (5.4%)	Medium	Minimal
Total urban residents		322.5 (26.1%)	Socially privileged	
Eastern/coastal China		171.2 (13.9%)	Desirable	Controlled
Rest of China		151.3 (12.2%)	Desirable	Controlled
Suburban rural residents[e]		42.1 (3.4%)	Medium	Minimal
Rural residents		872.2 (70.5%)	Low	Generally none
Total rural residents		914.3 (73.9%)	Undesirable	
Remote areas[f]		Rural & urban residents	Undesirable	Rewarded

SOURCES: SSB 2000, 347, 350–51; MPS 2001, 3–104.

[a]The four centrally administrated municipalities (Beijing, Shanghai, Tianjin, Chongqing) with 29.5 million urban residents and "separately planning cities" including the SEZs (Shenzhen, Zhuhai, Shantou, Xiamen, Haikou, Dalian, Qingdao, Ningbo) with 96.95 million urban residents. All (except for Chongqing) are on the East Coast. Migration to these cities is most tightly controlled.

[b]Mainly the provincial capital cities. Migration to these cities is highly controlled.

[c]With urban residents between 0.8 and 2 million.

[d]With urban residents between 300 and 800 thousand.

[e]Pockets of rural residents. Due to limited availability of data, only the "agricultural *hukou*" holders who live under the administration of the metropolises and provincial capital cities are counted here. Although not exactly an urban area, the outskirts of major cities are very attractive to rural residents due to their proximity to the urban centers.

[f]The towns and posts primarily on the Western borders, on the Tibetan Plateau, and in deep mountains.

TABLE 5.8

China's Horizontal Stratification

1. Elite Chinese—urban *hukou* holders living in the metropolises, provincial capitals, and large cities—6.3 percent of the total population.

2. High Class—urban *hukou* holders living in the medium cities—10.4 percent of the total population.

3. Middle Class—urban *hukou* holders living in the small cities and towns (18.2 percent) and rural *hukou* holders living in the suburban areas of the metropolises and provincial capital cities (3.4 percent)—21.6 percent of the total population.

4. Low Class—rural *hukou* holders living in the rural areas—70.5 percent of the total population.

tional opportunities between the various regions. In the late 1990s, the illiteracy rate in region 1 (the metropolises) was as low as 4–14 percent, but it was 14–52 percent in region 4 (the western provinces and regions). The government spent on average 2,308 Yuan RMB per student in region 1 but only 340 in region 4.[91] Another study showed that, by the late 1990s, the average education of the workers was eight to ten years of schooling in the metropolises and provinces in eastern and coastal regions but only three to six years of schooling in the western provinces.[92]

Utilizing its Human Development Index (HDI), the United Nations has sponsored studies to measure overall socioeconomic development throughout the world. In its reports of 1999 and 2001, the U.N. listed China's regional gaps in socioeconomic development as among the largest in the world. Out of 162 nations, China ranked number 98 in overall HDI in 1999 and number 87 in 2001, just above Jordan in the medium human development range.[93] By the same measurement, however, China's most developed regions, Shanghai, Beijing, and Tianjin (all metropolises in eastern or coastal China), ranked number 25, 27, and 30, in the high human development range, equivalent to Greece, Singapore, and Malta, respectively. China's least developed regions, Qinghai, Guizhou, and Tibet (all in western China), ranked number 135, 137, and 147, in the low human development range, equivalent to Haiti, the Sudan, and Angola, respectively.[94] In other words, developed societies and the poorest societies coexist within one nation not only vertically but also horizontally. This is indeed a mighty testament to the power of the PRC *hukou* system.

Despite the inherent and increasingly obvious moral and ethical problems of the *hukou* system, it may have created one positive effect in Chinese society through its forced institutional division and exclusion. In contrast to what has happened in many other large developing nations such as Brazil or India, as I will discuss in Chapter 6, China's rapid economic development and industrialization have been relatively orderly, with limited problems of urban slums, urban poverty, and homelessness that have plagued many other developing nations.[95] Massive slums have been deemed "an inevitable and expanding feature of cities in the developing countries."[96] Yet so far, in the Chinese cities, the urban slums are generally small, temporary, and insignificant,[97] as many of the slums are often forced to close down and their residents repatriated. For example, in the first half of 2001, in one Dongfeng township, the Chaoyang District of Beijing, the authorities forcibly demolished illegally constructed rental housing in sixty-six residential compounds to enhance the management of floating people.[98] For some more developed settlements of sojourning ruralites, such as Zhejiang Village in Beijing, the local government has invested in and even taken over the management to upgrade the settlement and integrate it.[99] Other, smaller but quasi-permanent settlements of migrants just outside major urban centers tend to attract people from one place or from same profession, and many of their residents are highly mobile.[100]

The PRC *hukou* system has other social consequences. One study believes that the dual society in China is producing a "reverse elimination" effect on national "population quality," decreasing the physical and mental quality of the Chinese nation, and "even threatening the survival of our nation," since the excluded "low-quality" and poorly educated but massive rural population grows faster: in the late 1980s, the rural population, excluded and poorer, had a 2.4 percent birth rate and 1.7 percent annual growth rate, whereas the supposedly higher-quality urban population had only a 1.4 percent birth rate and 0.9 percent annual growth rate.[101] Similarly, others believe that the *hukou* system has spoiled the supposedly lazy, arrogant urbanites, created inferiority complexes, helplessness, and blind prejudice and hatred among the ruralites, and encouraged inbreeding that has lowered the population quality in the rural areas.[102]

The excluded Chinese peasants still by and large accept their fate under the PRC *hukou* system as it is. The extent to which those who are excluded in the rural and backward areas, three-quarters of the total Chinese population, will continue in their role as the reservoir to hold the unskilled millions, hence to make a multigenerational sacrifice for rapid modernization of the Chinese urban economy, remains increasingly uncertain. Unemployment pressure alone, likely to be significantly worsened by China's new WTO membership,[103] may make *hukou*-based institutional exclusion even less bearable. The hundred-million-strong migrant (*liudong*) population—registered holders of temporary *hukou* and unregistered *mangliu* (blind floaters)—clearly a second-class citizenry outside their home towns in their own country, has already become a major source of the rising crime rate and even of organized crime in the PRC.[104] How much and how quickly trickle-down and spillover effects of prosperous, glamorous urban centers will be felt in rural areas will be key to the continuation of China's sociopolitical stability and economic growth under the PRC *hukou* system.

A Case Study of China's College Admissions

Under the PRC *hukou* system and with a highly unevenly developed economy, basic principles of equity and equality are fundamentally and institutionally challenged in China. Even the fairest systems and designs are bound to be affected, distorted, and compromised, hence becoming inherently unfair. China's much-cherished and highly valued college entrance examination and admissions system is one important example.

Ever since the 1950s, education in colleges and selected professional schools has been a main avenue for upward socioeconomic and political mobility as well as for horizontal mobility (internal migration) in China. The PRC's college entrance examination system functions like the imperial civil-service examination system before 1906. The chance to earn a college degree is the main hope for the few with ability in the excluded rural areas and less developed regions to legally change their *hukou* location and type. That way, they can resettle in the urban areas, especially the major cities, and thus improve life chances for themselves and their offspring. By passing the examination in subjects decided on and graded by the state and then managing to graduate from a state-accredited college—all are still state-run in the 2000s—anyone can acquire an urban *hukou*. Passing the entrance examination of a graduate school gives anyone national mobility today. Furthermore, although since the late 1990s college graduates have no longer been guaranteed state jobs,[105] college education still is the key to economic and social advancement in a nation filled with hundreds of millions of low-skilled and unskilled laborers.

The PRC has about 14 million middle-school graduates every year, less than half of whom go on to high school. Out of more than 3.5 million high-school graduates and a few million older applicants, the colleges in the early 2000s are admitting on average one to one and a half million students every year. Although the rural *hukou*-holders have always been the overwhelming majority of the Chinese population, they never contributed more than half of the college entrance examination takers until 2004, when the rural *hukou*-holding examinees outnumbered the urban ones for the first time.[106] College education is still considered a luxury that only a fraction of the population can enjoy, despite the fact that higher education in China has had considerable development in the past two decades. The college entrance examination is a narrow bridge for young Chinese to struggle to pass over to get anywhere in their lives, a major upward mobility avenue in an otherwise rigidly stratified society.

Beginning in imperial times, the Chinese invented numerous ways to ensure that people taking examinations would be treated fairly, that everyone would have an equal chance in imperial examinations, as likewise now in college entrance examinations. With an elaborate system to ensure secrecy of the questions, integrity of the delivery and handling process, blind hence objective grading,[107] and nonhuman hence fair computerized selection for admission based primarily on examination scores, today's Chinese college entrance examination is considered one of the few fair systems open to every Chinese citizen. The college entrance examination, administered in late June and early July each year, is a major event that brings millions of parents' lives virtually to a standstill well before and long after the three testing days. Every year, there are harsh punishments handed down for those caught cheating on the examination.[108] There are also young high-school graduates killing themselves for real or merely perceived failures in their examinations. In the 2000s, a new group of young Chinese has emerged in the major Chinese cities, professional students, high-school graduates studying full-time for further attempts at the college entrance examination or college graduates studying full-time for the entrance examinations for graduate school.

Although China's college entrance examination questions are largely nationally uniform,[109] when it comes to admissions the all-important fair entrance examination quickly becomes inherently unfair to applicants from rural and less developed regions because of the PRC *hukou* system. According to *hukou* rules, all college applicants must take their entrance examinations and then be admitted in their own *hukou* zones (where their permanent *hukou* is located) regardless of where they actually live and where they actually finish high school.[110] All localities, especially the provinces or provincial-level metropolises or regions, have very different numbers of people taking college entrance examinations and vastly different quotas for college admission. The distribution of college admission quotas is not based on the size of the applicant pool or student performance in one particular province. Rather, it is heavily based on where the colleges are located and often simply state directives.

The number of college students per ten thousand citizens in the PRC has grown from 8.9 in 1978 and 16.1 in 1985 to 24 in 1995 and 43.9 in 2000. The number of state-accredited colleges has remained relatively stable from 1985 to 2000.[111] The distribution of those colleges, however, has been heavily and increasingly uneven. In the early 2000s, China's 857 state-accredited colleges admitted a total of 1.54 million students. Of those colleges, 461 (53.8 percent) are located in eastern and coastal China plus the metropolis of Chongqing, where only about 40.1 percent of the total population resides. Out of China's colleges, 123 (14.4 percent), including most of the top universities in China, are located in the four metropolises, which contain only 2.9 percent of the total population. In 2001, there were about fifty thousand college applicants but over a hundred colleges in Beijing; in nearby Shangdong Province, there were four hundred thousand college applicants but fewer than fifty colleges.[112] Of the top fifty comprehensive universities, all are located in large cities, and only one (Petroleum University) is located outside the metropolises and the provincial capital cities.[113]

Each year, China's universities and colleges are required to admit a fixed number of students from state-mandated areas. Some universities are good enough to offer national or cross-provincial admissions; hence their admissions quotas for each province are handed down directly by the central government via the Ministry of Education. The government also dictates total admissions quotas for in-province colleges but leaves their admissions quotas, in the different areas of each province, to the provincial education bureaus to decide. Many of the insiders whom I interviewed reported that the decision on quotas is primarily political and made at a high level of the national planning process, involving the State Planning Commission and the Ministry of Education.

The details of regional admissions quotas and the breakdown of the origins of college students in China are classified as a state secret, for good reason. Such a secretive practice is in line with the still semisecretive nature of the PRC *hukou* system and is intended to disguise the unfairness of the seemingly fair college entrance examination and admissions

TABLE 5.9

College Admission Scores and Rates by Region

Regions	2001 score[a]	Above/below nat'l average	College applicants[b]	Admission rate (2000–2001)
National	492	—	3,499,026	53.2%–52%
4 Metropolises	482	−10		
Beijing	454	−38	64,479	80–70%
Tianjin	480	−12	38,123	92.8%
Shanghai	491	−1	78,289	
Chongqing	502	+10	62,285	
Eastern/coastal regions	511	+9		
Hainan	468	−24	13,653	64%
Jilin	474	−18	80,758	
Helongjiang	490	−2	103,189	
Fujian	494	+4	102,599	54.3%
Liaoning	500	+8	133,076	70%
Guangdong	501	+9	213,691	
Jiangsu	511	+19	247,308	65%
Hebei	538	+46	229,038	48.9%[c]
Zhejiang	538	+46	164,946	60%
Shangdong	594	+102	313,140	
Qingdao (metropolis)	589	+97		
Jinan (capital)	556	+64		
Western/interior regions	483	−9		
Tibet	385	−107	3,150	
Tibetans	255	−237		
Qinghai	395	−97	15,686	
Yunan	429	−63	79,033	50%
Ningxia	452	−40	30,166	54.3%
Muslims	403	−89		
Guizhou	453	−39	65.784	62.9%[d]
Xinjiang	457	−35	63,012	66%
Gansu	484	−8	67,046	
Inner Mongolia	485	−7	75,501	
Mongolians	419	−73		
Shangxi	494	+2	131,583	40.2%
Sichuan	494	+2	169,427	
Anhui	504	+12	185,562	47.1%[e]
Shanxi	514	+22	92,785	decreased
Hubei	517	+25	228,842	56.8%
Guangxi	521	+29	103,175	
Hunan	524	+32	177,296	50%
Jiangxi	527	+35	124,737	53.2%[f]
Henan	568	+76	203,551	

SOURCES: SSB 2001, 666–67; *Zhongguo qingnian bao* (Chinese youth daily), various days in July, 2000; announcements of college admission offices in the 31 provincial units, in various local newspapers or government bulletins, July–Aug. 2001.

[a]The score here is the weighted average of four sets of minimum admission scores: social sciences/humanities and sciences/engineering, each with two categories; top universities (*zhongdian daxue*); and regular 4-year colleges. In the early 2000s, the provinces tested their college applicants with two different combinations (3+1 or 3+2) of the following six subject areas: Chinese, math, and foreign language plus physics/chemistry or history/geography, and current affairs. Three provinces used "new" high school textbooks and curricula in 2001. They graded the tests in three ways (3+1, 3+2, or by a standard 900 scale). Hence the total possible test score and the minimum admission score reported vary in different provinces. I have weighed that factor and adopted the grading method used by most provinces (the so-called 3+2 test with a total possible score of 750). The remaining provinces' scores are calculated as the equivalent in that scheme, based on their published "raw" scores and their grading methods. Information on admission rates is only available in some regions.

[b]High school graduates in 2000 or registered college applicants.

[c]Was 44.9 percent in 1999   [d]Was 52.9 percent in 1999.

[e]Was 35.6 percent in 1999.   [f]Was 42.1 percent in 1999.

process, in the name of implementing state policies. From what we know, however, the quota allocation clearly favors the major urban centers. In 2000, for example, Beijing, with a permanent population of 10 million, was allocated 25,000 college admissions while nearby Shandong Province, with nearly a hundred million people, got only 80,000. Between 1998 and 2001, the prestigious Tsinghua University, often ranked number one in China, was required each year to admit 600 of about 60,000 college applicants from Beijing, versus only 100 of the more than 300,000 college applicants from Shandong Province and only 88 from Hubei Province, which had a population more than five times larger than Beijing's and nearly 200,000 college applicants.[114] The nationally top-ranked Department of English at the Shanghai University of International Studies was required to admit 91 of its 153 freshmen in 1998 from among fewer than 80,000 Shanghai college applicants, but only two from nearby Anhui Province, which had about 150,000 college applicants.[115] During the reform era of the 1980s and 1990s, the colleges and local education bureaus got more authority in running the schools and some leeway in their admissions practices (as will be discussed later), but their state-mandated quotas in different regions are still strictly followed in the 2000s.

Consequently, there is a strong *hukou*-based institutional discrimination in China's college admissions. The chances of going to a college, especially a top university, are significantly worse outside metropolises and specially favored areas, as can be clearly seen from the admission scores of the college entrance examination in different regions. A so-called local minimum admission score is announced by each of the thirty-one provincial-level college admissions offices shortly after the entrance examinations are held. An analytical report of Chinese college admissions data for 2001 is presented in Table 5.9. Consistent with the policy of granting mobility to those with talent, the postgraduate schools (master's and doctoral degree programs), on the rationale that they are training the most talented students, have nationally uniform admissions scores and admit applicants regardless of their original *hukou* location or type.

Table 5.9 clearly shows that the ostensibly fair college admissions process heavily favors applicants from some areas while discriminating against those from others. Policy-driven favor is shown to certain minority groups (e.g., Tibetans, Mongolians, Muslims) and the people in some remote and backward areas, mainly the scarcely populated northwestern and southwestern provinces. The favors that have caught most people's attention have been the much easier chances for urban *hukou* holders to get higher education if they live in a major urban center. The most populated provinces tend to have higher admissions scores and lower admissions rates, in line with the general nature of *hukou*-caused horizontal stratification analyzed previously. Beijing, for example, had a minimum admission score 140 points (or 28 percent of the national average minimum admission score, 492) lower than in Shangdong Province.

In a perhaps more transparent way, the central government routinely orders special favors in college admissions for selected examinees, such as the descendants of martyrs, military medal winners, returned overseas Chinese, and decorated model high-school students. Such favoritism in admissions is "no more than a 20-point difference."[116] Compared with that, the gap between the minimum admissions scores of the major urban centers and those of many provinces, commonly ranging from 20 to 140 points, is indeed very substantial.

A game of *hukou* relocation for the sake of higher education is, therefore, routinely played by those with the resources and connections. In one case, for example, several college applicants in Hefei, the capital of Anhui Province, scored far below the minimum admissions score set for their province and could get into only a small community college in 2000. Yet upon learning this, their families managed to relocate their urban *hukou* from Hefei to Beijing and soon became Beijing residents; then all were admitted to the Chinese University of Science and Technology (CUST), one of the best Chinese universities—located right there in Hefei. CUST is required to admit a certain number of students from the much smaller applicant pool in Beijing, where all the top universities are competing. These lucky Hefei applicants got into this highly selective university while their high-school classmates with much higher test scores ended up only in small local colleges. With a change of *hukou* papers, one's life chances are dramatically altered. One leading way to relocate *hukou* quickly, of course, has been to acquire a blue-seal *hukou* by purchasing upscale housing at the government-designated price in the city of choice. One local newspaper reported people spending several hundred thousand RMB each to buy Beijing *hukou* in this way right before the 2001 college entrance examinations in order that their children would immediately have dramatically much better chances in life.[117] I have often heard similar stories from interviewees who speak of themselves as resigned to an unfair fate.

The provincial units are not treated equally under China's college admissions system, since they have different minimum admissions scores for the same college slot. Within each provincial unit, the cities and counties are further unequally treated even though they all have the same minimum admissions scores (with the exception of Shangdong Province and a few multiethnic provincial units). The regions in each province are allocated different admissions quotas, not determined on the basis of the size of the applicant pool but is based on administrative decisions under the *hukou* system. This allocation traditionally and clearly favors the cities, especially the major cities. Such intraprovincial inequality is especially obvious in admissions to professional schools.[118]

Hukou-based systematic favor in college admissions for the residents of major urban centers is further compounded by two additional categories: the so-called *zoudusheng* (off-campus students) and *zifeisheng* (self-paying students).

In addition to state-mandated and thus state-subsidized admissions quotas, Chinese colleges, especially those with good reputations, have been authorized and paid by Beijing to admit some off-campus students each year with slightly lower-than-minimum test scores. Since Chinese college students are normally provided with subsidized on-campus housing, off-campus students must have a local residence, essentially a local *hukou*, to qualify. Therefore, residents of the urban centers where most colleges are located have another chance to go to college, with admissions scores even lower than the published minimum.

Self-paying admission has created another way for the rich, especially those living in major urban centers, to have a better chance for higher education. This is very much in line with the general adaptation of the *hukou* system aimed at granting national mobility for the rich, as discussed in Chapter 4. To allow colleges to earn extra revenue, the government decided in the 1990s that they could admit some students outside the state's mandate or planning. These self-paying students are charged higher tuition and fees and are responsible for room and board at a higher price (or live off campus). They can be admitted to college with substantially lower test scores, in proportion to a given college's regular admissions quota in a given region. Therefore, the urban rich who could not get into college under already reduced admissions scores, or further reduced admissions scores as off-campus students, were now given a third chance to get into college, by paying.

Finally, the PRC has had a *baosongsheng* (sure-admissions students) policy since 1985. Under this system, local education bureaus, working with the local high schools, send a select few high-school graduates to college without taking the college entrance examination. Some colleges are also authorized to send a select few of their graduates to graduate schools without entrance examinations. This appears to be in line with the adaptation of the *hukou* system to offer mobility and favors to the politically powerful and correct. Essentially, this is a leading way for local officials and the rich to acquire better and easier chances of mobility and higher education for their children. It also provides an incentive for high-school students to be politically correct in hopes of being selected as *baosongsheng*. Beijing University, often regarded as the best university in China, was given about two hundred such freshmen every year in the early 2000s.[119] Because of mounting criticism about the unfairness, politicization, and corruption involved,[120] in 2001 Beijing slashed the national *baosongsheng* quota from twenty-five thousand to only five thousand, to be selected from among provincial model students, science-contest winners, and graduates of thirteen foreign-language schools.[121]

The Chinese themselves have noticed and discussed the unfair college admissions process that follows upon the supposedly fair entrance examination. Some have publicly called for a uniform national admissions score to correct unfair practices, asserting that "these many top universities in Beijing are supported with national taxpayers' money and should not favor Beijing residents too much."[122] Some argue that it is necessary for an unevenly developed nation to use a seemingly unfair admissions process to assist the backward areas and have a balanced representation in the institutions of higher education for national political and social stability, a sort of affirmative action for the various regions. Others argue that the uniform college entrance examination does not really measure the true potential and real talents of many urban youth, who because of prior education and experience in developed urban areas tend to do well in colleges even with lower test scores, whereas many high-scoring students from rural and backward areas tend to have better test-taking skills rather than genuine talent and knowledge.[123] Most people I interviewed, however, tend to agree with the following statement:[124]

> The huge gap that sometimes exists in admissions scores in different regions reflects uneven regional distribution of higher education resources. It is the product of a long-term planned economy. It is the result of a state policy of developing education first in the core cities and regions like Beijing and Shang-

hai and using education to guarantee employment. ... It artificially creates injustice among the college applicants in different regions. ... Since we have a nationally uniform college entrance examination, it is only fair to eventually have a nationally uniform admissions standard.

Resentment and criticism against unfair college admissions have been rising, leading even to lawsuits against the government. In August 2001, three college applicants in Shangdong Province, which had the highest admissions score (28 percent higher than that in Beijing), sued the Chinese Ministry of Education. In their administrative lawsuit filed at the Chinese Supreme People's Court, three high-school graduates, through lawyers, charged the ministry with unconstitutionally violating their right of equal access to higher education. The three applicants had entrance examination scores of 457, 506, and 522, respectively, considerably above the minimum admissions score (454) of prestigious universities for applicants in Beijing, but they could not get into any college at all, being legally Shangdong residents.[125]

The Chinese government forecasts that higher-educational resources in the foreseeable future will remain in short supply as the college-bound population grows rapidly and will level off only in 2008. Since the government eliminated age and marriage restrictions on college applicants in 2001, the potential college-age population in China will reach a peak of over 120 million by 2010.[126] The unusually rapid expansion of college admissions after the end of the 1990s (1.1 million in 1998, 1.95 million in 1999, 2.2 million in 2000) has been much criticized; the total annual college admissions capacity is unlikely to grow at that pace for long.[127] The unevenness of China's development and power distribution in different regions is hopelessly large and growing. *Hukou*-based institutional exclusion and state policy manipulation in the supposedly fair college admissions process, however unfair they may be, are likely to continue.

Conclusion

Under *hukou*-based institutional exclusion and social control, essentially every PRC citizen is politically and socially, if not entirely economically, stratified and governed according to his *hukou* type and location on a near-permanent basis by the government. A comprehensive, stereoscopic, omnipresent framework of sociopolitical control with clear economic consequences ensures the PRC's political stability and generates for the state strong political power and ample room for policy manipulations. Under the *hukou* system, the best to be hoped for is only a limited elite democracy, if Chinese politics indeed moves toward genuine democratization. Recent actions by Chinese leaders—the so-called Three "Represents" and recruiting capitalists to join the CCP[128]—have literally codified the fact that, under a combined institutional exclusion of Type 2 (based on *what one has*) and Type 3 (based on *where one is*), a new ruling class has emerged primarily from Chinese urban *hukou* holders. China's "political elite, economic elite, and intellectual elite have all reached a consensus and joined an alliance" to rule China as an institutionally protected minority through the CCP's one-party monopoly of political power.[129] When the ruling elite, increasingly unable to mobilize political support, provide public goods, and manage internal tensions,[130] is encountering serious problems of governance, the *hukou* system has become an even more crucial tool of repression and control.

The PRC *hukou* system has enabled the seemingly puzzling coexistence of a rapidly developing, fairly diverse, dynamic market economy and a stable communist one-party authoritarian regime in an era of revolutionary information technology. By circumventing the Lewis Transition, China has so far achieved rapid economic growth and technological sophistication in a stable dual economy with relatively small and slow urbanization. Urban slums have so far remained insignificant in the PRC. Yet the *hukou* system directly perpetuates a duality in the Chinese economy and a market segmentation that together lead to inefficiency and waste. In the long run, the currently significant benefits of the *hukou* system may fade, as there is no guarantee of a real and speedy spillover or trickle-down effect of the "in," prosperous urban sector in coastal China upon the excluded rural and inland regions.[131] How long a *hukou*-based circumvention of the Lewis Transition can last, at the expense of excluding the majority of the population, remains a legitimate and profound question.

Another leading consequence is the vertical and horizontal social stratification of Chinese society. The PRC *hukou* system has developed a vertical differentiation of the people in each administrative unit based on their *hukou* type, agricultural versus nonagricultural. It has also created a horizontal stratification of the people across regions based on their *hukou* location, ranging from metropolises to small townships. The combination of these two stratifications not only has affected the allocation of resources, opportunities, and life chances in general for every Chinese, but also has largely shaped Chinese values, behavioral norms, and culture. A small, elite group, urban *hukou* holders living in the major urban centers, is master of this people's republic at the expense of excluding and discriminating against the majority of the people.[132] This is indeed a very peculiar class structure and social stratification in our time.

CHAPTER SIX

China's *Hukou* System
in Comparative Perspective

E ach nation is divided and then organized in its own ways; institutional exclusion hence exists in all states. Different types of institutional exclusion, however, set nations and states apart in terms of
governing effectiveness, national characteristics, achievements, and performance. As a Type 3 institutional exclusion (based on *where one is*), the
PRC *hukou* system has greatly contributed to China's peculiarities and
development: it has brought to the Chinese the benefits of rapid economic growth and sociopolitical stability through circumventing the
Lewis Transition, but it has also produced some of the worst exclusions
and discrimination in the world. Exclusion and discrimination against
peasants sojourning in the cities exist in many developing countries, but
"in many regards the level of discrimination experienced by China's ruralites residing in its metropolises exceeds that visited upon urbanizing
peasants in Latin America, Southeast Asia, or African cities."[1]

In this chapter I analyze China's *hukou* system in a comparative perspective so as to see better the commonalities and peculiarities of this system and its role. I will first trace the existence of residential registration
systems and internal migration controls in different historical and national settings to show that household registration systems are essentially
traditional and universal elements of statecraft; nothing compels them to
be institutionally exclusive like the PRC *hukou* system. I will cite the literature on the internal passport and *propiska* (registration) systems in the
former Soviet Union and Russia to show the similarities and differences
between the PRC *hukou* system and the Soviet and Russian registration
system. Whereas *hukou*-based institutional exclusion is alive and well in
the PRC, Soviet and Russian *propiska*-based control of internal migra-

tion has become both illegitimate and ineffective, with tremendous revelations about politics and governance in Russia in general.

The remainder of the chapter will be devoted to a comparative study of institutional exclusion in three large developing nations: Brazil, China, and India. China and India, very similar in that they both have a massive supply of low-skilled and unskilled labor in a dual economy, exhibit unique, important institutional exclusions based on politically or societally maintained fault lines, in addition to the universal division between haves and have-nots. In China, the PRC *hukou* system serves as the foundation of a powerful state-enforced institutional exclusion. India has its caste system, profound socially enforced institutional exclusion. Brazil, a large but much less densely populated developing nation with a dual economy that is also regionally very uneven, differs from China and India in many regards and may serve as a good contrast. The fault line between the rich and the poor has been the main basis for institutional exclusion in Brazil, just as in the developed nations and many other developing countries.

In its brief compass, this comparative study intends to raise rather than answer questions. It will, I hope, allow better assessment of the PRC *hukou* system, especially its implications, and a refinement of the theory of institutional exclusion. The independent variable here is the different types of institutional exclusion that exist in the three nations; the dependent variables are socioeconomic development and technological sophistication. My intention is to see whether there is any relationship between speed of development and type of institutional exclusion.

Residential Registration in the West

The use of state power to compel people's administrative registration, to regulate and restrict internal migration, and hence to fix population geographically—to divide and organize people—has a long history. It is not exclusively a Chinese or a communist phenomenon. Naturally, residential registration does not always lead to internal migration control and create institutional exclusions. The role and significance of residential registration and internal migration control seem to be directly and positively related to the speed of economic development, industrialization, and urbanization. The enforcement mechanisms of locational and residential registration and identification vary in different countries; many of them have practiced institutional division and exclusion through citizen registration and internal migration control at different times and in varying degrees. According to one nongovernmental international organization's study in 2001, at least thirty-three nations around the world used nationally uniform identification cards based on the bearer's location and residence in order to identify different racial, ethnic, and religious groups and maintain rural-urban divisions with clear characteristics of discrimination and exclusion.[2]

In the West, the Greeks (mainly in Athens) and the Romans started to register and then identify citizens so as to clarify the rights and duties of every resident. The Romans developed a national residential registration system, at first irregularly, during the republican era.[3] In 48 B.C., Julius Caesar declared his *Lex Julia Municipalis*, which started the comprehensive registration of citizens and their property in Italy. Augustus later institutionalized this important practice in A.D. 14, regularizing its occurrence to once every five years. Judged by role and style, Roman residential registration was quite similar to the imperial *hukou* system used by Chinese dynasties and was important for purposes of identifying citizens and enabling centralized taxation and military conscription. Augustus even listed the system as one of his major legacies.[4] Soon the system was implemented in other provinces of the Roman Empire, with varying degree of effectiveness.[5] The coming of the feudal system in Europe after the fall of the Roman Empire decentralized and even stopped residential registration for centuries, as citizen-based taxation and military service were minimized and replaced.

Toward the end of the Middle Ages, there were already laws restricting internal migration and punishing unauthorized migrants aimed at consolidating control of the peasantry by the monarchies and nobility of Western Europe. The advance of industrialization and especially the enclosure movement created a constant flood of dislocated peasants.[6] The continued existence of massive numbers of displaced and migrating peasants prompted states to increase their efforts at internal migration control. Such efforts subsided only in the nineteenth century, when massive overseas colonization and early social-welfare systems based on new taxes from prosperous new industrial economies began to alleviate the pressure caused by the floating surplus labor.

In England, for example, in addition to the firmly entrenched institutional divide between nobles and commoners, there were bloody, brutal antivagrancy laws under the Tudor Dynasty (1485–1603), especially during the reigns of Henry VIII (1509–47) and Elizabeth I (1558–1603), often prescribing mutilation, slavery, and death to deter vagrants or free migrating or floating people.[7] Only when the British state, under an increasingly capitalist Parliament in the Stuart and later Windsor eras, made active efforts to settle and employ displaced peasants and the urban poor through collecting poverty-relief taxes (e.g., the 1601 Poverty Relief Law, amended and completed in 1834) were the harsh and strict internal migration controls eased.[8] Massive emigration to British colonies all over the world and economic prosperity in the nineteenth and twentieth centuries eventually rendered such internal migration control obsolete,[9] even though displaced migrants and the associated urban poverty problem in the United Kingdom never entirely went away.[10] Regional differences and market segmentation remained important issues there toward the end of the twentieth century.[11] And the government has maintained a birth and death registration system in the United Kingdom since the nineteenth century.[12]

In the late twentieth century, European nations once again began another round of passportization to allow easier internal migration and social control. By 1977, thirteen European Union (EU) nations mandated a national personal identification card, to be inspected by police at any time, and the European Council was making efforts to standardize such personal identification cards.[13] By the 1990s, all EU nations except the United Kingdom, Ireland, and Luxembourg made registration of place of abode obligatory for all citizens and residents. "Failure to register, where stipulated," concluded a European scholar on passportization, "may entail a penalty."[14]

Contemporary residential registration in Western Europe, however, is very different from its ancestors and from that in the former USSR or today's China. It is not run by the police, and people can register automatically, albeit often as a mandatory duty, wherever they live without specific government approval. Such registration generally does not affect people's rights or freedom to move either internally or even beyond national borders but inside the EU.[15] Nevertheless, "modernization of society inevitably demands more passportization of one kind or another."[16] To identify people by their location and residence is still clearly a European phenomenon today. The system is there and can be used in different ways for different purposes. It is how such registration is used that sets it apart from the PRC *hukou* system or the Soviet and Russian *propiska* system. Although national identification cards and residential registration are not a form of institutional exclusion today, geographically based sociopolitical exclusion and discrimination against various minorities and regions still exist in Europe in the aftermath of the Cold War.[17]

There are perhaps only two major nations in the West, the United States and Australia, that have yet to require national registration and identification of their citizens. But even there, the widespread use of driver's licenses (and perhaps more important, Social Security numbers in the United States) has served much the same purpose as identification based on location or residence.[18] Until even as late as the 1970s, some of the United States actually required the bearer's race identified on driver's licenses as well.[19] Regional gaps and differentiations exist and matter significantly in American life without a national registration and identification system, even in law enforcement and capital punishment. One study showed that, in the United States, "the most telling factor in whether the death penalty will be handed down is the locality where the crime was committed" and where the case was tried.[20] In the 2000s, a nationally uniform identification card for every legal resident in the United States may be adopted in the aftermath of the September 11 tragedies.[21]

Location and residential registration in the United States are hardly a functional basis for a Type 3 (*where one is*) institutional exclusion. Instead, institutional exclusion in the United States is mainly of Type 2 (*what one has*), based on state-enforced and socially accepted property rights.[22] The fault line between haves and have-nots appears to be the main divide among Americans. "In the American justice system, as in so much else in this country," concluded the report of a major news magazine in the United States, "money changes everything, and huge amounts of money change things almost beyond recognition."[23] Of course, other forms of institutional exclusion, as for example exclusion and discrimination against women, against such behavioral minorities as homosexuals, and against racial minorities—the African slaves and their descendants in particular[24]—are by no means insignificant or less unjust.

Non-Chinese *Hukou* Systems

Residential registration has existed in many non-Western nations throughout history, serving various purposes including taxation, political and military mobilization, and social control. In only a few, however, has it functioned to restrict internal migration like the PRC *hukou* system.

In East Asia, nations learned from the Chinese to register their people for the same purposes of control, taxation, and conscription. Japan and Korea had their equivalents of the *hukou* system, even with the two exact same Chinese characters, before modern times. Copied directly from the Tang Dynasty, Japanese *hukou* rules were quite strict in controlling internal migration and mobility among eight strictly divided social strata also largely modeled after Chinese and Confucian ideals.[25] Peasants and other classes of people, except officials and samurai warriors, needed official permits to migrate and to reregister in their new locations in order to maintain imperial tax revenue. Peasants were allowed to move freely, but only from places with low tax and conscription rates to places with higher rates. If one wanted to move in the opposite direction, official permission was required.[26]

After the Meiji Restoration in 1868, the *hukou* system became an important part of Japan's post-Tokugawa institutions, altering Japanese society and culture profoundly. Japan's Law on Household Registration of 1871 (revised in 1898) instituted the practice of registering all Japanese citizens and residents, and commoners began for the first time to be recognized by family names.[27] Legally registered residents were allowed freedom of internal migration. Japan also modernized the administration of its *hukou* system to allow rapid industrialization and national mobilization for military expansion. Many similar administrative skills and techniques were later seen in the Republic of China (ROC) and PRC *hukou* systems.[28]

The Japanese *hukou* system does not restrict internal migration, although it does appear to have affected Japan's urbanization. Urbanization proceeded more slowly than industrialization in Japan, as the country's urban population was only 37.5 percent of the national total by 1950 (75.9 percent by 1975).[29] During World War II, tight, effective social control, helped by the *hukou* system, significantly assisted Japan's militarism and fascism.[30] The American occupation and reform of Japan started to diminish the social control of Japan's *hukou* system. Currently run by local governments with police assistance, Japan's *hukou* system is similar to that practiced in the EU, although Japanese *hukou* law stipulates more restrictive registration requirements.[31] Anecdotal evidence indicates that Japanese police are authorized to detain people who fail to produce proper identification papers upon random inquiry.[32]

Korea, as a largely Confucian society,[33] had institutions and practices similar to ancient China's to divide and organize the people and to control internal migration. After Japan annexed Korea through the 1894–95 Sino-Japanese War, a colonial version of the Japanese *hukou* system was implemented with more control and brutality, together with other colonial modernization measures.[34] In the years after World War II, the Koreans quickly developed as the main basis for institutional exclusion the fault line of property ownership, and Korea's urbanization proceeded rapidly, without much restriction via residential registration.[35] However, locational and residentially based divisions appear to remain important in Korean politics in the 1990s, as certain political parties tend to develop strong regional focuses and bases.[36] Under the management of the Ministry of Home Affairs, a mandatory residential registration (within two weeks of moving in) with fingerprints of every adult over age sixteen is still required by law in the 2000s, and residential identification can still mean differentiated taxes and rights, as well as different duties. For example, in order to discourage speculators a family owning more than one house or apartment in different cities will be required to pay more than local residents, and nonlocal residents sometimes have to pay additional taxes to purchase real estate in the controlled cities or areas.[37]

Taiwan was forced to alter traditional Chinese institutions and legal norms including the Qing *hukou* system during Japanese colonial rule (1895–1945).[38] The Japanese continued and enhanced the *baojia* (mutual responsibility) system for their rule of the island.[39] Taiwan moved away, however, from Japanese-style modernized residential registration and back to the ROC *hukou* system after World War II.[40] The defeated ROC central government found its new home on the island in 1949 and quickly improved an already tight *hukou* system to ensure effective control of the population and resources.[41] Taiwan's successful bloodless land reform in the 1950s stabilized the rural population into massive numbers of self-farming smallholders of land.[42] By law, there were institutional barriers erected between ruralites and city dwellers, as urban *hukou* holders were restricted from purchasing land or engaging in farming activities in the countryside. The stable rural socioeconomic structure provided great support to political and social institutions at a time when changes and shocks were numerous because of the advancement of the market and the impact of external events.[43]

Senior Taiwanese economists believed that the ROC *hukou* system contributed significantly to the island's sociopolitical stability and economic take-off in the 1960s and 1970s. By the mid-1990s, Taiwan still required everyone to register with the *hukou* authority and verified *hukou* records once a year. A *linli* (neighborhood) organization functions like the old Chinese *baojia* structure for social control and local governance.[44] Beyond that, Taiwan's *hukou* system has little impact on internal migration on the island.[45] The social control of Taiwan's *hukou* system, however, lasted well into the 1990s, when the rapidly developing young democracy effectively reduced the intrusiveness of personal identification cards the better to protect people's rights of privacy.[46] In the 2000s, Taiwan's *hukou* system has largely evolved into one similar to Japan's, losing much of its traditional function.[47]

Systems of residential registration and their function of social control and even control of internal migration are also found elsewhere.[48] In Indochina, for example, the French colonial government administered a very tight residential registration and identification system before the 1950s, under which not only internal migration but even internal travel had to be approved by the authorities with a stamp on the registration booklet. The French also used similar systems in Algeria and other former colonies.[49]

Residential registration is largely underdeveloped in most African (especially the sub-Saharan) nations, reflecting an overall problem of underdeveloped state capacity and governance in general.[50] Some African nations, however, do have fairly complete residential registration systems.[51] Institutional exclusion in these countries is often organized along strict tribal, ethnic, and racial lines, and, of course, the division between rich and poor. Internal migration in Africa generally resembles that in developing nations with weak states, where market forces and social considerations seem to be the main regulator.[52]

In South Asia, residential registration exists in India and other nations, but it has not nearly the power of the PRC *hukou* system and is generally unimportant as a basis of institutional exclusion. Much of the control of internal migration and geographically based exclusion and discrimination takes place at the hands of nonstate actors. In Latin America, residential registration is generally similar to that in Europe. It does not restrict internal migration, although in various countries it does frequently function in social control to varying degrees. Regulation of internal migration is largely left to the forces of the economy and the market.[53]

The Soviet and Russian Example:
Internal Passport and *Propiska*

As Dorothy Solinger has noted, the PRC's control of internal migration and discrimination against the rural population stemmed significantly from the Soviet example.[54] Indeed, other Soviet-style socialist countries also practiced residential registration and restricted internal migration.[55] Yet Soviet registration and control mechanisms based on internal passports and exclusive residential permits (*propiska*) were not nearly as rigid or as stringently enforced as the PRC *hukou* system. "The Soviet leaders were not always rigorous in checking [population] movement, because of the persistent labor shortage in their country, which fed a special ambivalence toward rural-to-urban migration and indeed towards geographical mobility in general."[56]

The Soviets, actually, did not invent internal passports or *propiska* registration. Both can be traced back to at least the time of Peter the Great, in the early eighteenth century, if not earlier. Tsarist control of internal migration was very similar to that practiced in ancient China, in that both were aimed at strengthening sociopolitical stability, tax collection, and conscription.[57] Shortly after the 1917 Revolution, the new regime quickly established an identification and registration system during the hard times of the 1920s. The Soviet Union, under Stalin, finally restored the internal-passport system in 1932.[58] Each internal passport has a *propiska* (residency) stamp showing the bearer's legal residence. "No change in residence could be made without official permission and failure to register was subject to fines or imprisonment. A valid *propiska* was required in order to work, get married or gain access to education or social services."[59] Even though the *propiska* was especially difficult to obtain in certain areas like Moscow, the Soviets did not maintain an enforced quota of migration, and people commonly used marriages (even fake marriages) as an effective way of changing *propiska*.[60]

The revitalization and reinstitutionalization of the tsarist internal-passport system in the USSR and the imperial *hukou* system in the PRC were indeed strong evidence supporting Andrew Walder's finding "communist neo-traditionalism" and its resultant "organized dependence" in Leninist-Stalinist countries."[61] More resilient and lasting than communist ideology or even the Communist Party itself, however, these two similar systems have continued into the twenty-first century in both countries, with varying effectiveness and scope.

The Soviet internal passport with its *propiska* stamp was an important tool for controlling population movement. It served several functions, such as limiting the urban population in specific areas (especially the major cities such as Moscow), implementing industrial development and relocation, and screening and persecuting political dissidents through forcing them into internal exile. It was not, however, very strictly enforced to effectively limit rural-to-urban migration or internal migration in general. The *propiska* system played only a limited role in the economic development of the USSR, largely because the Soviet Union was not a typical dual economy with a practically unlimited supply of unskilled labor. As a result, the USSR urbanized rapidly. From 1929 to 1941, over 23 million peasants left their villages and moved to the Soviet cities, increasing the urban population by nearly 100 percent and more than doubling the industrial workforce.[62] By the time the Soviet Union came to its end in the early 1990s, its urban population was already the majority.[63] The Soviet registration system required much less detailed information from the registrant and much less strict official surveillance of the people than does the PRC *hukou* system. Hence it was not nearly as profound, extensive, or effective as the PRC's system, not even justifying "the substantial social and economic costs of running it."[64]

The collapse of the USSR in 1991 did not end the internal-passport system completely. The *propiska* system also continued in most former Soviet republics even though it was officially abolished. Seven of these republics, including Russia, Belarus, Kazakhstan, and Ukraine, have continued to require citizens to register, although the need for permission to change registration is officially illegal and even unconstitutional. But the old system dies hard. In Russia, Articles 17 and 27 of the 1993 Russian constitution guarantee citizens' freedom of movement. The Russian Federation adopted a special law, *On the Right of the Citizens of the Russian Federation to the Freedom of Movement,* in 1993 and related regulations in 1995, and the Constitutional Court abolished the *propiska* five times by 2001. "Yet legislatures at various levels have continued to issue laws aimed at controlling migration and residency that are blatantly unconstitutional, and a *propiska*-like system is still in place across many parts of the country. Between 30 to 40 of Russia's 89 regions have laws unconstitutionally restricting local migration, including Moscow City, Moscow District, and St. Petersburg." These restrictive measures, unconstitutional and hence quite illegitimate, include local restrictions and hefty fees charged for the official change of one's residential registration. In 1996, Moscow decreased its fees for registering new residents to 25,000 rubles— still some three hundred times the minimum monthly wage in the city.[65] People who move to cities without a local *propiska* "are favorite targets of the Russian police for harassment, mistreatment and detention."[66]

In 1998 and 1999, when the Russian Constitutional Court twice declared measures controlling inmigrants to Moscow unconstitutional, the popular city mayor Luzhkov simply announced that he would refuse to obey the court's ruling and answered the criticisms and legal challenges of human-rights groups by conducting "Moscow registration," which is essentially the same old *propiska* renamed.[67] By the end of 2000, "Moscow maintains its *propiska* system" despite all legal rulings and lawsuits.[68] One report finds that Moscow registration carries an undertone of racial, ethnic, and gender bias against non-Russians and women who want to live in the city, violating the International Convention on the Elimination of Racial Discrimination.[69]

Therefore, internal passports and *propiska* both remain in today's Russia, resurrected despite their clearly and repeatedly declared illegality in the emerging Russian democracy.[70] Some members of the European Parliament were so concerned about the illegal *propiska* system that they actually proposed a motion in 1999 to condemn the Commonwealth of Independent States (CIS) for continuing this systematic discrimination and restriction of freedom of migration and residence.[71] The United Nations High Commission for Refugees also expressed concerns about the unfavorable impact the *propiska* system had on refugees in the CIS in 1999.[72] Numerous reports and studies published inside and outside Russia have severely criticized the stubborn persistence of the *propiska* system on the grounds of human rights, ethical and moral concerns, and a need for the rule of law in Russia and the CIS.[73]

Because of such strong external pressure and criticisms and the changed and fluctuating political and legal environment in the CIS states, especially Russia, the *propiska* now appears to be localized, ad hoc, and highly illegitimate. Hence the positive function of the system, arguably beneficial and even necessary for socioeconomic stability and development in Russia, is clearly undermined and incomplete and has lost much of its legitimacy and effectiveness. When the state is unable or unwilling to support it, and when the society has learned to condemn it,[74] the continued existence of this residence-based institutional exclusion is likely to generate profound negative consequences and high costs rather than perform any positive functions. One leading consequence has been the erosion of the rule of law, as the Russian federal government could not even enforce its own repeatedly declared laws and regulations granting people freedom of movement.

Russia's great regional unevenness is increasing in the 2000s. In addition to wealth, which is now the dominant fault line in Russia, spatial differences maintained by administrative means are strikingly prevalent. The two largest urban centers, Moscow and St. Petersburg, clearly have great advantages in government favor, spending, and investment. Residents there enjoy a much higher standard of living and seem besides to regard themselves as markedly superior to other Russians. Only a hundred kilometers away from a quickly developing Moscow, Russia looks depressingly poor and distinctively backward, pretty much still in a state of shock.[75]

The decline, dysfunction, and even withering away of the *propiska* system in the CIS states now have largely been the result of "social and moral pressures" with few "economic considerations."[76] As the old central planning and communist state control decrease, institutional exclusion in Russia has shifted to one primarily along the lines of rich versus poor, as the majority of the excluded in Russia now appears to be the "more than half of the population" that has sunk into poverty, with the rural population still the number-one group of the excluded.[77]

Institutional Exclusion in India: The Perpetual Caste System

As the second most populous nation in the world, India shares much in common with China: both are large and densely inhabited, both have a long history and are rich in culture and tradition, both had a backward economy and low technological development when they acquired modern statehood in the twentieth century, and both aim and compete with each other for world power and leadership.[78] Both China and India feature a typical dual economy and massive supply of low-skilled and unskilled labor from the agricultural sector; hence both need to pass the Lewis Transition in order to emerge from poverty and backwardness.

Yet there are just as many differences that set them apart. Their languages and cultures are very different. Created from the remains of British colonial rule, India has had a functioning political democracy, however limited and criticized, for over half a century, whereas China during the same time has been under a one-party authoritarian regime that won power after defeating another authoritarian government. China is largely a homogenous nation, with over 92 percent of its population belonging to the same Han ethnic group, whereas India displays one of the most complicated, diversified, and conflicting racial and ethnic collections in the world.[79] In short, China and India are institutionally different in that they divide and exclude—hence organize—their massive populations in very different ways.

By the early twenty-first century, China appears to have achieved significantly higher economic growth and technological sophistication than

TABLE 6.1

Brazil, India, and China: A Comparative Report Card

	Brazil	India	China	Developing nations
Size (,000 square km)	851.2	328.8	959.7	—
Population (millions, in 1975)	108.1	620.7	927.8	2,898.3
In 1999	171.9	1,000.8	1,264.8	4,609.8
In 2015 (projected)	201.4	1,230.51,410.2	5,759.1	
Annual growth rate (1975–99)	1.8%	2.0%	1.3%	1.9%
Urban population (1999)	80.7%	28.1%	26.1–33.8 %	38.9%
Urban population (1988)	75%	27%	18.7 %	23%
Administrative units	26 states, 1 district	25 states, 7 territories	31 provincial units	—
Official languages	1	14	1	—
GDP (by PPP method, billion US$)	1,182	2,242	4,534.9	16,201.9
Annual growth rate (1975–99)	0.8%	3.2%	8.1%	2.3%
Annual growth rate (1990–99)	1.5%	4.2%	9.5%	3.2%
Per capita GDP (PPP, 1999)	$7,037	$2,248	$3,617	$3,530
Export (1999, million US$)	47,140	37,598	194,931	—
Import (1999, million US$)	63,443	47,212	165,699	—
Trade balance (1999, million US$)	−16,303	−9,614	29,232	
Export/GDP in 1990	8%	7%	18%	26%
Export/GDP in 1999	11%	12%	22%	29%
Hi-tech export/export (1999)[a]	16%	16.6%	39%	—
Foreign direct investment/GDP (1999)	4.3%	0.5%	3.9%	2.9%
Foreign debt/GDP (1999)	9.0%	—	2.1%	5.8%
Foreign debt/export (1999)	110.9%	—	9.0%	22.3%
Foreign exchange reserve (1999–2000)[b]	$35.7 billion	$35.1 billion	$161.4 billion	—
Annual inflation rate (1999–2000)	253.5%	4.7%	−3%	—
Inequality (Gini Index)[c]	59.1	37.8	40.3 (29.3)	—
Human development index/rank (2001)	0.750/No. 69	0.571/No. 115	0.718/No. 87	0.647/Nos. 49–162
Human development index rank (1990)	0.784/No. 50	0.439/No. 93	0.716/No. 64	—/ Nos. 46–130
Technology achievement index (rank)	0.311/No. 34	0.201/No. 63	0.299/No. 45	—
Gender development index rank (1999)	Number 64	Number 105	Number 76	—
k–9th grade school enrollment	80%	56%	73%	61%
People living under poverty line	9–22%	35–44.2%	4.6–18.5%	—
Physicians (per 100,000 people)	127	48	162	—
Life expectancy (years)	67.2	62.9	70.2	64.5
Infant mortality rate (per 1,000 births)	34	70	33	61
Underweight children at age 5	6%	53%	10%	—
Undernourished people	10%	21%	11%	18%
Adult literacy rate	84.9%	56.5%	83.5%	72.9%
Per capita electricity use (kw, 1998)	1,793	384	746	757
Subjective happiness index[d]	77/100	72/100	78/100	62–77/100
Political system	democracy with intervals	weak democracy	one-party authoritarianism	
Military expenditure/GDP (1999)	9.0%	2.4%	2.1%	—
International status	strong regional power	strong regional power	weak world power	—

India. (See Table 6.1.) Indian leaders openly admit that "China has surpassed India in basically every aspect."[80] Even the widely noted socialist state of Kerala in southern India, which has made impressive advances in such areas as women's literacy, rural medicine, and family planning, has been no model of economic success or technological sophistication.[81] Whereas China has changed greatly since the 1980s, two Indian-studies scholars based in the United States told this author in the late 1990s that "almost nothing [had] changed in India since 1984 except that the pollution [had] gotten worse."[82] In the past two decades, Chinese city maps and tour-guide information have often become obsolete in just two to three years; an American sociologist visiting India in 2003 found that his 1981 edition of *The Lonely Planet Tour Guide for India* still worked, "except that some hotel phone numbers had changed and the prices had all gone up." An Indian-American in Mumbai (Bombay) in 2003 bluntly commented that in twenty years the city's population had grown much larger, and that "everything else is much worse than before."

It is intellectually stimulating and fruitful to compare China and India for any study in social sciences or humanities. Yet just the linguistic and logistical difficulties and the immensity of a comparative field study in both countries make an in-depth comparative study of them too daunting a task for a single book.[83] It is too simplistic to seek a clear-cut answer to why there exists such a difference in economic growth between China and India, as there are so many relevant factors and variables. Furthermore, the current performance gap between China and India may not last.[84] Nevertheless, the world's largest democracy is apparently, so far, lagging behind the world's largest nondemocracy in just about every aspect of socioeconomic development. This is indeed a profound enigma, demanding explanation.

To advance the effort of theorizing China's *hukou* system and in hopes

---

SOURCES OF TABLE 6.1: Interview with Li Yining in 2001; SSB 2001, 4; EIU 2001, 65–74; World Bank 2001; UNDP 1990, 128–143; UNDP 2001, 48–54 and 128–212; RBI 2001, Tables 113 and 140.

[a]China was listed as number 10 of the world's top 30 high-tech goods exporters in 1999, Brazil as number 27, and India was not on the list.

[b]China has been the second largest foreign exchange reserve holder (after Japan) and second largest FDI recipient (after the US) in the world since 1997.

[c] = perfect equality and 100 = perfect inequality. China's value (40.3) is the aggregate national Geni Index. The value inside parentheses (29.3) is the perhaps more accurate and applicable sectorial Geni Indices, separately calculated for the urban and rural residents in China's clear-cut dual economy. The PRC official data on income may report a smaller than actual Gini Index due to the difficulty in calculating household income figures. The real aggregate Gini Index may be as high as 45 after the mid-1990s (Bramall 2001, 703).

[d]Based on a comparative survey conducted by Inglehart and Klingemann (2000). As a reference, the US has a subjective happiness index of 89/100 and Spain 79/100.

of making a contribution to our understanding of the developmental gap between China and India, this section suggests that a main institutional difference between them may be one factor responsible. More specifically, India's peculiar institutional exclusion based on social divisions, namely the caste system, may have hampered effective circumvention of the Lewis Transition—hence India's less impressive socioeconomic development. The caste system in India remains well accepted, a deeply entrenched institutional exclusion, very relevant and powerful in how the people are divided and organized. For a nation needing to quickly pass or circumvent the Lewis Transition, in regard to economic growth and technological sophistication this socially based institutional exclusion seems more negative than the residentially based *hukou* system.

Naturally, both China and India have more than one type of institutional exclusion. A Type 2 institutional exclusion (based on *what one has*) is prominent and powerful in both countries. Additionally but profoundly, the PRC has its *hukou*-based Type 3 institutional exclusion (based on *where one is*), whereas India's caste system forms a unique institutional exclusion. The caste system affects Indians' daily life chances, socioeconomic stratification and changes, and internal migration. Certainly not everything that happens in India can be attributed to the caste system, but it is no exaggeration to say that this societally enforced Type 1 (*who one is*) institutional exclusion still functions extensively and continuously to affect virtually every aspect of Indian life decades after the Indian state declared it illegal.

The caste and subcaste system is a racially, ethnically, linguistically, religiously, professionally based, highly rigidified, permanently labeled identification of a onetime socioeconomic and political stratification that resulted from military and religious conquests. Based on the supreme principle of dharma (the law of all things) in Hindu religion, deeply rooted in Indian culture, and evolving over many centuries—some Indian scholars believe that the four *varna*s or main caste divisions can be traced back to 5,000 B.C.[85]—the caste system was created to denote geographic and professional identity for various social groups. To socially maintain the caste system, discriminatory "customs, traditions and rituals were developed ... [and] acquired the force of law." Muslim invasions and the later British colonization contributed to the caste system's rigidification and longevity.[86]

Under the caste system, four *varna*s (Brahmans, Kshatriyas, Vaishyas, and Shudras) and Avarna (untouchables) and some twelve hundred complicated castes, subcastes and creeds of these five categories exist in India to socially divide the people into fixed clusters of families. Each high-caste family has several permanently attached unpaid and specialized worker families, the so-called scheduled castes, to form a hierarchy for generations. At the bottom of the caste system are several kinds of sub-castes of the untouchables, considered spiritually, mentally, physically, and socially unclean and discarded.[87] "[T]he significance of caste ... more than anything else characterizes India. ... Every Hindu necessarily be-longs to the caste of his parents and in that caste he inevitably remains."[88]

Various caste systems can be identified at different times in different places in Myanmar, Iran, Fuji, Tonga, Samoa, Sri Lanka, parts of Africa, and ancient Egypt, Greece, Japan, and Rome.[89] The remarkable lon-gevity, rigidity, and sharp social stratification of the caste system, how-ever, is found nowhere else but in India.[90] To the Hindu majority of the Indian population (about 80 percent in 2001), it is a peculiarly powerful institution, since it is rooted in Hindu religious teachings and ceremonial rituals. But it also exists among Muslims and other non-Hindu Indians on the subcontinent.[91]

The caste system features a clear hierarchy among the layers of inher-ited social identification of families that have different rights and privi-leges as well as differing access to community services and provisions. The castes' religious standing and chances in life and afterlife are also predetermined, although people may theoretically have some freedom to escape their fate through personal effort, especially in the afterlife. The status and divisions are given and unchangeable according to religious teachings and folklore as well as social custom. In some communities, lower castes or subcastes are limited even in their daily consumption of food and water. With connubiality highly restricted, "there is no mobil-ity within the hierarchy of caste."[92]

The Indian government created after independence in 1947 set out to peacefully tackle the issue of caste through legal means. The Indian con-stitution prohibited caste-based discrimination, abolished untouchability, and banned trafficking in human beings and forced labor. It also allowed special assistance and rights for lower-caste people, the scheduled castes, once their status is declared and recognized by the government. The scheduled castes have had seats reserved in the parliament and state leg-islatures for fifty years. They also have special access to government jobs, welfare assistance, and legal protection.[93] By the early 1980s,[94] the Indian presidency recognized by declaration many scheduled castes and scheduled tribes, about 11 percent of India's total population (80 percent of them living in the countryside), to be specially protected and assisted by the state. The hope is that, gradually, the lower castes can escape from discrimination, control, and exploitation by the higher classes and castes. Indeed, some studies show that, after half a century of political effort in the form of special assistance (loans, college and training admissions, legislature seats, and quotas in government employment), many scheduled castes and tribes (including the officially recognized untouchables) have gained noticeably in political and economic power and social status.[95]

Yet gains by the scheduled castes have not changed the nature or role of the caste system itself in India. India's caste system seems a remarkably resilient, stable, and powerful basis for India's peculiar institutional exclusion fifty years after the government set out to politically reduce it. J. H. Hutton in the mid-twentieth century found the caste system "exceptionally constant for a human institution."[96] Ronald Segal's conclusion in the 1970s still rings true in today's India: "A society like *India with a caste system is easy to rule but difficult to change.*"[97] Rajendra Pandey found in 1986 that "through the centuries in India, caste has remained a force despite religious and political revolutions to uproot it." "[C]aste exists; whatever changes there are, these are only in the peripheral areas. There is continuance and reinforcement of old in new forms, … and new dimensions of stratification, … along with the caste are in the process of emerging. … Caste seems to be entrenched in almost all walks of our life after Independence."[98] Some Indian scholars even believed that the caste system was actually reinforcing itself, as socioeconomic stratification in India became even less vertically and horizontally flexible. The gaps widened among the castes, or between "in" people and excluded groups, and tensions among the castes increased.[99]

A former director of the Indian Council of Social Science Research, S. P. Agrawal, pointed out in 1991 that the caste system as a "social organization worked very well as a well-oiled smooth system." Without a written "ban on horizontal or upward mobility," the caste system still gave rise to "divisive forces" in India while serving important organizational and religious functions.[100] Brahmanism based on the caste system, argued a militant leftist pamphlet published in Bangalore in 1994, continued functioning powerfully, breeding racism and fascism that was "killing India."[101] Another study by Indian scholars concluded in 1996 that Indians' caste status "affected their ability to exercise basic citizenship rights" and that the caste system remained "India's principal category of social grouping ... one of the most entrenched structures of domination and subordination, with an in-built system of demarcation and exclusion."[102] "Caste," argued an Indian scholar in 1997, is "the controlling mechanism of the Indian society."[103] As much as 75 percent of India's population was believed to be the low castes, excluded from most economic and political opportunity, whereas the Brahmans, the small top caste, monopolized over 70 percent of all government jobs.[104]

By 2000, India watchers concluded that "the processes of urbanization, industrialization and modernization [had] ... not necessarily replaced old values" of caste and class structures and dynamics in rural India. "Caste and class nexus ... penetrated into Indian politics as well as the larger society," just as in the mid-1970s. The caste system, a mainly societally maintained division, has increasingly acted in concert with a class structure partitioning between rich and poor to provide the foundation of political, economic, and social activities for a billion-plus Indians in the new century.[105]

Caste-based institutional exclusion affects people's economic and social activities extensively and profoundly. One illuminating example is the sale of land. While higher-caste people have preference buying land from anyone, lower-caste or "outside" families have a hard time buying land from higher-caste families even though they may be very able farmers and have the money.[106] Fewer than 5 percent of newspaper personal ads seeking mates stated "caste creed is not a concern" or the like in the late 1990s, and hotel registration forms commonly require guests to report caste creed.[107] The caste system has apparently contributed to repeated failures of a much-needed population policy of the Indian government since the 1950s.[108]

Although the Indian government does not use a *hukou*-style administrative tool to control internal migration, and although caste-based discrimination against sojourning ruralites is illegal, India's urbanization has been nonetheless slow and low. In the second half of the 1980s, the annual cross-state migration rate in India was only slightly higher than China's cross-provincial permanent migration (*qianyi*) rate of 0.196 percent but much lower than the total internal migration rate in China, including *liudong renkou* (migrants not permanently changing their *hukou*).[109] India's urbanization was slightly below the Chinese level in 2001 but was already over 20 percent in 1970, twice what it was in China at that time.[110] This slow urbanization without formal government control of internal migration is perhaps due to several factors, and the caste system's informal but powerful restriction is likely crucial. As a British scholar based in southern India concluded, "there is no meaningful internal migration in India" under a "very alive and powerful caste system other than urban slums, beggars, and a few technical professionals."[111]

The generally low level of industrialization and the high degree of income inequality, combined with caste-based exclusion and discrimination in housing and employment and legal free internal migration and resettlement have created in Indian cities some of the worst urban poverty and slums in the world, despite slow and low urbanization.[112] In the 1980s, between 20 and 45 percent of Indian urban residents were already living in slums.[113] By the late 1990s, improvement in the situation was almost unnoticeable.[114]

Consequently, "India lags behind many other poor countries in general education standards and achievement, and also in health improvement."[115] Indeed, "too many Indian people are sleeping on the sidewalks of the cities," and while fewer than 20 percent of all Indians owned more than 70 percent of India's GDP, 30 to 40 percent of India's rural population were in starvation.[116] India's urban poverty, rural backwardness, environmental degradation, poor urban and rural sanitation, and widespread corruption and crime empirically appear more serious and extensive than in Brazil or China.[117] In the states of Kerala and West Bengal, under communist government, a weakened caste system may actually have been the key to relatively impressive social development despite continuing economic and technological backwardness.[118]

The caste system, together with other fault lines in the multiethnic, multilingual, multireligious Indian society, provides the foundation for perhaps the most delicate, decentralized, debilitating, discriminatory, and deepest institutional exclusion in the world. The people most excluded seem to be the rural, poor, and uneducated, and women.[119] The fact that the caste system is alive and well and still very influential in India has been good evidence of the power of social and religious organization and tradition in that country, of the weakness and incapability of the Indian government, of an absence of revolutionary institutional change, and of the caste system's functions and effective organizing service in this, the second largest nation, which features a typical dual economy and a burning desire to compete for power internationally.[120] The caste system may not completely account for India's functional but elite democracy and slow economic growth, but it appears to be a major cause, in need of further exploration. Compared with the PRC *hukou* system, the caste system lacks a major positive role in effectively regulating internal migration and protecting the "in" urban sector for a partial economic take-off, while sharing the same problems of irrationality and discrimination in a less uniform but more rigid, more lasting way.

Some Indian scholars have maintained that the caste system, as a mechanism to materially and ritually organize and rank people, can be and has been undergoing adaptation in the form of *jati*-(kind-)based political participation and social compartmentalization, and Sanskritization or national culture–oriented social mobilization. All these have provided sociopolitical organization and control of social mobility to the population during the modernization process under democratic politics in India, thereby giving the caste system value and utility in its perpetual existence.[121] Perhaps organizing a nation like India indeed requires an effective institutional exclusion in addition to the division between haves and have-nots. If a democratic but weak state cannot provide one, the society will simply keep its tradition of socially and racially based institutional exclusion.

Institutional Exclusion in Brazil: The Market Dominance

Brazil, occupying more than half of South America, is the largest Latin American nation and well blessed with natural resources, hence enjoying one of the best per-capita resource endowments in the world. Territorially, Brazil is fully comparable to China and India. In terms of population, Brazil's is large, but its population density is nowhere near China's or India's. Historically, Brazil is a new nation, primarily created by European colonial powers only after the sixteenth century. Politically, like India, Brazil has never experienced any major sociopolitical revolution. Brazil gained its independence relatively peacefully in 1822, peacefully and gradually ended its slavery system in the years between 1871 and 1888, and relatively nonviolently replaced Don Pedro II's monarchy with a republic in 1889.[122] Demographically, Brazil is similar to India in that it is multiracial and multiethnic. But it is much more homogeneous than India, since its dominant culture is rooted in a mixture of European, African, and Native American inputs, Portuguese as its common language, and the Catholic Church as its dominant religion. Racial division has not been as rigid as in India, as miscegenation has provided racial mobility, an escape hatch, for the nonwhite Brazilians.[123]

Not only did Brazil acquire political independence early; it also started its industrialization and urbanization early in the nineteenth century, when both China and India were still struggling violently for nationhood. By the mid-twentieth century, when the Republic of India and the PRC were barely established, Brazil was already a significant player on the world market. A so-called Brazilian miracle in the 1960 and 1970s propelled Brazil's economy to number ten in the world, equaling the GNP of Canada, only to be followed by massive foreign debt, great downturns and instability, and long stagnation.[124] By the early twenty-first century, Brazil is still listed as a developing nation, with generally the same socioeconomic ranking as China and India. However unfairly, in 2002 Brazil was even viewed during the latest round of its frequent financial crises as a nation that should have simply declared bankruptcy.[125] While Brazil fares well in comparison with China and India by some socioeconomic indicators, its economic growth is less impressive, given its rich natural endowment and long history of market economy.

Like China and India, Brazil has more than one fault line to base its institutional exclusion on. The Brazilians are divided, excluded, and organized, similarly, along the dominant cleavage of rich versus poor and also the perhaps less universal, less uniform, but not necessarily less powerful divisions of race, ethnicity, language or dialect, region, religion, and gender.[126] Unlike China and India, however, Brazil relies fundamentally on the market as the chief enforcer of its institutional exclusion, based primarily on wealth or property. For Brazilians, money, rather than *hukou* registration, caste, or other sociopolitical features, largely determines political power, socioeconomic stratification, vertical and horizontal mobility, and life chances and where to live.[127]

A quick glance at studies of the Brazilian political economy reveals the stubborn existence of massive urban poverty, polarization of the people into rich and poor,[128] environmental degradation, poor governance, and an erratic record of economic growth often mortally plagued by hyperinflation and capital flight,[129] extremely uneven income distribution and landownership, large socioeconomic disparities among regions,[130] foreign debt crises, and stubborn stagnation.

Such domestic problems, and the long-lasting criticisms of Brazil's dependent development under an unholy triple alliance of foreign investors, local business elites, and government at the expense of Brazil's economy and people,[131] all point to the predominant role of a poorly regulated market in Brazilian politics, economy, and foreign relations, as both the state and social forces are weak and marginalized.[132] In fact, the Brazilian style of urbanization itself is a direct result of foreign economic ties.[133] The process of deeper economic globalization weakens needed social spending for a decent social-welfare system.[134] Scholarly prescriptions against poverty in Brazil—such as agrarian reform, the reform of education, and labor legislation—all seem to call for a stronger and more effective role of the state.[135]

Under the invisible hand of the market, urbanization, economic development, and income distribution in Brazil are by no means regionally even. A dual economy is deeply entrenched in Brazil, where modern and prosperous urban centers are islands in a sea of poverty. The north (the Amazon Basin) is still largely an agrarian and raw-material producing area; the northeastern states are much poorer and more backward than the south and southeast. In the 1970s, average income in Rio de Janeiro was more than twice that in neighboring Minas Gerais and the northeast.[136] Whereas the real wages of Brazilian workers declined by more than half from 1980 to 1993, real wages in São Paulo, Brazil's largest urban center and industrial base, increased by more than 30 percent.[137] The northeastern region, with a per-capita GDP only 55 percent of the national average, had an illiteracy rate of 36 percent, much higher than the national average of 18 percent in the early 1990s.[138] Although much of Brazil exhibits characteristics of a typical developing nation, Curitiba, the capital city of the southeastern state of Paraná, boasts world-class public transportation, a well-designed, well-protected urban environment, impressive economic development, and comfortable living. For more than two decades, this city of 1.6 million residents (mostly European descendants) has maintained a per-capita GDP nearly twice as high as the remaining four million people of Paraná and more than double the average per-capita GDP of Brazil.[139]

As a result, uncontrolled internal migration has been taking place in a one-way flood from the poor states in the northeast to the rich ones in the south and southeast, mostly just to swell the urban slums there. The government, through its Northeast Development Agency (SUDENE, Superintendencia do Desenvolvimento do Nordeste), tried to use monetary incentives to keep people from blindly increasing the population in urban slums. But SUDENE officials admitted that such efforts had largely failed by the mid-1990s.[140] Some richer states did occasionally, unconstitutionally, resort to noneconomic means to exclude outsiders"[141] The model city of Curitiba has benefited from the progressive master plan of its stable socialist government and from its unique natural condition, located at a high altitude (3,000 feet above sea level on the plateau of Serra do Mar) and hence having quite un-Brazilian weather. The combined effect of leadership and nature so far seems to have been unusually successful in minimizing the negatives of Brazil's uncontrolled internal migration by keeping away poor migrants from the warmer regions.[142]

Internal migration in Brazil is much freer than in China or India. Brazilians often proudly declare that none of them can claim to have pure blood; hence it usually does not make much difference to divide and organize along racial or ethnic lines.[143] Racial or ethnic discrimination is indeed perhaps less noticeable, let alone effective, in Brazil. With little historical baggage and a nation largely of immigrants, Brazil's tradition of allowing racially mixed marriages and sexual relations, as well as the common practice of slaveowners' fathering children by African slaves, has prevented a widespread caste-type institutional exclusion.[144] The weak state and the fact that Brazil has a large ratio of land to labor has rendered *hukou*-style institutional exclusion and migration control ineffective and unnecessary.[145]

Consequently, Brazil has had a rapid urbanization, and its urban population surpassed the rural population in the mid-1960s.[146] Even one of the least developed states, Pernambuco in the northeast, achieved a very high urbanization level of over 74 percent in 1996, whereas the most developed province in the PRC, Guangdong, was only 31 percent urbanized in 1998.[147] Brazil's urbanization is now the same as a typical developed nation's. In 2001, it was 80.7 percent, higher than the average 70.4-percent level of nations belonging to the Organisation for Economic Cooperation and Development (OECD) and even higher than the 74.9-percent average urbanization of the richest, most developed high-income OECD nations.[148]

Brazil's high degree of urbanization and rich natural endowment, however, have not solved its dual-economy problem, nor have they made Brazil a developed world power as the nation's great potential seemed to foretell long ago and as Brazilian nationalists still hope.[149] Rather, a quick, unregulated, unfettered rush of low-skilled and unskilled labor to the cities seems to have Brazil only nominally past, though remaining actually stuck in, the Lewis Transition. Highly urbanized Brazil has some of the world's worst examples of urban poverty in the form of urban slums and shantytowns in and around the major urban centers of São Paulo and Rio de Janeiro, and in literally every Brazilian city of any size. In Rio de Janeiro, shantytowns called *favelas* emerged in significant numbers in the 1930s and peaked by the 1950s, when over 14 percent of the population in the Rio de Janeiro Federal District lived in *favelas* and more than 60 percent of these were new inmigrants.[150] Half a century later, *favelas* still exist prominently in Brazilian cities, shoulder to shoulder with or above (many are located on hills) the communities of middle-class and even upper-class Brazilians. The rich, as highlights the money-based exclusion of the poor next door, now customarily hire private armies to guard their fortresslike iron-gated compounds.[151]

Favela residents are generally free to move out, since there are few noneconomic forces keeping them there, but the actual mobility of those excluded is very low. Many slum dwellers are now second-generation, third-generation, and even fourth-generation residents born and raised there. Most are either unemployed or underemployed, living on family members' small incomes, charity donations, and incomes from informal economic activities. An economically functioning, socially excluded, and politically and legally autonomous and even independent community has taken deep root in the *favelas*. The more established *favelas*, with as many as a hundred thousand people each, have developed a sense of community membership and often refuse to accept unrelated newcomers or even receive visitors.

Field interviews of slum residents reveal that usually they freely choose to be stuck there for purely market-determined socioeconomic reasons. When asked why they do not leave urban poverty behind and move to the vast interior land to farm, many simply gave answers like "We are used to this [poor, excluded, but] urban life now"; "It's cheap and easy to live here and not too hard to find some income [from low-paying jobs, since living close to the rich people]"; "No reason for us to stay in the country [since land is highly concentrated in the hands of a few or owned by the government and there is no administrative means to keep them there]"; and "There is more culture [TV] and fun [football and beaches] in the cities."[152]

Brazilian scholars have dubiously honored their nation as the world champion of income inequality.[153] In the 1980s, 70 percent of the rural and urban populations had incomes below each area's average.[154] Forty-five percent of urban Brazilians (55 percent in the less developed state of Pernambuco) were employed in the so-called informal economy in the 1990s.[155] Fifty percent of Brazilians earned only about 10 percent of the national income. Uncontrolled rural-to-urban migration of landless peasants due to the lack of land reform seems to be a major cause of permanent urban poverty in Brazil.[156]

In the late 1990s, a well-trained white-collar professional in Brazil might make 2,000–5,000 reals a month, while 75 percent of Brazilian workers had monthly wages of only 150–300 reals. The monthly salary of a state police chief (or a federal minister) could be over 40,000 reals. One such rich official, whitish-mixed, owns several residences, one of them a luxury five-hundred-square-meter apartment by the ocean worth at least 500,000 reals, and six cars, and has two maids for his family of six. Merely two blocks away, a twenty-three-year-old single mother, whitish-mixed, lives in a thirty-square-meter hut divided into two rooms by a plastic curtain in a shantytown on an open sewage ditch with her fifteen-month-old son, elderly mother, and three siblings. She makes only 120 reals a month—the only family income—in the food court of a local mall, but she attends classes, hoping to get a company receptionist job that may double her pay.[157] The depth, stability, and longevity of the Brazilian Type 2 institutional exclusion (based on *what one has*) indeed rival any elsewhere.

Conclusion: How and Whom to Exclude

Residential registration systems have existed in many countries for centuries. But not all of them are effective Type 3 institutional exclusions (based on *where one is*) like the PRC *hukou* system. The closest case, the Soviet *propiska* system, is now dysfunctional and disgraced, replaced in Russia by a singular institutional exclusion of Type 2 (based on *what one has*). Brazil, China, and India, three large developing nations facing similar challenges of the Lewis Transition, have quite different institutional exclusions and varied mechanisms affecting their internal migration and population mobility. Table 6.1 provided a comparison of Brazil, China, and India in regard to economic development, technological sophistication, and sociopolitical features. I now present, in Table 6.2, a summary of these three nations' different institutional exclusions and varied socioeconomic development.

Institutional and performance discrepancies among the three nations certainly have many causes, some of them possibly temporary and not necessarily institutional or lasting. However, the roles of the different institutional exclusions seem obviously important and lasting, if not decisive, factors. From this standpoint, I propose a few thoughts below while

TABLE 6.2

In Addition to Money: Institutional Exclusion in Brazil, China, and India

Country	Brazil	China	India
Institutional Exclusion	Yes	Yes	Yes
Common type (nationally)	II	II	II
Fault line	*What you have*	*What you have*	*What you have*
Legitimacy	high	high	high
Main enforcer	market	market	market
Uniformity	high	high	high
Effectiveness	high	high	high
Rigidity[a]	high	medium	high
Unique type (nationally)	little	III (*hukou*)	I (caste)
Fault line	—	*Where you are*	
		Who you are	
Legitimacy	—	high	low
Main enforcer	—	the state	society
Uniformity	—	high	low
Effectiveness	—	high	medium
Internal migration control	relaxed	tight	medium
Performance/Implication			
Growth rate (1990–2001)	erratic	high	low
Technological sophistication	medium	medium	low
Urbanization	completed	slow/low	slow/low
Distribution of gains	polarized	uneven	uneven
Income inequality	high	medium	medium
Urban poverty/slum presence	high	low	high
Population growth	high	low	high
Formal democracy	yes	no	yes
Governance rank[b]	50.0	63.4	54.1
HDI rank	stagnation	rise	slow rise
Subjective happiness index	77/100	78/100	72/100
International standing	medium	high/rising	medium

[a]China had revolutionary land reforms that destroyed the landlord class. The basis of the Chinese new rich is less rigid since it is not associated with land-based property rights but more often with the ever changing political power and administrative control of the PRC *hukou* system. Brazil and India had no meaningful land reform, and the land-based entrenched rich class is hence more stable and rigid.

[b]As a comparison, Russia is 44.3 and the United States is 91.2. World Bank, *Governance Research Indicator Country Snapshot* (Washington, D.C.: World Bank, 2001).

summarizing this brief comparison of institutional exclusions in Brazil, China, and India. Further testing, obviously, is needed before solid knowledge can be ascertained about the implications of different institutional exclusions on economic and sociopolitical development across nations.

First, these three nations differ economically, socially, and politically. Brazil, with the best resource endowment, earliest start of industrialization, and least problematic surplus labor, has nominally passed the Lewis Transition, achieving a high degree of urbanization. But it appears not really to have solved the problem of a dual economy. Its economic growth and technological sophistication have stagnated for decades, and its social development has suffered from extreme income inequality and periodic financial crises. China and India have roughly the same problem of surplus labor in a typical dual economy. China has so far managed to circumvent the Lewis Transition with an authoritarian regime. The Chinese have had impressive economic growth and technological sophistication, as well as profound social development and improvements in living standards. India has struggled to maintain a functional formal democracy but so far has significantly lagged behind China in almost all aspects of socioeconomic development.

Second, money and market forces are or are becoming a major basis for institutional exclusion (of Type 2, *what one has*) in all three nations. There seems to be a strong convergence of these nations in that regard. Based on a market-oriented economy and supported by a market-friendly state, the rich now enjoy the greatest vertical and horizontal mobility in all three nations, whereas the poor have the least upward mobility or real freedom of internal migration.

Third, these nations all have powerful additional institutional exclusions: China the PRC *hukou* system and India the castes, with Brazil also divided along several other fault lines but much less uniformly. The existence or the lack of additional institutional exclusions may hold a key to our understanding of these nations' varied political development, socioeconomic achievement, and international standing. In nations with a low per-capita resource endowment and a massive supply of unskilled labor, as in China and India, market-based institutional exclusion may need supplementation of other types to allow fast economic growth and technological development while maintaining sociopolitical stability. However, these additional types of institutional exclusion, under the pressure of and being replaced by market forces, all have demonstrated trends of weakening and localization, and signs of change in the general direction of relaxation.

Fourth, in theory and in practice, all nations must have at least one type of institutional exclusion. All institutional exclusions create injustice, inequity, and inequality for the excluded. A consideration of how much and how strong a negative an institutional exclusion creates for how many people as opposed to how effectively and efficiently it performs its necessary and even positive functions may make sense as a comparative assessment. Just having a Type 2 (*what one has*) and of course also the implied Type 4 (*what one has done or does*) institutional exclusion may not be better than having an additional institutional exclusion, especially in a developing nation beleaguered with massive unskilled labor and a poor per-capita resource endowment. A need for additional institutional exclusions may be seen in the case of Brazil, which has the best resource endowment and the least problem of surplus labor but has nonetheless achieved roughly the same economic development as China and India and created similar, if not worse, social problems. From my sketchy study of the three nations, I suggest, more as a hypothesis than as a conclusion, that residentially based institutional exclusion (of Type 3, *where one is*) may be a lesser necessary evil than exclusion based on genetic, religious, or social group (of Type 1, *who one is*). A Type 1 institutional exclusion, with its tendency to support sociopolitical stability, perhaps also helps to smooth and circumvent the Lewis Transition required for a developing country's economic takeoff. But it appears to be less effective and less desirable than a Type 3 institutional exclusion, which allows a quick, targeted, and selected circumvention of the Lewis Transition.

Fifth, it seems that how uniform and how legitimate an institutional exclusion is makes a significant difference to its impact. The PRC's *hukou*-based institutional exclusion, being a deeply legitimate, nationally uniform, and hence simple system, has been rigid, stable, effective, yet cheap and even transparent in performing its important functions in resource prioritization, sociopolitical stabilization, and controlling urbanization and internal migration. India's caste-based division, exclusion, and discrimination are long lasting and complex but now politically illegitimate, operationally disorganized, and isolated. Like the PRC *hukou* system, the castes have been performing similar functions and producing equal, if not more, social injustice and inequity for the excluded, but with higher costs and lower effectiveness, as India's socioeconomic development is lagging noticeably behind China's. The key here seems to be the state, which may or may not have the willingness and capacity to maintain and enforce effective and efficient institutional exclusions, in addition to the easy and natural exclusion based on money and enforced by the market. It is interesting that a democratic regime in a nation needing additional effective institutional exclusions is often unable to afford any, as in the case of Brazil or India.

Sixth, all institutional exclusions can be highly rigid, but they can also have a certain flexibility. Type 1 (*who one is*) institutional exclusion understandably has the highest inherent rigidity, usually granting upward mobility to the excluded only in a promised afterlife. Type 2 (*what one has*) institutional exclusion may historically have demonstrated the greatest flexibility, since it sometimes can be altered by people's able and willing efforts. The existence of entrenched urban poverty in Brazil shows, however, that division between rich and poor can be stubborn and rigid for generations. The rigidity of a Type 2 institutional exclusion may be even more apparent if we consider the impact of globalization, under which capital and the rich have achieved quasi-global mobility while labor and the poor have not even had internal mobility. Type 3 (*where one is*) institutional exclusion usually is highly rigid, as our exploration of the PRC *hukou* system has demonstrated. Yet it could allow for authorized vertical and horizontal mobility for a selected few of the excluded, as was the case in the PRC even before reforms released the forces of the market. In concert with the market forces, Type 3 institutional exclusion has allowed more vertical and horizontal mobility than Type 1, especially in regard to the guided or directed moves of selected groups of people who meet state-determined and sometimes also market-determined qualifications.

Finally, it seems that an effective, suitable institutional exclusion, or a combination of several, is important to a nation's socioeconomic record. It appears to have been a crucial challenge of governance in latecomer developing nations to maintain a good balance between two seemingly opposing needs: to have an effective institutional exclusion and to minimize its negative effects through reducing the numbers and the suffering of the excluded. Political will and wisdom, state capacity, history, and sheer luck—say, the right leader—seem to be key. More specifically, a reasonable combination of Type 2 (*what one has*) and Type 3 (*where one is*) institutional exclusions seems to be a more effective and efficient way for a large, massively populated developing nation to rapidly develop its economy, meaningfully upgrade its technology and living standards, and still maintain its sociopolitical stability.[158] In view of China's higher achievement and lower per-capita natural-resource endowment as compared with Brazil's or India's,[159] the utility of *hukou*-based institutional exclusion in China, for all its dreadful consequences of inequality and discrimination, is even more apparent and impressive.[160]

CHAPTER SEVEN

The Future of China's *Hukou* System

In the early 2000s, China's *hukou* system appears to have entered a new era: The five-decade-old PRC *hukou* system remains a key component of the Chinese way of organizing the people through division and exclusion but has started to transform further under increased pressure. This chapter reports the latest reforming ideas and actions as well as the continuities and changes in the operation and function of the PRC *hukou* system. I will also make some concluding speculations about the future of the *hukou* system in China.

The PRC *hukou* system remains a strong pillar of the CCP authoritarian political regime and contributes to much of China's institutionalized social injustice, especially the institutional exclusion of the rural population. It is still the foundation of the uniquely Chinese Type 3 institutional exclusion (based on *where one is*), in addition to the advancing market forces that are increasingly creating a universal division between the haves and the have-nots. The CCP, through manipulation of the *hukou*-based internal-migration regulations and the *hukou*-based tiered management of the targeted groups of the population, controls a segmented nation and thereby implements its various development plans and policies. Apart from contributing to a rapid economic growth and technological sophistication in the urban sector, especially in the eastern and coastal region, the PRC *hukou* system maintains a regionally uneven development and a rural-versus-urban duality that are still hallmarks of today's Chinese political economy.

Significant strains in the PRC *hukou* system and increasing outside pressure have inevitably accumulated over the past decades as the market-oriented reform and opening brought rapid economic growth and considerable social diversification and liberalization to the PRC. In line with a general decay of the state capacity, the PRC *hukou* system has lost considerable efficacy and penetration. As mentioned in previous chapters, the *hukou* system itself has developed some adaptive measures that can be summarized here as three: first, the PRC *hukou* system, especially its implementation, has become less rigid and less exclusive in accommodating the needs of a national labor market and the pressure for population mobility. The control of internal migration has relaxed considerably, especially in small cities and townships, as the confining power of the *danwei* (work units) is now diminished and the communes have disappeared. Second, the sociopolitical control of the *hukou* system has become less ad hoc and less intrusive. The categorization of the *zhongdian renkou* (targeted people) has become more institutionalized. An awareness of the legal process and procedures as well as a general sense of individual rights and personal privacy are on the rise.[1] Third, the *hukou* system has reduced its discriminatory impact in the areas of resource and income distribution since its longtime role in determining urban rations has been greatly minimized. Grain and most other subsistence goods are now largely allocated through market mechanisms, and the *hukou* system has generally withdrawn from much of its once-mighty role of resource allocation in the PRC.

Despite the changes and softening developments, many ethically and practically troubling issues about the PRC *hukou* system remain with regard to freedom of internal migration, equal rights and treatment of citizens under the law, and the fate of political democracy, social liberty, and national unity. This Chinese institutional exclusion draws increasing fire and is a hot topic for reformist discourse. Currently, two major rationales appear to be driving for further reforms of the PRC *hukou* system. First, there is a strong economic logic for reform, as the *hukou* system and the related population immobility are considered to be creating economic irrationalities such as low labor efficiency, market segmentation and market retardation since the massive rural population is still significantly excluded from the new market economy and Chinese urbanization is still small and slow. Second, there is an increasingly powerful ethical concern over the incomplete citizenship of the excluded and the uneven regional development and horizontal stratification in the PRC. External factors, such as China's accession into the World Trade Organization (WTO) in 2001 and the required conformity to international standards, especially the WTO's call for national-citizen-equal-treatment of foreign investors and businessmen, have highlighted and energized these two rationales. Therefore, in the 2000s, there are intensified public discussions about the *hukou* system and extensive governmental actions of reform that may hint at the future of the *hukou* system in China.

The Words of Reform

As Premier Zhu Rongji's ambitious fifth-wave reforms (1998–2000) were largely stalled by the summer of 2000 with the notable exception of WTO accession,[2] Chinese media and academic circles became highly active in generating discussions, stories, and proposals on the need and ways to further reform the PRC *hukou* system (perhaps merely preparing for and also echoing Beijing's *hukou*-reforming actions, launched in early 2001). Some of the reports published indeed looked profound; news bulletins used sweeping headlines such as THE *HUKOU* SYSTEM IS UNFAIR and THE BARRIERS OF THE *HUKOU* SYSTEM ARE COLLAPSING.[3] Overall, however, the words and the actions they have reflected are still largely reformist rather than abolitionist.

In the late 1990s, after two decades of economic reform, Chinese academicians and journalists started to criticize the PRC *hukou* system for creating injustices, especially in regard to the excluded rural population. The *hukou* system is often clearly and unequivocally termed a frozen and obsolete historical relic of the pre-1980s central-planning economy, although some published pieces still mention the administrative or historical rationality and necessity to have the *hukou* system in a country that has many people but few resources. The *hukou* system is also commonly believed to have restricted China's economic growth and is widely viewed as an obstacle to the further development of China's new market system, a fertile soil for corruption, and a detriment to China's new international image. Few, however, ever publicly advocated how to reform the *hukou* system until after March 2001, when the central government approved major national reforms of the PRC *hukou* system in small cities and towns.

When it became politically correct and permitted, there was a sudden gush of opinions and reports on *hukou* reform in the Chinese media. With a tacit approval and an official green light from the CCP authorities, newspapers (mainly local and commercial newspapers), magazines, and especially Internet-based bulletin boards, news websites, and discussion groups have engaged in active coverage and debates on the negative consequences of the *hukou* system, the necessities and urgencies of its reform, and the bold reform measures already taken since the end of the 1990s.[4] Much of this, however, appears to be an officially sanctioned and orchestrated propaganda campaign to prepare the people for actions of *hukou* reform and to explain the nature of these reforms. These words of *hukou* reform may also be some preemptive gestures for China's accession to the WTO, which was only scarcely discussed in China and may generate tremendous resistance from the affected populace once the accession terms and conditions are published and enforced.[5]

One author who appears to be well informed wrote on the website hosted by the *Renmin Ribao* (People's daily), the mouthpiece of the CCP Central Committee, in 2001:[6]

> Residence and migration are two basic human rights. ... The nature of the *hukou* system is closely linked to the planned-economy system. ... While restricting population mobility, the *hukou* system also restricts China's economic development and further intensifies the urban-rural gap. ... It is extremely incompatible with the current economic development in China, and has to a great extent damaged China's image of reform and opening. ... The *hukou* system also produces corruption ... [as] some cities even openly auction local *hukou* to solve local financial problems. ... To abolish the existing *hukou* system is inevitable, [as] the market economy demands population mobility and migration, and China needs to have a more liberal image. From this perspective, the *hukou* system will soon become a symbolic remnant of China's [former] planned economy.

One essay in *Chinese Youth Daily* asserted: "The cities will become truly filled with energy and hope only when [we] abolish the artificial barriers [of the *hukou* system] and allow laborers from rural areas to compete in an orderly and rational fashion with the urban labor on equal terms."[7] Many others expressed similar attitudes toward the *hukou* system and complained, often emotionally, about the sufferings and inconveniences that outsiders experience in the major urban centers when they do not have local *hukou*. Some argued that the *hukou* system is an extremely unfair system that is floating outside the PRC constitution and is legally problematic.[8] Others call for freedom of migration so as to give every Chinese citizen social equality, equality of opportunity, and conditions free from discrimination.[9] A major criticism focuses on police treatment of the so-called three-no people, migrants who have no legal *hukou* papers, no permanent job, and no permanent residence.[10] One summarized the five leading flaws and problems of the *hukou* system as follows:[11]

First, [the *hukou* system] hinders agricultural modernization and urbanization. ... Second, it is unfavorable to a nationally unified labor market. ...
Third, *hukou* management gives the Chinese people different identities of
[agricultural and nonagricultural *hukou*, permanent and temporary resident]
and different treatments. ... Fourth, [it] blocks the further takeoff of the consumer market [as the *hukou* system suppresses the spending of the migrant
workers since they] can never acquire the same opportunity and social status
as the urban residents, and do not have even a basic sense of personal security—having to watch out for the frequent police checks of identification and
papers, failure to produce which could mean detention and repatriation. ...
Fifth, the existing *hukou* system has already lost its ability to effectively manage people's migrations.

Some have attempted to reason and rationalize a deep reform of the
hukou system. One economic reporter declared the *hukou* system "a relic
of the Cold War era" and emphasized its great negative impact on
China's economy, environment, social and cultural progress, and legal development.[12] An economist argued for overcoming the resistance of the
minority urbanites to open the city gates to the young ruralites because
the excluded rural youth were becoming the most explosively rebellious
group in Chinese politics.[13] One essay in a local newspaper described the
hukou system as an old legacy "happily inherited by all rulers" in China
for two thousand years, which "has been tattooed deeply into the Chinese traditional culture." It compared the excluded rural residents under
the *hukou* system to the untouchables of India and argued that "if we do
not abolish the *hukou* system, at least theoretically, we can all sooner or
later become *mangliu* [blind floating migrants] [to be abused and mis-
treated by the police for not having proper local *hukou* registration]."[14]

Critics of the *hukou* system, however, sometimes seem to be criticizing
the ineffectiveness of the *hukou* system rather than the system itself. The
many millions of migrant workers from interior provinces represent a
massive drain of educational investment from already backward western
China, and the *hukou* system could neither stop them nor give them a
permanent new *hukou* in the eastern cities. The abundant but artificially
cheap migrant labor in the eastern cities thus prevented the investors in
the east from chasing cheap labor to the poor regions in the west. Hence
the trickle-down and spillover effect of China's segmented-development
strategy is greatly hampered.[15]

To some thoughtful Chinese scholars, the key problem of the PRC
hukou system has been its creation and maintenance of inequality and
discrimination among the people. To fundamentally rectify the problem,

the reform must move beyond just relaxing internal-migration control or mitigating its rigidity. The reform needs to focus on a long-term and comprehensive effort to construct a new citizenship in China. Through forming a civil society with new resident-class or middle-class citizens as the basis of Chinese citizenship, the PRC *hukou* system will eventually be transformed and become a new and normal system of administratively registering the people—no more, no less.[16]

Only very few publications have contradicted the overwhelming criticisms against the *hukou* system. One Internet posting accuses the *hukou* critics of being selfish hypocrites who are just trying to stay in the major urban centers after college and do not want to go back to their home towns to help the backward economies there.[17] An essay in an influential magazine for the PRC intelligentsia asserts that the *hukou* system "played a positive and irreplaceable role" in China's industrialization in the past, will only be reformed gradually in a "long and painful process," and cannot be realistically abolished anytime soon.[18]

Although it is clearly politically correct and popular to talk about the problems, flaws, and failures of the *hukou*-based internal-migration control and the need for its reform and even abolition, few in Chinese academic circles or policy-making communities have the naïveté to believe that the *hukou* system can or should be changed overnight or abolished. The PRC *hukou* system somehow appears to enjoy a higher level of legitimacy among the Chinese elite, including the CCP leadership itself.[19] At the same time, some have called for administrative and technical reforms and enhancements to improve the *hukou* system, especially in the poorly administered rural areas.[20]

To move gradually and to replace administrative quotas with economic means have been some of the most noticeable suggestions about *hukou* reform. One of the best-known Chinese authorities on *hukou* studies, Zhang Qingwu, who was a senior official of the *hukou* management at the Ministry of Public Security (MPS) for many years, has argued since the late 1980s that the *hukou* system has its important uses in regulating the undesirable mechanical growth of the cities. He has insisted that *hukou* reform be gradual, orderly, and in the general direction of "shedding the irrational add-ons" such as state subsidies for urban residents and opening the gates of small cities and towns first.[21] Another *hukou* scholar suggested that the government should rely mainly on economic means rather than the *hukou*-based administrative quotas as the way to control and direct internal migration.[22] One of the top economists in China, Li Yining, openly argued as early as the mid-1990s that proper regulation and restriction of internal migration have historical and practical justifications and positive effects in China and should be maintained.[23] Those mainstream ideas seem to be guiding the *hukou* reforms of the late 1990s and the early 2000s.[24] To gradually mitigate the negatives of the *hukou* system, such as the urban-rural gap, regional inequalities, and labor immobility, as much as possible and to reform the system at the low level of small cities and towns while maintaining a selective migration for the large cities seem to be the dominant views.[25]

So far, talk of reforming the PRC *hukou* system has almost exclusively focused on the system's function of regulating internal migration and the socioeconomic inequalities it created. It appears that, by 2004, most insiders and experts still firmly believe in the rationality and necessity of *hukou*-based institutional exclusion based on some type or types of restriction of internal migration, especially in major urban centers.[26] *Hukou*-based sociopolitical control through tiered management of the targeted people by the police (outlined in Chapter 4), however, has never even been mentioned in any open publications in the PRC.[27] This highly valuable function of the *hukou* system is still a topic too sensitive and too secretive to be even discussed in public. Internally, the general opinion of discussions has actually been advocating for a more effective sociopolitical-control role of the *hukou* system, primarily in the name of public security and crimefighting.[28]

The Actions of Reform

The basic political forces and rationale that created the PRC *hukou* system in the 1950s largely remain in the 2000s, as does the *hukou* system itself. But the much-changed social and economic landscape of the PRC since the 1980s has altered much of the CCP's political calculation and capacity, and hence has led to intentional and unintentional changes and reforms of the *hukou* system, especially its rigidity. The *hukou* system's longtime and much-examined function of resource allocation and subsidization to the urbanites has now been reduced and even replaced by the advancing market forces, as the urban rations of food and many other supplies have now either disappeared or become insignificant. The administration of the well-known function of internal-migration control is now increasingly localized, with clear regional characteristics. Regional variations, distortions, exceptions, and lapses hence have developed in the *hukou* system in the various parts of China, giving rise to increased mobility of the population in general and the rural laborers in particular.[29] The other leading albeit much less known but highly crucial function of the *hukou* system, the management of the targeted people (*zhongdian renkou*), however, remains highly centralized, rigid and forceful, and nationally uniform.

Of the two main functional roles of the PRC *hukou* system, restricting internal migration and managing the targeted people, the internal-migration control so far has seen most of the reform actions launched by the government. Appearing to be aware of the political consequences and the cost of the *hukou*-based administrative exclusion and discrimination against the majority of the Chinese, the CCP began to craft a general plan to reform the *hukou* system, mainly its restriction of internal migration, shortly after the political scare in 1989.[30] At the end of 1992, Beijing formed an interministry task force to study *hukou* reform. Several months later, the task force completed its *General Plan for the Reform of the Hukou System*, which was then issued by the State Council as a policy directive in June 1993.

The 1993 general plan on *hukou* reform calls for a gradual overhaul of the *hukou*-based control of internal migration and an eventual eradication of the rural-urban duality in the *hukou* system. The *hukou* system's function of resource allocation and urban subsidies is to be gradually eliminated. The long-term objective is to have just one type of *hukou*, of the PRC resident, without the distinction of agricultural versus nonagricultural types, under a much-anticipated but yet to be made PRC *hukou* law. There will be eventually only three categories of residential or household registration: permanent *hukou*, temporary *hukou*, and guest or visitor *hukou*. The *hukou* authority at the destination *hukou* zones, however, will continue to have the power to regulate and restrict the inmigrating permanent residents, depending on the local socioeconomic considerations. The *hukou* location differences and varied degrees of restriction among the major cities, medium cities, and small cities and towns are to be maintained at least for a very long time to come. For that, the general plan insists on the need to continue regulation of China's internal migration and proposes the basic principles of such a regulation to be observed. Not surprisingly, the general reform plan does not even mention the *hukou*'s role of managing targeted people.[31]

Action to reform the PRC *hukou* system has basically followed the spirit of the 1993 general plan. Many of this general plan's proposals were later converted into new policies and experiments. From 1997 to 1998, the State Council approved several directives by the MPS to gradually implement new reform measures. I have outlined and reported most of those actions as adaptive measures of the *hukou* system in Chapters 3, 4, and 5.

Building upon the momentum of the 1990s, during 2001–4, new reform actions took place to replace migration quotas with locally defined entry conditions in small cities and towns. Some medium and large cities also followed suit. Several measures were also adopted to address some of the needs of the millions of temporary migrants in the urban sector and to improve the public relations of the *hukou* system. Internal migration, especially rural-to-urban migration at the level of small cities and towns, has become significantly less restricted. The social-control function of the *hukou* system, the management of targeted people, however, has yet to be on Beijing's agenda of relaxation.

To open the small cities and towns. Based on the 1993 general plan of reform, on June 10, 1997, the PRC State Council approved the MPS's *Experimental Plans on Reforming the Hukou System in Small Cities and Towns* and *Suggestions on Improving Rural Hukou Management.* These two documents allow migrant ruralites who have been in small cities or towns for more than two years and who have a stable income and permanent residence to automatically get a local urban *hukou*, without being subjected to any quota limit. In two years, in 328 such experimental cities and towns,[32] over 540,000 former peasants gained their urban *hukou* and formally became full citizens of the small cities and towns where they had only been temporary *hukou* holders.[33] A few additional directives and documents from Beijing relaxed migration controls for certain selected groups of people such as elderly parents, newborns (they can now adopt the father's as well as the mother's *hukou*), and highly educated talents and skilled workers. But the migration quota system is still maintained, especially in large cities. These gradual and controlled reforms have relaxed the *hukou*-based regulation of internal migration at the level of small cities and towns yet have kept the quota-based migration restrictions largely intact for large cities.

On March 30, 2001, the State Council approved the MPS's *Suggestions on Promoting Reforms of the Management of the Hukou System in Small Cities and Towns.* The directive set October 1, 2001, as the starting date for a national reform of internal-migration regulations by abolishing the migration-quota system in all small cities and towns (defined as county-level cities, county seats, and established towns). Anyone, along with his immediate family members, including migrant ruralites, who has a stable nonagricultural income and a permanent residence in a small city or town for two years will automatically qualify to have a local urban *hukou* and become a permanent local resident.[34] Some medium and even large cities were also authorized to do the same, with a higher requirement of income and more specific types of employment as well as residence for an applicant to qualify.[35] The central government plans to use five years to deepen the *hukou* reform to "establish an integrated labor market for urban and rural labor in the eastern region where the conditions are ready" in order to eliminate market segmentation in eastern China.[36] To achieve this goal, naturally, many other reforms, including a more flexible user's right of land (or even a private ownership of land) to be more easily circulated and exchanged, are needed.[37] The Chinese media have carried lengthy and exciting reports to cheer on process with phrases like "fundamental changes" and "a historic moment."[38]

Yet this new round of *hukou* reform appears to be highly limited and controlled. According to a *hukou* expert associated with the MPS, the 2001 reform only barely touches upon the internal-migration regulations of the *hukou* system and only covers the migrant ruralites in small cities and towns. "The *hukou* system has not been abolished but only enhanced and improved with scientific means." The universal residential registration and the uniquely Chinese style of social control through the management of targeted people, or public-security management, of the *hukou* system continue and will be further enhanced. Migration quotas in the large cities will continue in use for the foreseeable future. *Hukou* reform should be "well-synchronized, smooth, and steady; must consider the rational flow and allocation of talents and labor; and guarantee the stability of socioeconomic order." The eventual goal should be to legally achieve a freedom of internal migration conditioned by state laws, not just free migration.[39] Furthermore, as I will show later, the 2001–4 *hukou* reform in the small cities and towns soon had to face harsh reality and pause.

Improved migration regulations in the major cities. While these historic reforms take place in small cities and towns, major urban centers retain their migration quotas and openly set high prices for their much-sought-after *hukou*. The most attractive cities such as Beijing and Shanghai have repackaged and polished their quota-based migration restrictions and have created ways to selectively grant certain migrants local urban *hukou* (the so-called blue-seal *hukou*) in a scheme nicknamed Using *Hukou* in Exchange for Talent and Investment.[40] So far, these improvements have basically been enhanced efforts to allow the rich and the talented, educated, or skilled to move in permanently while keeping the poor, unskilled, or uneducated out of China's urban centers.[41] The municipal governments in the urban centers are authorized to set and adjust their ever-changing standards and criteria measuring a migrant's net worth and talent or skills. For the much-needed manual labor and workers in those special industries like restaurants, hotels, and entertainment businesses, the *zanzhuzheng* (temporary-resident permit) remains the tool of *hukou* management.

In Beijing, a new sort of selective migration scheme took effect on October 1, 2001. Any outsider can now apply for Beijing's urban *hukou* but must meet a few very restrictive conditions and have a crime-free record. For a set of three urban *hukou* (self, spouse, and one child) in one of the eight central districts of Beijing, one must be a private entrepreneur who pays local taxes of more than 800,000 Yuan RMB a year for at least three years (or a total three-year tax payment that exceeds three million Yuan) and must hire at least a hundred local workers (or at least 90 percent of the employees must be local *hukou* holders). If applying for the same set of three Beijing urban *hukou* in the rest of the city outside the eight central districts, the tax payments and employment requirements can be halved (400,000 Yuan a year and fifty workers or 50 percent local hires).[42]

Such a requirement essentially means that qualified applicants must be multimillionaires, still a tiny minority in China.[43] Therefore, in the first week after the long-anticipated implementation of this reformed policy, not even one applicant emerged.[44] More than two months later, on December 4, 2001, Beijing taxation authorities certified only one rich business owner as the first qualified applicant for a set of Beijing urban *hukou* under the new regulation.[45]

The alternative is the housing-purchasing scheme first adopted in the mid-1990s. Any migrant may obtain a set of three Beijing urban *hukou* by purchasing a commercial housing unit,[46] in a designated area,[47] at a designated market price (at minimum a 100-square-meter apartment that costs at least 500,000 Yuan RMB, about fifty times the average annual income in Beijing), still subject to the available migration quota. A purchase of such high-end housing must be made with cash, since only local *hukou* holders can apply for mortgage loans and borrow from their pension plans to make the down payment.[48] In a city that has at least 2.37 million temporary *hukou* holders, in 1999, only 715 families made such designated housing purchases in Beijing.[49] Furthermore, to openly show off such wealth in a nation with hundreds of millions of poor people may be an unwise invitation to blackmail and kidnapping.[50] Indeed, wealthy outsiders who glamorously bought their way in have already caused resentment from the original local residents in some cities.[51]

Perhaps to improve the international image of the *hukou* system, Beijing's municipal government ordered all local employers to stop putting Beijing *hukou* as a requirement in hiring ads in mid-2001. But all relevant Beijing regulations limiting the hiring of nonlocal residents still apply completely.[52] Essentially, this is a reform in name only. Furthermore, the Chinese capital decided to offer its permanent urban *hukou* to any Chinese newcomer (along with spouse and any number of children under 18) who earned a bachelor's degree or higher from any recognized foreign college.[53]

Shanghai has had a similarly nominal reform of its *hukou* relocation control. The municipal government simply changed the name of its *hukou* system to the residential location (*juzhudi*) system in propaganda materials in 2001 as a gesture of reform. Shanghai's newly adopted *2001 Municipal Regulation on Hukou Management*, however, still uses the legal name "*hukou* system." The 1993 (revised 1998) blue-seal *hukou* measure was also updated to reflect a similar strategy to attract talent and money. The required price, however, appears to be lower than that in Beijing. An investor of one million Yuan RMB or U.S. $200,000 who has been in operation for more than two years may apply for a blue-seal Shanghai *hukou* for one of his employees. In the five outer districts and three counties of Shanghai, the requirement is lowered to 300,000–500,000 Yuan in investments. Alternatively, commercial housing unit purchasers might buy an apartment in a designated area with prices ranging from 100,000 to 350,000 Yuan to qualify for a set of three Shanghai blue-seal *hukou*. Such a low price attracted too many outsiders to Shanghai, so in April 2002, the Shanghai government stopped issuing blue-seal *hukou* to those who purchased a commercial housing unit. The rumor was that those who purchased the high-end units for foreigners only (*waixiaofang*) could still hope for a blue-seal *hukou*. The *hukou*-for-talent and *hukou*-for-investment/jobs schemes, however, are continuing.

All the blue-seal *hukou* holders, however, are still subject to the limits set by the citywide annual quota and may only apply for a regular and permanent Shanghai *hukou* after three to five years.[54] In 2001, as a major reform of social-welfare, medical, and pension provisions, the Shanghai municipal government established a social-security-card system that still covers only permanent Shanghai urban *hukou* holders.[55] Hiring ads in 2003–4 still commonly require the prospective applicants to have Shanghai local permanent *hukou*.

On March 17, 2003, a young migrant from Wuhan in Hubei Province named Sun Zhigang was arrested for having no identification papers by the police in Guangzhou, where he was lawfully employed. He was in typical manner abused by the police, and he was brutally beaten to death three days later by fellow inmates during the repatriation process. The case was reported by influential Chinese news outlets and led directly to a public outcry against the irrationality and injustice generated by the *hukou* system, especially the practice of forced repatriation. A dozen perpetrators, including several police officers, were sentenced to death or long jail terms. As a result, the PRC State Council canceled the 1982 "Measures of Detaining and Repatriating Floating and Begging People in the Cities," issued "Measures on Repatriation of Urban Homeless Beggars" on June 18, 2003, and "Measures on Managing and Assisting Urban Homeless Beggars without Income" on June 20, 2003, establishing new rules governing the handling and assisting of destitute migrants. Many cities, including the most controlled Beijing municipality, decided soon after that *hukou*-less migrants must be dealt with with more care; they are no longer automatically subject to detention, fines, or forced repatriation, unless they have become homeless, paupers, or criminals.[56]

National waves of replacing quotas with entry conditions for selected migration. Other provinces have made *hukou*-reform efforts as well since 2000. In Jiangsu, one of the most developed provinces, over 978 towns and small cities had abolished their migration quotas, and an estimated 3.35 million migrant ruralites had received new urban *hukou* in the small cities and towns, by late 2001. The large cities of the province basically followed Beijing's and Shanghai's examples and established stringent conditions to attract the rich and talented.[57] The provincial capital, Nanjing, has roughly the same entry conditions as other major urban centers for its blue-seal *hukou*, with a slightly lower price tag than that, say, in Shanghai and Guangzhou.

In Guangdong, one of the richest provinces, all cities replaced their migration quotas with entry-permitting conditions that are area-specific.

Hence, the attractive urban centers of Shenzhen and Guangzhou have established much higher entry conditions than the small cities and towns.[58] In Guangzhou (with over 4 million migrating population in the early 2000s),[59] one must buy at least a hundred-square-meter commercial apartment and pay a one-time fee of 30,000–40,000 Yuan RMB for a set of three blue-seal *hukou*, or buy a fifty-square-meter apartment for just one blue-seal *hukou*.[60]

Several provinces have adopted a similar Jiangsu/Guangdong-style policy. Anhui adopted an identical entry-condition model. Guizhou, one of the poorest provinces, decided to give a small city/town urban *hukou* to anyone who meets the income and residence requirements immediately, waiving the usual two-year residence requirement. Shangxi, another less developed province, has used urban *hukou* to reward migrant ruralites who have moved to the province's remote and poor regions to reclaim desert land through tree planting or grass growing.[61]

Ningbo, a large city in Zhejiang Province, was chosen as the national testing ground for *hukou* reforms and replaced the old migration quota ahead of time in 2000. A migrant may get local urban *hukou* by meeting the requirements of stable income (at least a five-year contract of employment or a certain amount of investment) and permanent residence (own a self-built housing unit for more than five years or purchase a hundred-square-meter commercial housing unit priced at least 250,000 Yuan RMB). However, only about 30 thousand migrant ruralites, a small fraction of the two million migrants from the countryside (who constitute one-third of the total population in the city) are expected to qualify.[62]

Shijiazhuang in Hebei Province was the first provincial capital to be a testing ground for the new round of *hukou* reforms. It replaced its migration quota with entry conditions in the mid-1990s. Migrant ruralites could apply for a local urban *hukou* by meeting the two requirements of stable income and permanent residence and paying a fee of 30,000 Yuan RMB (substantially reduced in 2001). The old annual rural-to-urban migration quota for the city was only about six hundred (0.15 percent of the city's rural population). Under the new regulation, from 1992 to 2000, over sixty thousand migrants obtained local urban *hukou*.[63] This reformed migration control was further relaxed in 2001. The entry conditions, however, are still too high for most migrant ruralites. Several months into the new round of reforms, only eleven thousand (out of the 300,000 migrant workers in the city) had applied, falling far short of the ambitious expectations of doubling the 1.2 million urban residents through *hukou* reforms in a few years. A key problem appears to be the difficulty for a migrant to have a stable job in the city, which has already been plagued by high unemployment for years.[64]

At the end of 2001, Fujian Province decided to even abolish the categorization of agricultural versus nonagricultural *hukou* and register every citizen in the province under a uniform categorization of resident versus temporary *hukou*. Each city or town was allowed to establish its own entry-permitting conditions to determine who could be registered as a new resident in that location. These conditions were to be based on an applicant's legal residence, employment, and legal income. For the larger cities in the province such as the capital, Fuzhou, and the special economic zone (SEZ) of Xiamen, however, controls of total migration or migration quotas were to be continued.[65]

In 2002, Hunan Province and Nanjing, the capital of Jiangsu Province, decided to convert the current blue-seal urban *hukou* to permanent urban *hukou* for all the qualified holders, without the three to five years of probation. Shanghai planned to experiment with a Shanghai Green Card system to allow a medium-high-level talent to have a local temporary *hukou* identification card after only a half-year residency.[66]

Education for migrant children. Under the PRC *hukou* system, only people with permanent local *hukou* can send their children to the local public schools at the state-subsidized cost. In 1996, to enforce the national policy of mandatory education among the millions of migrants, the State Education Commission issued a regulation to address the education of migrant school-age children. The *hukou* police were first required to restrict the migration of school-age children so they could continue their mandatory education in their home town or home village, if any relatives there could be found to serve as nonparent guardians.[67] In March 1998, the MPS and the Ministry of Education (formerly the State Education Commission) jointly issued a new regulation that requires the public schools of all cities to organize guest classes for the migrant children, with appropriate and reasonable additional fees. The regulation also legalizes the previously illegal private schools created exclusively for migrant children.[68]

The 1998 regulation acknowledged the serious problem of no education for massive numbers of migrant school-age children and outlined new policies to accommodate that fact. Yet "different localities have reacted very differently: some support but some stop the implementation" of the 1998 regulation.[69] Most frequently, the urban schools simply charge the guest students hefty fees to keep them away.

In Beijing, the guest-class tuition averages 500 Yuan RMB, in addition to a one-time entrance fee of 2,000–6,000 Yuan, plus other fees, making the annual cost 1,080–2,580 Yuan per student, a hefty sum for most migrant families, whose annual savings average only 2,400 Yuan per household (out of an average annual income of 15,600).[70] In 1999–2000, there were as many as 114 private schools established in Beijing exclusively for migrant children (half of them opened after 1998). All were run by nonprofessionals (including some illiterates) and often without the most basic equipment. These substandard schools charged only 300–600 Yuan per year. But more than 87.5 percent of the estimated 100,000 school-age migrant children in Beijing were still excluded from any type of schooling for the lack of money to attend even those low-quality private schools.[71] The largest and best-run private school for migrant children, the Beijing Xingzhi School (established in 1994 and with 2,000 students in 2000), was banned and forced to relocate three times by local governments in three years. In 1997, police in the Fengtai district of Beijing closed down over one dozen private schools for migrant children so as to control and reduce the migrant population in the district.[72] Migrant shop owners in Beijing interviewed in November 2003 believed that they would never become real Beijing residents as long as their children were excluded from local schools and college admissions.

The lack of proper education has been a major reason for many relatively well-off migrant ruralites to take advantage of the new reforms and apply for an urban *hukou* in the cities where they meet the entry conditions. In Zhengzhou, the capital city of Henan Province, among the former migrants who applied for new urban *hukou*, 80 percent did that because they wanted to send their children to the local public schools without additional fees. Consequently, just two months into the 2001 *hukou* reform, the already underfunded and crowded local public schools were suddenly stretched far beyond their capacity by the flood of new students, while the hope for new funds to make improvements was nowhere in sight.[73] Apparently, even a limited relaxation of the *hukou*-based institutional exclusion needs to be backed up with significant new resources that may not be present in many of China's cities today.

An Early Assessment

Sweeping and profound as they may appear, Chinese criticisms against the PRC *hukou* system so far are still very limited. There are few comprehensive and in-depth analyses of the nature, degree, and scope of the *hukou*-based institutional exclusion and its roles in the Chinese political economy. Many of the published essays and reports on *hukou* reforms are rather typical examples of the traditional role of the PRC media, which is to justify the CCP's decisions, explain government policies, promote official programs, mobilize popular support, project a new image, and educate the masses. The lack of knowledge and true analysis is apparent in the Chinese discourse on the *hukou* system, as has been the increasingly popular and strong sense of human rights and equality. A posting on a major Chinese news website in October 2001 angrily lashed out at the injustice inflicted upon the excluded rural residents in life and even in death:[74]

> [Background: On August 23, 2001, a bus accident in Shangxi Province killed thirty-two passengers from Gansu Province. Days later, local newspapers reported that the victims' families got damage compensation "according to the standard of 50,000 Yuan RMB per urban-*hukou*-holding victim and 30,000 Yuan per rural-*hukou*-holding victim, based on relevant official regulations."]
>
> Wow, what kind of regulation is that? What sort of rationale is that? ... Is there a different price of life for the same passengers on the same bus [because of their different *hukou* types]? Is it true that the lives of urban *hukou* holders are more valuable than those of the rural *hukou* holders?
>
> I will never understand why the peasants who painstakingly produce grain, vegetables, and fruits for us have to face outrageous discrimination at every turn. We are all taxpayers, all citizens of the republic; but who has ever offered the peasants any welfare, living subsidies, or pension plans?
>
> Our peasant friends leave home to work in the cities to make a living and earn some money for their kids' school tuition. Such a reasonable and rational move only brings upon them groundless discrimination by the city dwellers. ... Even when they encounter misfortune and die far away from home, their identities are categorized and the value of their lives is measured by their rural *hukou*. How brutal and how sad is that?!

Emotional and radical venting of criticisms against the PRC *hukou* system has its impact but is still rare in the mainstream Chinese media in the 2000s. The secrecy surrounding the operation of the *hukou* system effectively prevents the public from a complete examination and an adequate assessment of the system. Since basically all the educated, wealthy, and powerful in the PRC are or can become privileged urban residents, the excluded rural population lacks the ability, resources, knowledge, and information to fundamentally challenge and repudiate the *hukou* system. The Chinese discourse on the *hukou* system and its roles, therefore, remains to be ultimately shaped by the CCP's political decisions. Popular opinion may justify the reforms of the *hukou* system by revealing and discrediting some of the *hukou*-based exclusions and discrimination but can hardly guide the reforms or generate viable alternatives. The really relevant and meaningful discussions about the status and future of the *hukou* system are still clearly reformist and primarily conducted internally inside the PRC government.

Knowing that the PRC *hukou* system performs key functions crucial to China's sociopolitical stability, governance, and economic development, most Chinese academicians and policy makers do not believe in or call for abolishing the *hukou* system. The approved actions of *hukou* reform so far have been limited, controlled, and localized, primarily focused on image fixing and rationalization of the internal-migration-control function of the *hukou* system, featuring improved implementation of the four principles governing China's internal-migration regulation (see Chapter 4).[75] The main structure and operational mechanisms of the *hukou*, especially its function of social control of targeted people, are still intact. In the foreseeable future, it is highly unlikely for Beijing to completely abolish the *hukou* system. A senior official from the MPS summarized the objectives of China's *hukou* reforms this way:[76]

> Our main goal is to gradually break the dual-*hukou* structure of urban versus rural and establish a uniform *hukou* system for urbanites and ruralites; to ease the restrictions of *hukou* relocation to create a more relaxed environment for the cross-regional movement of urban and rural populations, especially talented people; to enhance the management of the two identification documents, the personal identification card and the *hukou* booklet; to speed up the creation of a *hukou* law so as to put *hukou* management on the tracks of rule of law; and to gradually peel off the various irrational functions assigned to the *hukou* system under the central-planning economy so as to restore the original and glorious image of the *hukou* system.

Even the limited reforms of relaxing rural-to-urban migration ran into great difficulties shortly after their national implementation in 2001. By mid-2002, only eight months into the national waves of merging the rural *hukou* with urban *hukou* to form a uniform "resident" and "temporary" *hukou* registration and identification, most provinces were forced to suspend the reforms and "wait for further directives" from Beijing. At the center of the "resistance and difficulties," inadequacy of resources for the newly "urbanized" ruralites who met those "entry conditions" seems to be the key. In Fenghua, a city in Zhejiang Province, for example, 13,000 "qualified" former rural residents were granted urban *hukou* in eight months of the reform in 2001–2. The city government suddenly lost over 20 million Yuan RMB income in additional school fees and had to come up with new investment for the expansion of schools for the new city dwellers, not to mention the massive funds needed to pay for the additional social security, unemployment insurance, medical care, and other expenses. The city, like many of its sisters throughout China, simply could not afford the inflow of these new urban residents.[77] By mid-2004, about one dozen, out of 31, provincial units in the PRC were reported to be resuming the reform of merging the agricultural and nonagricultural *hukou* types into one "residential *hukou*," opening the small cities and town to qualified migrant ruralites, and allowing all cities to use their "entry conditions" to regulate inmigrating registration.

A politically motivated or CCP-ordered "urbanization" through the change of names cannot accomplish much without a sufficient and sustainable growth of nonagricultural employment. Many rural residents seem to have seen the hollowness of the 2001–2 reform and started to show only limited enthusiasm. In Henan, a province with a massive rural population, only one-third of the total "rural-to-urban *hukou* relocation quota" allocated by the reforms was used from 1999 to 2002, and the province's urban population increased at the same pace as before the reforms. Without a solid urban economy to back it up, permanent urban-bound migration inevitably remains just an ideal for the ruralites.[78] Some local cadres in that province have cooked up ambitious plans to administratively double their urban population in five years by allowing the unskilled peasants to move into their small cities and towns that have already had significant problems of unemployment and underemployment. Such urbanization plans will likely become political bubbles to burst in no time, probably with disastrous socioeconomic and environmental consequences.[79]

Apparently, not only is there a strong political motivation for the continuation of the PRC *hukou* system as a form of institutional exclusion and social control; there are also real economic and social barriers to the diminution of the system. Urbanization and free internal migration without adequate resources to back them up would mean either a rapid decay of the existing urban sector or simply just a nominal change of the *hukou* type without any real benefits to the excluded rural population. Chinese rural residents are estimated to be currently treated differently and unfairly in at least forty-seven areas of rights and benefits; in the next twenty years, at least 300 million rural residents are poised to become urban residents through internal migration, hence to double the Chinese urban population.[80] To lift the *hukou*-based institutional exclusion for so many people and in so many realms, there must be either a massive spending of public funds or a massive resource reallocation and redistribution—neither, however, is easy, since the interest of the minority but powerful and organized urbanites will be directly impaired. Whether the PRC can genuinely achieve the modest goals of creating a uniform category of *hukou* registration for the rural and urban residents and relaxing internal-migration control by its planned deadline of 2008, therefore, remains to be seen. The 2001 reform, which was suspended in 2002 and began to continue with noticeably less hyperbole and haste in 2004, has yet to have a full resumption. Both political rationale and economic logic seem to point to at best a nominal and cosmetic reform of the *hukou* system and limited relaxation of internal-migration control; the essence of institutional exclusion of the PRC *hukou* system continues.

Epilogue: The Trends and the Future

The *hukou* system, for its crucial political values and socioeconomic functions, is likely to continue in the PRC to be the basis for organizing the Chinese people through administrative division and exclusion, in addition to the now increasingly important division between the haves and have-nots. Not only is it "impossible to relax *hukou* management and control in Beijing for a long time to come";[81] the whole *hukou* system "cannot possibly be abolished regardless" of how many efforts may be made to gradually ease internal migration in China.[82] When the 2001–2 *hukou* reforms had just begun, MPS officials already called for further enhancements of the *hukou* system, primarily for its "original and main" functions of identification and social control, after lessening the "undue" burdens of resource and job allocation through reforms.[83]

On account of internal and external pressures, the Chinese government wants and has attempted, to a degree, to reform certain aspects of the PRC *hukou* system, primarily for the purpose of narrowing regional gaps, promoting urbanization, and improving public relations and China's international image. The relaxation of *hukou*-based internal-mi-

gration control has been and will likely continue to be controlled, localized, and gradual. The government has proposed that Chinese urbanization should grow slowly by one percentage point a year to reach a 54.5-
percent urbanization level by 2020. The eastern and coastal regions may
have a higher urbanization level of 60.3 percent (about the average urbanization level of middle-income developed nations in the 1990s),
whereas the central regions should achieve 54 percent and the western
provinces should have only 48.5 percent by 2020, about the same level as
the eastern/coastal region's projected urbanization level in 2010.[84]

The most notoriously unfair and unsightly rural-urban distinction and
identification may be the first to be remade, and the ruralites may gain
even more freedom to enter small cities and towns as permanent residents. The PRC may work to blur or even eradicate the legal and nominal distinctions of rural and urban *hukou* types (the agricultural and
nonagricultural types) by using the same type of personal identification
cards, hence psychologically erasing that ugly mark of institutional exclusion and discrimination against the majority rural population. Yet the
locally defined but nationally enforced "entry conditions" or "requirements" for acquiring a permanent urban *hukou*, primarily property ownership and education/skill levels, will serve as an effective and more efficient economic tool to regulate China's internal migration based on the
hukou system than the old administratively maintained migration quotas.
The key factor that affects urbanization speed and urban development in
China remains the urban industrial structure and strength, as well as a
more productive new agriculture that requires many fewer peasants and
a greater amount of capital. Without the development of more labor-in-
tensive tertiary-sector or service industries to absorb unskilled labor from
the rural areas, a mere change of name cannot alter the reality of China's
rural-urban division.[85]

Furthermore, throughout the reform years, the PRC *hukou* system has
proven to be useful for the policy-motivated relocation of the Chinese
population. It has been effectively used to relocate many residents of
Shanghai, for example, away from the city center to allow for a revitalization of commercial and financial centers there.[86] The Three Gorges
Project relocated over one million people by 2003 when the first phase of
the dam project was completed. Some of the people who lived in the
reservoir area were relocated to places as far away as Arkersu in Xinjiang. This could not have been completed without the *hukou* system.[87]

As a major battle against poverty, nearly two million people in the extremely harsh natural environment of Sanxi in Ningxia and Gansu provinces have been targeted for relocation through *hukou*-based population administration since 1983.[88]

The Chinese government may be right to pin its hopes of eventually overcoming the dual-economy problem on the development of small cities and towns while allowing the major cities to continue to "get rich first." Jiang Zemin repeatedly emphasized that the construction of more small towns "is a major strategic issue that affects the economic and social developments in China." A fast urbanization at the level of small cities and towns has been listed, together with science and technology and sustainable development strategy, as three of the "six major strategies" of the tenth Five-Year (2001–5) Plan of the PRC.[89] But the potentials for urbanization through developing small cities and towns and rural industrialization have appeared to be limited. The widely promoted Sunan (southern Jiangsu Province) Model of small-town urbanization and industrialization has encountered troubles of economic stagnation, local falsification of data, and the exhaustion of development niches in recent years.[90] A study of the floating population in China using robust logic models to describe interprovincial and intraprovincial migration has shown that the township and village enterprises (TVEs, rural industries, hailed as a major avenue of small-town urbanization) have not reduced rural-to-urban migration and have important limits to their size, viability, and labor-absorption capacities.[91] TVEs created five to six million nonagricultural jobs every year from the early 1980s to the mid-1990s but only 94,000 annually after 1995.[92] In the early 2000s, the TVEs exhibited a nationwide stagnation and withering, even before the external competition after China's WTO accession was genuinely felt.[93] Therefore, most of the migrant ruralites are still flowing to the large cities rather than the small towns.[94]

The Chinese dual economy with its "unlimited" supply of unskilled labor will continue to exist for a long time, as will the political and economic justification for a continued circumvention of the difficult Lewis Transition with the help of the *hukou*-based institutional exclusion. For a political regime that lacks the legitimacy and loses the effectiveness of governance,[95] the CCP now is somehow caught between the need for a rapid albeit uneven economic growth through circumventing the Lewis Transition, hence to deliver rising living standards to the Chinese elite in the cities, and the need to address the growing grievance and pressure from the excluded majority of the rural population so as to avoid massive rebellious actions outside the city gates. To maintain the control and exclusion functions of the *hukou* system while gradually relaxing the control of internal migration seems to be the way out. Whether the CCP has what it takes to walk the fine line to reform the *hukou* system for the two somewhat conflicting objectives may be a key factor determining the CCP's political fortune.

The proven tradition of social control under the PRC *hukou* system, especially the tiered management of the targeted people, is unlikely to be relaxed as long as China remains under an authoritarian government (even a non-CCP one). The rise of crime in China today has been conveniently used by the government as a powerful justification for the enhancement of this function of the *hukou* system. Electronic equipment, laser scanning and graphic technologies, and computer networks have become new ways to supplement the significantly demoralized old system of personal informants and low-tech eavesdropping. In 2001, Beijing reaffirmed its national directive requiring all *hukou* files to have complete photographic information of the registered persons and reprimanded several cities for their incomplete compliance. All hotels, inns, and guesthouses with more than fifty beds must have scanners and computers directly linked to local police stations to instantaneously scan and transmit the photos of all guests who have completed the check-in registration.[96]

Widely believed to be irrational and unethical and an international public-relations liability, the *hukou* system is likely to be further examined and criticized in China. Some inside the CCP, in their desperate effort to salvage and strengthen the Party's governing legitimacy, may work to reduce further *hukou*-based discriminations as an obvious and easy way to appease an increasingly restive population, especially the excluded rural residents. Yet the secretive nature of the system's operation, the limited but meaningful adaptive measures,[97] and the firm support from the authoritarian CCP-PRC state apparatus may be enough to control and suppress the criticisms. The urban-based Chinese elite seems to be with the CCP on the issue of perpetuating the PRC *hukou* system. One leading sociologist in Beijing believes that the current *hukou*-based divisions and exclusions among the urban residents, the rural residents, and the migrant population are likely to continue to 2040 or even the end of the twenty-first century.[98] Senior officials in Shanghai simply assert in private that the *hukou* system "is highly useful" and "absolutely cannot be abolished."[99] In 2002 and again in 2004, Deputy Minister of Public Security

Bao Suixian formally announced in Beijing that the *hukou* system will exist for a long time in China. It "will not be abolished—not now, and not in the future."[100]

Therefore, the consequences of the PRC *hukou* system, discussed in Chapter 5, continue in China. A stable authoritarian one-party politics, rapid but segmented and uneven economic growth, rural-urban divisions, and horizontal socioeconomic stratification are likely to persevere. Due to the selective relaxation of internal-migration controls that has been the favorite reform measure in major urban centers, we may actually see an even higher concentration of capital and talent or educated labor in the few major urban centers like Beijing and Shanghai, creating even more internal brain drains and capital drains on the rest of the country.[101] In Shanghai, about 30 percent of college graduates who are originally from other provinces, usually the cream of the crop, are routinely "selected" to become Shanghai *hukou* holders each year and stay in the prosperous city permanently.[102] As a "special favor" granted by the education minister who was from Shanghai, Shanghai started in 2002 to openly siphon talent at a much younger age. Some thirty Shanghai "top high schools" were allowed to recruit fifty best middle-school graduates each from other provinces for a hefty fee of 50,000 Yuan RMB per pupil (two to five years' average wages in Shanghai). The main lure is that those outsiders can participate as local residents in Shanghai's much easier college admissions process twice.[103] In 2000, under the selective migration schemes that offered mobility to the rich and the talented, Beijing took in 1,400 "talents" (nearly 80 percent of them had a master's degree or higher) from other provinces and kept 11,000 college graduates who originally came from other provinces, while 2.3 million migrant workers with less education and no money could only work in Beijing as eternally "temporary" and discriminated residents. Increasingly, the reforms appeared to be replacing the Type 3 institutional exclusion of "the urban-rural *hukou* duality" with one of a "rich-poor *hukou* divide" in the PRC.[104]

With its deep roots, proven utilities, and many rationalizations and justifications, the PRC version of China's *hukou* system is here to stay, even if the CCP is reduced and removed from the scene. The consequences of the *hukou* system will continue to constitute the peculiarities of Chinese institutions and the Chinese way of life. Further development of the Chinese political economy and China's external relations may reduce the intensity and extent of the *hukou*-based institutional exclusion as market forces quickly redraw the Chinese landscape of institutional division and organization. A more democratic and liberal polity in China may further decrease the utility and increase the cost of *hukou*-based sociopolitical control. The PRC *hukou* system may then possibly have a genuine transformation from a Type 3 (*where one is*) institutional exclusion and administrative social control to merely a system of simple residential registration and identification.

After more than two decades of economic reform and development, indeed, the market has largely replaced the PRC state as the main form of economic transaction and resource allocation in China.[105] A market-based Type 2 (*what one has*) institutional exclusion is quickly supplementing and even greatly replacing the PRC *hukou* system as the main basis for China's internal organization through division and exclusion. The advancing market by itself may never be able to erase the *hukou*-based institutional exclusion and offer everyone in China an equal citizenship.[106] Based on the division between the haves and the have-nots, the poor, in the cities as well as in the countryside, are now uniformly excluded across the nation, whereas the rich may now overcome the *hukou*-based exclusion with ease.[107] While minimization of the numbers and the sufferings of the institutionally excluded is indisputably imperative, there will never be full citizenship,[108] or completely equal treatment, for *everyone* in China, or in any other nation as a large and organized human grouping. The increasingly combining and merging evolution of the *hukou*-based institutional exclusion with the money-based institutional exclusion appears to be forming a two-dimensional structure as the new basis for dividing and organizing the Chinese in the years ahead.

Notes

Preface

1. China's rural population was 807.4–914.2 million in 2000, out of the total population of 1,236.7–1,265.8 million (MPS 2001, 3, and SSB 2001, 101).

2. As an easy target, the land-based peasants are levied with disproportionately heavy taxes that have seriously stripped the peasants' ability to accumulate capital. Chinese central government sets the total tax burden in the rural areas at 5 percent of the peasants' generally low income. But in reality, the peasants are commonly forced to pay as much as 20–40 percent of their incomes as various taxes and fees (Cao Jinqing 2000, 64, 253, and 389; also see Chen Dongyou 1999, 168–79 and 193–206; Zhong Dajun 2001, 14; Liang Jun 2000, 3–38; and Shen Laiyun 2001, 20–21). According to one influential report, the rural population paid a total of 8.79 billion Yuan RMB taxes in 1996; four years later, the rural tax ballooned 4.5 times to reach 46.53 billion Yuan in 2000. On average, a rural resident paid 146 Yuan in tax in 2002, whereas an urban resident only paid 37 Yuan, but with an average income six time that of the rural resident (chapter 4 of Chen Guili and Chun Tao 2004). Whereas China's rural population grows by over 10 million every year, China's per capita acreage of cultivated land shrank by about 50 percent from 1949 to 2000 (Wen Tiejun 2001, 18) and was only 0.103 hectares (or about 0.25 acre) per person in 2001 (SSB 2001, 5 and 101) or, according to Committee for the National Institute for the Environment (www. cnie.org, Dec. 31, 2001), only 32 percent of the world average. China's per capita shares of fresh water and forests were also very low, only 28 and 14 percent of the world average respectively (SEPB 1994, 107).

3. The Chinese rural population has acquired extensive access to TV broadcasts, and nearly 90 percent of rural households had at least a black and white TV set by 2000 (SSB 2001). One survey study found that an average Chinese peasant watched TV for 79 minutes every day in the late 1980s, more than the total time he spent for social interactions, child education, and sports, or equivalent to his total cooking and meal time (Liu Ying 1993, 299–305). The popular programs on the rural TV were news, miniseries, and made-for-TV movies mainly about Chinese and foreign urban life (Huang Ping 1997, 71–72).

4. For a journalistic report on the rural-to-urban migration in China, see Roberts 2000. Incomplete citizenship holders or "noncitizens" are often viewed as second-class citizens (Solinger 1999, 4 and 7).

5. In Beijing, for example, out of the 13 major professions/industries, only jobs in three industries (garbage picking and recycling, agricultural and animal husbandry/fishery, and construction) are available without strict restrictions to migrant workers from the rural areas (Li Qiang 2000, 165).

6. Ministry of Labor, *Regulations on Employment Registrations*, Beijing, Sept. 12, 1995. In 2002, the officials rarely released the rural unemployment rate (20 percent as opposed to the 3–5 percent in the cities), and only in the English newspaper of *China Daily* (Feb. 7, 2002).

7. Although the sojourning ruralites in Chinese cities earn twice the average rural laborers' income, their average income was only 48 percent of the permanent urban residents' in the same city, and on average they worked 55 hours a week, 13 hours more than the urban average (Cai Fang et al. 2000, 83 and 90).

8. The officially defined special industries include garbage recycling, pawn stores and auction firms, and the hospitality industry (hotels, discotheques, night clubs, video alleys, and massage parlors). Liu Jiarui 1998, esp. 16–17, and Shanghai Municipal Government, *Shanghai shi tezhonghangye he gonggong changsuo zhian guangli tiaolu* (Measure on the management of special industries and public areas in Shanghai city), *Xin fagui yuekan* (New laws and regulations monthly), Shanghai, Feb. 2001, 43–47. The employees in these special industries consist disproportionately of "outsiders," especially those from rural areas. One internal study reported that 66 percent of all prostitutes in China (90 percent in Guangdong, 83 percent in Fujian) are nonlocal residents or "floaters" (Mu Xinshen et al. 1996, 5).

9. Months after the much publicized case of Sun Zhigang, a legally employed and properly registered migrant worker who was arrested for having no papers on him at the time and later beaten to death in Guangzhou while being deported in March of 2003, Beijing and a few other cities suspended forcible deportation of permitless migrants who are not paupers or convicts. *Changsha wanbao* (Changsha evening news), June 13, 2003; China News Agency, Beijing, June 15, 2003; *Zhongguo qingnian bao* (Chinese youth daily), Beijing, Apr. 14, 2004.

10. Personal ads and matchmaking ads in urban centers like Beijing often include the statement "do not contact if you do not have a local urban *hukou*." The very few rural-urban marriages usually take place between older urban men and young, attractive rural women. Author's field notes, 1998–2003. For China "dual circles of marriages," see Lu Yilong 2003, 351–96. For stories about how the *hukou* system has twisted love and marriages, see Tian Bingxin 2003, 150–84.

11. Starting in 2001, the migration quota in small cities and towns was gradually replaced with entry conditions but is still maintained in most medium and large cities. As an alternative to the "asset and talent" requirements, the small cities and towns mainly have two entry conditions to admit new residents: a stable local job and a permanent local residence for two years. PRC State Council, *Approval of the Ministry of Public Security's Suggestions on Promoting the Reform of the Management of the Hukou System in the Small Cities and Towns,*

Beijing, Mar. 30, 2001. However, as critics in China have already pointed out, those entry conditions are just a different way to exclude the poor and unskilled rural population, and hence have little impact in genuinely improving the rural residents' lives. *Qingdao zhaobao* (Qingdao morning news), Qingdao, Aug. 4, 2003; *Nanfang dushi bao* (Southern metro daily), Guangzhou, Dec. 1, 2003; *Zhongguo qingnian bao* (Chinese youth daily), Beijing, Dec. 26, 2003; and *Gongren ribao* (Worker's daily), Beijing, Jan. 4, 2004.

Chapter 1

1. Usually multiple political and socioeconomic stratifications (Max Weber 1978, esp. 251–54, 302–7; also Parsons 1951).

2. "Nation" refers to a sizable and independent human grouping that is clearly beyond the scope of the body politic and family lineage. Here, it is synonymous with terms such as "society," "tribe," "state," "country" or simply "human grouping" (Anthony Smith 1993). "Organization" means that the individual humans are arranged, linked, assigned, and controlled under one set of rules backed by a common public authority. "Division" is the existence of differentiated and sometimes even confrontational subgroups and the different treatment and power these subgroups and individuals receive in a common mother grouping.

3. Of course, many other factors such as resource endowment, geographic location, technological sophistication, and sheer chance all matter. Even the size of a nation seems to be a relevant factor as well (Wittman 2000 and Alesina and Spolaore 1997, 1027–56). But it is how a group of people and their activities (division of labor) are organized—the human institution or institutional setting—that makes the fundamental differences (Fei-Ling Wang 1998 *Institutions*, 1–2).

4. Daniel Little 1989, 3.

5. "Division of labor" or "specialization" of skills, practice, and information "is a basic structural aspect, not merely of the economic world, but of all other social worlds" (Kenneth Arrow 1979, 154, 156).

6. Various classic thoughts on social division and organization may indeed be interpreted in a synthesized fashion to harvest their insights. For a masterful attempt at reinterpreting Marx, Durkheim, and Weber, see Giddens 1977.

7. Many of the classic thinkers may disagree on the inevitability and desirability of the division of labor, but few fail to recognize the fundamental role played by the division of labor in organizing and powering human civilization. Adam Smith (1776) 1994, Émile Durkheim (1893) 1997.

8. Williamson 1985 and Williamson and Masten 1999.

9. Collins 1977.

10. Wilson 1978, ix–x. Of course, human organizations and hierarchies are mainly a product of institutional or legal arrangement (and its internalized versions or norms and values) that is primarily constructed and maintained by the discriminatory use of force and rewards, rather than by the involuntary alteration of body chemicals of the individual members like in the cases of bees and ants. Humanlike institutionalized hierarchy and organizations based on force can be

seen among some animals, but usually with much smaller scope (often just a clan or a pack).

11. Marx and Engels 1998 and Marx 1992.

12. The concept of "social structuration" recognizes and describes well the inevitability and crucial role of social stratification and division in human organization (Giddens 1986, esp. 110–61 and 227–80).

13. Keohane 1986 and Baldwin 1993.

14. Rodgers 1995, 8.

15. In the United States, even the proponents for immigration conceded that they only wanted the other nations to "give us your best and brightest" (Stephen Moore, "Give Us Your Best, Your Brightest," in *Insight*, Washington, DC, Nov. 22, 1993).

16. Scott 1976, William Booth 1993 and 1994, and Arnold 2001.

17. Gewirth 1982.

18. For racial and ethnic relations and their implications, see Feagin and Feagin 1993. For the lingering effect of racial division in the United States, see Entman and Rojecki 2000. Fukuyama (1993) is a frequently cited work on history being dominated and "ended" by one ideological divide. Huntington (1999) is perhaps the most well-known work on civilization-based international division and confrontation.

19. Compaine 2001 and Norris 2001.

20. Schmitter and O'Donnell 1986 and Huntington 1993.

21. Almond 1991. For a review of the latest scholarship on this, see Linda and Kapstein 2001, 264–96.

22. Here, "institution" is understood as a set of "humanly devised constraints that shape human interaction" and "a set of rules, compliance procedures, and moral and ethical behavioral norms designed to contain the behavior of individuals in the interest of maximizing the wealth or utility of principals" (North 1990 "Institutions and Transaction-cost," 182 and 1981, 201–2).

23. For social exclusion, see Jordan 1996 and Booth and Ainscow 1998. For an international effort addressing the issue of "social exclusion," see Rodgers et al. 1995 (esp. 1–29), Tchernina 1996, and Appasamy et al. 1996, the *Social Exclusion and Development Policy Series* under the auspices of the International Labor Organization.

24. For an elaboration on Max Weber's concept of social closure and its complementary role to Marxism, see Murphy 1988.

25. For the concept of exclusion, see Riggins 1997. For the concepts of citizenship and exclusion, see Bader 1997.

26. Rousseau (1755) 1992, 848–912.

27. For examples, Barbalet 1988, Eckstein 1991, Brubaker 1992, Meehan 1993, Bryan Turner 1993, Bader 1997, Ong 1999, and Castles 2000. Solinger (1999) impressively applied a citizenship analytical framework in studying China's migrant population.

28. Eckstein 1991, 346. For the consequential division between the "in" people and the "outsiders" in the context of Italy, see Sniderman et al. 2000.

29. It should be noted, as Solinger did (1999, 110–46), that some "public

goods" cannot be realistically excludable. In China, for example, certain subsidized resources and services are also readily available to the sojourning peasants and temporary visitors. Yet the nonexcludable public goods, important as they can be, do not constitute much of the life-chance-shaping resources and services discussed here.

30. Flanagan and Rayner 1988.

31. The masses, other than slaves, however, did not all enjoy the same political or social rights in Athenian democracy, let alone under the oligarchy regimes (Ober 1991).

32. For "artificial" or political creations of boundaries among people and their implications, see Manzo 1996.

33. For a discussion of gender-based stratification and exclusion, see Blumberg 1984, 42–47.

34. Max Weber (1978) explored and discussed exhaustively many of the political, economic, social, racial, and cultural divides and strata in his general theory of economy and society.

35. The suburban versus inner city division, for example, vividly illustrates this point (Langdon 1997 and Duany et al. 2001).

36. Fei-Ling Wang 1998 Institutions, chapter 1.

37. Naturally, being "inevitable" and "necessary" does not mean that we should not work to minimize the inequities and inequalities produced by an institutional exclusion. The imperative moral and ethical concerns can often be further intensified by a cost-effective analysis for the minimization of those negative externalities. For a general discussion on the reduction of "social exclusion," see Rodgers 1997, 253–309.

38. Of course, in reality, the four types listed here often overlap with one another and create hybrid variations in reality. Indeed, as will be elaborated later, few nations have only one "pure" type of institutional exclusion.

39. Genovese 1989, esp. 1994, and Smith 1999.

40. Herman and Chomsky 1988 and Chomsky 1989 and 1997.

41. For example, a person in the United States can be imprisoned for violating others' property rights. This Type 4 exclusion is a direct extension of the dominant Type 2 institutional exclusion. Further, the dominant Type 2 institutional exclusion may, ironically, work wonders to reward the Type 4 excluded, if the excluded and her case somehow drew great publicity and she hence became a marketable celebrity. The dominant institutional exclusion thus may override the secondary exclusion and the punishment may actually elevate the punished to a higher status in a money-dominated society if her books and movie rights sell well.

42. Different city-states at different times had different laws and policies on this matter. Not all the Greek states allowed for the purchase of freedom (MacDowell 1986).

43. For a report about America's poor in the 2000s, see Rodger Doyle, "Quality of Life: Is the U.S. the Best Place to Live?" *Scientific American*, Oct. 2002, 32.

44. Fei-Ling Wang 1998 Institutions, 18–20.

45. The much-admired democracy in the Greek city-state of Athens was a good example of elite democracy for the minority of the population. It took 130 years for the American democracy to include half of the U.S. population when women gained voting rights in the 1920s and nearly two hundred years to include the African Americans during the civil rights movement in the 1960s. Swiss women did not have voting rights in the long-standing Swiss democracy until as late as 1971 (*Time* magazine, Aug. 28, 1995, 25).

46. Capital accumulation has always been regarded as the number one "pushing" factor for economic development (Meier 1984, 137).

47. In Marxist terminology, the so-called primitive accumulation of capital (Marx 1992).

48. Osterfield 1992, 195; emphasis in original.

49. For a concise description of the dual-economy concept and its modifications, see Meier 1984, 151–58.

50. One group of Chinese economists and strategists declared that the serious problems of the backward rural sector were "the most fundamental problem" for China's great power dream (Hu and Yang et al. 2000, 285–350).

51. This is what was later named the Lewis Model of economic development, after the development economist W. Arthur Lewis. For his original treatment of the dual economy model, see Lewis 1954, 1965, 1974 and 1983. For modifications and amendments of the Lewis Model, see Fei and Ranis 1999, Todaro 1969 and 1999 and Schultz 1976 and 1986. For a Chinese version of the "four-dimensional" (agriculture, rural nonagriculture, urban formal economy and urban informal economy) type of Lewis transition, see Zhu Nong 2001, 44–52.

52. Lewis 1983, 319 and 320–63.

53. Azizur Khan 1994, 27–69.

54. Lewis 1983, 327.

55. Lewis 1983, 389.

56. Huang Renlong, "Zhongguo de feifa yimin wenti" (China's problem of illegal emigration), *Renkou yu jingji* (Population and economics), Beijing, no. 124 (Jan. 2001), 12–22. The "cost" figures are reported in *South China Morning Post*, Hong Kong, Feb. 15, 2001, 9.

57. Field reports from China (Wang Jun 2001) and the author's personal interviews in Brazil (1997) and in China (2000–2003) revealed a high degree of economic irrationality in rural-to-urban migration that inevitably creates urban slums and poverty, as well as retarding the development of an urban middle class.

58. Lewis 1954, 193–96.

59. Lewis 1966, 273; emphasis in original.

60. Wang Chunguang 2001, 67–68. For similar but general findings on this, see Osterfield 1992, 201–2.

61. Williamson 1988, 425–29.

62. An interesting place to see an insider's view on this is George Soros 2002.

63. Lewis 1966, 77–78.

64. Meier 1984, 156–58.

65. The Chinese appear to have realized this logic. A leading Chinese economist, Li Yining, commented in 2001 that a developing nation like China has two developmental gaps to close in its pursuit of modernization: the gap with the developed nation and the gap between sectors/regions within the country itself. It can only manage to close one at a time and the international gap needs to be worked on first, and the internal gaps can be narrowed much more easily later once part of the nation has developed. This "trickle down" or "spillover" argument, of course, can be viewed as the justification of Deng Xiaoping's famous proposal of "letting some people get rich first" in the early 1980s (Deng Xiaoping 1985 and 1992).

66. Lewis 1954, 145, and 429, and 1966, 68–75.

67. Meier 1984, 166.

68. For a discussion of the state's role of "governing the market," see Wade 1990. For discussions of "strong state," see Myrdal 1968 and Migdal 1988.

69. This line of thinking benefits from the insights developed by the "world system" theorists. For the crucial role of divided international politics in the development of the capitalist world economy and the conceptualization of the included "core" versus the excluded "periphery" of the world economy, see Wallerstein 1974. John G. Ruggie made a similar argument about the role of Westphalia world politics ("Continuity and Transformation in the World Politics: Toward a Neorealist Synthesis," in *World Politics* 35.2 [1983], 261–84). For varied international mobility of capital and labor, see Sassen 1988.

70. UNDP 2001, 144 and 157. G8 Okinawa Summit 2000, i.

71. The deep gulf between rich and poor nations has become common knowledge. The U.S. Department of Defense's annual budget ($289 billion for 2000) alone is nearly three times as large as the total estimated cost ($100 billion) for providing safe water, adequate nutrition, and basic education for the whole of humankind (*Time* magazine, Sept. 27, 1999, 33). The 7 percent of the world's population living in North America consumes 30 percent of the world's energy ("Earth Pulse—Insatiable Appetites," *National Geographic*, Mar. 2001), and 20 percent of the world's population living in the OECD nations has per capita productive land of 20 acres (the United States has 30.2 acres) while the remaining 80 percent only has 5 acres per person ("Earth Pulse—We Leave More than Footprints," *National Geographic*, July 2001).

72. Money-based Type 2 institutional exclusion never fully disappeared in the Mao era and has become increasingly prominent in the PRC in the past two decades. In addition to the money-based and the *hukou*-based exclusions, another unique form of Type 3 exclusive barrier in the PRC is the now reduced and withering *danwei*-(work unit-)based divisions and exclusions. For more on the *danwei* system and its role, see Walder 1986, Bian 1994, Lu and Perry 1997, Fei-Ling Wang 1998 *Family*, and esp. Li and Li 2000.

73. "Legitimacy" refers to the acceptance, de jure or de facto, by the practically meaningful majority of the population.

74. Cheng and Selden 1994, 644.

75. Yu Depeng 2002, 1–2.

76. Peng Yiyong: "Shehui zhuyi shichang jingji yu hukou tizhi gaige" (Socialist market economy and the reform of the *hukou* system) in *Xuehai* (Sea of learning), Nanjing, no. 5 (1994), 39.

77. For how the meritocracy worked in China in the 1990s, see Bakken 1999, 254–76.

78. For the status and prospects of China's labor allocation, see Fei-Ling Wang 1998 *Family*.

79. "Internal" estimates concluded that nearly 50 percent (80 percent in the Northeast and more than a quarter in Shanghai) of the Chinese state-owned enterprises were losing money. Massive underemployment (estimated to be more than 30 percent of the state employees) has been deemed the main cause of the problem. Author's interviews in Shanghai and Beijing, 1998–2003.

80. "Surplus" laborers in the Chinese rural areas are currently estimated to be 150 to 240 million, out of a total of about 900 million rural residents that grows by more than ten million every year (Wang Guichen 1988, 92–112, Zhang Siqian 1988, 98–114, SSB 1992, 15–18, SSB-PB 1993, 66 and 88, Niu Renliang 1993, 145–49, and SSB 2001). As a comparison, the total rural labor force of the fifty-two countries of Africa in the 1980s was only 117 million and the total rural labor force in the twenty-seven European nations was only 31.29 million (Wang Guichen 1988, 112).

81. Cheng Tiejun 1992, 393.

82. From Jan. 1, 1996 to Jan. 9, 2002. Author's online search at www.nytimes.com, Jan. 10, 2002.

83. Many works on Chinese political economy and reform have mentioned various aspects of it, although few engaged in an in-depth exploration of the whole system. Notable examples of recent Western scholarship that address the *hukou* system and its functions include Bian 1994, Cheng Tiejun 1992, Harry Wu 1994, Cheng and Selden 1994 and 1997, Dutton 1988 and 1999, Mallee 1995, Shaw 1996, Cheng Li 1996, Khan and Ruskin 1997, Sharping 1997, Zweig 1997, Davin 1999, Solinger 1999, Chan and Zhang 1999, Rozelle 1999, Guang 2001, Liu et al. 2001, and Fei-Ling Wang 2004.

84. The term "dual economy" has sometimes been used to describe the coexistence of a market economy and a nonmarket economy in the PRC. See the argument about "two parallel" Chinese economies in Studwell 2002.

85. For an institutional exclusion to have any "positive" impact in a dual economy, naturally, there must be a market economic system to allow the "in" urban sectors to grow efficiently. The PRC *hukou* system affected the Chinese economy before the reform era; but since it was then under a grossly inefficient central planning economy, the "positive" effects were largely limited to some Soviet style rapid development of heavy industries and infrastructure.

86. Cohen 1996, xiii and 236–65.

87. Cheng Tiejun 1992, 393.

88. Zweig 2001. The commercial polling firm Gallup China has a very low 1 percent response rate for its marketing surveys, primarily conducted by door-to-door visits and telephone calls. To survey people on social and political issues is

simply "too expensive and too risky." Author's interview with Gallup senior staff in Beijing, 1998.

89. As workers in the China field are generally aware, the official statistics published by the PRC often need to be carefully selected and weighed before being used to draw conclusions. For example, RAND believes that the Chinese GDP growth rate is generally overstated while its real GDP size is often underreported. RAND 2000, 34–36. For a penetrating Chinese discussion on the inaccuracies in Chinese statistics and the reasons for that, see Cui Naiwen 1995, 7–10.

90. The selection of interviewees was primarily done through friends, relatives, colleagues, and acquaintances, not necessarily random but sufficiently representative and highly informative. For a discussion of the necessity and usefulness of such a method of field study in China and an impressive product based on that, see Cao Jinqin 2000, esp. 3–5, 14–15, 475, 487–88, and 761–62.

91. The Ministry of Public Security specifically classified most of this information as "public security secrets," to be protected as an "important part of the state secrets." Liu Donglin 1989, 426–27. Even an "in-depth" case study of a *hukou* zone in Anhui Province by a PRC scholar appears to be unable to gather such information (Lu Yilong 2003, 165–221).

92. For an authoritative explanation of the uncertainty principle, see Hawking 1996, 69–77.

93. For example, see the UN-sponsored multivolume study on global employment and unemployment, Simai 1995 and 1996. For an argument of "sharing the world's wealth" with its excluded workers, see Kapstein 1999.

94. Of course, China's *hukou*-based institutional exclusion is not nearly as exclusive or unfair as the nation-states-based institutional exclusion in a globalized world economy. The central government in Beijing has significant power and resources for national redistribution, and the excluded low-skilled ruralites can still float to the cities to find some income. Internationally, globalization so far is at best incomplete, where the capital and goods may be achieving a worldwide mobility for maximum efficiency and profit for the property owners but the labor, especially the massive low-skilled labor in the less developed countries, is highly immobile and there is no world governing authority to levy a world tax for global profit redistribution.

95. Hardt and Negri 2001.

96. For a forceful argument of closing the relatively open U.S. doors to new immigrants, see Daniel James, "Close the Borders to All Newcomers," in *Insight*, Washington, DC, Nov. 22, 1993. After September 11, 2001, the United States indeed started to enhance its border controls and monitoring of foreigners, just like all other nations (U.S., *The Anti-Terrorism Act of 2001*, Sept. 19, 2001).

97. For example, while the citizenship-based institutional exclusion on the international level may be inevitable and even desirable for the common good of humankind, much still can be done to devise ways to minimize, not enlarge, the size and the sufferings of the excluded in the poor nations.

98. The late Robert Warren Barnett (1915–97) is remembered for personally inspiring and encouraging the author on this point.

Chapter 2

1. Fei-Ling Wang 1998 *Institutions*, 93–104.
2. The population was recorded to be over 13 million. Sima Qian, *Shiji* (History), vol. 2.
3. *Shangshu* (Ancient books), Chapter Duoshi.
4. Liu Yizheng 1988, 131; *Zhouli—Qiuguan* (Rites of Zhou—Autumn officials).
5. *Zhouli—*dasitu (Rites of Zhou—Chapter Dasitu) and *Zhouli—*suiren (Rites of Zhou—Chapter Suiren).
6. Guan Zhong, *Guanzi* (Guan book) Chapter Jincang (Prohibit hiding).
7. Jin Jingfang, *Jinshu qiantang* (Preliminary analysis on the classics) (Beijing: Zhonghua Press, 1984), 46. Cited in Zhong Nian 1994, 92.
8. Guan Zhong, *Guanzi,* Chapter Jincang. Also see *Guoyu—*Qiyu (State books—book of Qi).
9. Sima Qian, *Shiji: Shangjun liezhuan* (History: story of Lord Shang). Scholars outside China have different views on when the *baojia* system was adopted in China. Some started to mention it only after the Song Dynasty (Fairbank and Goldman 1998, 97). Others found it was not used in the remote regions to restrict and manage the migrants until the Ming Dynasty (Leong 1998, 106–7).
10. *Shangjunshu—Jingneipian* (Book of Lord Shang—internal tranquility).
11. Wan Chuan 1998.
12. *Hanlu* (Codes of Han). For more, see Lu Simian 1947, 493–96.
13. Lu Deyang 1997, 219–24.
14. For a treatment of the gentry class and its sociopolitical role, see Hsiao 1980.
15. Leong 1998, 21.
16. Solinger (1999, 28) avers that the people in the Qing Dynasty were "free" to move.
17. James Lee's conclusion (in McNeil and Adam 1978, 22) on China's internal migration in the imperial time seems to have missed this point.
18. *Beishi—Zhou wudi ji* (History of the North—record of Emperor Wu).
19. For an account of this and a few other smaller officially sanctioned reregistrations of migrants in history, see Lu Deyang 1997, 212–15.
20. *Suishu—Shihuozhi* (History of Sui—trade and industry).
21. Song Jiayu, *Tangchao hujifa yu juntianzhi yanjou* (A study on the *hukou* laws and land redistribution system in the Tang Dynasty) (Beijing: Shangwu, 1988), 74 and 76.
22. Yao Yuan 2000.
23. *Jiutangshu—Shihuozhi: Juntian* (Old history of Tang—trade and industry: land distribution). *Juntian,* a cyclical phenomenon coinciding with the rise of a new dynasty, has played a very important role in perpetuating the traditional Chinese institutional arrangement.
24. *Tanghuiyao—jizhang* (Collection of essentials of Tang—records and rulings) and *Tanghuiyao—xianglin* (Countryside and neighborhood).
25. Meng Xianshi, "Zhongyang, difang de maodun yu changan sannian kuo-

hu" (The conflicts between the central and local governments: the household inclusion campaign in the third year of Changan Era), *Lishi Yanjiu* (Studies of History), Beijing, no. 4 (2001).

26. Wu Songdi, "Songdai hukou de zong fabu xitong" (The general *hukou* reporting system in the Song era), *Lishi Yanjiu* (Studies of History), Beijing, no. 4 (1999).

27. *Mingshi—shihuozhi* (History of Ming: trade and industry).

28. Migrating merchants, however, survived and even prospered, often with the support of the imperial regime and local officials. A famous example was the *huishang* (merchants from Anhui) who dominated commerce for several centuries in the Ming and Qing Dynasties. For a recent study of the *huishang*, see Wang Shihua 1997.

29. Yu Depeng 2002, 321–31.

30. This reform appears to be a direct result of the decline of the Ming imperial power in enforcing the *hukou* system. The declining Tang Dynasty also did the same in its final years through the so-called *liangsuifa* (law of two kinds of taxes), attempting to collect taxes outside the *hukou* system.

31. *Qingchao tongzhi—Shihuo lue 3* (General books of the Qing Dynasty—outline of trade and industry 3). Also see Chen Dengyuan (1938) 1984, 198–205.

32. Ni Jin and Li Fang 1988, 364, and Chen Pengshen 1991, 410. For the *baojia*'s role in fighting against the numerous rebellions in the Qing, see Philip Kuhn 1980.

33. For analyses of this factor and other factors that powered the rapid population growth in the Qing Dynasty, see Zhao Wenlin and Xie Shujun 1988, 385–95, Tian Xueyuan 1997, 20–23, and Ge Jianxiong et al. 1999, 87–94.

34. Scholars have long debated the exact meaning of *ding* and the related issue of the accuracy of the detailed demographic data collected by the Ming and early Qing dynasties. See, for example, Ping-ti Ho 1959. A detailed summary of this debate is in Cao Shuji 2001, 9–16 and 51–68.

35. Sun Xiaofen 1997, 26–28.

36. *Shengzhu renhuangdi shilu* (Records of Emperor Kangxi), vols. 36, 58, 149, and 250. Cited in Sun Xiaofen 1997, 22–23.

37. Cao Shuji 2001, 722.

38. Li Debin et al. 1994, 2–338, and Ge Jianxiong et al. 1999, 150–71 and 191–203. For a general discussion of China's emigration and "colonization" history, see Li Changfu (1937) 1984, esp. 2–20.

39. One study estimates that Beijing extracted about 600 billion RMB from the excluded peasants in the 1950–80s, equivalent of the PRC's total fixed capital investment in the thirty years (Cheng Tiejun 1992, 402–3).

40. For an extensive study of the history of the *baojia* system in China until the Qing Dynasty and its related operational mechanisms, see Wen Juntian 1935 and Zhou Zhongyi 1947.

41. For the Wang reform and the *baojia* system, see Fairbank and Goldman 1998, 97, 132–33, and 297–98.

42. *Songshi—Wang Anshi zhuan* (History of Song—story of Wang Anshi).

43. Yu Depeng 2002, 328–29.

44. *Qingshigao—shihuozhi* (Draft history of Qing—trade and industry).

45. For a selected collection of Qing's *baojia* documents, see Xu Dong and Ding Richang (1871) 1968.

46. Fei Xiaotong 1986, *Jiangchun jingji*, 78–79. For the KMT *baojia* in the rural areas and the Japanese use of *baojia* in the occupied Chinese cities, see Schurmann 1966, 368–71.

47. For the *baojia* system and its use by the KMT, the Japanese, and the CCP in North China in the 1930–40s, see Zhu Dexin 1994.

48. Sun Yao 1994, 27.

49. Yu Depeng 2002, 337.

50. For the objectives of the ROC *hukou* system, see Guo Yanxian et al. 1952, 1–3, 58–60.

51. The ROC promulgated over three dozen laws and regulations governing the *hukou* system in 1911–49 (Gu Daoxian et al. 1996).

52. Xi Guoguang et al. 1997, 38–39 and 108–109.

53. Sun Yao 1994, 29.

54. For the CCP's takeover of the police network and *hukou* files in the cities, see Xi Guoguang et al. 1997, 152–57, 162–64, and 167.

55. In Haerbin alone, over 8,000 arrests were made through *hukou*-based population inspections. In 1946, in Northern Manchuria Province, 12,000 "enemies" were arrested through *hukou*-based investigations (Xi Guoguang et al. 1997, 141–43).

56. Sun Yao 1994, 30.

57. Ma Fuyun 2000, 36.

58. Schurmann 1966, 371–80, and White 1989, 90. Solinger (1999, 43) seemed to share the PRC official view that the *hukou* system was established for statistical purposes; yet the CCP started the system well before 1949.

59. Sun Yao 1994, 31.

60. Xi Guoguang et al. 1997, 163.

61. Solinger 1999, 32–34.

62. Cheng and Selden 1994, 655.

63. Since the mid-1980s, there have been "internal discussions and proposals" on establishing a separate ministry in charge of the *hukou* system and related population management, including birth control, to reduce the "increasingly heavy workload" of the police. So far, such views clearly remain a minority scholarly opinion in Beijing. Wang Taiyuan 1997, 112–15.

64. At Chen Yun's suggestion, the PRC adopted this policy in the fall of 1953, setting the stage for agriculture collectivization (Chen Yun 1983, 209).

65. For one account of the rural consequences of the disastrous Leap, see Friedman et al. 1991, 226–52.

66. Basil Ashton et al., "Famine in China: 1958–61," in *Population and Development Review*, 10.4 (Dec.) 1984, 613–45; John Aird, "The Preliminary Results of China's 1982 Census" in *The China Quarterly*, no. 96 (Dec. 1983), 613–40. A thorough study concluded that the "abnormal death toll" during the three years of the Leap was around thirty-five million. Ding Shu, *Renhuo* (Man-made disaster) (Hong Kong: Nineties Press, 1995).

67. For the initial years of the PRC *hukou* and its role in the development of a "spatial hierarchy" in the Chinese society, see Cheng and Selden 1994 and 1997.

68. Sun Yao 1994, 33.

69. For instance, see the following official publications: Sun Weibeng 1992, 664–65; Ying Songnian 1992, 117; Cao Haibo and Li Weimin 1989, 62–63; and The Supreme People's Court of the PRC 1989–99.

70. Cheng and Selden 1994, 663–66.

71. For the CCP's consideration of and decision on the move, see Zhang Shenbin 2001, 373–84.

72. Schurmann 1966, 400–402; Huang Daoxia 1989, 159. The legal basis of this action was CCP Central Document no. 61–460 (*Notice on several issues of reducing workers from the CCP Central Committee*), issued on June 28 of 1961 and collected in Labor Ministry 1986, 199–203.

73. For an extensive study of people's communes in the Chinese countryside, see Zhang Lutian 1998.

74. Yuan Lunqu 1989, 135–37; Zhang Shenbin 2001, 384.

75. Ma Xia 1994, 239; MPS 2001, 3.

76. The *yinong-yigong* scheme was a pragmatic solution to the dilemma of developing the economy in a nation with a huge population, little capital, and low labor mobility. Under Liu Shaoqi and Deng Xiaoping, many urban enterprises were allowed to hire workers from the rural areas on a contractual or temporary basis. When the contract expired, these workers had to leave for their original communes or villages where their permanent *hukou* was located. It was a measure to obtain a certain labor mobility without impairing the overall institutional exclusion against the rural residents, thus minimizing the state subsidies to the urban population. For more on this policy, see Yuan Lunqu 1989, 138–40. Similar but less extensive measures are still in use in today's PRC.

77. For the "paralysis" of the police networks and the "brutal treatment" of many police officers at the beginning of the Cultural Revolution and Zhou Enlai's effort of restoring order, see Xi Guoguang et al. 1997, 329–39.

78. They included housing policy, employment policy, and grain rations (Wang Guixin 1997, 304–5). Some of these were offshoots of the *hukou* system, like the grain ration system, and were discontinued in the 1990s; others, like the housing policy, were still being reformed in the early 2000s.

79. Zhong Yicai, "Chengxiang eryuan shehui de yonghe yu yingnong jingcheng" (The merging of the dual urban-rural societies and the pulling of the peasants into the cities), *Shehui kexue* (Social sciences), Shanghai, no. 1 (1995), 55–58.

80. For a collection of the stories of the "sent-down" urban youth, see Li Guangping 1993.

81. Hu Ping 1993, 452–53.

82. Ma Fuyun 2000, 57.

83. A *hukou* police official wrote to assert that "the increase of migrant population has directly motivated the reform of the *hukou* system." Liu Tie 1998, 54.

84. Kam Wan Chan and Li Zhang 1999, 831–40; Fei-Ling Wang 2004.

85. Solinger 1999; Delia Davin 1999; Michael Dutton 1992; Lei Guang 2001; Jianhong Liu, Lening Zhang, and Steven Messner 2001; Hein Mallee, "China's Household Registration System under Reform," *Development and Change* 26.1 (Jan. 1995); Chan and Zhang 1999, 818–55; David Zweig 1997; and the special issue of *Chinese Law and Government*, May–June 2001.

86. For agricultural reforms in the 1980s and 1990s, see Kelliher 1992, Kate Xiao Zhou 1996, and Walder 1998.

87. MPS-TB 1993, 98.

88. For a lengthy reportage with colorful anecdotes about the massive amount of *liudong renkou* in the 1990s, see Hao Zaijing 1996.

89. The various regulations governing the blue-seal *hukou* issued by the municipal governments of the PRC are officially listed at www.news.china.com, last accessed Oct. 20, 2003. The blue-seal *hukou* holders can be viewed as what Solinger called "proto-citizens" in the Chinese cities (1999, 289).

90. Gao Shangquan et al. (vol. 1) 1993, 92.

91. *Baokan wenzhe* (Newspaper and magazine digest), Shanghai, June 18, 1998, 2. For an examination of the Chinese urban housing issue, see Wang and Murie 1999.

92. For the official rules and regulations on the urban-only social security and welfare programs, along with other state subsidized benefits, see State Council-MLSS 1999.

93. Supreme People's Court of the PRC (vol. 4) 1992, 11–17. The regulations on the personal ID card and its specifics were revised and reissued in 1999.

94. Still, if the father's or stepfather's *hukou* is in a major city, the child would have to wait for the available quota. State Council–approved MPS Document *Guanyu jiejue dangqian hukou guanli gongzu zhong de jige tuochu wenti de yijian* (Suggestions on solving some of the pressing issues in current *hukou* management work), Beijing, July 1998.

95. Gao Shangquan 1993, 674–75.

96. Shue 1988, 105. Shue argues that due to the heavy legacy of the past, China today is still basically an enduring, localistic, solitary and resistant cellular society. This view is the antithesis of Walder's argument (1986) in which he states that contemporary China is a new, party-dominated, divided, yet compliant network society—although both of them agreed that, fundamentally, the Chinese economy was a nonmarket economy, which shaped patterns of social and political relationships in China for centuries. For summaries and critiques of both views, see Perry 1989, 581–84.

97. Jin Guangtao 1987 and Zhang Minyuan 1990, 6–7. For an influential early discussion of "the spirit of the Chinese people" in English, see Gu Hongmin (1915) 2001, esp. 25–66.

98. Chen Duxiu, "Dongxi minzhu genben sixiang zhi chayi" (The fundamental differences between Western and Eastern thought), *Xin qingnian* (New Youth), 1.4 (Winter 1915), cited in Su and Yang 1991, 4–7.

99. Weber, "Konfuzianismus und Taoismus," cited in Moore 1967, 220. Also see Degrute 1910.

100. For instance, in the famous Xuankongsi (Midair Temple) in Shanxi

Province in North China, all the three major Chinese religions are enshrined and worshipped together in the same complex. *Shanxi ribao* (Shanxi daily), Mar. 15, 1992. In Taipei, the famous Lunshan Temple enshrines not only Buddhist gods and goddess, Taoist figures, but also the local Goddess Mazhu and many other legendary gods. For further examination of religion in China by Chinese and foreign scholars, see Tang Yijie 1992.

101. This is very different from India, whose caste-based institutional exclusion is closely related to the dominant Hindu religion (see Chapter 6 of this book).

102. Chen Hua (1996, 34–35) found that there was the division of "eight economic regions in the Qing Dynasty" that are still clearly seen in today's PRC.

103. Gu Chaolin 1999, 15–27.

104. For example, the capital city of the Song Dynasty (10th to 12th centuries), Bianjing, with 1.5 to 1.7 million people, was the largest in the world. Liu Junde and Wang Yuming 2000, 20.

105. Jiang Yimin and Guo Yaxing, "Xiaochengzheng jianshi yu nongcun chengshihua" (The construction of small towns and the urbanization of the countryside), *Shihui gongzhu yanjou* (Studies of social works), Beijing, no. 4 (1994), 10–11. Also Gu Chaolin 1999, 24.

106. Ma Fuyun 2000, 29.

107. For an argument that claims "China's dual socioeconomic structure started in the 1860s," see Lu Zhaohe 1999, 184–87.

108. Skinner 1977, 229; Zhang Shanyu 1997, 294.

109. Ma Xia 1994, 236–40; MPS 2001, 3.

110. Wang Jianchu 1987, 4.

111. Chen Zhen 1961, 53.

112. Peng Huei En 1995, 239–40 and 243–51; Li Chen and Wu Hui-Ling 1993, 236.

113. For a historical survey of the Chinese cities, see Liu Junde and Wang Yuming 2000, 6–50.

114. Solinger 1999, 33–34.

115. For the role of *guanxi* in Chinese politics, see Xuezhi Guo 2001, 69–94.

116. Turner et al. 2000, 328.

117. It is not very difficult to alter one's *hukou* record through local *hukou* police or even establish a whole new identity through sympathetic or bribed *hukou* police, especially in the rural areas and in small towns. For example, see the reports on such incidents in *Nanfang zhoumu* (Southern weekend), Guangzhou, May 10, 2001, 7.

118. There are countless anecdotes about "illegal" but very "Chinese" ways of bending the *hukou* system: "swapping" *hukou* with illegal and under-the-table payments, bribing local officials for *hukou*-changing permits with money and sex, and falsifying documents.

119. For a collection of Chinese self-examinations on the Chinese culture and "national characters" in the past century, see Su and Guo 1991, esp. 4–151; also Sa Lianxiang 1988.

120. Luo Guoji, President of the Chinese Society on the Study of Ethics,

"Quanju yishi, zhengti jingshen—tan zhonghua minzhu lunli sixiang hexin" (Overall viewpoints, sense of entirety—on the core of Chinese ethics), *Renmin ribao—haiwaiban* (People's daily)—*Overseas*, July 29, 1995, 3.

121. Central Party School of CCP 2001, 1, 16–19 and 51–89.

122. As part of the CCP's organized effort, there were numerous Chinese scholarly publications on Chinese culture and its role in Chinese institutions in the 1990s. For example, see Sheng and Feng 1995, Zhou Yongliang 1995, Shang et al. 1996, and Lu Zheng 1996.

123. One historian identified two major "factors" that contributed to the stability of traditional Chinese social life: the family structure and "a relatively flexible class system" (Shu-min Huang 1989, 3).

124. Wang Chunguang 2001, 68–70.

125. Ni Jin and Li Fang, 1988, 637. This may also be interpreted to be that the *PRC Constitution* finally became more relevant to legal reality.

126. The *hukou* system is generally not included in the authorized experimentation rights of those zones. Gao Shangquan 1993, 141–43.

127. See, for example, the six essays and articles on the *hukou* system in the Hong Kong–based journal *Ershiyi shiji* (Twenty-first century), no. 5 (1999).

128. For example, *Banyue tan* (Fortnightly chat), an official journal by the state-run Xinhua News Agency, published a short essay titled "*Hukou* reform is inevitable" by Han Jun in its 11th issue in 1994. The essay outlined most of the "talking points" repeated by many *hukou*-reform articles published in the years after that.

129. See, for example, a collection of such articles in www.news.china/zh_cn/ focus/hjzd, a website of the official *Renmin ribao* (People's daily), Aug. 2001–Dec. 2003. Further examination of the latest Chinese discourse of *hukou* reform is in Chapter 7 of this book.

130. China New Agency News Dispatch, Guangzhou, Sept. 24, 2001; *Renmin ribao* (People's daily), Sept. 6, 2001, 9; and *Nanfang dushibao* (Southern metro daily), Guangzhou, Sept. 8, 2001 and May 11, 2004.

131. China News Agency News Dispatch, Beijing, Aug. 9 and Aug. 20, 2001.

Chapter 3

1. The most "comprehensive" study openly published on the *hukou* system is still the very sketchy and largely made-for-propaganda booklet by Zhang Qingwu (1983, English edition in 1988, translated by Michael Dutton) and its various reincarnations and expansions. Zhang, an authority on the *hukou* system and a senior official in charge of the *hukou* management at the MPS for many years, did author or advise on a number of in-depth "internal" publications and reports on the *hukou* system, which have been frequently utilized by this book. Yu Depeng (2002), a college teacher in Zhejiang Province, attempted to make a scholarly examination of the *hukou* system from quasi-official perspectives. Tian Bingxin (2003), a formal Xinhua News Agency Guangzhou bureau chief and a public speaker, had an interesting journalistic treatment of the *hukou* system and called the study of the system a "taboo" in the PRC. Lu Yilong's book (2003), a

published Beijing University Ph.D. dissertation, represented perhaps the latest, albeit still very underdeveloped, PRC scholarship of the *hukou* system.

2. Recent examples include Bian 1994, Cheng Tiejun 1992, Cheng and Sleden 1994 and 1997, Dutton 1988 and 1999, Guang 2001, Liu et al. 2001, Mallee 1995, Shaw 1996, Scharping 1997, Davin 1999, Solinger 1999, Wang 1998 *Family*, Zweig 1997, and the special issue of *Chinese Law and Government*, May–June 2001.

3. The "internal only" materials are not available to the public or foreign scholars but legally are not "state secrets," and their leaking to "outsiders" generally does not trigger criminal investigation but may bring disciplinary actions against a leaker if caught (Gao Guiting 1994, 322). Occasionally, scholarly works published inside the PRC are seen citing such internal publications (e.g., Lu Yilong 2003, 455).

4. For example, unreleased *hukou* data and local data on the targeted people are classified as secrets, the national data base of the targeted people is classified as critical secrets, and the national data of arrested criminals, especially the "counterrevolutionaries" or antistate criminals, are classified as top secrets (MPS regulations in Liu Donglin 1989, 424–25). These three types of classifications usually expire in 10, 20, and 30 years respectively although a particular piece of information can be classified "indefinitely." The legal basis for classifying information in the PRC is the *PRC Law on Protecting State Secrets* of May 1, 1989 (Gao Guiting 1994, 323).

5. Many restricted but highly useful "internal" publications are readily available in Chinese and foreign bookstores and libraries these days. Using them is in no violation of any Chinese law and does not affect the PRC citizens who may have helped to locate and interpret them as long as the identity of these Chinese is protected. Attempting to collect currently classified information, I believe, may endanger the integrity of an academic research like this one. Furthermore, the few "classified" documents and publications about the *hukou* system that can be found are either too old or too incomplete to be very useful.

6. Jiang Xianjin et al. 1996, 218; MPS-BPT 2000, 5.

7. Jiang Xianjing et al. 1996, 220; MPS-BPT 2000, 161–73.

8. MPS-BPT 2000, 122.

9. Jiang Xianjin et al. 1996, 225.

10. Ying Zhijin and Yu Qihong 1996, 55–60.

11. The latest bills for a PRC *Hukou* Law proposed to the National People's Congress (NPC) by the NPC deputies were reported in 2003 and 2004. The MPS was also reported to be working on an early draft of such a law in 2004. *Huasheng bao* (Huasheng daily, Beijing, Nov. 28, 2003; *Xinjing bao* (Xinjing daily), Beijing, Mar. 15, 2004. But such bills have yet to be included in the legislative agenda. Author's interviews with *hukou* officials and NPC officials, 2002–4.

12. Yao Weizhang 2003 *Gongan paichusuo*, 123–48.

13. A family-household is defined by the police as people with blood relations and especially those living together and sharing income (MPS-EB 1997, 57).

14. *Renmin ribao* (People's daily), Beijing, Feb. 26, 1998, 1.

15. MPS-BPT 2000, 46; SSB 2000, 98–99.

16. Interviews in Beijing, 2001.

17. As a major reform for entering the WTO (World Trade Organization), the MPS streamlined the passport application procedure. Now every Chinese citizen may apply for a passport for overseas trips by only showing his personal ID card and his *hukou* booklet, with no more requirement of "overseas invitation letters." *Fazhi ribao* (Legal daily), Beijing, Nov. 23, 2001, 1.

18. These are the MPS's 1985 regulations. In the 2000s, there is a great regional variation in their enforcement (Li Rujian 2001, 20–21).

19. Yu Jin 1991, 55, and MPS-BPT 2000, 121.

20. In the 2000s, in the major urban centers, nonlocal *hukou* holders, even with a legitimate job and residence, could only get prepaid cell phone service instead of a much cheaper local cell phone account. Author's field notes in Beijing and Shanghai, 2002–4.

21. "Qualified" newlyweds usually get birth-quotas easily. For the rural couples or special urban couples who want to have a second or even a third child, a birth-quota must be granted before labor (sometimes even before pregnancy). For migrant people, the PRC State Council issued a special *Management Measures on the Birth-Planning of Migrant People* in 1991 that mandated any birth-age migrant to carry a valid birth-planning card (issued by the birth planning authorities in one's permanent *hukou* zone) that certifies the carrier's birth history. The card is required when applying for temporary *hukou,* jobs, or business licenses. Married migrants may ask for reimbursement from the local government of their permanent *hukou* zone for contraception and abortion costs. Empirically, the birth planning of migrant people has been highly problematic and ineffective nationwide since the 1980s (Gui Shixun 1992, 2–5). In 1998, some places in the PRC started to relax birth quota restrictions and birth control itself. Elisabeth Rosenthal, "China Relaxes 'One Child' Controls," *International Herald Tribune*, Nov. 3, 1998.

22. Gao Shangquan et al. (vol. 1) 1993, 92.

23. *China Daily*, Beijing, Jan. 22, 2001, 4.

24. Some of these goods, like the urban public transportation system (Solinger 1999, 110–46), have become nonexcludable public goods, and the state subsidies on their provision are thus shared by migrants as well. Yet even though migrants can ride on subsidized buses and subway trains in cities for the same fare, they still do not have access to the numerous monetary "transportation subsidies," including bicycle allowances and local discounts on various monthly passes.

25. Just the teachers' wages needed to maintain a substandard six-to-nine-year education could take as much as 60–75 percent of the total revenue of the financially already burdened township governments in central China (Cao Jinqing 2000, 360–61, 459 and 525).

26. Chinese universities have different admission standards in different *hukou* zones. For example, a high school graduate with a Beijing urban *hukou* could get into the top Beijing University with a college entrance exam score 20 percent lower than that of a rejected applicant who has a rural *hukou* from Hubei or Anhui provinces, even though they had exactly the same tests on the same state-mandated curricula and textbooks. The details of such disproportionate quotas

are classified and vary across the region. More on this later in Chapter 5 of this book.

27. Wang 1998 *Family*, 262–64.

28. For example, Shijiazhuang and Ningbo launched such reforms in 2001 (*Xinhua Daily Telegraph*, Beijing, Aug. 20, 2001). More on this later in Chapter 7 of this book.

29. To combat rising crime and manage the increasingly mobile population, Chinese police have since the mid-1990s started to set several outposts, policing zone (*jingqu* or *jingwuqu*), or security zone (*zhian xiaoqu*) under each police station in large cities to have more "on the spot" and integrated police presence. For internal discussions and reports on this new structure of the police network, see Kang Damin et al. 1998, 71–91, 184–90, 303–33, and 375–86.

30. MPS-EB 1997, 409.

31. Full-time *hukou* police were first assigned to police stations in 1909 when the Qing Government set up modern police stations in Beijing. For every station, one police officer was designated *hukou* police. Qing Government, *Jingcheng paichusuo guiding* (Police station regulations in Beijing), 1909.

32. MPS-PD 1997, 127, and MPS-PD 2001, 185–86.

33. See, for example, Li Zhongxin 1998, 82–85.

34. *Renmin ribao—haiwai ban* (People's daily—overseas edition), Beijing, Jan. 28, 1997, 1.

35. Wang Yongping 1998, 142.

36. To protect the privacy of the elite and the senior officials, the old *hukou* dossiers of those residents who later become exempted from the *hukou* dossier requirement are required to be sealed (MPS-EB 1997, 87).

37. MPS-BPT 2000, 142–43, 58–61.

38. For the complete rules and detailed regulations as well as some court-case rulings on the permanent *hukou* registration, see MPS-BHM 1996.

39. Article 24 of *The Implementation Details of the PRC Personal Identification Card Regulation*, Beijing, MPS, 1999.

40. Wang Hongjun 1999, 18–19.

41. MPS-PSMB 2001, 482–90. The personal ID card, which looks like a credit card, is indeed much easier to carry than the *hukou* booklet, which resembles a normal passport. Counterfeiting of the ID card is still very common in the PRC. In a ten-month period in 1993, for example, the police in Shenzhen Airport alone caught about one thousand passengers using fake personal ID cards at the boarding gates (MPS *Zhifa shou ce*, vol. 15, 1995, 890). In the late 1990s and early 2000s, the sale of fake personal ID cards was still a common occurrence in most Chinese cities. In Guangdong, a "good quality" fake personal ID costs only 150 RMB, about a quarter of the average monthly income of manual laborers in the region. Author's interviews in Dongguang, Guangdong, 1998. In Beijing, a repeat offender using a fake personal ID card was sentenced to jail for 15 years in 2004 (*Beijing Youth Daily*, May 26, 2004).

42. Wang Hongjun 1999, 55–56. People's *hukou* information changes frequently, but the current PRC personal ID cards are issued only to people aged 16 and up and are effective for 10 years (for people aged 16 to 25), 20 years (for

people aged 26 to 45), or indefinitely (for people aged 46 and up). The cards hence cannot reflect various *hukou* changes. If the ID card can be made to carry people's complete *hukou* information and less expensive, thus easier to change and update, the high-tech plastic card may replace the low-tech paper booklet at some point. In the 2000s, the use of both the personal ID card and the *hukou* booklet is still routinely required to legally and fully identify a person, especially the *hukou* location and type for important purposes like applying for a passport (Chinese News Agency News Dispatch, Jan. 5, 2002).

43. In one Gaobeidian City in Hebei Province, over 2,000 people had two different *hukou* booklets and in one Xiaoguanying Township, half of the official copies of the 30,000 *hukou* registrations were "lost" in 1997. *Nanfang zhoumu* (Southern weekend), Guangzhou, May 10, 2001, 7.

44. The strict family planning and birth control policy that commonly levies heavy fines against those who exceed their authorized birth quota is chiefly responsible for nonregistration of newborns, especially in rural areas. Chinese peasants' desire to have at least one male child has fueled their resistance to the birth control policy since the 1970s. In one province in central China, unauthorized and unplanned births occurred to as many as 25–36 percent of the married couples in the mid-1990s. The fines for one such "extra birth" could be as high as one year's total household income (usually payable in 5–7 years). As a result, in some villages, "hidden" children could number as many as one per every 10–15 households (Cao Jinqing 2000, 16, 65, 109–13, 211–23, 347, 389, 520–21, 588, and 643).

45. Report by the MPS, in Wang Zhongfang 1993, 119.

46. By the mid-1990s, all of the sought-after special economic zones and major cities had developed such blue-seal *hukou* systems. Wu Changping 1996 and Wang Jianmin and Hu Qi 1996, 262–63. See the various regulations governing blue-seal *hukou* issued by the municipal governments of Dalian, Guangzhou, Nanjing, Shanghai, Taiyuan, 1992–2001. www.news.china.com, Dec. 5, 2001.

47. By late 2002, some medium- and small-size cities had eliminated the migrating-in quota and started to allow anyone "who meet[s] the requirements/conditions" to move in and get a permanent local *hukou* (Knight Ridder, "Residency Reforms to Ease Plight of Rural Poor," *The South China Morning Post*, Sept. 29, 2001). More on this in Chapter 7 of this book.

48. Interviews with *hukou* police in Haidian and Xicheng districts of Beijing, 1998–2002.

49. In Supreme People's Court of the PRC (vol. 1) 1989, 102–3.

50. The hospitality industry is officially designated a "special industry" that requires special attention and management from the police. Police regulations require all hotels to keep duplicates of check-in forms, as temporary *hukou* registrations, and guest lists for the police to inspect (Liu Jiarui 1998, 42–100).

51. Computers do not necessarily mean increased efficiency. For one report on that, see "Yige zhitou yu xiaolu" (One finger and efficiency), *Renmin gongan bao* (People's public security news), Beijing, Oct. 12, 2001.

52. A registration for temporary *hukou* is good for only three months before

a visitor must apply for *zanzhuzheng*. If a visitor plans to stay for more than one month, he should apply for a *zanzhuzheng* while registering for a temporary *hukou* within three days of arrival (Article 3 of the MPS's *Measure on Zanzhuzheng Application*, June 2, 1995).

53. Wu Changping 1996, 5. In Shenzhen, temporary *hukou* holders were more than 69 percent of the "registered" population of 2.6 million. In addition, there were at least 460 thousand unregistered "*manliu*" people (blind floaters) (Li Zongjian 1993, 50–51).

54. Shenzhen City Personnel Bureau 1994–97.

55. *Guanyu dajie he qudi feifa laowu zhongjia huodong de tonggao* (Notice on opposing and eliminating illegal labor referral activities), Urumqi, May 5, 1998. This notice, still effective in 2000, was based on the 1998 instructions from the PRC "Central Commission on Comprehensively Managing Public Security." It did not, however, wipe out the fairly common private and "unauthorized" hiring of outsiders in the city. Author's interviews in Urumqi, 2000.

56. For field studies and reports about the massive migrant population in the three major cities of Beijing, Shanghai, and Guangzhou, see Wang Ju et al. 1993, 38–42; Zhu Baoshu 1999, 38–45; Wang Guangzhou et al. 2000, 51–55; and Li Ling et al. 2001, 46–52.

57. Li Rujian 2001, 20–21.

58. Since the 1990s, local governments often organize contests to rank the households in terms of law-abiding, family harmony, hygiene, living standard, and even decoration. A three-, five-, seven-, or ten-star ranking system is commonly used, especially in rural areas. In the cities, the residential committees and groups also have similar contests but only rank the households with simpler labels such as "Harmonious Family" and "Good Hygiene Household." Better-ranked households, especially in rural areas, could get preferential treatment from the government in the form of employment, relief subsidies, loan guarantees, and even direct rewards of goods and money. Author's field notes, 1995–2002. For a justification of that practice and its "positive" role of social control and crime fighting, see Zhou Liangtuo 1991, 48–49. For an official case report on "Ten Star Rural Household" contests in Hunan Province, see *Qiushi* (For truth), CCP Central Committee Journal, Beijing, no. 245 (Apr. 2002), 39–41.

59. It has become a common belief in the PRC that migrants commit most of the crimes. While migrants indeed have a higher crime rate than local residents, their inclination for committing crimes may have been exaggerated due to statistical and psychological factors (Yu Depeng et al. 1998).

60. In one city, Xiamen, where 79–90 percent of all crime suspects arrested were migrant "outsiders," a new intranet of the *hukou* police was reported to be a very effective weapon that led to the reduction of the crime rate in the city for the first time in 2000–2001. *Xiamen ribao* (Xiamen daily), June 25, 2001, 5.

61. Li Zhongxin 1999, 11–13 and 23–24. For case studies of the newly focused police work on migrant people in various regions, see ibid., 40–42, 106–9, 116–18, 142–45, and 189–90.

62. Zhou Guoxiong 1995, 164–65.

63. Mu Xinshen et al. 1996, 5.

64. Author's interviews in Jiangsu and Anhui, 2001. Therefore, in many places, the police treat and "protect" the "illegal" but widespread prostitution as an endless source of "extra income" like Chinese chives that can be "cut" again and again. The fines, if documented, are to be divided between the local taxation bureau and the police station, which typically takes about one-third (Li Zhongxin 1998, 111).

65. Many of them are not properly registered or not registered at all. Thus the estimate of the size of the *liudong renkou* (migrant population) is not easy. An effort is made in Solinger 1999, 15–23, and later in Solinger 2001. Foreign reporters estimated as early as in 1994 that there were 100 million migrants already (Kuhn and Kaye 1994). Officially, Beijing believes the size to have been over 80 million by the mid-1990s and generally about 100 million by 2001 (Wu Xiaoping 2001, 146). For an in-depth academic study of China's migrant population, see Wang Jianmin and Hu Qi 1996. In 2004, Chinese media reported that in some major cities, "more than 30 percent of the population are not living in their own *hukou* zones." *Xian wanbao* (Xian evening news), Xian, Feb. 13, 2004.

66. The remote city of Lhasa, the capital of Tibet, had about 300 thousand permanent residents in 1998 but over 100 thousand migrant population. The small town of Gongga in Tibet also has dozens of migrants working in the restaurants near the airport. Author's interviews in Tibet, 1998.

67. Zhou Yi 1998, 85–86.

68. Nationally in 1995, there were about 80 million migrant people in China, but only about 44 million were registered with the police as "temporary residents." *Jingji ribao* (Economic daily), July 24, 1995, cited in Wang Jianmin and Hu Qi 1996, 41.

69. In one metropolis, Chongqing, for example, the police estimated internally that a staggering 52.3 percent of the migrant people in the city were "missed" in the temporary *hukou* registration in 1999 (Li Zhongxin 1999, 41). Similarly, 50–60 percent of Beijing's then over three million migrants were estimated as "not properly registered" by the *hukou* police in the mid-1990s (Ji Dangshen and Shao Qin 1995, 150–51, and Wang Jianmin and Hu Qi 1996, 262).

70. Most of China's private schools (primary to high schools and some colleges), fast growing after the 1980s, are mainly catering to the new rich only. For a report on that see Jing Lin 1999.

71. Matthews 1993, 63.

72. Hebei Province, for example, published its government fee schedules in 1998, and the fee was 6–8 RMB for a regular *hukou* booklet, 6 RMB for a *zanzhuzheng* (temporary resident permit), 30 RMB for a collective *hukou* booklet, and 10–20 RMB for a personal ID card. But there was also a 15 RMB per month fee for "managing" a temporary *hukou* holder. *Hebei ribao* (Hebei daily), Shijiazhuang, June 4, 1998, 12. The per capita income in the late 1990s was about 420–500 RMB per month for Hebei urban residents and 160–90 RMB per month for rural residents (SSB 2000, 293–315).

73. The MPS requires the police to complete uncomplicated *hukou* registra-

tion in one trip and at most in two trips (MPS-PD 1997, 127; MPS-PD 2001, 185). Yet, for a *zanzhuzheng* application, it is common to require the applicants to get official approval in the form of as many as 11 official seals. *Dadi* (Earth), no. 11 (Oct. 10, 2003).

74. The fee includes a onetime application fee and a monthly maintenance fee. In order to "reduce the size of the migrant population in the city," Beijing city raised its monthly fee for "temporary *hukou* management" from 15 RMB to 30–50 RMB in 1999 (*China Daily*, Beijing, Jan. 4, 1999, 3).

75. Such as in Beijing in 2003. The rationale of shorter-term *zanzhuzheng* is to prevent the employees in high-turnover industries to leave the original employer too soon.

76. Huang Mengdi 1997, 32–34.

77. *Guangming ribao* (Guangming daily), Beijing, Aug. 3, 1995, 4. In Beijing, a payment of 300–400 RMB would often be enough to make the police ignore an expired *zanzhuzheng*, and many migrants without *zanzhuzheng* asserted that they had "never been stopped by the police [for a check of their papers] unless [they had been] caught for something else" (author's interviews, 2003–4).

78. Author's interviews in Beijing and Guangdong, 1998–2002. For journalistic stories of *hukou*-related crime and corruption, see Tian Bingxin 2003, 185–232.

79. Figures calculated based on the information in Li Zhongxin 1999, various pages and MPS 2001, various pages.

80. Shanghai initiated this practice in 1991. Shanghai Bureau of Public Security, *Provisional Regulations on 24-hour Reception of Hukou Matters at Police Stations*, Shanghai, Dec. 28, 1990.

81. The conclusion by an official study in Beijing (Ji Dangshen and Shao Qin 1995, 148).

82. Li Ling 2001, 46 and 50.

83. MPS-BPT 2000, 115–16.

84. Sun Yao 1994, 49–51 and 155–57; MPS-BPT 2000, 127–31. For detailed specification of the migrant registration, see MPS-PSMB 2001, 472–81.

85. Sun Yao 1994, 159–62; MPS-BPT 2000, 131–35.

86. Like the Migrant *Hukou* Certificate's 30-day legal effect, the *Hukou* Relocation Permit's 40-day expiration limit is not very seriously enforced in practice. For voluntary or involuntary reasons (such as the lack of a current quota in the new *hukou* zone), migrants were observed holding the Certificate and the Permit for up to a year or even longer before completing the migration registration. Author's field notes, 1996–2001.

87. MPS-EB 1997, 86.

88. Author's interviews with *hukou* police in Anhui, Beijing, Guangdong, Jiangsu, and Shanghai, 1993–95 and 1998–2003. The *hukou*-related fees and fines are only part of the police's "created" extra income. The budgetary constraints and rising living cost have forced some police stations to devote as much as 70 percent of their time to "create" more extra income. For example, see the case report on police work in a county seat of Jiangxi Province in Li Zhongxin

1998, 111. For a discussion on such common "collective violation" of law and regulations by a *danwei* (work unit) in the PRC, see Lei Hong 1998.

89. Although internal migration is strictly controlled and hence remains low in the PRC, the absolute size of population movement has been very large. Chinese scholars estimate that from the 1950s to the 1990s, on average about 20 million Chinese moved throughout the *hukou* system every year (Li Debin et al. 1994, 339–45). Among them, the *qianyi* (permanent *hukou* relocation) was only less than 10 percent (Wang Guixin 1997, 306–8). Cross-province *qianyi* was about 400 thousand a year in the second half of the 1980s (Zha Ruichuan et al. 1996, 18).

90. *Nanfang Zhoumuo* (Southern weekend), Guangzhou, Aug. 31, 2001.

91. Hebei Province, for example, published its fees for migration registrations. In 1998, the fee was 3 RMB for each migrant *hukou* certificate or each *hukou* relocation permit. *Hebei ribao* (Hebei daily), Shijiazhuang, June 4, 1998, 12.

92. In the late 1990s, the fee was 3,000 to 10 thousand in the relatively less expensive Tianjin and 20 to 25 thousand in the moderately attractive Fuzhou. *Zhongguo qingnian bao* (Chinese youth daily), Beijing, Apr. 15, 1997, 7. In the remote large city of Urumqi and small city of Shihezhi in Xinjiang, the fee was 8,000 and 5,000 RMB respectively. Author's interviews in Xinjiang, 2000. In the 2001 reform of the *hukou* system, the small cities and towns in the PRC started to waive their previously required urban construction or expansion fees.

93. Yu Jing 1991, 56.

94. MPS-PD 1997, 127; MPS-PD 2001, 185.

95. The MPS started to establish an electronic database for the *hukou* system in 1986, and the PRC state set up a special fund for computerization of the *hukou* database in 1992. That effort was largely completed by 1999 (MPS-DOP 1999, 75–76).

96. *Zhongguo qingnian bao* (Chinese youth daily), Beijing, Jan. 5, 2002.

97. *Xinhua Daily Telegraph*, Beijing, Sept. 1, 2000.

98. Author's interviews with police in Beijing, Chongqing, Hefei, and Shanghai, 2000–2004.

99. Author's interviews in Beijing, Chongqing, Guangdong, Jiangsu, and Shanghai, 2000–2003.

100. For an examination of the Chinese labor market, see Meng 2000.

Chapter 4

1. For examples, see Solinger 1999, Darvin 1999, Wang 1998 *Family*, Chan and Zhang 1999, and Dutton 1999.

2. Wang Huaian 1989, 1502.

3. The PRC currently has a *hukou*-based categorization of the population: nonagricultural *hukou* holders versus agricultural *hukou* holders. It also has a statistical categorization of urban population (those who live in cities or townships) and rural population. The concept of "urban population" may include some agricultural *hukou* holders who live inside the boundaries of a city or a

township. That is, "urban population" is likely to be larger than "nonagricultural population" while the latter is the legally meaningful term in the *hukou* system (tables 7 to 13 of Tian Xueyuan 1995, 291–97). For a rather problematic interpretation of these two sets of categorization, see Harry Xiaoying Wu 1994, 674–75. By 2004, the *hukou* reforms since 2001 had begun to merge the two categorizations in the small cities and towns.

4. MPS-BPT 2000, 118.

5. Wang Taiyuan 1997, 233, and Lu Yilong 2003, 115–16.

6. MPS-BPT 2000, 119, and Wang 1998 *Family*, 87–162.

7. Wang Taiyuan 1997, 234.

8. Even in Shanghai, one of the most developed and open cities in China, all agricultural *hukou* holders as well as all non-Shanghai urban *hukou* holders are still clearly excluded from housing benefits, public schools, many college education opportunities, and newly socialized pension and health care plans. Author's field notes, 1998–2004.

9. Wu Zhongmin and Lin Juren 1998, 71–81. Urban migrants, however, tend to be better off than rural migrants primarily due to the relatively easier change of their *hukou* location and their better education and higher working skills.

10. The mostly talked about official reasons have been "to maintain an orderly construction of the urban economy," "to avoid overburdening the urban infrastructure," and "to ensure enough grain producing manpower in the countryside" (Sun Yao 1994, 139–47).

11. Sun Yao 1994, 141.

12. *Renmin ribao* (People's daily), Beijing, Sept. 24, 2001, 9; *South China Morning Post*, Sept. 29, 2001; China News Agency News Dispatch, Guangzhou, Sept. 24, 2001; and *Nanfang dushibao* (Southern metro daily), Guangzhou, Sept. 8, 2001 and May 11, 2004. More on this in Chapter 7.

13. Sun Yao 1994, 147–50.

14. Wang Zhongfang 1996.

15. MPS-BPT 2000, 121; Wang Taiyuan 1997, 235.

16. MPS-BPT 2000, 139; emphasis added.

17. Solinger 1999, 55.

18. For a study on the active and targeted use of the *hukou* system to move and relocate people in the PRC before 1979, see Tian and Lin 1986.

19. According to an internal assessment, the "chaotic" operation of *hukou* relocation is a major problem that needs to be addressed nationwide (Wang Taiyuan 1997, 243).

20. CCP Central Organization Department et al., *Notice on Reaffirmation of Restricting Cadres Moving into Beijing*, May 1, 1981, in CPB-PB 1985, 236–38.

21. Ibid., 237.

22. Gutherie 1999.

23. See, for example, the various regulations governing blue-seal *hukou* issued by the municipal governments of Dalian, Guangzhou, Nanjing, Shanghai, Taiyuan, 1992–2001. www.news.china.com, accessed Feb. 19, 2002.

24. In some places, blue-seal *hukou* holders still report that they cannot access

certain locally subsidized benefits such as job training and placement. Author's interviews in Shanghai and Beijing, 2000–2002.

25. In Shenzhen, internal regulations require a blue-seal *hukou* holder to pass an annual verification of qualifications. A blue-seal *hukou* holder may apply for a permanent local *hukou* if he is "younger than 45 years old," maintains his qualifications for four years, and has a good record of birth planning (Shenzhen City Personnel Bureau, *Shenzhen renshi*, no. 6 [1995], 22–24).

26. By the mid-1990s, all of China's sought-after special economic zones (SEZs) adopted localized but largely similar regulations on the blue-seal *hukou* (Wu Changping et al. 1996).

27. The most expensive locations have been Beijing, Shanghai, and Shenzhen. For some smaller cities, the mentioned monetary requirement can be substantially less.

28. For example, when the government of Wuxi City in Jiangsu Province devised a similar scheme that seemed to resemble an "auction" of its blue-seal *hukou*, Beijing ordered the Jiangsu Provincial Government to stop the Wuxi initiative and reprimanded the responsible cadres in a nationwide circular. Interview in Jiangsu, 1998. Also see MPS-PSMB 2001, 252–55. For more on the illegal auction of urban *hukou* in other areas and the central government's reaction to it, see Lu Yilong 2003, 149–52.

29. The author's interviewees on this also revealed that rich but mediocre students could secretly "purchase" such local *hukou* quotas as were allocated to the departments of the top colleges at graduation time, with the rough equivalent of four-year tuition, if they could manage to get local job offers. Interviews in Beijing and Shanghai, 1997–2000. For reports about similar "purchase of *hukou* quotas" from authorized employers in Beijing, see *Zhongguo qingnian bao* (Chinese youth daily), Beijing, Jan. 12, 2004, and *Gongren ribao* (Worker's daily), Beijing, Jan. 14, 2004.

30. Wang Hongjun 1999, 33.

31. Martin King Whyte, "Book Review," *The China Journal*, issue 45 (Jan. 2001), 162.

32. For the special *hukou* policy regarding Ph.D. degree holders and their families, see Personnel Ministry documents (1992) 11, 16, and 23, in Legal Bureau of Personnel Ministry 1993, 393–420.

33. Not do only many urban centers use their attractive *hukou* to selectively admit "useful" migrants, but some wealthy rural communities (such as the highly promoted and very prosperous Jinghua Corporation or Group no. Five of Eastern Street of Xiaoji Township of Xinxiang County in Henan Province) also "use [local] *hukou* to attract and reward outside talents" (Cao Jinqing 2000, 442).

34. To mitigate the internal brain drain, the government also requires that the universities admit some *daipei sheng* (students educated specifically for their home towns). They are paid for their education by their home towns/provinces and must return after graduation or face a heavy fine. Author's interviews with university officials in Beijing and Shanghai, 2000–2004.

35. See the cases reported in Yang Shoujian 2001, esp. 95–143 and 187–303.

For an investigation about the "dark inside" of graduate program admissions, see *Zhongguo qingnian bao* (Chinese youth daily), Beijing, Nov. 28, 2000.

36. State Council directives in 1984, 1987, and 1993, cited in Ma Fuyun 2000, 67.

37. Wang Hongjun 1999, 34.

38. MPS-BPT 2000, 124.

39. Still, if the father's or stepfather's *hukou* is in a major or large city, the child will have to wait for the available quota. State Council–approved MPS Document *Guanyu jieju dangqian hukou guanli gongzu zhong de jige tuochu wenti de yijian* (Suggestions on solving some of the major issues in the current *hukou* management work), Beijing, July 1998. In Beijing, for example, only an "approved" child born after July 22, 1998 can adopt a father's local *hukou* (Xinhua, Mar. 12, 2002). This reform itself, however, has been rightly praised by many as a victory for the rural women as well as a sign of social progress in general. Interviews in China, 2000.

40. Ji Chuanpai, "Yidi hunyan duo qilai" (Cross-region marriages increased), *Beijing ribao* (Beijing daily), Aug. 17, 1999.

41. *Beijing wanbao* (Beijing evening news), May 13, 2003.

42. Some of those "special" workers, such as sailors on the overseas ocean liners, may be granted *nongzhuanfei* permits for their agricultural *hukou*-holding spouses. See State Council document (1992) 65, and Personnel Ministry documents (1992) 11, 16, and 23, in Legal Bureau of Personnel Ministry 1993, 548–51.

43. The PRC's national network of religious associations and bureaus of civil affairs is responsible for accrediting and registering "*bona fide*" religious organizations.

44. Wang Hongjun 1999, 45–46; MPS-PSMB 2001, 565 and 571–72.

45. Author's interview in Shanghai, 1996 and 1997.

46. For a sketch of this kind of internal migration, see Chan and Zhang 1999.

47. The so-called "three-no" people (people who have no legal *hukou* papers, no permanent local residence, and no permanent local job) are often termed *mangliu* (blind floaters). In the 2000s, there were still plenty of horror stories of the forced repatriation of "undocumented" floating people. For a personal account of being mistakenly treated as a floating peasant, see Huang Qian, "Ermeng bande qiansong" (Nightmarish repatriation), www.overseasforum.com.cn, Oct. 2, 2001. For more on the repatriation policy and its latest development in 2003-2004, see Chapter 7 of this book.

48. Li Mengbai et al. 1991, 55. Forcible repatriation was officially reformed in 2003 and replaced with anti-pauper policies in 2004. Author's field notes, 2002–2004.

49. The PRC central government formally issued three regulations governing those rotating workers in 1984. See Gao Shangquan 1993, 648.

50. Usually, the author has observed, those peasant workers have often become the most productive segment of the employees.

51. MPS 2001, 302.

52. *The State Council's Notice on the Issues of Peasants Residing in Towns,* issued on Oct. 13, 1984, in Wang Huaian 1989, 1552–53.

53. Chen Chunnong 1986, 166–67.

54. Wang Hongjun 1999, 48–49.

55. Sun Yao 1994, 151–52, and MPS-BPT 2000, 125–26.

56. For a survey and an explanation of China's widespread corruption, see Xiaobo Lu 2000.

57. For how the detained floaters can be physically abused and even group-raped, see *Zhonguo qingnian bao* (Chinese youth daily), Beijing, July 26, 2001. For how a permitless migrant was beaten to death in the process of deportation, see China News Agency News Dispatch, Beijing, June 15, 2003.

58. For public discussion of the *hukou* system in the 2000s, see Chapter 7 of this book.

59. Wang Taiyuan 2000, 237–57.

60. As recently as 1992, a state cadre who dared to write a letter to the government complaining about the unfairness of the *hukou* system could lose his job and get two years in prison. *Nanfang zhoumo* (South weekend), Mar. 7, 2002, 6.

61. For reports on some of those centers and stations, see *Zhongguo minzhen* (China civil affairs), Beijing, no. 1 (2001), 55–56, and no. 11 (2001), 56.

62. *Shehui* (Society), Shanghai, no. 9 (2001), 9.

63. MPS *Zhifa shouce* (vol. 15) 1995, 909–10. The sale of urban *hukou* apparently was significant. One study reported that, from 1978 to 1993, various local government "sold" about three million urban *hukou* to rural residents with a total revenue of 25 billion RMB for the local governments (Jiang Yimin and Guo Yaxin 1994, 12).

64. Gao Shangquan 1993, 675. For the 1988 prohibition, see the State Council notice dated Oct. 29, 1988, in Supreme People's Court of the PRC (vol. 3) 1990, 23–24.

65. *Renmin ribao* (People's daily), Beijing, Sept. 24, 2001, 9; *South China Morning Post,* Sept. 29, 2001; *Nanfang ribao* (Southern daily), Guangzhou, Apr. 1, 2004; and *Zhongguo qingnian bao* (Chinese youth daily), Beijing, Apr. 14, 2004.

66. www.news.china/zh_cn/focus/hjzd, a website of the official *Renmin ribao* (People's daily), accessed Jan. 16, 2002; *Nanfang dushibao* (Southern metro daily), Guangzhou, Sept. 8, 2001; and China News Agency News Dispatch, Guangzhou, Sept. 24, 2001.

67. For the details of these duties, see MPS-BPT 2000, 148–51.

68. The police assistants are commonly called *lianfang duiyuan* (joint-defense team members) or *zhian yuan* (public security personnel) and are generally recruited from local communities. They are considered and used as supplemental law-enforcement agents and can be twice as many as the regular police officers in some police stations. They normally get paid about one-third to half of a police officer's salary. Some of their pay comes from the income of the various fines collected by the police station, which gets to use 60 percent of the fines it has collected (Cao Jinqing 2000, 464–65).

69. Those informants play crucial, albeit "secretive," roles in the operation of

targeted people management and Chinese police work in general. For instructions to the local police on how to recruit, cultivate, manage, and utilize informants, see MPS-PTB 1999, 234–52.

70. Chen Chunlong 1986, 112–13. The residential committee system was set up in the 1950s (Shurmann 1966, 374–80) and continued in the 2000s.

71. Feng Xiaoying, "Beijing chengshi shequ guanli de chuangxin: jingyan, wenti yu duice" (Innovation in Beijing's community management: lessons, issues and measures), *Qianxian* (Frontier), Beijing, no. 3 (2001).

72. For an internal case study of cultivating and utilizing informants, see Li Zhongxin 1999, 192–93.

73. Interview with *hukou* police in Chongwen and Haidian Districts, Beijing, 1999–2001.

74. Sun Yao 1994, 104 and 37.

75. Sun Yao 1994, 105.

76. MPS-BPT 2000, 195.

77. Sun Yao 1994, 107.

78. Author's interviews, 1998–2001.

79. For example, some communities in Hainan's Haikou city were reported to assign each CCP member in the community a few households to be "assured" of being free of illegal activities such as the use of narcotics. "Women de xiaoxiang 'zongguan'" ("General manager" of our little lane), *Hainan ribao* (Hainan daily), June 25, 2001, 8.

80. A leading cause for that rapid and "sudden" surge of crime, according to the police's internal study, was the relaxation of *hukou*-based migration control and the massive numbers of the migrant population that may or may not be on the *hukou* police's radar screen (Li Zhongxin 1999, 9–13, 18–19).

81. Yao Weizhang 2003, *Gongan zhifa*, 154–58.

82. Since the 1990s there has been a noticeable increase of legal cases in which Chinese citizens sue to settle disputes even with the government. For one case report, see Elisabeth Rosenthal, "Chinese, Too, Start to Sue to Protect Their Rights," *International Herald Tribune*, June 18, 2001, 2.

83. The local information on the targeted people is classified as "public security secrets" and "an important part of the state secrets" (Liu Donglin 1989, 426).

84. MPS-BPT 2000, 162–64.

85. Chongqing police reports in 1998, in Li Zhongxin 1999, 43.

86. Criminals apprehended in the Chinese cities often are mostly (60 to even 90 percent) rural migrants, with or without a temporary *hukou*. A case-study on this is Hong Lu and Shunfeng Song, "Rural Worker Migration and City Transient Crime," a conference paper, Xiamen, 2001.

87. Since 1983 (Xi Guoguang and Yu Lei et al. 1997, 371–80) and with increased frequency (from once every 1–2 years in the mid-1980s to more than once a year by the late 1990s), the PRC has launched many "harsh striking" campaigns for various reasons, sometimes just to "clean things up" for important dates such as National Day, Hong Kong and Macao's returns to China in 1997 and 1999, or when the National People's Congress is in session (every March).

Author's field notes 1997–2004. For the rise of crime in China and especially organized crime, see Liu Shangyi 1997 and Huang Yiding 2001, 30–33. For the reemphasis on "continuing the harsh striking policy" by Luo Gan, the CCP's public security boss, see *Beijing ribao* (Beijing daily), Nov. 13, 2003, 2.

88. MPS-BPT 2000, 170. For the instructions to the police on how to specially manage the employees and customers of these industries, see MPS-DOP 1999, 96–112.

89. In one urban *hukou* zone, we were informed that "about 1 percent" of the population should be on the list. Too many could mean the "security environment is bad" there, too few would mean "sloppy police work" in the police station, and neither would be praiseworthy in the eyes of the superiors. Author's field notes, 2001.

90. Police internal reports from Chongqing and Henan, in Li Zhongxin 1999, 43 and 144.

91. Tianjin's Gansu Road police station internal report in 1998, in Li Zhongxin 1999, 180, 186, and 190.

92. Police report from Xinxiang City of Henan Province, in Li Zhongxin 1998, 60–61. In a county in Jiangxi Province, one police station was found in 1996 to have only two out of its 23 targeted people effectively monitored and controlled. Li Zhongxin 1998, 108.

93. Wang Taiyuan 1997, 319–23.

94. A 1998 police report from Shijiazhuang, the capital of Hebei Province, in Li Zhongxin 1998, 53.

95. MPS-EB 1996 and MPS-Team 1997. The often clandestine police work of "political investigation," however, is banned inside the CCP itself (Gao Guiting 1994, 142).

96. National data on the targeted people is classified as *jimi* (critical secrets), more secretive than just "state secrets (*mimi*)" (Liu Donglin 1989, 425).

97. Liu Jiarui 1998, 7–41 and 47–70; Mu Xinshen 1996, 173; and *Xin fagui yuekan* (New laws and regulations monthly), Shanghai, Feb. 2001, 43–47.

98. The police internally reported that many of the special industry establishments have now been penetrated and even controlled by organized crime. In Shenzhen, for example, among the 139 karaoke halls and dancing floors, at least 32 were found to be controlled by organized crime in the mid-1990s (Liu Shangyi 1997, 132–33).

99. Classified police case reports concluded that the *hukou* database and the targeted people management were highly useful in the destruction of several terrorist cells in Xinjiang (Cheng and Bo 2000, 129–30, 164, and 253–54).

100. Author's interviews, 2000–2002.

101. Interviews reported by China Net's News Center on www.newsw.china.com, Aug. 20, 2001, accessed Feb. 19, 2002.

102. The police concluded that lack of good management of the targeted people in many remote towns and villages was a major reason for "unnecessary" delays and police casualties in the campaigns against several terrorist cells, since some of the cell members were on the targeted-people list but somehow slipped out of police monitoring and control (Cheng and Bo 2000, 147–48, 214, 316, and 331).

103. By 2003, Falungong's once powerful organization and mobilization ability were largely destroyed on the Chinese mainland, thanks in no small part to the work of the *hukou* police.

Chapter 5

1. Minxin Pei 2002, 96–109.

2. Nationally, over 50 percent of all cadres and officials, 20 percent of the military, 50 percent of college faculty, and 10 percent of college students were CCP members in the mid-1990s. Author's interview in Beijing, 1996. The rural CCP members, often the demobilized draftees of the PLA and usually the political elite in the villages, are generally poorly organized and much less active than the CCP cells in the cities (Cao Jinqing 2000, 390).

3. The PRC government has four layers below the central government: province/metropolis, prefecture/city/district, county/city, and township. The county and especially the township government often appoints or affects the elections of the heads of administrative villages that are usually large villages or collections of a few small "natural" villages.

4. CCP Central Committee and State Council joint directives in 1983, 1986–87, and 1991–92, in Renshibu and Zhongzhubu 1993, 131–44.

5. A joint report by the Helongjiang Province Personnel Bureau and CCP Helongjiang Provincial Committee's Organizational Department, in Renshibu and Zhongzhubu 1993, 82–83, 87–88.

6. Renshibu and Zhongzhubu 1993. In practice, however, some of those *pinyong* cadres got promoted to be "formal state cadres" and eventually became permanent urban *hukou* holders.

7. *The PRC Law on NPC and People's Deputy Election at All Levels*, Beijing, Feb. 1952, revised Feb. 1995. For an examination of the CCP's design of an unequal election system in the PRC, see Yu Depeng 2002, 178–80.

8. Chen Chunnong 1986, 123–24.

9. A speech by Qiao Xiaoyang, the Vice Chairman of the Legal Committee of the NPC, at a press conference in Beijing on May 19, 1995. He further stated that "as an eventual goal, we will have the same ratio of representation" in the rural and urban areas (*Xinhua Daily Telegraph*, May 19, 1995). By 2004, this promise had yet to be fulfilled. This is, indeed, an interesting reversal of the similarly disproportional election system in Japan before its 1990s election reforms.

10. Chinese scholars seem to have also realized and openly admitted this (Zhu Qingfang 1998, 63).

11. Economic growth with the "assistance" of institutional exclusion may be viewed as a peculiar case of economic growth based on a certain combination of the market and the state or societal forces (Wade 1990 and Haggard 1990). For an attempt to describe it in the Chinese context, see Justin Lin et al. 2003.

12. For an examination of the "population" pressure as the "most basic of China's basic national conditions and the most difficult of China's difficulties," see Tian Xueyuan 1997.

13. Zhang Siqian 1988, 98–114; SSB 1992, 15–18; SSB-PB 1993, 66 and 88; Niu Renliang 1993, 145–49; and SSB 2001. The Chinese rural labor force was

seven times larger than the combined rural labor force in the fifty-two African countries in the 1980s and about 29 times larger than the total rural labor force in the twenty-seven European nations in the late 1980s (Wang Guichen 1988, 112).

14. Ma Hong and Wang Mengkui 2001, 190.

15. Chinese economists seem to have realized this. See Ma Xia 1994, 188–89.

16. Estimates of China's growth rate vary, but most agree that the Chinese economy grew at an average of above 8 percent annually for the past two decades (Lardy 2002, 11–13). According to the *Financial Times* (Oct. 13, 2003, 6), China's GDP growth was perhaps underreported and could have been as high as 11 percent in 2003 despite a severe epidemic.

17. Hu and Yang et al. 2000, 294–95. The Chinese government acquired its strong capacity for direct and indirect value-extraction in the early years of the PRC (Shaoguang Wang 2001).

18. Such a state capability may easily be abused. From the 1950s to the end of the 1970s, for example, Beijing carried out its economic development programs in a nonmarket fashion and literally wasted much of the capital it accumulated in many projects such as the "Third Front" developments.

19. Cook and Maurer-Fazio 1999.

20. For the labor-absorbing and stabilizing effect of the family-based labor allocation in the Chinese countryside, see Wang 1998 *Family*, 66–76.

21. Solinger 1999, 37 and 54.

22. There have been reports of how those migrant rural laborers are exploited and abused in cities and development zones. For example, see Solinger 1999. For a published account by Chinese scholars, see West and Zhao 2000. For a report on the deterioration of workers' rights in China, see Erik Eckholm, "Workers' Rights Slip Away in China," *International Herald Tribune*, Aug. 23, 2001, 1.

23. For example, in the increasingly common demonstrations and riots that sometimes stopped railway and highway traffic for many hours in the Lower Yangtze River Delta region, the "outside" or migrant workers who suffered most actually participated least, out of the six social groups of residents identified (Ding Yuanzhu 2000, 136).

24. The exploitation of the migrant peasant masses has been a hallmark of the economic prosperity in many of the Eastern/coastal regions. For reports on the migrant workers and their treatment in the Pearl River Delta, see Wang 1998 *Family*, 257–58 and 265–72, and Tan Shen 2000.

25. Deng Xiaoping 1983, 222. Jiang Zemin reaffirmed Deng's strategy and called for "allowing and encouraging some regions and some people to get rich first through honest work and law-abiding operations." Jiang's speech at the Fifth Plenum Meeting of the Fourteenth CCP Central Committee, Sept. 28, 1995. Jiang repeated these words in his speech at the celebration of the 80th anniversary of the CCP on July 1, 2001 (Jiang Zemin 2001, 179). Some PRC theorists think this is a "must" strategy and a "socialist grand policy" for China's modernization (Yu Xiaoqiu et al. 1994, 64–65, and Zhou Shangwe et al. 1997, 116–28), while others believe the strategy offers the "right recipes for economic development" everywhere (Chung ed. 1999).

26. Zhang and Song 2001.

27. Hugo Restall, "Decision Time Approaches on the Yuan," *Asian Wall Street Journal*, Oct. 31, 2003. Many have similarly argued for a drastic appreciation of the Chinese currency in a way similar to the 1985 Plaza Accord for the Japanese yen. For a different view, see Fei-Ling Wang, "Chinese and American Currencies: Pegging for Stability," *Aspenia*, The Aspen Institute, Rome, Italy, no. 24 (English edition) (May) 2004.

28. For example, Zhang Shanyu et al. 1996, 124–38.

29. For the rural reform and development in the 1980s, see Kelliher 1992.

30. Harry Xiaoying Wu 1994, 691–92.

31. For a report on the migrant workers in the rural industries in Southern Jiangsu Province, see Hu Haili 1998, 34–38. For an extensive examination of the *hukou*'s role of institutional exclusion in the villages, very tight in some places, see Zhang Jing 2000, 90–105. For a sociological investigation of the discrimination and exclusion against the migrant workers in the rural areas of the coastal provinces, see Yao Yang 2001, 32–41.

32. Wang 1998 *Family*, 163–220.

33. For a study of the Nanjie experience, see Liu Qian, "Renmin gongshe zhidu yichan yu zhongguo tese de shichang jingji" (Legacy of the people's commune system and market economy with Chinese characteristics), *Zhongguo shehui kexue jikan* (Chinese social science quarterly), no. 31 (Fall 2000), 177–86. For the "leftist" summaries and praises of this socialist "revolutionary" model of economic development, see "Wei jianshi gongchan zhuyi xiao shequ er fengdou" (To struggle to construct a communist small community) by Wang Hongbin, the party secretary of Nanjie Village, and the accompanying four articles and essays in *Zhongliu* (Midstream), Beijing, no. 139 (July 2001), 22–32.

34. Cao Jinqing 2000, 141–48. Such local *hukou*-based community benefits exist in all prosperous rural communities. In Qizhong Village, a "model" rural community outside Shanghai that also employed a large number of "outside" laborers, the village sells its one to two million RMB worth of cottages only to village *hukou* holders for a low price of 10–70 thousand RMB. Author's field notes in Shanghai, 2000–2002. Apparently, rural communities that have developed strong industries and become prosperous have greatly benefited from the cheap outside laborers. In the "star" rural communities, like Nanjie, Zhulin, and Jinghua in Hennan, Daqiu in Tianjin, and Huaxi and Shengzhi in Jiangsu, outside laborers commonly outnumber the privileged local laborers manyfold (Zhou Yi 1998, 85; Cao Jinqing 2000, 158–59 and 425–42).

35. An A. T. Keaney study in 2002 concluded that China replaced the U.S. as the most "attractive" place for foreign investors (Chris Giles, "China Attracts More Investors than the U.S.," *The Financial Times*, London, Sept. 23, 2002).

36. Yasheng Huang, "FDI in China," *Case Study Series*, Cambridge, MA, Harvard Business School, 2003, 8.

37. *Dadi* (Earth), Beijing, no. 96 (Dec.) 1999, 50–52. For a comment on the "confrontational" political and economic reforms in Venezuela, see *Economist*, Nov. 24, 2001, 38. For the Mexican problems, see the special reports in *The New York Times*, May 25 and Aug. 21, 2001. For troubled Argentina, a "country in

Chapter 11" and in "an epic of frustration" that had five presidents in two weeks (Dec. 20, 2001–Jan. 2, 2002), see the relevant reports and articles in *The New York Times*, Dec. 22, 2001, and Jan. 5–6, 2002.

38. China's bold and arguably hastily decided accession to the WTO (World Trade Organization) in 2001 has sparked the still largely "underground" discussions among Chinese intellectuals about the danger of a Latin-Americanization in China. That is, China may repeat the Brazilian and Argentinean stories and get stuck in the predatory net of the international financial system. That way, as one well-known scholar commented privately, China "would forever lose its chance of breaking out to be a real economic power." Author's interviews in Beijing and Shanghai, 2001–3. For one scholarly discussion, see Pan Wei 2003, especially 410.

39. UNDP 2001, 144 and 157; G8 Okinawa Summit 2000, i.

40. APMRN 2001, 2–4.

41. Wang Fang, "Chengshihua yu renkou xiandaihua de guangxi" (Relationship between urbanization and population modernization), *Renkou yanjiu* (Population research), Beijing, vol. 25.1 (2001), 31.

42. China's urban population in the mid-19th century (according to Skinner 1977), however, could be significantly exaggerated since Skinner only calculated the urban population figures in the 18 relatively more developed provinces, excluding the provinces in the more backward Northeast, Northwest, Inner Mongolia, and Tibet.

43. According to Yang Fan, a senior researcher at the Institute of Economic Studies, Chinese Social Science Academy, Oct. 2001.

44. Forgel 1999, 1–2.

45. Zhong Yicai, "Chengxiang eyuan shehui de yonghe yu yingnong jingcheng" (The merging of the dual urban-rural societies and the pulling of the peasants into the cities) in *Shehui kexue* (Social sciences), Shanghai, no. 1 (1995), 55–58.

46. SSB 2001, "Cong gini xishu," 29.

47. PRC State Statistical Bureau data, *Zhongguo guoqing guoli* (China's national conditions and strength), Beijing, no. 97 (Jan. 2001), 28.

48. Liu Cuixiao, "Zhongguo nongmin de shehui baozhang wenti" (The issue of social security for Chinese peasants), *Faxue yanjiu* (Legal studies), Beijing, no. 2 (2002).

49. Among the 259 thousand poor that were protected in 2001 in that city, 230 thousand were rural *hukou* holders. *Nanfang zhoumu* (Southern weekend), Guangzhou, Oct. 18, 2001, 2.

50. Official figures in *Zhongguo guoqing guoli* (China's national conditions and strength), Beijing, no. 97 (Jan. 2001), 28.

51. Meng and Zhang 2001.

52. For example, the families of many fresh Ph.D. degree earners simply pressured them to "just get a job" in a major urban center, usually the metropolises like Beijing and Shanghai, so the whole family could settle there, forgoing the many years of highly specialized study and research. Author's field notes, 1999–2003. In Chongqing, a metropolis in Southwestern China, when the state-

owned Chongqing Department Store wanted to hire 100 sales clerks (with a meager pay of 500–800 Yuan RMB a month but high job security) from local *hukou* holders, over 3,000 people applied and an unbelievable 70 percent of them were overqualified college graduates. *Chongqing wanbao* (Chongqing evening news), Chongqing, Oct. 24, 2001. In Shenzhen, as many as 12.34 percent of the unemployed were college graduates, crowded in the prosperous urban center. *Xinhua ribao* (Xinhua daily), Nanjing, Oct. 12, 2001.

53. Hu Angang et al. 1995, 223.

54. There are, naturally, many other factors responsible for the East-West gap in China. Dali Yang (1999) described a Chinese political system in which the PRC has been led by an east coast "oligarchy" and the interests of the East dominate.

55. Lu Wenlong and Huang Minyou 1998, 21. The "developed region" sometimes includes the later-created Chongqing Municipality. For a minority dissenting view that believes the studies on China's regional disparity are largely inconclusive and the situation may not be very serious, see Yanrui Wu 1999, 17–19.

56. Officially, the PRC calls all twelve provinces/metropolises along the Chinese coast "Eastern China": Beijing, Fujian, Guangdong, Guangxi, Hainan, Hebei, Jiangsu, Liaoning, Shandong, Shanghai, Tianjin, and Zhejiang. See Anhui Provincial Government 1995, 93.

57. Guo Tong, "Keji touru: Dongzhongxibu bupingheng" (R&D investment: Uneven among the east, central and west), *Zhongguo xinxibao* (China journal of information), Beijing, Aug. 3, 1995, 1; SSB 2000 and SSB 2001, chapter 2.

58. SSRC 1998 # 273, 22.

59. Hu and Zou 2000, 5.

60. Data provided by Yang Fan, a senior researcher at the Institute of Economic Studies, Chinese Social Science Academy, Oct. 2001.

61. SSB, "1993 shehui fazhan shuiping baogao" (Report on social development in 1993), *Liaowang* (Outlook), Beijing, Feb. 10, 1995, 10–11.

62. Observations revealed that the technological level was much lower in the western provinces and vertical income inequality there was also larger than in the east (Xu Fongxian and Wang Zhengzhong 1995, 5; MPS 2001, 3; and SSB 2001, 49, 56–57).

63. Zhu Qingfang 1998, 63.

64. Hu and Zou 2000, 3.

65. State Statistical Bureau data, *Zhongguo xinxibao* (Chinese journal of information), Beijing, Aug. 1, 1995, 1.

66. State Planning Commission figures, *Jingji gongzhuzhe xuexi ziliao* (Study materials for economic workers), Beijing, no. 68 (1994), 7.

67. *Hunan ribao* (Hunan daily), Changsha, Apr. 18, 2001.

68. Li Rujian 2001, 21.

69. Tibet actually even had a different tax system until 1994 when the PRC adopted a new and uniform tax system for the nation. *Renmin ribao* (People's Daily), Beijing, May 20, 1994.

70. Bureau of Economic Analysis, U.S. Department of Commerce, www.bea.doc.gov/bea/newsrel/SPINewsRelease.htm, accessed Nov. 25, 2003.

71. For the detailed state-mandated regional differentiation (by county) in pay

and subsidies in the different regions from 1954 to 1977, see Ministry of Personnel (vol. 2) 1986, 22–25, 86–126, and 478–87.

72. Data provided by Yang Fan, a senior researcher at the Institute of Economic Studies, Chinese Social Science Academy, Oct. 2001. Rural residents of the central province of Henan were commonly charged two to three times as much as urban residents for electricity (Cao Jinqing 2000, 601 and 744).

73. Some provincial and prefectural governments set up and enforce quotas for shipping in goods from outside (Chen Dongyou 1999, 206). Even the official journals start to list various "striking" cases of regional and local protectionism that damages law enforcement and market development. *Dadi* (Earth), Beijing, no. 101 (May 2001), 46–47.

74. One author even estimates that by 2020, the "Greater Chinese Economy" may form up to ten distinctive economic regions (Keng 2001, 607–10). In 2004, it was reported that the PRC government was planning to formally create eight relatively distinctive economic regions in the country. *Jinghua shibao* (Jinghua times), Beijing, June 6, 2004.

75. Lubman 1999.

76. One early effort was the State Council's *Directive on Breaking down Regional Blockade of the Market*, Nov. 10, 1990. A later such effort was the almost identically titled State Council Decree 303 of Apr. 12, 2001.

77. Hu Angang et al. 1995, 27–31, 90–97, and 258–78; Minxin Pei 2002.

78. Zhen and Li et al. 1997, esp. 83–161.

79. *Zhongguo minhang bao* (Chinese civil aviation daily), Beijing, July 17, 2000, 6. Ni Jianmin, Deputy Director of China Institute of Policy Studies, a front organization of the CCP's Central Policy Study Office, speech in Singapore, Sept. 27, 2001.

80. A Gini index of 0.45–0.5 is considered the alarming point in China (SSB 2001 "Cong gini xishu," 29–30).

81. SSB 2001 "Cong gini xishu," 30, and according to Li Yining (interviewed in 2001), an economic authority in the PRC.

82. Including "living standard" and "profession," this ratio would be even higher (Liu Xin 2001, 11).

83. Not all agree on the degree and trend of China's regional disparities. Some think that the regional gap is neither serious nor expanding in China (Hu Dayuan 1998).

84. In 1955, the State Council defined a "city" as the seat of province or prefecture administration, a population settlement with more than 100 thousand people (at least half of whom must be nonagricultural *hukou* holders), or a major industrial center (Cao Shuji 2001, 723). In 1986, the city criterion was reset to be any settlement that had at least 60 thousand nonagriculture *hukou* holders (Tian Xueyuan 1997, 158–61).

85. MPS 2001, 302, and Liu Junde and Wang Yuming 2000, 6–8.

86. Perhaps because some of the county seats are sometimes counted as "county-level cities," or perhaps because of simple statistical error, there is a statistical discrepancy (a difference of 35) in different places in the same authoritative source about the exact number of China's county-level cities (MPS 2001, 105 and 302).

87. Figures are from SSB 2001, 339, and MPS 2001, 97–104. In 1955, the State Council defined a "town" as the seat for county administration, a settlement with 2,000 people (at least half of them nonagriculture *hukou* holders excluding military personnel), or an industrial center. That criterion was revised to be 3,000 residents (at least 75 percent with nonagriculture *hukou*) in 1963. In 1984, the criterion was relaxed to include any settlement that had over 20 thousand people (at least 2,000 nonagriculture *hukou* holders). Tian Xueyuan 1997, 158–61.

88. For the state division of and authorization to the cities, see Liu Junde and Wang Yuming 2000, 256–68. For the latest gaps among the cities, see *Beijing qingnian bao* (Beijing youth daily), Beijing, Nov. 15, 2003, A13.

89. Wang Guixin 1997, 308–52.

90. Sargeson 1999, 17.

91. Xue and Shi 2001, 117–21.

92. Tan Youlin 2001, 57.

93. UNDP 1999 and 2001.

94. According to the calculation by Hu and Zou 2000, 7–9, based on UNDP 1999, *The China Human Development Report*, 58–62, and in comparison to the world listing in UNDP 1999 and 2001 *Human Development Report*.

95. For an examination of urban poverty in the developing nations, see Nelson 1979.

96. Desai 1990, 2.

97. More lasting and even semipermanent slums have emerged in places, primarily to house the floating peasants in the outskirts of cities—for example the famous and perhaps the best organized and most studied Zhejiang Village in Beijing (Zhou Xiaohong 1998, 260–66 and Solinger 1999, 231–34, 249–56), Nanjin Village in Guangzhou (Zhou Daming et al. 2001, 104–7), and the "Garbage Village" in Honghu (Wang Jun 2001, 58–69). But few of them are comparable to the urban slums in Brazil or India in terms of size, poverty, longevity, and "independence."

98. *Fazhi ribao* (Legal daily), Beijing, Nov. 21, 2001, 2.

99. Author's field notes in Beijing, 2001.

100. In Beijing, in addition to Zhejiang Village, there were Xinjiang Village, Anhui Village, Henan Village, and "Painter's Village." About 40 percent of their residents leave in six months. *Benyue tan* (Fortnightly chat), Beijing, no. 9 (1997).

101. Xia Jizhi and Dang Xiaoji 1991, 110, and Tian Bingxin 2003, 127–49.

102. Cheng Tiejun 1992, 408.

103. China's entry into the WTO (World Trade Organization) in December of 2001 will liberalize the Chinese market for imported agricultural products. This is expected to worsen the already deteriorating economic situation of the excluded Chinese peasants in the next few years (Fewsmith 2001, 576–91). Furthermore, the investment firm of Salomon, Smith Barney estimated that 40 million Chinese workers would lose their jobs in the first five years after WTO entry (*Far Eastern Economic Review*, Hong Kong, Oct. 5, 2001).

104. Li Zhongxin 1999, 11–13 and 23–24.

105. Chinese college reform started in 1988–89 with the new policy that the college students would start to pay some part of their tuition. Incidentally, that

understandably unpopular reform directly contributed to the student unrest, which culminated in the June 4 tragedy of 1989. By 1997, all state-run colleges started to charge tuition and the state job-guarantee became a safety net and last resort for those who could not get a job on the market on their own. Zhou Daping, "Gaoxiao biyeshen 'fengpei' zaidanghua" (The fading of the "assignment" of college graduates), *Liaowang* (Outlook), Beijing, no. 30 (Aug. 1995), 21–22; *Beijing Review*, Sept. 25–Oct. 1, 1995, 15–20; also, *Renmin Ribao—Overseas* (Beijing), Feb. 18, 1997, 3.

106. *Dadi* (Earth), Beijing, no. 101 (May), 2000, 42. In 2004, there were 1.1 million more college entrance examination takers than the year before; out of the 7.23 million examinees (for a college admission quota of about four million , up by 180,000 from 2003), the rural *hukou* holders were for the first time more than 50 percent. *Xinjing bao* (Xinjing daily), Beijing, June 6, 2004, A09; Chinese Central Television (CCTV), Morning News, Beijing, June 6, 2004, and CCTV, Joint News, Beijing, June 7, 2004.

107. The college entrance exam graders I interviewed all talked about their life of being isolated in those "grading camps" during the grading weeks for the sake of preventing corruption. Author's field notes, 1999–2003. For examples of the elaborate measures taken to ensure the integrity of the examination, see *Jinghua shibao* (Jinghua times), Beijing, June 6, 2004, 7, and *Beijing qingnian bao* (Beijing youth daily), Beijing, June 6, 2004, A5.

108. In Guizhou Province, 328 exam takers were caught cheating and penalized while 296 more answer sheets had identical answers in 2000. *Guizhou ribao* (Guizhou daily), July 27, 2001. Only one month after the 2001 exams, several high-profile cheating students and corrupt officials were already indicted in Guangdong, Shangdong, Sichuan, Hainan, Jiangsu, Hunan, Henan, Hubei, and Xinjiang. Reports in *Xin kuaibao* (New express news) and www.sina.com.cn, Aug. 2001.

109. The questions are based on a set of more or less identical textbooks and curriculum design mandated by the state. Since the early 1990s, certain provinces/metropolises such as Shanghai have been allowed to have their own curriculum and textbooks, hence slightly different exams.

110. In 2001, Beijing started to allow some students to take the exam in places where their families must be at the time of the exam, subject to approval. But they still have to be admitted under the quota in their home *hukou* zones (Ministry of Education 2001, 2).

111. SSB 2001, 303, 649, and 657.

112. SSB 2001, 660–61.

113. "Zhongdian daxue 2000 niandu paihang bang" (Ranking of the national major universities, 2000), www.edu.sina.com.cn/netbig2000.html, Nov. 2, 2001, accessed Feb. 19, 2002.

114. *Zhongguo qingnian bao* (Chinese youth daily), Beijing, Feb. 24, 2000, 5; MPS 2001, 2; author's interview with officials in Beijing, July 2001.

115. Author's interview in Shanghai, July 2001.

116. Ministry of Education 2001, 9; *Haerbin ribao* (Haerbin daily), Haerbin, June 5, 2001.

117. Pan Hongqi, "Tongyi gaokao xuyao tongyi luqu biaozhun" (Uniform college entrance exam needs a uniform admission standard), *Beijing qingnian bao* (Beijing youth daily), July 7, 2001. Some, in a scheme called "migration for college admission" (*gaokao yimin*), simply pay for a fake *hukou* paper or an illegal *hukou* relocation to a place where the admission score is lower. To protect the *hukou* system and its role in college admission, the government has used harsh measures against such *gaokao yimin* schemes (Tian Bingxin 2003, 120–26). In May 2004, the Ningxia government reportedly disqualified 225 takers of the 2004 college entrance examination (to be held in June) because of their "unlawful" *gaokao yimin. Beijing qingnian bao* (Beijing youth daily), Beijing, June 3, 2004, A15.

118. Author's interviews with education officials in Anhui and Jiangsu, 1998–2002.

119. *Guangmin ribao* (Guangmin daily), Beijing, Mar. 22, 2001.

120. For examples, see "Yanjiusheng baosong heimu jiujin duohei?" (How dark is the dark side of sure admission of graduate students?), *Zhongguo qingnian bao* (Chinese youth daily), Beijing, Nov. 28, 2000, and "Baosongsheng cailiao shuifen you duo da?" (How much water was added in the files of the sure-admitted students?), *Zhongguo qingnian bao* (Chinese youth daily), Beijing, Mar. 5, 2001.

121. *Beijing qingnian bao* (Beijing youth daily), Beijing, Feb. 13, 2001; *Jiangnan shibao* (Jiangnan times), Nanjing, Feb. 26, 2001.

122. Yang Zengxian, "Tongyi gaokao bu tongyi luqu fenshuxian gongping ma?" (Is the uniform college entrance exam fair without a uniform admission score?), *Zhongguo qingnian bao* (Chinese youth daily), Beijing, Aug. 1, 2001.

123. Xin Haiguang, "You nanbei bang shijian kangaokao fenshuxian" (View the college admission scores from the perspective of the south-north selection incident of the year 1397), *Qingnian shixun* (Youth times), Beijing, July 27, 2001.

124. Pan Hongqi, "Tongyi gaokao xuyao tongyi luqu biaozhun" (Uniform college entrance examination needs a uniform admission standard), *Beijing qingnian bao* (Beijing youth daily), July 7, 2001.

125. The lawyers cited Articles 9.2 and 36.1 of the *PRC Constitution* that stipulate "equal rights" of education for all PRC citizens. They also reported that at least 40–50 additional college applicants were interested in joining the effort. The lawsuit, however, was not even formally accepted by the Court and was later ignored by the Court and the media. Li Li, "Jiaoyuebu rishang gaokao guansi" (Ministry of Education got sued over college entrance exam), *Xinwen zhoukan* (News weekly), Beijing, reprinted in *Huaxia wenzhai* (China news digest), New York, no. 564 (Feb. 18, 2002).

126. Report by the State Council's Center for Education and Development Studies, *Renmin ribao* (People's Daily), Beijing, Aug. 7, 2001.

127. Ministry of Education officials plan to increase admission before leveling off by 2005 at 2.5–3 million each year. *Xinhua Daily Telegraph*, Fuzhou, Oct. 19, 2000.

128. Jiang Zemin, *Lun sange daibiao* (On "three represents") (Beijing: Zhongyang Wenxian Press, 2001). Three represents refers to the revisionist mis-

sion statement that the CCP "should represent the development requirements of China's advanced social productive forces, the progressive course of China's advanced culture, and the fundamental interests of the overwhelming majority of the Chinese people." *Communiqué of the 6th Plenum of the 15th CCP Central Committee*, Xinhua, Beijing, Sept. 26, 2001.

129. Kang Xiaoguang, "Weilai 3–5 nian zhongguo dalu zhengzhi wending-xing fengxi" (Analysis of the political stability issue on the Chinese Mainland in the next 3–5 years), *Zhanlue yu guanli* (Strategy and management), Beijing, no. 3 (2003), 1–2 and 10.

130. Minxin Pei 2002, 99–108.

131. As reported by *Financial Times* (James Kynge, "Chinese Workers Transform Fortunes of Home Towns," Nov. 9, 2003), the remittance of the migrant workers has indeed contributed noticeably to the improvement of the rural economy, albeit in a slow way. The government estimated that migrant families' average income is 17 percent higher than that of farming families (www.stats.gov.cn/tjshujia/zggqgl/200210240199.htm, accessed on Nov. 18, 2003).

132. Incidentally, among my interviewees, privileged urban dwellers tend to take the PRC *hukou* system for granted and assert that the *hukou* system "really does not make much difference in life," while the excluded "outsiders," especially the ruralites, insist that the *hukou* system affects their lives personally, persistently, and profoundly. Author's interviews, 1999–2003.

Chapter 6

1. Solinger 1999, 5. Some, however, have found that the migrant workers from rural areas working in the "informal" (or low-paying) sector of the Chinese urban economy actually enjoy "much better" working and living conditions and a "much higher" income than those in other large developing nations like Brazil, India, Indonesia, and Mexico (Zhu Nong 2001, 45, and Zhu Jingde 1996). One reason may be precisely that the *hukou* system reduced the supply of migrant labor.

2. Jim Fussell (Education Director of Prevent Genocide International), "Group Classification on National Cards," a report presented to the Conference of Prevent Genocide International, June 20, 2001.

3. Crook et al. 1994, 572–688.

4. Bowman et al. 1996.

5. Nicolet 1991. In Egypt, the system apparently was very well enforced (Bagnall 1999).

6. For a classic examination of the profound impact of the enclosure movement, see Polanyi 1957.

7. Pound 1971 *Poverty* and Beier 1983.

8. Leonard 1965, Beier 1983. Yet the anti-"paupers" Settlement Act of 1662 continued to be a "powerful weapon against vagrancy ... until well into the 19th century." Davin 1999, 157.

9. Leonard 1965.

10. Rose et al. 1969.

11. See, for examples, Bradbury and Mawson 1997 and McNabb and Whitfield 1998.

12. From 1854 to the 1990s, the UK had adopted five versions of birth and death registration law, in MPS-BHM 1996, *Guowai minshi*, 189–232.

13. Council on European Legal Affairs, *Establishment and Harmonization of National Identity Cards*, Strasbourg, 1977, 26, cited in Matthews 1993, x; Miles et al. 1995.

14. Matthews 1993, ix–xi.

15. Jean-Claude Sache, *Freedom of Movement in the Community, Entry, and Residence*, EEC, Luxembourg, 1988, 7. Cited in Matthews 1993, x.

16. Matthews 1993, ix–xi.

17. For exclusions against Eastern and Southern Europeans, see Joly 1997. For exclusions in the urban settings in the West, see Musterd and Ostendorf 1998. For a discussion of the geography of exclusion in the West, see Sibley 1995. For an examination of the "prejudice" against "outsiders" in Italian politics, see Sniderman et al. 2000.

18. Matthews 1993, xi.

19. Jim Fussell (Education Director of Prevent Genocide International), "Group Identification of National Cards," a report presented to the Conference of Prevent Genocide International, June 20, 2001.

20. Bryan Naylor, "VA Death Penalty," *NPR News—Morning Edition*, National Public Radio, Washington, DC, Dec. 28, 2001.

21. Leading U.S. news journals including *Time* and *Newsweek* magazines and *The New York Times* all carried extensive discussions on the issue of alien control through a national ID system in 2001–2002. A national survey in the United States showed that 68 percent of the respondents favored a "national ID system for all U.S. citizens" (*Business Week*, Nov. 5, 2001, 42). For a representative argument, see Margaret Carison, "The Case for a National ID Card: Big Brother Already Knows Where You Live, Why Not Let Him Make You Safer?" (*Time* magazine, Jan. 21, 2002, 52).

22. For an examination on American institutional exclusion as reflected in the U.S. legal system, see Minow 1991. For a study on the money-based divisions and exclusions in the U.S., see Hacker 1997.

23. Elizabeth Gleick, "Rich Justice, Poor Justice," *Time* magazine, June 19, 1995, 41.

24. By the 17th century, a racial slavery was established in North America (later the United States) under which all Africans were by law slaves except where and when they could show appropriate papers to prove their freedom. And Africans were banned from enslaving the European migrants with very rare exceptions (Stampp 1989, 194–95). For the lasting effect of the racial divide in America, see Hacker 1995 and Entman and Rojecki 2000.

25. For a historiography of the Japanese social strata and classes and their changes before the Meiji Restoration, see Howland 2001, 353–80.

26. *Japan Pension Decrees*, Article 15. Cited in Meng Xianshi, "Zhongyang, difang de maodun yu changan sannian kuohu" (The conflicts between the central

and local governments: the *hukou* inclusion campaign in the 3rd year of the Changan Era), *Lishi yanjiu* (Studies of history), Beijing, no. 4 (2001).

27. Before the Restoration, only the nobles and e samurai could have family names. After the Restoration, commoners were all required to have family names registered, so many of them simply gave themselves a family name based on their residence or occupation. Author's interviews in Tokyo and Kyoto, 1995.

28. Many of today's Chinese *hukou* management procedures are clearly seen in the *Details on the Implementation of the Japanese Household Registration* (1947 version, amended in 1984), MPS-BHM 1996, *Guowai minshi ...*, 35–78. On the way the Japanese installed their version of residential control in China during World War II, see Schurmann 1966, 369–70.

29. Asia-Pacific Center 2000, 81–82. For more detailed treatments of Japan's urbanization, see Wilkinson 1965 and Mosk 2001.

30. For the "lingering" effect of the historically tight social control and sense of compartmentalization in Japan, see Garon 1997.

31. The Japanese *hukou* law (articles 110 and 121) required that people who have moved register within ten days of their arrival or face a fine. MPS-BHM 1996, *Guowai minshi ...*, 28 and 30. This is different from the situation in France, for example, where the mandatory personal registration is more relaxed. Author's interviews with a French diplomat, 2001.

32. Author's interviews in Tokyo, 1998.

33. Peterson 1996.

34. Shin and Robinson 1999, especially the chapter by Chul-Woo Lee on legal modernization and rural penetration by the Japanese rulers.

35. For an analysis on the rapid urbanization process and urban center-bound internal migration in Korea, see Asia-Pacific Center 2000, 144 and 158.

36. For example, Korean President (1999–2003) Kim Dae-Jung's political base was for a long time solidly located in his home prefecture of Kwangju. Author's interviews in Korea, 1992 and 1997.

37. Author's interviews with a Korean scholar, 2001. As the result of a reform in the 1990s, a registering resident now only has to make thumbprints instead of ten-finger prints. One full-year stay will automatically grant local residency to any Korean citizen and hence the same tax rates and rights.

38. For the "blood and family" and territory-based social organizations in pre-1895 Taiwan, see Dung-Sheng Chen 2001, 63–80. For the Japanese-imposed legal changes in Taiwan, see Wang Tay-Sheng 2000.

39. Fairbank and Goldman 1998, 338.

40. For a glimpse of the Taiwanese *hukou* system in the 1950s, see Guo Yanlin et al. 1952.

41. The 1970s version of Taiwan's *hukou* law still stipulated in detail the different registrations of "permanent residents" versus "migrant/temporary residents." Wang Jianmin and Hu Qi 1996, 2.

42. In 1948, self-farming rural households were only 34.5 percent. By 1979, they were 84.8 percent (Wen Guanzhong 1992, 58).

43. For more on the Taiwanese land reform and rural development, see Brown and Lin Sein 1968 and Woodruff and Brown 1971.

44. Huang Xiaoming 1996, 76–77.

45. Taiwanese scholars described a pattern of internal migration in Taiwan from the 1950s to the 1980s as largely dictated by market forces and the urbanization process. Lin Yihou, "Taiwan renkou jizhong qushi jiqi yingxiang" (Population concentration and its impact in Taiwan), cited in Tian and Lin 1987, 350–69. A more detailed examination of Taiwan's urbanization is Speare et al. 1988. For an account on social mobility and family/clan structure in Taiwan, see Wang Hong-Zen 2001, 328–58.

46. Until the mid-1990s, the mandatory ID card of a Taiwanese resident, in addition to the common information about the bearer's address, age, and registration number, displayed his marital status and spouse's or parents' contact information. This "personal" and private information is now mostly stored on the card with a computer-read-only barcode. Author's interviews in Taiwan, 1995, 1999, and 2004.

47. For more on the demographic changes and the population policies in Taiwan, see Chen Shaoxin 1995. For a view that today's Taiwanese and Japanese *hukou* systems are very similar, see Yu Depeng 2002, 368.

48. Internal migration, naturally, is not all orderly or politically controlled in the developing world; see Skeldon 1993. For a report on the historical characteristics of labor migration in Southeast Asia and especially in the Philippines, see Francis A. Gealogo, "Historical Demography of Southeast Asian Labor Migration," a conference paper, Xiamen, 2001.

49. Author's interview with Anne Raffin, a French sociologist, 2001. Vietnam, after its independence in the 1950s and its unification in 1975, largely maintained the registration system and the related internal migration control.

50. African nations in general lack a comprehensive residential registration system and internal migration control, although discrimination and urban biases against sojourning workers from rural areas are commonplace (UNCTAD 1999 and Wohlmuth et al. 1999).

51. Morocco, for example, established a household registration system as early as 1951. MPS-BHM 1996, *Guowai minshi*, 365–91.

52. Caldwell 1969.

53. For an examination of the Mexico case, see Sernau 1994.

54. Solinger 1999, 27, 33–34. The Soviet experience, however, was perhaps more an ideological justification for China's indigenous *hukou*-based institutional exclusion than a source of it.

55. In the early 2000s, North Korea is one of the few that still practice comprehensive and tight control of internal migration and travel. For the case in Albania before the 1990s, see Sjoberg 1994.

56. Solinger 1999, 33.

57. Matthews 1993, 1–8.

58. *The Decree on Internal Passport* by the Central Executive Committee and the Council of People's Commissars, USSR, Moscow, Dec. 27, 1932.

59. Brazier 2001.

60. Matthews 1993, Buckley 1993, Brazier 2001.

61. Walder 1986.

62. Hoffmann 1994.

63. For more on internal migration and population distribution in the former USSR, see Lewis and Rowland 1979. For Soviet urbanization, see Medvedkov 1990.

64. Matthews 1993, 86–87, 98–99.

65. This could be interpreted as an attempt at granting mobility to the rich, as the Chinese are now doing nationwide (see Chapters 4 and 7 of this book). In the 1990s, Moscow, whose *propiska* is the most sought-after in Russia, openly auctioned its *propiska* or granted its *propiska* to the rich through the selling of officially owned housing properties. Matthews 1993, 83.

66. Information and quotations in this paragraph are mostly from Brazier 2001.

67. Filipp Sterkin, "Changes in Registration," *Current Digest of the Post Soviet Press* 52, issue 45 (Dec. 6, 2000), 10; Damian S. Schaible, "Life in Russia's Closed City," *New York University Law Review* 76, issue 1 (Apr. 2001), 344.

68. Human Rights Watch 2000, 317.

69. The Memorial Human Rights Center Moscow, "Racism in Russia: Compliance of the Russian Federation with the Convention on the Elimination of All Forms of Racial Discrimination," Report by International League of Human Rights, New York, Nov. 2000, 8–12.

70. Rubins 1998.

71. European Parliament, *Motion for Recommendation*, Doc. 8566, 1999.

72. "UNHCR Targets *Propiska* in Its Report," Reuters, Moscow, May 14, 1999.

73. For examples, see Olga Brednikova and Oleg Patchenkov, "Economic Migrants from Azerbaijan in St. Petersburg: Problems of Social Adaptation and Integration," *Caucasian Regional Studies* 4, issue 1 (1999); David Hoffman, "Objective: Work to Establish the Rule of Law," *Washington Post*, Sept. 9, 1999, A01.

74. As early as 1989, one limited survey found that 76 percent of the respondents wanted to "abolish" the *propiska* while 60 percent wanted to abolish the internal passport system. Matthews 1993, 52–53. One lengthy and well-researched posting titled "A Few Words on the Freedom of Movement" by Sergei Briyukov at www.nelegal.ru in 2001 declared strongly that "the current [Russian] system of registration (earlier known as *propiska*) is nothing else but the survival—no, not even of the Soviet Union, but of the Russian Empire. ... [Since Czarist Russia] we have all remained land-bound serfs to this day." Accessed on Feb. 19, 2002.

75. Author's field notes in Russia, 2003.

76. Matthews 1993, 85.

77. Tchernina 1996, 2 and 94–96.

78. For the "protracted" China-India rivalry, see Garver 2001, 110–37 and 368–90. For a Chinese view on the Sino-Indian strategic rivalry over being a "world leader" and on the "need to study each other carefully," see He Sen, "Indo kai 'ruanjian' qiangguo" (India relies on software to empower), *Zhongguo*

guoqing guoli (China national conditions and strength), Beijing, no. 103 (July 2001), 39–40.

79. For a recent account on the ethnic conflicts in India in general and the Sikhs' relationship with the Indian state in particular, see Gurharpal Singh 2000.

80. Quotes from Indian Defense Minister, George Fernandes, in the New York–based www.chinanewsnet.com, accessed Jan. 16, 2001. For a Chinese response to this admission and India's "great power ambition," see *Zhanlue yu guanli* (Strategy and management), Beijing, no. 3 (2001), 43–46.

81. Although Kerala scores significantly better than India's national averages of life expectancy, adult literacy, infant mortality reduction, and birth rate reduction, its per capita GDP and economic growth rate are actually lower than India's already low national averages. Furthermore, a Hong Kong–based scholar who visited Kerala in 2001 commented to the author in 2002 that "in terms of technological sophistication, Kerala looks like China in the 1960s and 1970s." For a general argument that social development can be achieved with a low level of economic development, using Kerala as an example, see Sen 1995 and 2000.

82. Author's conversation with David Croker and Michael Kruze in Madras (Chennai), 1997.

83. For a collective effort to comparatively study Indian and Chinese rural development and governance, see Baum and Mohanty 2004. For examples of cross-nation comparative studies, see Rozman 1973 (on social networks in China and Japan), Martine et al. 1998 (on reproductive trends in Brazil and India), and Anita Chan et al. 1999 (on reforms in China and Vietnam).

84. Yasheng Huang and Tarun Khanna, "Can India Overtake China?" *Foreign Policy*, July–Aug. 2003; Ma Ya, "Will Rising India Catch up with China: A Dialogue with Four Scholars," *Fenghuang zhoukan* (Phoenix weekly), Hong Kong, no. 145 (Apr. 25), 2004.

85. Gupta 1991, 13–14. According to a Tamil Nadu–based British scholar of Indian studies, Michael Lockwood, India's upper castes, mainly English-speaking and about 5–10 percent of the population, are descendents of the conquerors/rulers of India in ancient times. The lower castes are largely non-English-speaking and mostly illiterate. Their ancestors were either the conquered people or the escaped refugees. The lowest social groups of "untouchables" are the descendents of the rebels who rose unsuccessfully against the conquerors. The religious origin of the castes is used later as a "political adornment." Author's interviews in India, 1997.

86. Gupta 1991, 35–44.

87. They tend to have inherited low-ranking jobs such as working at the burning sites of fire burial on the banks of the Ganges River. Author's interviews in Varanasi (Banarasi), India, 1997.

88. Pandey 1986, 1.

89. Hocart 1950 and McCord and McCord 1977, 36–37.

90. Pandey 1986, 1–15.

91. Singh 1977 and Ahmad 1978. For the political favors bestowed on the lower castes by the Indian Government after 1947, many other ethnic and reli-

gious groups in India also tend to simply rename their internal socioeconomic stratification as caste system. Ahmad's description of castes in the Muslims is actually applicable to other Muslim nations including the Arab nations where a highly fixed social stratification and exclusive barriers among the layers of the population exist and are often justified and upheld by the religious establishment.

92. Pandey 1986, 3–9.

93. *Constitution of the Republic of India*, 1949, Sections 15–17, 23, 29, 164, and 330–42.

94. Gupta 1991, 46.

95. For the gains and progress of the scheduled castes, see Singh 1987.

96. Hutton 1946, 123.

97. Segal 1971, cited in Pandey 1986, 14–15; emphasis added.

98. Pandey 1986, 15 and 175.

99. Pandey 1986, 167–74. In the 2000s, physical mistreatment of lower caste people at the hands of higher caste people was common in places like Varanasi and old Delhi. In some Southern cities, especially Bangalore, the caste system seems to be somewhat less influential. Author's interviews in India, 1997 and 2003.

100. Gupta 1991, 7. Agrawal's view is quite representative of the Indian government's official opinion, which often tends to downplay or even dismiss the role played by the caste system in India. Many conservative and religious fundamentalist forces in India actually launched campaigns against the scheduled castes for their "unfair" rights and power. Author's interviews in India, 1997 and 2003.

101. Rajshekar 1994. Many Indian college professors and students believe that the conflicts between higher and lower castes were not diminishing but "rising" in the 1990s. Author's interviews in Calcutta, Madras, Varanasi, and New Delhi, 1997 and 2003.

102. Appasamy et al. 1996, 85. For statistical data on the caste-based socioeconomic exclusion against the low caste people, see Appasamy et al. 1996, 88–97. For examples of radical pamphlets and essays published in India in the 1980s–90s advocating revolutionary ways to destroy the "evil" caste system, see Ambedkar 1987, Rajshekar 1994, and the articles in the fortnightly journal *Dalit Voice*, Bangalore, various issues, 1981–97.

103. Author's interview with Badrinath Krishna Rao, in Madras, 1997.

104. Author's interview in New Delhi and Madras, 1997.

105. Selvam 2000, 121–58 and 179–89.

106. Selvam 2000, 119–20. Incidentally, this serves as a good comparison with real estate transactions in China, where the PRC *hukou* system literally led to housing prices being drastically higher for nonlocal buyers.

107. Author's field notes and content analysis of the personal ads in the English newspapers such as *Indian Express*, *Economic Times*, and *Saturday Statesman* of Jan. 1997.

108. Narayana and Kantner 1992.

109. Zha Ruichuan 1996, 18 and 86–87.

110. Table 5.2 of this book and Gowariker 1993, 175.

111. Author's conversation with Michael Lockwood at the Mamallapruma Relics in Tamil Nadu, 1997.

112. The massive urban slums in major cities like Bombay (Mumbai), Calcutta, and Madras are among the best known examples of urban poverty in the world (Desai 1990, 125–248).

113. De Souza 1983, xiii–xiv.

114. Misra et al. 1998, vol. 1, 1–70.

115. Joshi and Little 1997, 219.

116. Author's interview with P. S. Jacob and Badrinath Krishna Rao, two Indian professors of development studies, in Madras, 1997.

117. Author's field notes in Bombay, Calcutta, Madras, Varanasi, Agra, and New Delhi, 1997 and 2003.

118. For an academic discussion of "social inclusion" as a leading cause for Kerala's social achievements, see Heller 1999. Author's interviews in West Bengal, 2003.

119. Jayaraman 1981 and esp. den Uyl 1995.

120. For an officially endorsed Indian examination of the multidimensional causes of the inability of governance and changes, as reflected by the lack of success in population control and labor resource utilization, see Gowariker 1993.

121. Gould 1988, esp. his second volume.

122. Skidmore and Smith 1997, 147–56.

123. Skidmore and Smith 1997, 162. A group of Brazilian college students of mixed racial and ethnic backgrounds insisted, for example, that the main problem in Brazil was class divisions whereas the racial and ethnic divisions were only secondary. Author's interviews in Brazil, 1997.

124. Cavalcanti 1996, 95–96; Skidmore and Smith 1997, 184–85.

125. Richard N. Cooper, "Chapter 11 for Countries?" *Foreign Affairs* 81.4 (Jul.–Aug. 2002), 90–103.

126. The descendents of the former slaves and the *mulattos*, for example, are especially often subject to subtle discriminations based on race (Conniff and McCann 1989, 193–94).

127. For the "supremacy of economic over other dimensions of social life," see Jose de Souza Martin, "The Alliance between Capital and Property in Brazil: The Trend to Backwardness," in Kinzo et al. 1995, 131–52.

128. As much as 70 percent of the population was estimated as "poor" lower class in Brazil in the 1980s (Conniff and McCann 1989, xviii).

129. For example, Brazil scored some of the highest inflation rates in peacetime in the world, as high as 1,783 percent in 1989 and averaging 62 percent annually in the early 1990s (Kinzo 1993, 25–29, 101).

130. One-third of Brazil (the South and Southeast), with 58 percent of the total population, had 76 percent of Brazil's GDP in the mid-1990s. *Mobilization Forces for Progress* (Recife, PE, Brazil: SEBRAE-PE, 1997), tables 1.2 and 1.4. For an examination on the regional disparities and their impact on labor in Northeastern Brazil, especially in Pernambuco, see Chalmers 1997, 95–114.

131. Cardoso and Faletto 1979 and Evans 1979.

132. The "weak" and limited role of the state and the fragmented and marginalized social actors in an era of strong "neoliberal" economics have been a major reason for scholars' pessimistic views about Latin America in general (Smith and Korzeniewicz 1991, esp. 57–97). The Brazilians seem to have also realized that the lack of appropriate state efforts may have been a key factor of the "exclusions" the poor states in the Northeast experience (SDN 1995, 12–13).

133. Gilbert 1992.

134. Kaufman and Segura-Ubiergo 2001, 554–55.

135. Kinzo 1993, 77.

136. Dickenson 1982, 135.

137. Smith and Korzeniewicz 1997, 221 and 223.

138. SDN 1995, 90 and 108.

139. Curitiba's economic growth rate, however, has been only slightly higher than that of the rest of Paraná and Brazil since the 1970s (www.cic-curitiba. com.br/domestic_product.htm). For more on this "exceptional model city in Latin America" and its "visionary mayor," Jaime Lerner, see Cassio Tanguchi, "Transport and urban Planning in Curitiba," *DISP* 147 (2001), 14–19; www. dismantle.org/curitiba.htm and www.globalideasbank.org/BI/BI–262.HTML, accessed Nov. 22, 2003.

140. Author's interviews with SUDENE officials in Recife, Brazil, 1997.

141. In 1992, for example, the state of Rio Grande de Sul, which happened to be "more whitish" than the Northeastern states, sent officials to the bus terminals to "advise" (with some payment and pamphlets) the newcomers from the Northeast to return home. "It was very successful" until months later it was revealed in the media and the local governments were forced to abandon their operations. Author's interviews in Brazil, 1997.

142. According to Kirk Bowman, a Latin American specialist who studied Curitiba, 2003.

143. Author's interviews in Brazil, 1997. Of course, the ruling elite in Brazil has been largely whitish-looking "Europeans" whose land-based properties can often be traced back to the colonial times (Conniff and McCann 1989).

144. Indeed, in cities like Rio de Janeiro, people can easily see perhaps the most complete collection of all kinds of mixed-blood people imaginable including the fabled *mulattos*. Author's field notes in Brazil, 1997.

145. However, one comparative study of Brazil concluded that often "the cost of [government] nonintervention is bound to be higher than any potential government failure" (Moreira 1995, 139).

146. World Bank 1982, 77.

147. CONDEPE 1997, 11; MPS 2000, 3.

148. UNDP 2001, 155–57.

149. For nearly a century many Brazilians have believed that Brazil is "the country of the future." Author's interviews with Brazilian politicians and academicians in Brazil and the United States, 1997 and 1999.

150. Desai and Pillai 1990, 83.

151. Author's field notes in Brazil, 1997. Also see "Nice Cops, Nasty Cops," *The Economist*, London, Sept. 8, 2001.

152. Dickenson 1982, 138–41. Author's field notes in Pernambuco, Rio de Janeiro, and Sao Paulo, 1997.

153. Comments made by Leonardo Sampaio, a Brazilian professor of economics and management, in 1997.

154. Dickenson 1982, 135–36.

155. CONDEPE 1997, 3.

156. Kinzo 1993, 63, 76; Duquette 1999, 175.

157. Author's interviews in Recife, Pernambuco, Brazil, 1997.

158. Naturally, there should still be Type 4 (*what one has done/does*) institutional exclusion to punish and even to eliminate the law and rule violators through time-specific and issue-specific exclusions and discriminations.

159. For one thing, the per capita arable land in China is only 33 percent of the world's average, and 20–24.5 and 40–42.2 percent of that in Brazil and India respectively. Hu and Yang 2000, 300 and the Washington-based National Institute for the Environment, www.cnie.org, accessed Feb. 19, 2002.

160. Some readers may infer further and come to a conclusion that a heavily populated large developing nation today is better off with an authoritarian regime than a democracy since a Type 3 (*where one is*) institutional exclusion can hardly sustain or function well in a mass democracy. I would suggest that, first, an effective role of the state in legitimizing a Type 3 institutional exclusion is not necessarily impossible under a political democracy, especially a common elite democracy. Second, an effective mass democracy is generally a rarity in the developing nations anyway. Third, it takes more than an authoritarian or effective state to implement a Type 3 institutional exclusion. History and social and cultural factors, as I have demonstrated in the Chinese case, matter greatly. Finally, although it is beneficial for a dual-economy nation to grow fast, a Type 3 institutional exclusion is not the ideal or sufficient condition for socioeconomic development, probably not even a universally necessary condition.

Chapter 7

1. The increased awareness of personal privacy has been listed as a reason for underreporting in China's 2000 Census. *Renkou yanjiu* (Population research), Beijing, 25.3 (May) 2001, 28. For an example of Chinese publications defending citizens' personal rights to privacy, see Zhang Xinbao 1998, esp. 80–89. In March 2004, the PRC added, for the first time, a clause to its constitution guaranteeing citizens' "human rights."

2. Zweig 2001, 233–37. Much of Zhu's reform package, such as reforms of state-owned enterprises, has had a direct impact on the *hukou*-based institutional exclusion.

3. Reports on *hukou* reforms in different localities at www.news.china.com, accessed Oct. 28, 2003. Foreign media picked up the changes and the new mood. See, for example, Elisabeth Rosenthal, "China Eases Rules Binding People to Birth Regions," *The New York Times*, Oct. 23, 2001.

4. For journalistic coverage of the "unusual" discussion of the *hukou* system and its reforms, see Erik Eckholm, "China's Controls on Rural Workers Stir Some

Rarely Seen Heated Opposition," *The New York Times,* Mar. 10, 2000, A10. For PRC publications summarizing the reform views and proposals, see Party History Department of the CCP Central Party School, "Dandai zhongguo huji zhidu xingcheng yu yange de hongguan fenxi" (A macro analysis of the formation and evolution of the current Chinese *hukou* system), *Zhonggong dangshi yanjiu* (Studies of CCP history), Beijing, no. 3 (Dec. 15), 2003; *Guangming ribao* (Guangming daily), Beijing, Dec. 12, 2003; and the highly critical and controversial web postings calling for an abolishment of the *hukou* system by Zhang Yinghong (a Hunan CCP journal editor who was dismissed in July 2003 for criticizing the CCP's intervention in the PRC judicial system) during 2001–2003 in places such as www.asiademo.org, www.mlcool.com, and www.chinaelections. org.

5. China formally entered the WTO in Dec. of 2001, yet the details of the widely speculated "massive and major" concessions made by Beijing in that effort still remained largely a state secret in 2004.

6. He Jun, "Huji zhidu zuizhong jiangchengwei jihua jingji de canyu biaozhi" (The *hukou* system will eventually become the symbolic remnant of the planning economy"), www.people.com.cn, Aug. 28, 2001, accessed Feb. 19, 2002.

7. "Yiwei zhe shenfen butong? tequan? jiedu hukou zhenshi yiyi" (Does it mean different identity? Privileges? Understanding the real meaning of *hukou*), *Zhongguo qingnian bao* (Chinese youth daily), Beijing, Aug. 12, 2001.

8. Liu Juhua, "Zhuanjia cheng huji zhidu yiuliyu <xianfa> zhiwai jibupingdeng" (Experts say that the *hukou* system is floating outside the constitution and extremely unfair), *Renmin ribao* (People's Daily), Beijing, Sept. 4, 2001.

9. www.news.china.com/zh_cn/focus, Oct. 15, 2001, accessed Feb. 19, 2002.

10. For example, see the reports in *Zhongguo qingnian bao* (Chinese youth daily), Beijing, July 26, 2001.

11. Zen Wenhong, "Xianxing huji zhidu de wuda bibin" (The five problems of the existing *hukou* system), *Xinwen zhoukan* (News weekly), Beijing, Aug. 9, 2001.

12. Zhong Dajun 2001, 14–18.

13. Dang Guoying, "Qingnian nongmin shi dangjin zhongguo de zuida zhengzhi" (Young peasants are the biggest politics in today's China), *Zhongguo guoqing guoli* (China's national conditions and strength), Beijing, no. 101 (May 2001), 4–7.

14. "'Guocui' huji zhidu yu mangliu" ("National treasure" *hukou* system and the blind floating people), *Jingji guanca bao* (Economic observer news), Beijing, Aug. 9, 2001.

15. Wu Pengseng 2001, 4–6.

16. Yu Depeng 2002, esp. 394–406.

17. Penny, "Hukou, gaokao, gongmin quanli" (*Hukou,* college entrance exam, and citizens' rights), www.people.com.cn, Aug. 15, 2001, accessed Jan. 16, 2002.

18. Zheng Pingsheng, "Huji zhidu gaige de lingyizhong silu" (Another way of thinking of *hukou* reform), *Dushu* (Reading), Beijing, no. 2 (2003), 120–25.

19. I discussed the *hukou* issue with groups of Chinese academicians and of-

ficials in seminar and conference settings in 1997 and 1999–2002 in Beijing, Chengdu, Guangzhou, Kunming, Shanghai, and Xiamen. It impressed me that none would justify or defend the *hukou* system at the meetings but in private all of them believed that there is little people can do about it.

20. For a criticism against the poor management of the *hukou* system in the countryside and some small towns, see Cao Jingchun 2001, 10–11 and 16–17.

21. Zhang Qingwu 1992 and 1993 and his interviews with newspapers in the late 1990s. For a summary of his views on *hukou* reform, see *Renkou yu jingji* (Population and economics), Beijing, no. 127 (Apr. 2001), 78–79.

22. Ding Shuimu 1999.

23. Li Yining "Guanyu shehui liudong" (On social movement), Ji Dangshen and Shao Qin 1995, 12–20. Li reaffirmed his view in an interview with me in 2001.

24. For expressions of the mainstream reform view on the *hukou* system, see Mu Xinshen 1996, 6–7; Xu Ming 1997, 432–35; and Zhou Yi 1998, 85–91.

25. For representative "designs" and proposals of *hukou* reform, see Zhang Ping 2000, Ban Maosheng and Zhu Chengsheng 2000, and esp. Cao Jingchun 2001, 12–16.

26. For an extensive collection of the "internal" but dominant views on the *hukou* system and its necessity, see Wang Taiyuan 1997.

27. Some academic writings have only indirectly hinted at this role of the *hukou* system in their debates on how to improve "community construction."

28. For examples, see Wang Taiyuan 1997, Li Zhongxin 1998 and 1999, MPS-PTB 1999, Cheng and Bo 2000, and MPS-PD 2001.

29. Kam Wan Chan and Li Zhang 1999, 831–40.

30. The major lesson the CCP "learned" from the June 4 Incident of 1989 is that sociopolitical stability, control, and the unity of the leadership are absolutely the top priorities. Such a belief is still widely shared by senior officials in the 2000s. Author's interviews in Beijing and Shanghai, 2001–2004.

31. Ying Zhijin and Yu Qihong 1996, 59–60, 82–98. As of 2004 the full text of the 1993 general plan of *hukou* reform had yet to be publicly released.

32. According to Article 2 of the *Experimenting Plans*, no more than 20, 15, and 10 small cities and towns ("with good economic conditions") were to be selected from each provincial unit in the eastern, central, and western regions respectively to run the experiments for two years (1998–2000).

33. *Shenhuo shibao* (Life times), Beijing, Aug. 9, 2001.

34. But "all the migration registration procedures are still to be followed strictly." *Zhongguo minzhen* (China civil affairs), Beijing, no. 11 (Nov. 2001), 57.

35. *Renmin ribao* (People's daily), Beijing, Sept. 4, 2001.

36. Shen Wenmin, "Guanyu huji zhidu gaige de wenda" (Q&A on the *hukou* system reforms), *Renmin ribao—huadong ban* (People's daily—Eastern China edition), Shanghai, Aug. 29, 2001, 3.

37. Cao Jinqing 2000, 463. This way, the land "allocated" to former farmers can be reallocated to the remaining farmers, increasing the scale and, hopefully, the productivity of agricultural production, hence raising rural income and helping to overcome the dual economy (Wu Caisheng 1999, 200). After the 1978–82

decollectivization, the "user's right" to land was allocated to farming families under a "responsibility" system for 15 years. In 1993, the allocation began to be extended for another 30 years. By 1998, the CCP formally guaranteed a 30-year extension of the allocations (Chen Dongyou 1999, 114–19).

38. See, for example, the reports in *Nanfang zhoumo* (Southern weekend), Guangzhou, Aug. 31, 2001.

39. Wang Taiyuan's interview on Oct. 1, 2001, www.news.china.com, accessed Feb. 19, 2002.

40. Chinese Central TV, *Jingji banxiaoshi* (Half hour on the economy), Beijing, Aug. 9, 2001.

41. The PRC Ministry of Education and three other ministries issued a directive to abandon migration quotas in cities smaller than provincial capitals for any college graduate employed from outside (Xinhua, Beijing, Nov. 22, 2002).

42. To generate 800,000 Yuan RMB of taxes, a business must have assets exceeding 16 million Yuan. However, the average asset size of private businesses in China was only 530,000 Yuan in the late 1990s (China News Agency, Beijing, Oct. 1, 2001). In 2004, this requirement was reduced in the outer towns of the Beijing Municipality. Author's interviews in Beijing, 2004.

43. According to one accounting expert's calculations, to be able to live in Beijing and own a business that employs 100 workers and pays 800,000 Yuan RMB tax a year, one must have a net worth of at least eight million RMB (www. news.china.com, Oct. 15, 2001, accessed Feb. 19, 2002).

44. "Daodi suixiang jingjing?" (Exactly who wants to enter Beijing?), *Beijing qingnian bao* (Beijing youth daily), Beijing, Oct. 9, 2001.

45. The main motivation for such efforts was reported to be the successful fast-food chain owner's desire to bring his 13-year old son from his home town in Hunan Province to Beijing so that the boy could take advantage of the "much better" education opportunities in the nation's capital. www.news.china.com/zh_cn/focus/hjzd, Dec. 5, 2001, accessed Feb. 19, 2002.

46. As opposed to "cost-priced" housing or economy housing or *anju* (peaceful living) housing that is subsidized for local urban residents only. *Business China*, Hong Kong, Aug. 30, 1999, 4, and *China Daily*, Beijing, Apr. 24, 2001.

47. The PRC Ministry of Construction prohibits unauthorized sale of housing in urban districts where there is a "*hukou* freeze" (no new residents). *Renmin ribao* (People's daily), Beijing, May 6, 1999, 2.

48. Chinese People's Bank, *Provisional Measure on the Management of Individual Housing Loans*, Apr. 28, 1997. The maximum amount of a housing mortgage is 70 percent of the purchase price.

49. "Jiujing sui caishi zuixuyao beijing hukou de ren?" (Exactly who needs a Beijing *hukou* the most?), www.news.china.com, Oct. 7, 2001.

50. Author's interviews in Beijing, Shanghai, and Shenzhen, 1999–2003.

51. Mark O'Neil, "Dislike Grows for Incomers as Wealth Casts Shadow on City," *South China Morning Post*, Hong Kong, June 25, 2001.

52. Interview with officials from Beijing Personnel Bureau, *Chengbao* (Morning news), Beijing, Aug. 22, 2001.

53. Beijing Municipal Government's *Regulations on Encouraging Chinese Who Studied Overseas to Work or Open Business in Beijing*, May 1, 2000; *Shengzhou xueren* (Chinese scholars), Beijing, June 2000, 47.

54. Shanghai Municipal Government, *Shanghai shi lanying hukou guanli zanxing banfa* (Provisional rules on the management of blue-seal *hukou* in Shanghai city), www.news.china.com, Oct. 15, 2001, accessed Feb. 19, 2002.

55. Shanghai Municipal Government, *Shanghai shi shehui baozhang ka guangli banfa* (Measure on the management of Shanghai city social security card), Directive 100. May 5, 2001, in *Xin fagui yuekan* (New laws and regulations monthly), Shanghai, July 2001, 37–39.

56. Zhang Yinghong, "Sun Zhigang zhisi yu zhidu zhier" (The death of Sun Zhigang and the evil of the [*hukou*] system), Apr. 28, 2003, www.mlcool.com; *Caijing shibao* (Financial and economic times), Beijing, June 15, 2003; *Changsha wanbao* (Changsha evening news), June 13, 2003; Xinhua *Daily Telegraph*, Beijing, June 21, 2004; Author's interviews in Beijing, 2004.

57. *Jiangsu ribao* (Jiangsu daily), Nanjing, Oct. 16, 2001.

58. *Nanfang dushi bao* (Southern metro daily), Guangzhou, Sept. 8, 2001.

59. *Dongfang ribao* (Oriental daily), Hong Kong, July 29, 2001, 30.

60. *Guangzhoushi goumai shangpinfang shenban lanying hukou zanxing guiding* (Provisional rules on blue-seal *hukou* through purchasing commercial housing units in Guangzhou), Jan. 8, 1998, www.news.china.com, Dec. 5, 2001, accessed Feb. 19, 2002. Such entry conditions were lowered in 2004. *Nanfang ribao* (Southern daily), Guangzhou, Apr. 1, 2004.

61. *Xinhua Daily Telegraph*, Beijing, Aug. 9, 2001.

62. "Ningbo hukou bilei hongran daota" (The *hukou* barriers collapsing in Ningbo), *Nanfang zhoumu* (Southern weekend), Guangzhou, Aug. 31, 2001; *Zhongguo qingnianbao* (Chinese youth daily), Sept. 17, 2001.

63. CCTV (Chinese Central TV), *Evening news*, Oct. 25, 2001.

64. *The Independence Daily*, Sydney, Australia, Aug. 14, 2001, 4; Josephine Ma, "Farmers Turn Noses up at Life in the City," *South China Morning Post*, Hong Kong, Oct. 17, 2001.

65. *Xinhua Daily Telegraph*, Beijing, Dec. 24, 2001.

66. *Hunan ribao* (Hunan daily), Changsha, Jan. 20, 2002, and *Renmin ribao—huadongban* (People's daily—East China edition), Shanghai, Jan. 9 and Feb. 26, 2002. Beijing started to issue its "green cards" in 2003 (author's interview in Beijing, 2004).

67. State Education Commission, *Chengzhen liudong renkouzhong shining ertong shaonian jiuxue banfa (shixing)* (Provisional regulations on the education of school age children among the migrant population in the cities), Beijing, 1996.

68. MPS, *Liudong ertong shaonian jiuxue zanxing banfa* (Provisional measures on the education of migrant youth), Beijing, 1998.

69. Wu Xiaoping 2001, 147.

70. Wu Xiaoping 2001, 147–48, and Lu Shaoqing and Zhang Shouli 2001, 100–101 and 104.

71. Some of the schools had over one thousand students; others only had seven students (the average enrollment was 93 per school). Lu Shaoqing and

Zhang Shouli 2001, 95–96, 98, and 103. In Shanghai, such "self-run" schools for migrant children were reported to number about 400 in 2001. *Huanqiu shibao* (Global times), Beijing, May 22, 2001, 4.

72. Wu Xiaoping 2001, 147–48.

73. In many local elementary schools, class sizes doubled to as many as 70 students per teacher; sometimes three children had to share one seat. *Gongren ribao* (Worker's daily), Beijing, Dec. 27, 2001. For a report about how some new urban residents were disillusioned and considered returning to the villages, see *Qingdao zhaobao* (Qingdao morning news), Qingdao, Aug. 4, 2003.

74. "Tongyang shi gongmin, weishimo shimin pei 5 wan nongmin pei 3 wan?" (Same citizens—why does the urban dweller get 50 thousand RMB compensation and rural resident only 30 thousand RMB?), www.people.com.cn, Oct. 8, 2001, accessed Feb. 19, 2002.

75. "Huji zhidu gaige shizaibixing" (*Hukou* reform is inevitable), *Renmin ribao* (People's daily), Beijing, Sept. 24, 2001, 9. Some have interpreted Beijing's calls for "orderly" rural-to-urban migration as a new effort to "reconstitute" China's rural-urban divide (Guang 2001, 489–93).

76. Interview with Bao Suixian, deputy bureau chief of public security of the MPS, CCTV, Beijing, Jan. 5, 2002.

77. *China News Weekly*, Beijing, Sept. 6, 2002, and *Huaxi dushi bao* (Western China metro news), Chengdu, Sept. 5, 2002.

78. Sometimes only a few people, or no one at all, applied for urban *hukou* in the small cities or towns under the new "entry conditions." They either could not find a stable job to support them in the cities or found artificial "urbanization" meaningless since there were few new jobs or new markets for them in the cities. Li Junde, "Nongzhuanfei shou lengdan" (Rural-to-urban change is cold-shouldered), Xinhua New Agency, Zhengzhou, Jan. 5, 2002.

79. An uncontrolled internal migration or a politically motivated "Great Leap Forward" style rapid urbanization is viewed by many in China as likely, at the minimum, to cause enormous waste of resources and at the maximum lead to a so-called "Latin Americanization" of China, with massive urban slums, political instability, and uncertain economic development. Author's interviews in Anhui, Beijing, Jiangsu, Shanghai, and Tianjin, 2002–3. Also, Pan Wei 2003, 410.

80. Interviews with Wang Taiyuan, a senior *hukou* official and expert. *Huaxi dushi bao* (Western China metro news), Chengdu, Sept. 5, 2002.

81. Beijing Bureau of Public Security official statement, *Cheng bao* (Morning news), Beijing, Aug. 25, 2001.

82. Interview with Central Government official, *Cheng bao* (Morning news), Beijing, Aug. 9, 2001.

83. Interviews with the *hukou* chief of the MPS, *Cheng bao* (Morning news), Beijing, Aug. 20, 2001.

84. Liu Guoguang ed. 2000, 31. Liu is one of the top economic advisors to the PRC government. Another more optimistic "design" suggests that, by 2050, China should have 80 percent of its estimated 1.6 billion population living in the cities (Cao Jingchun 2001, 14–15).

85. For a critical report on the popular "name-changing only urbanization"

schemes, through which local officials "urbanize" their jurisdiction by simply renaming their counties to be "cities," in the 1990s, see Xie Ying 1996 and *Guangming ribao* (Guangming daily), Beijing, Dec. 12, 2003.

86. Wu Li 2001.

87. Dong Fan and Deng Jianwei, a conference paper on the Three Gorges relocation program, Xiamen, 2001, 4. For a study on the Three Gorges relocation program, see Zhu Nong and Wang Bin 1999, 264–86. For details of the PRC policy on Three Gorges population relocation, see State Council 2001 *Changjiang sanxia*.

88. Over 400,000 people were relocated and rid of poverty in the first decade of the project. See the Sanxi Relocation assessment report in Zhang Zhiliang 1996. For a report on the relocations in Ningxia, see Zhang Tongji et al. 1998.

89. SCESB 2000.

90. Gu Jiekang, "Lun 'sunan muoshi' de jiben tezhen jiqi chuangxin fazhan" (On the basic features of the Sunan model and its further innovations and developments), *Qunzong* (Masses), Beijing, no. 12 (1997). For Sunan small town development, see Wu Caisheng et al. 1999.

91. Goodkind and West 2001.

92. Huang Bincheng 2001, 39.

93. Author's interviews in Anhui, Beijing, Chongqing, and Jiangsu, 2001–3.

94. Zai Liang 1999.

95. Minxin Pei 2002.

96. "E jingcha kaishi liangxian, huji dangan jiang dianzihua" (E-police starts to emerge and *hukou* files will be electronic), www.news.china.com, Sept. 21, 2001, accessed Feb. 19, 2002. The police asserted that several high-profile criminal cases in 2002 were solved due to the *hukou* police's routine but now faster gathering and monitoring of hotel registration information. Author's interviews in Beijing and Shanghai, 2002–3.

97. One study concludes that *hukou* reforms and adaptations have already provided a "high degree of freedom of [temporary] population movement (*liudong*)" in China even though the state still maintains tight control on permanent internal migration (*qianyi*) or *hukou* relocation (Ma Fuyun 2000, 71). Another study reports that the surveyed residents of small cities and townships view the difference between urban and rural types of *hukou* as something already insignificant (Lu Yilong 2003, 417–18).

98. Author's interview with Li Qiang, a professor at Tsinghua University, 2001. Li says the *hukou* system is "a good legacy of the Mao era and works wonders to stabilize the society" and hence will certainly be well maintained by the urban *hukou*-holding Chinese elite.

99. Author's interviews in Shanghai, 2001. Only a few months after the government ordered a halt to forcible repatriation of the floaters in the major urban centers in June 2003, some in Beijing already started to worry that such "cheap and easy" measures of pleasing people through weakening the *hukou* system may lead to a premature collapse of the CCP's ability of control and mortally damage China's much-needed sociopolitical stability. Author's interviews in Beijing, 2004.

100. Reported by the official Xinhua News Agency, *South China Morning*

Post, Hong Kong, Feb. 26, 2002. Bao reaffirmed this position in his interview with Chinese Central Television, Mar. 10, 2004.

101. Financially, major urban centers have long benefited from the "capital drain" of inland regions. In 1996–97, for example, more than half of the massive investments in Shanghai's impressive Pudong New Area were from inland provinces. Author's interviews in Shanghai, 1998.

102. *Fudan bao* (Fudan University daily), Shanghai, June 10, 1998, 2.

103. Author's interview with Shanghai's Nanyang Model School faculty, Nov. 2003.

104. www.news.china.com, Aug. 20, 2001; *Cheng bao* (Morning news), Beijing, Aug. 25, 2001; and Kang Jin, "'Chengxiang hujizhi' gaiwei 'pingfu hujizhi' bushi jinbu" (Reforming "urban-rural *hukou* system" to "rich-poor *hukou* system" is no progress), *Zhongguo qingnian bao* (Chinese youth daily), Beijing, Dec. 26, 2003.

105. By the mid-1990s, the state only controlled 4.5 percent of China's industrial production, down from 40 percent in 1980, and only 5.9 percent of commercial wholesale and retail. *Renmin ribao* (People's daily), Beijing, May 10, 1994, 1.

106. Solinger 1999, 1, 10, and 227–90.

107. As an indicator, the Chinese police reported that, by the late 1990s, 80 percent of processed criminal cases were violations of property rights (65 percent were simple thefts), up from less than 30 percent twenty years earlier (Kang Damin 1998, 448).

108. Full citizenship, as defined in Brubaker (1992, 180) and cited and elaborated in Solinger (1999, 4–5 and 293), means "not only political rights but also the unconditional right to enter and reside in the country, complete access to the labor market, and eligibility for the full range of welfare benefits." For an optimistic semiofficial account estimating a ten-year total reform of the *hukou* system to allow a "basic freedom of internal migration for all citizens" so as to promote human rights in China, see *Xinjing bao* (New capital daily), Beijing, Jan. 2, 2004.

Bibliography

Agrawal, Pradeep, et al. *Economic Restructuring in East Asia and India*. London: Macmillan Press, 1995.

Ahmad, Imtiaz. *Caste and Social Stratification among Muslims in India*. New Delhi: Manohar, 1978.

Alesina, Alberto, and Enrico Spolaore. "On the Number and Size of Nations," *The Quarterly Journal of Economics* (Cambridge, MA) 112.4 (1997), 1027–56.

Almond, Gabriel A. "Capitalism and Democracy," *PS: Political Science and Politics* (Sept. 1991), 467–74.

Ambedkar, B. R. *Annihilation of Caste*. Bangalore: Dalit Sahitya Akademy, 1987.

Amin, A. T. M. Nurul. *Economic Logic of Resource Flows between the Rural-Agricultural and the Urban-Industrial Sector*. Bangkok: Asian Institute of Technology, 1994.

Amos, F. J. C. *Contemporary Perspectives on Urbanization*. New York: Pergamon, 1996.

Anhui Provincial Government. *1995 Anhui Shengqing Shouce* (Provincial situation handbook of Anhui, 1995), internal publication. Hefei, 1995.

APMRN (Asia-Pacific Migration Research Network). *Migration Issues: Issues Paper from the People's Republic of China*. Wollongong, Australia: APMRN, 2001.

Appasamy, Paul, et al. *Social Exclusion from a Welfare Rights Perspective in India*. Geneva: International Labour Organization, 1996.

Arnold, Thomas C. "Rethinking Moral Economy," *American Political Science Review* 95.1 (Mar. 2001), 85–95.

Arrow, Kenneth J. "The Division of Labor in the Economy, the Polity, and Society," in Gerald O'Driscoll Jr., ed., *Adam Smith and Modern Political Economy*. Ames, Iowa: The Iowa State University Press, 1979.

Asia-Pacific Center. *A Comparative Study on the Urban Systems in Asian Countries: System of Cities in Japan, Korea, and Malaysia*. Fukuoka, Japan, 2000.

Asia-Pacific Urban Forum. *Living in Asian Cities: The Impending Crisis, Causes, Consequences and Alternatives for the Future*. New York: United Nations, 1996.

Azrael, Jeremy R., and Emil A. Payin, eds. *Cooperation and Conflict in the Former Soviet Union: Implications for Migration.* Santa Monica, CA: Rand, 1996.

Bader, Veit, ed. *Citizenship and Exclusion.* New York: St Martin's Press, 1997.

Bagnall, Roger S. *The Demography of Roman Egypt.* Cambridge, UK: Cambridge University Press, 1999.

Bajpai, Nirupam. *India's Economic Reform: Some Lessons from East Asia.* Cambridge, MA: Harvard Institute for Economic Development, 1996.

Bakken, Borge. *The Exemplary Society: Human Improvement, Social Control, and the Dangers of Modernity in China.* Oxford: Oxford University Press, 2000.

Baldwin, David, ed. *Neorealism and Neoliberalism.* New York: Columbia University Press, 1993.

Ban, Maosheng, and Zhu Changsheng. "Huji gaige de yanjiu zhuankuan ji shiji jingzhan" (Current study of the *huji* reform and its development), *Renkou yu jingji* (Population and economics), Beijing, no. 114 (Jan.), 2000.

Banister, Judith. "China: Population Dynamics and Economic Implications," in *China's Economic Future: Challenges to U.S. Policy*, ed. U.S. Congress Joint Economic Committee. Armonk, NY: M. E. Sharpe, 1997, 339–60.

———. *China's Changing Population.* Stanford, CA: Stanford University Press, 1987.

Bao, Yueyang, and Li Haibin. *Zhongguo jingji de ruoshi* (Weaknesses of China's economy). Beijing: Jingji Daily Press, 2000.

Barbalet, J. M. *Citizenship: Rights, Struggle, and Class Inequality.* Milton Keynes: Open University Press, 1988.

Baum, Richard, and Manoranjan Mohanty, eds. *Local Governance in China and India: Rural Development and Social Change.* New York: Sage, 2004.

Bayley, David H. *Social Control and Political Change.* Princeton, NJ: Center for International Studies, 1985.

Becker, Charles M. *Indian Urbanization and Economic Growth since 1960.* Baltimore: Johns Hopkins University Press, 1992.

Beier, A. L. *Problem of the Poor in Tudor and Early Stuart England.* London: Routledge, 1983.

Bernstein, Thomas P. *Up to the Mountains and Down to the Villages: The Transfer of Youth from Urban to Rural China.* New Haven, CT: Yale University Press, 1977.

Bian, Yanjie. *Work and Inequality in Urban China.* Albany, NY: SUNY Press, 1994.

Blumberg, Rae Lesser. "A General Theory of Gender Stratification," in R. Collin, ed., *Sociological Theory 1984.* Hoboken, NJ: Jossey-Bass, 1984.

Body-Gendrot, Sophie. *The Social Control of Cities: A Comparative Perspective.* Malden, MA: Blackwell, 2000.

Booth, Tony, and Mel Ainscow, *Inclusion and Exclusion: An International Comparison.* London: Routledge, 1998.

Booth, William Jones. "On the Idea of the Moral Economy," *American Political Science Review* 87 (Dec. 1994), 949–54.

————. *Households: On the Moral Architecture of the Economy.* Ithaca: Cornell University Press, 1993.

Bowman, Alan K., et al. *The Cambridge Ancient History: The Augustan Empire, 43 B.C. – A.D. 69.* 2nd ed., vol. 10. Cambridge, UK: Cambridge University Press, 1996.

Bradbury, Jonathan, and John Mawson, eds. *British Regionalism and Devolution: The Challenges of State Reform and European Integration.* London: Jessica Kingsley, 1997.

Bramall, Chris. "The Quality of China's Household Income Surveys," *The China Quarterly,* no. 167 (Sept. 2001), 689–705.

Brazier, Susan. "Propiska," www.nelegal.net/articles, Nov. 8, 2001.

Brown, Alan A., and Egon Neuberger, eds. *Internal Migration: A Comparative Perspective.* New York: Academic Press, 1977.

Brown, James R., and Lin Sein, eds. *Land Reform in Developing Countries.* Hartford, CT: University of Hartford Press, 1968.

Brown, Lester, et al. *State of the World.* London: World Watch Institute, 2000.

Brubaker, Rogers. *Citizenship and Nationhood in France and Germany.* Cambridge, MA: Harvard University Press, 1992.

Buckley, Cynthia. *The Myth of Managed Migration: Migration Restrictions and Marketization in the Russian Republic.* Austin, TX: Texas Population Research Center, 1993.

Cai, Fang, et al., eds. *Zhongguo renkou wenti baogao: Nongcun renkou wenti jiqi zhili* (Report on China's population issue: the rural population issue and its solutions). Beijing: Social Science Documents Press, 2000.

Caldwell, John C. *African Rural-Urban Migration.* New York: Columbia University Press, 1969.

Cannon, Terry, ed. *China's Economic Growth—The Impact on Regions, Migration and the Environment.* New York: Macmillan/St. Martin's Press, 2000.

Cao, Haibo, and Li Weimin, eds. *Sifa cidian* (Dictionary of law enforcement). Beijing: Zhongguo Gongren Press, 1989.

Cao, Jingchun. "Jiaqiang huji gaige, chujing renkou qianyi he chengzhenhua jingcheng" (Enhancing *hukou* reform and promoting population movement and urbanization process), *Renkou yanjiu* (Population research), Beijing, 25.5 (Sept. 2001), 9–17.

Cao, Jinqing. *Huanghe biande zhongguo: yige xuezhe dui xiangcun shehui de guanca yu sikao* (China by the Yellow River: a scholarly observation and reflection of the rural society). Shanghai: Shanghai Wenyi Press, 2000.

Cao, Shuji. *Zhongguo renkou shi-Qing shiqi* (Population history of China: the Qing era). Shanghai: Fudan University Press, 2001.

————. *Zhongguo yimin shi-Qing, minguo shiqi* (Population history of China: the Qing and republican eras). Fuzhou: Fujian Renmin Press, 1997.

Cardoso, Fernando E. *Charting a New Course: The Politics of Globalization and Social Transformation.* Lanham, MD: Rowman & Littlefield, 2001.

————, and Enzo Faletto. *Dependency and Development in Latin America.* Berkeley, CA: University of California Press, 1979.

Castles, Stephen, and Alastair Davidson, eds. *Citizenship and Migration: Globalization and the Politics of Belonging.* London: Routledge, 2000.

CAUD (Chinese Association for Urban Development), ed. *Zhongguo chengshi nianjian* (Yearbook of Chinese cities). Beijing:, CAUD, 1999.

Cavalcanti, H. B. "Brazil at the End of the Century: Presidential Impeachment and Economic Integration in First World Markets," in Satya R. Pattnayak, ed., *Globalization, Urbanization, and the State*. Lanham, MD: University Press of America, 1996.

Central Document Study Office of the CCP. *Shisanda yilai* (Since the 13th party congress), 3 vols. of documents. Beijing: Renmin Press, 1990–92.

Central Party School of the CCP. *"Yifa zhiguo" yu "yide zhiguo" xuexi wenda* (Q & A for the study of "rule by law" and "rule by morals"). Beijing: Central Party School of the CCP Press, 2001.

Centre for Asian Studies. *Economic Bluebook of the PRC, 1999*. Hong Kong: University of Hong Kong, 2000.

Chalmers, Douglas, et al., eds. *The New Politics of Inequality in Latin America: Rethinking Participation and Representation*. New York: Oxford University Press, 1997.

Chan, Anita, et al., eds. *Transforming Asian Socialism: China and Vietnam Compared*. Lanham, MD: Rowman & Littlefield, 1999.

———. *Chen Village, under Mao and Deng*. Berkeley, CA: University of California Press, 1992.

———. "Urbanization and Rural-urban Migration in China since 1982: A New Baseline," *Modern China* 20 (July 1994), 243–82.

Chan, Kam Wan, and Li Zhang. "The *Hukou* System and Rural-Urban Migration in China: Processes and Changes," *The China Quarterly*, 1999, 818–55.

Chan, Kam Wing. "Rural-Urban Migration in China, 1950–1982," *Urban Geography* 9.1 (1988), 53–84.

Cheema, Shabbir, and Sandra E. Ward, eds. *Urban Management: Policies and Innovations in Developing Countries*. Westport, CT: Praeger, 1993.

Chen, Chunnong: *Gongmin fali guwen* (Legal reference for citizens). Harbin: Heilongjiang Renmin Press, 1986.

Chen, Dengyuan. *Zhongguo tianfu shi* (History of China's land taxation). Shanghai: Shangwu Press, (1938) 1984.

Chen, Dongyou, ed. *Zhongguo nongmin* (Chinese peasants). Nanchang: Jiangxi Gaoxiao Press, 1999.

Chen, Dung-Sheng. "Taiwan's Social Changes in the Patterns of Social Solidarity in the 20th Century," *The China Quarterly*, no. 165 (Mar. 2001), 61–82.

Chen, Guili, and Chun Tao. *Zhongguo nongmin diaocha* (Investigation of Chinese peasants). Beijing: Renmin Wenxue Press, 2004.

Chen, Hua. *Qingdai quyu shehui jingji yanjiu* (Study on the regional socioeconomics in the Qing dynasty). Beijing: Zhongguo Renmin University Press, 1996.

Chen, Pengshen, ed. *Zhongguo gudai fali sanbei ti* (Three hundred issues in the ancient legal system of China). Shanghai: Guji Press, 1991.

Chen, Shaoxin. *Taiwan de renkou bianqian yu shehui bianqian* (Demographic and social changes in Taiwan). Taipei: Jinglian, 1995.

Chen, Xiangyi. "Huji guanli mianling de kunjing yu xunzhi" (The dilemmas and choices of *hukou* management). *Neibu wengao* (Internal drafts), Beijing, no. 9 (1993), 7–12.

Chen, Yun. *Chen Yun wenxuian 1949–1956* (Selected works of Chen Yun). Beijing: Renmin Press, 1983.

Chen, Zhen, ed. *Zhongguo jindai gongye shi ziliao* (Historical data on Chinese modern industry), vol. 4. Beijing: Sanlian Books, 1961.

Cheng, Tiejun. "Dialectics of Control: The Household Registration (Hukou) System in Contemporary China." Ph.D. diss., SUNY-Binghamton, 1991.

———. "Zhongguo hukou zhidu de xiangzhuang yu weilai" (The current status and the future of China's *hukou* system), in Li Shaomin, ed., *Zhongguo dalu de shehui, zhengzhi, jingji* (Society, politics, and economy of the Chinese Mainland). Princeton, NJ: Center for Modern China, 1992.

Cheng, Tiejun, and Mark Selden. "The Origins and Social Consequences of China's *Hukou* System," *The China Quarterly* (1994), 644–68.

———. "The Construction of Spatial Hierarchies: China's *Hukou* and *Danwei* Systems," in Timothy Cheek and Tony Saich, eds., *New Perspectives on State Socialism in China*. Armonk, NY: M. E. Sharpe, 1997.

Cheng, Zhiyong, and Bo Xiao, eds. *Qiangzhan yu qiangan* (Gun-battles and gun-cases: selections of case reports on anti-terrorism in Xinjiang), internal publication. Beijing: Qunzhong Press, 2000.

Chomsky, Noam. *Media Control: The Spectacular Achievements of Propaganda*. New York: Seven Stories Press, 1997.

———. *Necessary Illusions: Thought Control in Democratic Societies*. New York: South End Press, 1989.

Christiansen, Flemming. "The Legacy of the Mock Dual Economy: Chinese Labor in Transition, 1978–1992," *Economy and Society* 22.4 (1993), 411–36.

Chung, Jae Ho, ed. *Cities in China: Recipes for Economic Development in the Reform Era*. London: Routledge, 1999.

CNI (Confederação Nacional da Indústria). *The Brazilian Economy: Performance and Prospects, 1996/97*. Rio de Janeiro, RJ, Brazil, 1997.

Cohen, Robin, ed. *Theories of Migration*. Cheltenham, UK: Edward Elgar, 1996.

Collins, Randall. "Some Comparative Principles of Educational Stratification," *Harvard Educational Review* 47.1 (1977), 1–27.

Compaine, David. *The Digital Divide*, Cambridge, MA: MIT Press, 2001.

CONDEPE (Instituto de Planejamento de Pernambuco). *Pernambuco 2010: Estrategía de Desenvolvimento Sustentável*. Recife, PE, Brazil: CONDEPE, 1996.

———. *Pernambuco em Dados*. Recife, PE, Brazil: CONDEPE, 1997.

Conniff, Michael L., and Frank D. McCann, eds. *Modern Brazil: Elites and Masses in Historical Perspective*. Lincoln: University of Nebraska Press, 1989.

Cook, Susan, and Margaret Maurer-Fazio, eds. *The Workers' State Meets the Market: Labor in China's Transition*. London: Frank Cass, 1999.

CPB-PB (Chinese People's Bank—Personnel Bureau), ed. *Renshi gongzuo wenjian xuanbian* (Selected documents on personnel works), internal publication. Beijing: Zhongguo Jinrong Press, 1985.

CPS (Chinese Police Society). *Gongan shi wenda* (Q & A on the history of public security). Beijing: Qunzhong Press, for law-enforcement use only, 1994.

Crook, J. A., et al. *The Cambridge Ancient History: The Last Age of the Roman Republic, 146–43 B.C.* Cambridge, UK: Cambridge University Press, 1994.

Cui, Naiwen. "Diaocha tongji shuzi kexingdu you duoda" (How reliable are the statistical and survey data), *Xinshiji* (New century), Beijing, Dec. 1995, 7–11.

Dai, Yuancheng, and Chen Dongqi. *Laogong guoshen jingji de jiuye yu shouru* (Employment and income in an economy with surplus labor). Shanghai: Shanghai Yuandong Press, 1996.

Davin, Delia. *Internal Migration in Contemporary China.* New York: Palgrave, 1999.

Day, Lincoln H., and Ma Xia, eds. *Migration and Urbanization in Modern China.* Armonk, NY: M. E. Sharpe, 1994.

Degrute, J. J. M. *Chinese Religion.* New York: Macmillan, 1910.

Deng, Xiaoping. *Deng Xiaoping wenxun 1975–1982* (Selected works of Deng Xiaoping 1975–82). Beijing: Renmin Press, 1983.

———. *Deng Xiaoping wenxun* (Selected works of Deng Xiaoping), vols. 1–2. Beijing: Renmin Press, 1985 and 1992.

den Uyl, Marion. *Invisible Barriers: Gender, Caste, and Kinship in a Southern Indian Village.* The Netherlands: International Books, 1995.

Desai, A. R., and S. Devada Pillai, eds. *Slums and Urbanization.* London: Sangam Books, 1990.

De Souza, Alfred. *The Indian City: Poverty, Ecology and Urban Development.* New Delhi: Manohar, 1983.

Dickenson, John. *Brazil.* London: Longman, 1982.

Dikotter, Frank, ed. *The Construction of Racial Identities in China and Japan.* London: Hurst, 1997.

Ding, Shuimu. "Huji guanli yu shehui kongzhi: Xianxing huji guanli zhidu zaiyi" (Another view on the management of the current *hukou* system), *Shehui* (Society), Shanghai, no. 3 (1989), 26–29.

———. "Xianxing huji zhidu de gongneng jiqi gaige zouxiang" (The function of the current *hukou* system and the trend of its reform), *Shehuixue yanjiu* (Sociological studies), no. 5 (1992), 100–104.

———. "Yong jingji shouduan tiaojie renkou liuxiang" (To use economic means to adjust the directions of migration), *Ershiyi shiji* (Twenty-first century), Hong Kong, no. 5 (1999).

Ding, Yuanzhu. "Tiaozhan yu jiyu: WTO xia zhongguo shehui fazhan de ruogan wenti" (Challenge and opportunity: several issues of China's social development under the WTO), *Zhongguo shehui kexue jikan* (Chinese social science quarterly), Hong Kong, no. 32 (Winter 2000), 133–39.

Duany, Andres, et al. *Suburban Nation: The Rise of Sprawl and the Decline of the American Dream.* New York: North Point Press, 2001.

Duquette, Michel. *Building New Democracies: Economic and Social Reform in Brazil, Chile, and Mexico.* Toronto: University of Toronto Press, 1999.

Durkheim, Émile. *The Division of Labor in Society*, originally published 1893. New York: Macmillan, 1933/Free Press 1997.

Dutton, Michael R. *Policing and Punishment in China: From Patriarchy to "The People."* New York: Cambridge University Press, 1992.

———, ed. "Policing the Chinese Household: A Comparison of Modern and Ancient Forms," *Economy and Society* 17.2 (May 1988).

———, ed. *Streetlife China*. Cambridge, UK: Cambridge University Press, 1999.

Dyrberg, Torben Bech. *The Circular Structure of Power: Politics, Identity, Community*. London: Verso, 1997.

Eckstein, Harry. *Regarding Politics: Essays on Political Theory, Stability, and Changes*. Berkeley, CA: University of California Press, 1991.

EIU (The Economist Intelligence Unit). *Country Profile 2000: China and Mongolia*. London: EIU, 2001.

Elvin, Mark, and G. William Skinner, eds. *The Chinese City between Two Worlds*. Stanford, CA: Stanford University Press, 1974.

Entman, Robert M., and Andrew Rojecki. *The Black Image in the White Mind: Media and Race in America*. Chicago: University of Chicago Press, 2000.

Evans, Peter. *Dependent Development, the Alliance of Multinational, State and Local Capital in Brazil*. Princeton, NJ: Princeton University Press, 1979.

Fairbank, John King, and Merle Goldman. *China: A New History*. Cambridge, MA: Harvard University Press, 1998.

Faist, Thomas. "States, Markets, and Immigrant Minorities," *Comparative Politics* 26.4 (1994), 439–60.

Fan, Ping. "Zhongguo chengzheng de di shouru qunti" (The low income groups in the Chinese cities and towns), *Zhongguo shehui kexue* (Chinese social sciences), Beijing, no. 4 (1996), 64–77.

Feagin, Joe, and Clairece B. Feagin. *Racial and Ethnic Relations*. Englewood Cliffs, NJ: Prentice Hall, 1993.

Fei, John C. H., and Gustav Ranis. *Growth and Development from an Evolutionary Perspective*. London: Blackwell Publishers, 1999.

Fei, Xiaotong. *Xiao chenzhen siji* (Four records of small towns). Beijing: Xinhua Press, 1985.

———. *Jiangcun jingji* (The economy of the Jiang village). Nanjing: Jiangsu Renmin Press, 1986.

———. *Small Towns in China: Functions, Problems and Prospects*. Beijing: New World Press, 1986.

Fewsmith, Joseph. "The Political and Social Implications of China's Accession to the WTO," *The China Quarterly*, no. 167 (Sept. 2001), 573–91.

Fitzpatrick, Stephen, ed. *Work and Mobility: Recent Labour Migration Issues in China*. Wollongong, Australia: Centre for Asia Pacific Social Transformation Studies, 1999.

Flanagan, James G., and Steve Rayner, eds. *Rules, Decisions, and Inequality: In Egalitarian Societies*. Aldershot, UK: Avebury, 1988.

Fleisher, Belton M. "The Coast-noncoast Income Gap, Productivity, and Regional Economic Policy in China," *Journal of Comparative Economics* 25 (Oct. 1997), 220–36.

Fogel, Robert W. "Aspects of Economic Growth: A Comparison of the U.S. and China," conference paper, Chengdu, China, 1999.

Frank, Andre Gunder. "The Development of Underdevelopment," *Monthly Review* 18.4 (1966), 17–31.

Friedman, Edward, et al. *Chinese Village, Socialist State.* New Haven, CT: Yale University Press, 1991.

Fukuyama, Francis. *The End of History and the Last Man.* New York: Avon Books, 1993.

Gao, Guiting, ed. *Baowei gongzuo tonglun* (General discourse on protection work), internal publication. Beijing: Police Education Press, 1994.

Gao, Shangquan, et al., eds. *Zhongguo jingji gaige kaifang dashidian* (Events of Chinese reforming and opening), 2 vols. Beijing: Beijing Gongye University Press, 1993.

Garcia, Soledad. "Cities and Citizenship," *International Journal of Urban and Regional Research* 20.1 (1996), 7–21.

Garon, Sheldon. *Molding Japanese Minds: The State in Everyday Life.* Princeton, NJ: Princeton University Press, 1997.

Garver, John W. *Protracted Contest: Sino-Indian Rivalry in the Twentieth Century.* Seattle: University of Washington Press, 2001.

Ge, Jianxiong, et al. *Jianmin zhongguo yimin shi* (A short history of China's internal migration). Fuzhou: Fujian Renmin Press, 1993.

———. *Renkou yu zhongguo de xiandaihua* (Population and China's modernization). Shanghai: Xuelin Press, 1999.

Ge, Xiangxian, and Qu Weiying. *Zhongguo mingong chao* (The tides of Chinese peasant labor). Beijing: Zhongguo Guoji Guangbo Press, 1990.

G8 Okinawa Summit. *Global Poverty Report.* IMF and World Bank, July 2000.

Genovese, Eugene D. *The Political Economy of Slavery: Studies in the Economy and Society of the Slave South.* Boston: Wesleyan University Press, 1989.

———. *The Slaveholders' Dilemma: Freedom and Progress in Southern Conservative Thought, 1820–1860.* Charleston: University of South Carolina Press, 1994.

Gewirth, Alan, *Human Rights.* Chicago: University of Chicago Press, 1982.

Ghosh, B. N., ed. *Contemporary Issues in Development Economics.* London: Routledge, 2001.

Gibbs, Jack P. *A Theory about Control.* Boulder, CO: Westview, 1994.

Giddens, Anthony. *Capitalism and Modern Social Theory: An Analysis of the Writings of Marx, Durkheim and Max Weber.* New York: Cambridge University Press, 1973.

———. *The Constitution of Society: Outline of the Theory of Structuration.* Berkeley, CA: University of California Press, 1986.

Gilbert, Alan. *Cities, Poverty, and Development: Urbanization in the Third World.* 2nd ed. New York: Oxford University Press, 1992.

Goldman, Merle, and Roderick MacFarquhar, eds. *The Paradox of China's Post-Mao Reforms.* Cambridge, MA: Harvard University Press, 1999.

Goldscheider, Calvin, ed. *Urban Migration in Developing Nations: Patterns and Problems of Adjustment.* Boulder, CO: Westview, 1983.

Goldstein, Alice, and Wang Feng. *China: The Many Facets of Demographic Change.* Boulder, CO: Westview, 1996.

Goldstein, Sidney. *Population Mobility in the People's Republic of China.* Honolulu: East-West Center, 1985.

———. *Surveys of Migration in Developing Countries: A Methodological Review*. Honolulu: East-West Center, 1981.

Goodkind, Daniel, and Loraine A. West. "China's Floating Population—Definitions, Estimates, and Implications for Urbanization," conference paper, Xiamen, 2001.

Gould, Harold A. *The Hindu Caste System*, vol. 1: *The Sacralization of a Social Order*; vol. 2: *Caste Adaptation in Modernizing Indian Society*. Delhi: Chanakya Publications, 1988.

Gowariker, Vasant. *The Inevitable Billion Plus*. New Delhi: Vichar Dhara, 1993.

Griffin, Keith, and Zhao Renwei, eds. *The Distribution of Income in China*. London: Macmillan, 1993.

Groll, Elisabeth, and Ping Huang. "Migration for and against Agriculture in Eight Chinese Villages," *The China Quarterly* 149 (1997): 128–46.

Gu, Chaolin, et al. *Zhongguo chengshi dili* (Urban geography in China). Beijing: Shangwu Press, 1999.

Gu, Daoxian, et al. *Qingchao moqi zhi zhonghua minguo huji guanli fagui* (Laws and regulations on *hukou* management from the late period of the Qing Dynasty to the Republic of China). Beijing: Qunzhong Press, 1996.

Gu, Hongmin. *Zhongguoren de jingshen* (Spirit of the Chinese people), translated by Huan Xintao and Song Xiaoqing. Guilin: Guangxi Normal University Press (1915) 2001.

Gu, Jin, et al. *Changyong renshi guanli falifagui* (Common laws and regulations on personnel management). Beijing: People's Court Press, 1999.

Gu, Shengzhu, and Li Zhengyou. "Zhongguo zhixia ershang chengzheng hua de zhidu fengxi" (An institutional analysis of China's bottom up urbanization), *Zhongguo shehui kexue* (Chinese social sciences), Beijing, no. 2 (1998), 60–70.

Gu, Xin. "Revitalizing Chinese Society: Institutional Transformation and Social Change," in Gungwu Wang and John Wong, eds., *China: Two Decades of Reform and Change*. Singapore: Singapore University Press, 1999, 67–100.

Guang, Lei. "Reconstructing the Rural-Urban Divide: Peasant Migration and the Rise of 'Orderly Migration' in Contemporary China," *Journal of Contemporary China* 10.28 (2001), 471–93.

Gugler, J. *The Urbanization of the Third World*. Oxford: Oxford University Press, 1988.

Gui, Shixun. *Zhongguo liudong renkou jihua shengyu guanli yanjiu* (Study on the management of birth-planning among the migrant population). Shanghai: Huadong Normal University Press, 1992.

Guo, Dehong, et al., eds. *Dang he guojia zhongda juece de licheng* (The process of the party and state's major decisions). Beijing: Hongqi Press, 2 vols., 1998.

Guo, Guanghua, "Ruhe jiaqiang liudong renkou guanli" (How to enhance the management of migrant people). *Renmin gongan* (People's public security), Beijing, no. 16 (1995), 18–19.

Guo, Xuezhi. "Dimensions of *Guanxi* in Chinese Elite Politics," *The China Journal*, issue 46 (July 2001), 69–94.

Guo, Yanlin, et al., eds. *Jingca yu huzheng* (Police and *hukou* administration). Taipei: Taiwan Jingmin Daobao Press, 1952.

Gupta, Shanti Swarup. *Varna, Castes and Scheduled Castes: A Documentation in Historical Perspective*. New Delhi: Concept Publishing, 1991.

Gutherie, Doug. *Dragon in a Three-Piece Suit: The Emergence of Capitalism in China*. Princeton, NJ: Princeton University Press, 1999.

Hacker, Andrew. *Two Nations*. New York: Ballantine Books, 1995.

———. *Money: Who Has How Much and Why*. New York: Scribner, 1997.

Haggard, Stephan. *Pathways from the Periphery—The Politics of Growth in the Newly Industrialized Countries*. Ithaca, NY: Cornell University Press, 1990.

Hamer, Andrew M. *Decentralized Urban Development and Industrial Location Behavior in Sao Paulo*. Washington, DC: World Bank, 1985.

Han, Jun. "Chengxiang geli bixu dapo: zhongguo huji guanli zhidu gaige zaiji" (Urban-rural separation must be broken: reform of the *hukou* system is imminent), *Shidian* (Viewpoint), Beijing, no. 8 (1996), 6–11.

Han, Shaogong. "Meiyou quanqiu shui de quanqiuhua" (Globalization without global tax), *Tainya* (Frontier), Haikou, Hainan, no. 4 (2001), 190–91.

Hao, Zaijing. *Baqianwan liumin buluo* (Eighty million migrant tribes). Beijing: Zhongguo Shehui Press, 1996.

Hardt, Michael, and Antonio Negri. *Empire*. Cambridge, MA: Harvard University Press, 2001.

Hare, Dennis. "'Push' versus 'Pull' Factors in Migration Outflows and Returns: Determinants of Migration Status and Spell Duration among China's Rural Population," *Journal of Development Studies* 35.3 (1999), 45–72.

Hawking, Stephen. *A Brief History of Time*. New York: Bantam Books, 1996.

He, Tieguang. "Kongzhi zhian 'shikongcun'" (To control the 'uncontrolled village'), *Renmin gongan* (People's public security), Beijing, no. 12 (1996), 18–20.

Hein, Laura, and Mark Selden, eds. *Citizenship and Memory in Japan, Germany, and the United States*. Armonk, NY: M. E. Sharpe, 2000.

Heller, Patrick. *The Labor of Development: The Workers and the Transformation of Capitalism in Kerala, India*. Ithaca, NY: Cornell University Press, 1999.

Henry, Stuart, ed. *Social Control: Aspects of Non-State Justice*. Aldershot, UK: Dartmouth, 1994.

Herman, Edward S., and Noam Chomsky. *Manufacturing Consent: The Political Economy of the Mass Media*. New York: Pantheon, 1988.

Ho, Ping-ti. *Studies on the Population of China, 1368–1953*. Cambridge, MA: Harvard University Press, 1959.

Hocart, Arthur M. *Caste: A Comparative Study*. London: Methuen, 1950.

Hoffmann, David L. *Peasant Metropolis: Social Identities in Moscow, 1929–1941*. Ithaca, NY: Cornell University Press, 1994.

Honig, Emily. *Creating Chinese Ethnicity: Subei People in Shanghai, 1850–1980*. New Haven, CT: Yale University Press, 1992.

Hou, Yangfang. *Zhongguo renkou shi—1910–1953* (Population history of China: 1910–53). Shanghai: Fudan University Press, 2001.

Howland, Douglas R. "Samurai Status, Class, and Bureaucracy," *The Journal of Asian Studies* 60.2 (May 2001), 353–80.

Hsiao, Tung Fei, ed. *China's Gentry: Essays in Rural-Urban Relations*. Chicago: University of Chicago Press, 1980.

Hu, Angang, and Chang Zhixiao. "Zhongguo de chengzheng pingkun yu xinde fanpingkun zhanlue" (China's urban poverty and new anti-poverty strategy), *Zhongguo shehui kexue jikan* (Chinese social science quarterly), Hong Kong, no. 32 (Winter 2000), 107–16.

Hu, Angang, Wang Shaoguang, and Kang Xiaoguang. *Zhongguo diqu chaju baogao* (Report on China's regional disparities). Shengyang: Liaoning Renmin Press, 1995.

Hu, Angang, Yang Fan, et al. *Daguo zhanlue: zhongguo liyi yu shiming* (Great power's strategy: China's interest and mission). Shengyang: Liaoning Renmin Press, 2000.

Hu, Angang, and Zou Ping. *Shehui yu fazhan: zhongguo shehui fazhan diqu chaju yanjiu* (Society and development: A study of China's regional gap of social development). Hangzhou: Zhejiang Renmin Press, 2000.

Hu, Dayuan. "Zhuan gui jingji zhong de diqu chayi: dui 'diqu chayi kuoda lun' de zhiyi" (Regional gap in a transitional economy: questioning the "opinion that the regional gap enlarges"), *Zhanlue yu guanli* (Strategy and management), Beijing, no. 1 (1998), 35–41.

Hu, Haili. "Sunan wailai laodongli zhuangkuan ji xingbie bijiao de fengxi" (A situational and gender-based analysis of migrant laborers in Sunan), *Jianghai xuekan* (Jianghai journal), Nanjing, no. 3 (1998), 34–40.

Hu, Zhaoliang, et al. *Zhongguo quyu jingji chayi jiqi duice* (China's regional economic gaps and mitigating measures). Beijing: Qinghua University Press, 1997.

Huang, Bincheng. "Jiakuai xiao chengzhen jianshe" (Speed up the construction of small cities and towns), *Zhongguo guoqing guoli* (China national conditions and strength), Beijing, no. 100 (Apr. 2001), 39–40.

Huang, Daoxia, et al. *Zhonghua remin gongheguo dashiji 1949–1989* (The chronicle of the PRC). Beijing: Guangming Daily Press, 1989.

Huang, Mengdi, ed. *Xingzheng zhifa dianxing anli yu chuli quanshu* (Complete collection of typical cases of enforcing the administrative laws and regulations). Beijing: Zhongguo Renkou Press, 1997.

Huang, Ping, ed. *Xunqiu shenchun: dandai zhongguo nongcun waichu renkou de shehuixue yanjiu* (In search for survival: a sociological study of rural outmigrants in China). Kunming: Yunnan Renmin Press, 1997.

Huang, Shu-min. *The Spiral Road: Changes in a Chinese Village*. Boulder, CO: Westview, 1989.

Huang, Xiaoming, ed. *Zaikan taiwan: zhengzhi, shehui, jingji he liangan guanxi* (Another look at Taiwan: politics, society, economy, and the cross-strait relations). Hong Kong: Social Science Press, 1996.

Huang, Xiyuan. *Zhongguo jinxiandai nongye jingji shi* (Modern history of agriculture in China). Zhengzhou: Henan Renmin Press, 1986.

Huang, Yiding. "Jingti heishili" (Watch out for organized crime), *Zhongguo guoqing guoli* (China national conditions and strength), Beijing, no. 100 (Apr. 2001), 30–33.

Human Rights Watch. "The *Propiska* System Remains *de facto* in Places in Several Regions (2000)," *World Report 2001*, London, Dec. 2000.

Huntington, Samuel P., ed. *The Third Wave: Democratization in the Late 20th Century*. Norman: University of Oklahoma Press, 1993.

———. *The Clash of Civilizations and the Remaking of World Order*. New York: Touchstone Books, 1998.

Hutton, J. H. *Caste in India: Its Nature, Function and Origins*. Cambridge, UK: Cambridge University Press, 1946.

Ingelhart, Ronald, and Hans-Dieter Klingemann. "Genes, Culture, Democracy and Happiness," in E. Dienerand and E. M. Suh eds., *Culture and Subjective Well-being*. Cambridge, MA: MIT Press, 2000, 165–85.

Ingram, Larry C. *The Study of Organizations: Positions, Persons, and Patterns*. Westport, CT: Praeger, 1995.

Jayaraman, Raja. *Caste and Class: Dynamics of Inequality in Indian Society*. New Delhi: Hindu Publishing Corp, 1981.

Ji, Dangshen, and Shao Qin. *Zhongguo renkou liudong taishi yu guanli* (The trends and management of China's population movement). Beijing: Zhongguo Renkou Press, 1995.

Jiang, Lihua. "Guowai 'minshi dengji' yu woguo 'huji guanli'" (Foreign countries' civil registration and our nation's *hukou* management), *Zhongguo guoqing guoli* (China's national conditions and strength), Beijing, no. 105 (Sept. 2001), 37–38.

Jiang, Tao. *Lishi yu renkou—Zhongguo chuantong renkou jiegou yanjiu* (History and population—study on the traditional Chinese demographic structure). Beijing: Renmin Press, 1999.

Jiang, Xianjin, and Luo Feng, eds. *Jingca yewu shiyong quanshu—zhian guanli juan* (Complete guide of police works—volume on public security management). Beijing: Qunzhong Press, for MPS use only, 1996.

Jiang, Yimin, and Guo Yaxin. "Xiao chengzheng jianshe yu nongcun xiandaihua" (Construction of small cities and towns and the modernization of the countryside), *Shehui gongzuo yanjiu* (Studies on social works), Beijing, no. 4 (1994), 10–13.

Jiang, Zemin. *Lun sange daibiao* (On "three representing"). Beijing: Zhongyang Wenxian Press, 2001.

Joly, Daniele, ed. *Scapegoats and Social Actors: The Exclusion and Integration of Minorities in Western and Eastern Europe*. New York: St. Martin's Press, 1997.

Jordan, Bill. *A Theory of Poverty and Social Exclusion*. New York: Polity Press, 1996.

Joshi, Vijay, and I. M. D. Little. *India's Economic Reforms: 1991–2001*. Delhi: Oxford University Press, 1997.

Kang, Damin, et al., eds. *Lun zhongguo tesi de gongan* (On public security with Chinese characteristics). Beijing: Qunzhong Press, 1998.

Kapstein, Ethan B. *Sharing the Wealth: Workers and the World Economy*. New York: Norton, 1999.

Kaufman, Robert R., and Alex Segura-Ubiergo. "Globalization, Domestic Politics, and Social Spending in Latin America: A Time-Series Cross-Section Analysis, 1973–97," *World Politics* 53.4 (July 2001), 553–87.

Kelliher, Daniel. *Peasant Power in China: The Era of Rural Reform, 1979–1989*. New Haven, CT: Yale University Press, 1992.

Keng, C. W. Kenneth. "China's Future Economic Regionalism," *Journal of Contemporary China* 10.29 (Nov. 2001), 587–612.

Keohane, Robert O. *Neo-Realism and Its Critics*. New York: Columbia University Press, 1986.

Khan, Azizur Rahman. *Overcoming Unemployment*. Geneva: International Labor Office, 1994.

Khan, Azizur Rahman, and Carl Riskin. "Income and Inequality in China," *The China Quarterly*, no. 154 (June 1998).

Kinzo, Maria D'Alva, ed. *Brazil: The Challenges of the 1990s*. London: British Academic Press, 1993.

Kinzo, Maria D'Alva, and Victor Bulmwe-Thomas, eds. *Growth and Development in Brazil: Cardoso's Real Challenge*. London: Institute of Latin American Studies, 1995.

Kirkby, R. J. R., et al., eds. *Small Town China: Governance, Economy, Environment and Life Style in Three Zhen*. London: Ashgate, 2001.

Knight, John, and Lina Song. *The Rural-Urban Divide: Economic Disparities and Interactions in China*. Oxford: Oxford University Press, 1999.

Kuhn, Anthony, and Lincoln Kaye. "Bursting at the Seams: Rural Migrants Flout Urban Registration System," *Eastern Economic Review* 157 (Mar. 10, 1994), 27–29.

Kuhn, Philip A. *Rebellion and Its Enemies in Late Imperial China: Militarization and Social Structure, 1796–1864*. Cambridge, MA: Harvard University Press, 1980.

———. *Origins of the Modern Chinese State*. Stanford, CA: Stanford University Press, 2001.

Labor Ministry, ed. *Renshi gongzhu wenjian xunbian* (Selected documents on personnel works), an internal publication, vol. 3. Beijing: Laodong Renshi Press, 1986.

Langdon, Philip. *A Better Place to Live: Reshaping the American Suburb*, Amherst, MA: University of Massachusetts Press, 1997.

Lardy, Nicholas R. *Integrating China into the Global Economy*. Washington, DC: Brookings Institution, 2002.

Lawrence, Roderick J. *Sustaining Human Settlement: A Challenge for the New Millennium*. North Shields: Urban International Press, 2000.

Lee, James Z., and Wang Feng. *One Quarter of Humanity: Malthusian Mythology and Chinese Reality*. Cambridge, MA: Harvard University Press, 1999.

Legal Bureau of Personnel Ministry, ed. *Renshi gongzuo wenjian xunbian (15)* (Selected documents on personnel works—15), an internal series. Beijing: Zhongguo Renshi Press, 1993.

Lei, Hong. "Jiti yuegui: zhongguo yingxing shehui wenti zhiyi" (Collective violation: one of China's hidden social problems), *Jianghan luntan* (Jianghan tribune), Wuhan, no. 4 (1998), 70–74.

Leonard, E. M. *The Early History of English Poor Relief*. New York: Frank Case Co., 1965.

Leong, Sow-Theng. *Migration and Ethnicity in Chinese History: Hakkas, Pengmin, and Their Neighbors*, ed. Tim Wright. Stanford, CA: Stanford University Press, 1997.

Leontaridi, Marianthi Rannia. "Segmented Labour Market: Theory and Evidence," *Journal of Economic Surveys*, U.K., 12.1 (Feb. 1998), 63–101.

Lewis, Robert A., and Richard H. Rowland. *Population Redistribution in the USSR: Its Impact on Society 1897–1977*. New York: Praeger, 1979.

Lewis, W. Arthur. *The Theory of Economic Growth*. London: George Allen & Unwin, (1954) 1956.

———. *Dynamic Factors in Economic Growth*. New York: Advent Books, 1974.

———. *Development Planning: The Essentials of Economic Policy*. London: George Allen & Unwin, 1966.

———. *Selected Economic Writings of W. Arthur Lewis*, ed. Mark Gersovitz. New York: New York University Press, 1983.

Li, Changfu. *Zhongguo zhiming shi* (History of Chinese colonization). Shanghai: Shangwu Press (1937) 1984.

Li, Chen, and Wu Hui-Ling: "Taiwande laogong fali yu cangye fazhan" (Labor laws and industrial development in Taiwan), in Yu Zong-Xian, ed., *Canye Fazhan yu Zhengci Yantaohui* (A Conference on Industrial Development and Policies). Taipei: Chinese Economic Academy, 1993.

Li, Cheng. "Surplus Rural Laborers and Internal Migration in China: Current Status and Future Prospects," *Asian Survey* 36.11 (1996), 1122–45.

Li, Debin, et al. *Jingdai zhongguo yimin shiyao* (A short history of migration in modern China). Harbin: Harbin Press, 1994.

Li, Guangping, ed. *Zhongguo zhiqing beihuan lu* (The record of the joy and sorrow of the Chinese educated youth). Guangzhou: Huacheng Press, 1993.

Li, Ling, et al. "Dachengshi renkou liudong tezhen ji guanli: yi guangzhou weili jianyu beijing, shanghai bijiao" (Features and management of migrant population in major cities: the case of Guangzhou in comparison with Beijing and Shanghai), *Renkou yanjiu* (Population research), Beijing, 25.2 (Mar. 2001), 46–52.

Li, Lulu, and Li Hanlin. *Zhongguo de danwei zhuzhi: ziyuan, quanli yu jiaohuan* (China's *danwei* [work unit] organization: resources, power, and exchange). Hangzhou: Zhejiang Renmin Press, 2000.

Li, Mengbai, et al., eds. *Liudong renkou dui dachengshi fazhan de yingxiang ji duice* (Floating population, its impact on the development of major cities, and the response to it). Beijing: Jingji Ribao Press, 1991.

Li, Nan, and Li Shuzhuo, eds. *Quyu renkou chengzheng hua wenti yanjiu* (Study on regional urbanization). Shanghai: Huadong Normal University Press, 1996.

Li, Qiang. "Zhongguo chengshi zhong de eryuan laodongli shichang yu dicheng jingying wenti" (The dualistic labor market in China and the issue of elites at the bottom), *Qinghua shehuixue pinglun* (Tsinghua sociological review), Beijing, special issue 1 (June 2000), 151–67.

———. *Dandai zhongguo shehui fengcheng yu liudong* (Social stratification and movement in contemporary China). Beijing: Jingji Press, 1993.

Li, Rujian. "Difang wailai renkou guanli fagui chubu tangtao" (Preliminary study on the regulations of the local management of migrant population), *Renkou yu jingji* (Population and economics), Beijing, no. 128 (May 2001), 17–22.

Li, Shangfeng. "Dangdai zhongguo chengxiang guanxi de shizheng yanjiu" (Empirical study of China's current urban-rural relationship), *Shehuixue yanjiu* (Sociological studies), Beijing, no. 3 (1989), 31–38.

Li, Si-ming, and Wing-shing Tang, eds. *China's Regions, Polity, and Economy: A Study of Spatial Transformation in the Post-Reform Era*. Hong Kong: The Chinese University Press, 2000.

Li, Wenhai, and Wang Feng. *Renlei de sifen zhiyi: Maersasi shenhua yu zhongguo de xiangshi, 1700–2000 nian* (A quarter the mankind: the Malthusian myth and China's reality, 1700–2000). Beijing: Sanlian Press, 2000.

Li, Yining. *Chaoyue shichang yu chaoyue zhengfu: lun daode liliang zai jingji zhong de zuoyong* (Beyond the market and beyond the government: on the role of ethics in the economy). Beijing: Jingji Kexue Press, 1999.

Li, Zhongxin. *Shiqu jingwu yu paichusuo gongzuo gaige lunwenji* (Collection of essays on the reform of community policing and police stations). Beijing: Qunzhong Press, for law enforcement agencies only, 1998.

———, ed. *Zhongguo shequ jingwu yanjiu* (Study on China's community policing). Beijing: Qunzhong Press, for law enforcement agencies only, 1999.

Li, Zongjian. "Shenzhen renkou jiegou de shehuixue fengxi" (A sociological analysis of Shenzhen's demographic structure), *Tequ lilun yu shijian* (SEZ theory and practice), Shenzhen, no. 50 (June 1993), 50–53.

Liang, Fangzhong. *Zhongguo lishishang de hukou, tudi yu tudishui ziliao* (Historical data on *hukou*, land and land tax in China). Shanghai: Shanghai Renmin Press, 1980.

Liang, Jun, et al. *Cunmin zizhi: huangtudi shang de zhengzhi gemin* (Villager self-governance: political revolution on yellow soil). Beijing: Zhongguo Qingnian Press, 2000.

Liang, Zai. "Changing Patterns of Migration in China: 1982–1995," conference paper, Chengdu, China, 1999.

Liang, Zai, and Michael J. White. "Internal Migration in China," *Demography* 31 (1996), 525–48.

Lin, Jing. *Social Transformation and Private Education in China*. Westport, CT: Praeger, 1999.

Lin, Justin Yifu, et al. *The China Miracle: Development Strategy and Economic Reform*. Hong Kong: The Chinese University Press, 2003.

Linda, Dimitri, and Ethan B. Kapstein. "Inequality, Growth, and Democracy," *World Politics* 53.2 (Jan. 2001), 264–96.

Little, Daniel: *Understanding Peasant China*. New Haven, CT: Yale University Press, 1989.

Liu, Donglin, ed. *Gongan baowei shouce* (Handbook on public security protection). Beijing: Qunzhong Press, 1989.

Liu, Guoguang, ed. *21 shiji zhongguo chengshi fazhan* (China's urban development in the 21st century). Beijing: Hongqi Press, 2000.

Liu, Jianhong, Lening Zhang, and Steven F. Messner, eds. *Crime and Social Control in a Changing China.* Westport, CT: Greenwood, 2001.

Liu, Jiarui, *Tezhong hangye zhian guanli* (Public security management in the special industries). Beijing: Qunzhong Press, for MPS use only, 1998.

Liu, Junde, and Wang Yuming. *Zhidu yu chuangxin: zhongguo chengshi zhidu de fazhan yu gaige xinlun* (Institution and innovation: a new view on the development and reform of China's city system). Nanjing: Dongnan University Press, 2000.

Liu, Shangyu, ed. *Heishehui fanzui yu duice* (Organized crime and countermeasures). Beijing: Qunzhong Press, internal publication, 1997.

Liu, Tie. "Liudong renkou yu huji zhidu gaige" (Migrant population and the reform of the *hukou* system), *Xuesu jiaoliu* (Academic exchange), Haerbin, no. 2 (1998), 54–56.

Liu, Xin. *In One's Own Shadow: An Ethnographic Account of the Condition of Post-Reform Rural China.* Berkeley, CA: University of California Press, 2000.

———. "Zhuangxinqi zhongguo dalu chengshi jumin de jiecheng yishi" (People's strata consciousness in urban China during the transformation era), *Shehui kexue yanjiu* (Sociological Research), Beijing, 16.3 (May 2001), 8–17.

Liu, Ying, et al., eds. *Dangdai zhongguo nongcun jiating* (The rural families in contemporary China: a survey in 14 provinces). Beijing: Shehui Kexue Wenxian Press, 1993.

Liu, Yizheng. *Zhongguo wenhuashi* (Cultural history of China), vol. 1. Beijing: Minzhu Press, 1988.

Liu, Zhixian. "Huji guanli jiang zouxian renkou guanli" (Hukou management moves to population management), *Ershiyi shiji* (Twenty-first century), Hong Kong, no. 5 (1999).

Lloyd, Peter. *Slums of Hope? Shanty Towns of the Third World.* Manchester, UK: Manchester University Press, 1979.

Lu, Deyang. *Liumin shi* (History of migrants). Shanghai: Shanghai Wenyi Press, 1997.

Lu, Shaoqing, and Zhang Shouli. "Chengxiang chabie xiade liudong ertong jiaoyu" (Education of the migrant children under the urban-rural disparity), *Zhanlue yu guanli* (Strategy and management), Beijing, no. 4 (2001), 95–108.

Lu, Simian. *Qinhan shi* (History of the Qin and Han). Shanghai: Kaimin Press, 1947.

Lu, Wenlong, and Huang Minyou. "Qian fada diqu jingji fazhan qianyi" (Preliminary discussion on economic development in the less developed region), *Shehui kexuejia* (Social scientist), Guilin, no. 69 (Jan. 1998), 21–26.

Lu, Xiaobo. *Cadres and Corruption: The Organizational Involution of the Chinese Communist Party.* Stanford, CA: Stanford University Press, 2000.

Lu, Xiaobo, and Elizabeth J Perry, eds. *Danwei: The Changing Chinese Workplace in Historical and Contemporary Perspective.* Armonk, NY: M. E. Sharpe, 1997.

Lu, Yilong. *Huji zhidu-kongzhi yu shehui chabie* (Hukou system-control and social disparities). Beijing: Shangwu Press, 2003.

Lu, Yixue. "Nongmin bushi nongzhong liao" (Peasants are not caged birds), *Gaige neican* (Internal reference of reform), Beijing, no. 19 (1996), 23–36.

Lu, Zhaohe. *Zhidu bianqian yu renkou fazhan* (Institutional changes and population development). Beijing: Zhongguo Shehui Kexue Press, 1999.

Lu, Zheng. *Zhongguo chuantong shehui xintai* (Mentality of the traditional Chinese society). Hangzhou: Zhejiang Renmin Press, 1996.

Lubman, Stanley B. *Bird in a Cage: Legal Reform in China after Mao.* Stanford, CA: Stanford University Press, 1999.

Ma, Fuyun. "Zhongguo huji zhidu bianqian yanjiu" (A study on the evolution of China's *huji* system). Ph.D. diss., Beijing, Chinese Social Science Academy, 2001.

Ma, Hong, ed. *Zhongguo shichang fazhan baogao, 1999–2000* (China market development report 1999–2000). Beijing: Zhongguo Fazhan Press, 2000.

Ma, Hong, and Wang Mengkui, eds. *Zhongguo shichang fazhan baogao, 2000–2001* (China market development report 2000–2001). Beijing: Zhongguo Fazhan Press, 2001.

Ma, Xia. *Zhongguo chengzheng renkou qianyi* (Migration of China's urban population). Beijing: China Renkou Press, 1994.

MacDowell, Douglas M. *The Law in Classical Athens.* Ithaca, NY: Cornell University Press, 1986.

Mallee, Hein. "China's Household Registration System under Reform," *Development and Change* 26.1 (Jan. 1995).

Manzo, Kathryn A. *Creating Boundaries: The Politics of Race and Nation,* Boulder, CO: Lynn Reinner, 1996.

Martine, George, Monica Das Gupta, and Lincoln C. Chen, eds. *Reproductive Change in India and Brazil.* Delhi: Oxford University Press, 1998.

Marx, Karl. *Capital: A Critique of Political Economy.* New York: Penguin, 1992.

———, and F. Engels: *The Communist Manifesto.* New York: Signet Classic, 1998.

Matthews, Mervyn. *The Passport Society: Controlling Movement in Russia and the USSR.* Boulder, CO: Westview, 1993.

McCord, William, and Arline McCord. *Power and Equity: An Introduction to Social Stratification.* New York: Praeger, 1977.

McNabb, Robert, and Keith Whitfield. "Testing for Segmentation: An Establishment-level Analysis," *Cambridge Political Economy Society,* 1998, 147–63.

McNeil, William H., and Ruth S. Adams, eds. *Human Migration: Patterns and Policies.* Bloomington, IN: Indiana University Press, 1978.

Medvedkov, Olga. *Soviet Urbanization.* London: Routledge, 1990.

Meehan, Elizabeth. *Citizenship and the European Community.* London: Sage, 1993.

Meier, Gerald M. *Emerging from Poverty.* New York: Oxford University Press, 1984.

Meng, Xin. *Labor Market Reform in China.* Cambridge, UK: Cambridge University Press, 2000.

Meng, Xin, and Junsen Zhang. "The Two-Tier Labor Market in Urban China:

Occupational Segregation and Wage Differentials between Rural Residents and Urban Migrants in Shanghai," conference paper, Xiamen, 2001.

Migdal, Joel S. *Strong Societies and Weak States: State-Society Relations and State Capabilities in the Third World*. Princeton, NJ: Princeton University Press, 1988.

Miles, Robert, et al., eds. *Migration and European Integration: The Dynamics of Inclusion and Exclusion*. UK: Fairleigh Dickinson University Press, 1995.

Ministry of Education. *2001 putong gaodeng xuexiao zhaosheng gongzhu guiding* (Regulations of normal college admission work in 2001), Beijing, Apr. 2001.

Ministry of Labor and Social Security. *Laodongli shichang guangli guiding* (Regulations on the management of labor market), Directive 10. Beijing, Dec. 14, 2000.

Ministry of Personnel. *Renshi gongzuo wenjian xuanbian* (Selected documents on personnel works), multivolume, internal publication. Beijing: Laodong Renshi Press, 1984–96.

Minow, Martha. *Making All the Difference: Inclusion, Exclusion, and American Law*. Ithaca, NY: Cornell University Press, 1991.

Mishra, Anil Kant. *Rural Tension in India*. New Delhi: Discovery Publishing, 1998.

Misra, R. P., and Kamlesh Misra. *Million Cities of India: Growth Dynamics, Internal Structure, Quality of Life and Planning Perspectives*, 2 vols. New Delhi: Sustainable Development Foundation, 1998.

Moore, Barrington. *Social Origins of Dictatorship and Democracy*. Boston: Beacon, (1967) 1993.

Moors, Hein, and Rossella Palomba, eds. *Population, Family, and Welfare: A Comparative Survey of European Attitudes*. New York: Oxford University Press, 1995.

Moreira, Mauricio M. *Industrialization, Trade and Market Failure: The Role of Government Intervention in Brazil and South Korea*. New York: St. Martin's, 1995.

Mosk, Carl. *Japanese Industrial History: Technology, Urbanization, and Economic Growth*. Armonk, NY: M. E. Sharpe, 2001.

Moss, William W. "Dang'an: Contemporary Chinese Archives," *The China Quarterly* 145 (Mar. 1996), 112–29.

MPS (Ministry of Public Security). *1999 Quanguo fengxianshi renkou tongji ziliao* (Statistical information of the population by cities and counties in the PRC, 1999). Beijing: Qunzhong Press, 2000.

———. *2000 Niandu Quanguo fengxianshi renkou tongji ziliao* (Statistical information of the population by cities and counties in the PRC, 2000). Beijing: Qunzhong Press, 2001.

———. *Zhifa shouce* (Law-enforcement handbook), multivolume, for law enforcement only. Beijing: Qunzhong Press, 1980–2000.

MPS-BHM (Ministry of Public Security—Bureau of *Hukou* Management). *Chushen dengji xiangguan fagui zhengce* (The relevant rules and policies on birth registration). Beijing: Qunzhong Press, for MPS use only, 1996.

———. *Guowai minshi dengji he huji guanli fagui* (Foreign laws and regulations on civil registration and *hukou* management). Beijing: Qunzhong Press, 1996.

MPS-BPT (Ministry of Public Security—Bureau of Personnel and Training). *Huzheng guanli jiaocheng* (The textbook on *hukou* management). Beijing: Qunzhong Press, for MPS use only, 2000.

MPS-BSM (Ministry of Public Security—Bureau of Security Management). *Gongmin shenfeng haoma gongzuo wenjianji* (The collection of documents on the citizen ID number). Beijing: Qunzhong Press, for MPS use only, 2000.

———. *Quanguo zhanzhu renkou tongji ziliao huibian* (The collection of national statistical information of temporary residents). Beijing: Qunzhong Press, 1999.

MPS-DOP (Ministry of Public Security–Department of Politics). *Gongan yewu jichu zhishi* (Basic knowledge of public security works). Beijing: Qunzhong Press, for MPS use only, 1999.

MPS-EB (Ministry of Public Security—Education Bureau), ed. *Zhengzhi zhenca* (Political investigation). Beijing: Qunzhong Press, for MPS use only, 1996.

———. *Zhian guanli* (Public security). Beijing: Qunzhong Press, for MPS use only, 1997.

MPS-PD (Ministry of Public Security—Political Department). *Gongan jiguan renmin jingca jiben shuzhi kaoshi fuxi tiyao* (Abbreviated preparation guide of the basic quality exams for the people's police in the public security agencies). Beijing: Qunzhong Press, for MPS use only, 1997.

———. *Xianshi gongan jiguan lingdao zhiwu zhige kaoshi fuxi tiyao* (Abbreviated preparation guide of the qualification exams for the leading officers of the public security bureaus at the county and city levels). Beijing: Qunzhong Press, for MPS use only, 2001.

MPS-PSMB (Ministry of Public Security—Public Security Management Bureau). *Hukou guanli fagui guizhang zhengce huibian* (Collection of *hukou* laws, regulations and policies). Beijing: Zhongguo Renmin Gongan Daxue Press, for MPS use only, 2001.

MPS-PTB (Ministry of Public Security—Personnel Training Bureau). *Zhian jicheng jichu jiaocheng* (Basic textbook on public security in the local communities). Beijing: Qunzhong Press, for MPS use only, 1999.

MPS-TB (Third Bureau of the Ministry of Public Security). *Hukou guanli ziliao huibian* (Collections of *hukou* management materials), vol. 4. Beijing: Qunzhong Press, for MPS use only, 1993.

MPS-Team (Ministry of Public Security writing team). *Baowei gongzuo* (Protection work). Beijing: Qunzhong Press, for MPS use only, 1997.

Mu, Xinshen (Vice Minister of Public Security). *Guanyu gaige he wanshan zhongguo xiaochengzheng huji guanli zhidu de jiben silu* (Basic reasoning on the reform and perfection of the *hukou* management system in the small cities and towns), *Cunzheng jianshe* (Village and town construction), Beijing, no. 79 (Feb. 1996), 6–7.

———, et al. *Zhili maiying piaochang duice* (Measures for dealing with prostitution). Beijing: Qunzhong Press, internal publication, 1996.

Murphy, Raymond. *Social Closure: The Theory of Monopolization and Exclusion*. New York: Oxford University Press, 1988.

Musterd, Sako, and W. J. M. Ostendorf, eds. *Urban Segregation and the Welfare State: Inequality and Exclusion in Western Cities*. London: Routledge, 1998.

Myrdal, Gunnar. *Asian Drama*, New York: Oxford University Press, 1968.

Nam, Charles B., et al. *International Handbook on Internal Migration*. Westport, CT: Greenwood, 1990.

Narayana, G., and John Kantner. *Doing the Needful: The Dilemma of India's Population Policy*. Boulder, CO: Westview, 1992.

Nee, Victor, and David Mozingo, eds. *State and Society in Contemporary China*. Ithaca, NY: Cornell University Press, 1983.

Nelson, Jon M. *Migrants, Access to Power: Politics and the Urban Poor in Developing Nations*. Princeton, NJ: Princeton University Press, 1979.

Ni, Jin, and Li Fang, eds. *Zhonghua shiyong faxue dacidian* (Practical encyclopedia of the Chinese laws). Changchun: Jilin University Press, 1988.

Nicolet, Claude. *Space Geography and Politics in the Early Roman Empire*. Ann Arbor: University of Michigan Press, 1991.

Niu, Renliang. *Laoli: Yongyuan, shiye yu qiye xiaoli* (Labor force: underemployment, unemployment, and enterprise efficiency). Beijing: Zhongguo Caijing Press, 1993.

Norris, Pippa. *Digital Divide: Civic Engineering, Information Poverty, and the Internet Worldwide*. New York: Cambridge University Press, 2001.

North, Douglass. *Structure and Change in Economic History*. New York: Norton, 1981.

———. "Institutions and a Transaction-cost Theory of Exchange," in James Alt and Kenneth Shepsle, eds., *Perspectives on Positive Political Economy*. New York: Cambridge University Press, 1990.

———. *Institutions, Institutional Change and Economic Performance*. New York: Cambridge University Press, 1990.

Ober, Josiah. *Mass and Elite Democratic Athens*. Princeton: Princeton University Press, 1991.

Oi, Jean. *Rural China Takes Off: The Political Foundation for Economic Reform*. Berkeley, CA: University of California Press, 1999.

Oliga, John C. *Power, Ideology, and Control*. New York: Plenum Press, 1996.

Ong, Aihwa. *Flexible Citizenship: The Cultural Logics of Transnationality*. Durham, NC: Duke University Press, 1999.

Osterfield, David. *Prosperity versus Planning: How Government Stifles Economic Growth*. New York: Oxford University Press, 1992.

Page, Joseph A. *The Brazilians*. Reading, MA: Addison-Wesley, 1995.

Pan, Wei. *Nongmin yu shichang: zhongguo jiceng zhengquan yu xiangzhen qiye* (Peasants and market: grassroots government and township and village enterprises). Beijing: Shangwu Press, 2003.

Pan, Yiyong. "Lun xianxing hukou zhidu dui zhongguo xiandaihua shida weihai" (On the ten major damages of the current *hukou* system on China's modernization), *Gaige yu zhanlue* (Reform and strategy), Beijing, no. 4 (1995).

Pandey, Rajendra. *The Caste System in India*. New Delhi: Criterion Publications, 1986.

Parish, William L., and Martin King Whyte, eds. *Village and Family in Contemporary China*. Chicago: University of Chicago Press, 1978.

Parsons, Talcott. *Toward a General Theory of Action,* Cambridge, MA: Harvard University Press, 1951.

Pei, Minxin. "China's Governance Crisis," *Foreign Affairs* 81.5 (Sept.–Oct. 2002), 96–109.

Peng, Huei En. *Taiwan fazhande zhengzi jingji fenxi* (The political economy of Taiwan's development). Taipei: Fengyun Luntang Press, 1995.

Peng, Sen. *Zhongguo jingji tequ kaifaqu nianjian 1999* (Yearbook on China's special economic zones and development zones, 1999). Beijing: Gaige Press, 2000.

Peng, Xizhe, and Guo Zhigang, eds. *The Changing Population of China*. Malden, MA: Blackwell, 2000.

Perkins, Dwight H. *Agricultural Development in China, 1368–1968*. Chicago: Aldine, 1969.

———, ed. *China's Modern Economy in Historical Perspective*. Stanford, CA: Stanford University Press, 1975.

Perry, Elizabeth: "State and Society in Contemporary China," *World Politics,* July 1989.

———, and Wong, C. *The Political Economy of Reform in Post-Mao China*. Cambridge, MA: Harvard University Press, 1985.

———, and Li Xun. *Proletarian Power: Shanghai in the Cultural Revolution*. Boulder, CO: Westview, 1997.

Peterson, Mark A. *Korean Adoption and Inheritance: Case Studies in the Creation of a Classic Confucian Society*. Ithaca, NY: Cornell University Press, 1996.

Piore, Michael J. *Birds of Passage: Migrant Labor and Industrial Societies*. Cambridge, UK: Cambridge University Press, 1979.

Polanyi, Karl. *The Great Transformation*. Boston: Beacon, 1957.

Potter, Sulamith Heins, and Jack M. Potter. *China's Peasants: The Anthropology of a Revolution*. Cambridge, UK: Cambridge University Press, 1990.

Pound, John. *Poverty and Vagrancy in Tudor England*. London: Longman, 1971.

Powell, Walter W., and Paul J. DiMaggio, eds. *The New Institutionalism in Organizational Analysis*. Chicago: University of Chicago Press, 1991.

Preston, P. W. *Political/Cultural Identity: Citizens and Nations in a Global Era*. London: Sage, 1997.

Rajshekar, V. T. *Brahminism: Father of Fascism, Racism, Nazism*. Bangalore: Dalit Sahitya Akademy, 1994.

Ramsay, Meredith. *Community, Culture, and Economic Development: The Social Roots for Local Action*. Albany, NY: SUNY Press, 1996.

RAND. *Cooperation and Conflict in the Former Soviet Union: Implications for Migration*. Santa Monica, CA: Rand, 1996.

———. *Asian Economic Trends*. MR-1143, Santa Monica, CA: Rand, 2000.

RBI (Reserve Bank of India). *Handbook of Statistics on Indian Economy 1999–2000*. New Delhi: RBI, 2001.

Redding, S. Gordon. *The Spirit of Chinese Capitalism*. New York: Gruyter, 1990.

Renkou Yanjiu Editors. "Zhongguo huji gaige: shichang jingji fazhan de biyou zhilu" (Reform of China's *hukou* system: a must route for the development of market economy), *Renkou yanjiu* (Population research), Beijing, no. 3 (1997).

Renmin Ribao, editor-in-chief. *Neibu chanyue* (Internal reference), internal publication, selected issues, 1990–2000.

Renshibu (Personnel Ministry), ed. *Guojia gongwuyuan zanxing tiaoli shiyi* (Explanation of the state provisional regulation of civil servants). Beijing: Renmin Press, 1993.

Renshibu and Zhongzhubu (Personnel Ministry and CCP Central Organization Department), eds. *Xiangzheng ganbu pingyongzhi guanli jingyan yu zhengce huibian* (Policies and lessons in the management of hired township cadres). Changsha: Hunan Keji Press, 1993.

Riggins, Stephen Harold, ed. *The Language and Politics of Exclusion: Others in Discourse (Communication and Human Values)*. London: Sage, 1997.

Robert, Dexter. "The Great Migration: Chinese Peasants Are Fleeing Their Villages to Chase Big-city Dreams," *Business Week*, Dec. 11, 2000.

Roberts, Bryan R. *The Making of Urban Citizens: Cities of Peasants Revisited*. London: Arnold, 1995.

Rodgers, Gerry, et al. *Social Exclusion: Rhetoric, Reality, Responses*. Geneva: International Labor Organization, 1995.

Rose, Lionel, et al. *Vagrant Underworld in Britain, 1815–1985*. London: Angus and Robertson, 1969.

Rousseau, Jean-Jacques. *Discourse on the Origin and Foundation of Inequality among Men* (1755), in Michael L. Morgan, ed., *Classics of Moral and Political Theory*. Indianapolis: Hackett Publishing, 1992.

Rowe, William T. *Hankow: Community and Conflict in a Chinese City, 1796–1895*. Stanford, CA: Stanford University Press, 1984.

Rozelle, Scott, et al. "Leaving China's Farms: Survey Results of New Paths and Remaining Hurdles to Rural Migration," *The China Quarterly* 158 (1999), 367–93.

Rozman, Gilbert. *Urban Networks in Ch'ing China and Tokugawa Japan*. Princeton, NJ: Princeton University Press, 1973.

Rubins, Noah. "Recent Development: The Demise and Resurrection of the *Propiska* I," *Harvard International Law Journal* 39.545 (Spring, 1998).

Russell, Sharon Stanton. *International Migration: Implications for the World Bank*. Washington, DC: World Bank, 2001.

Sa, Lianxiang. *Zhongguo minzhuxing* (Chinese national characteristics). Beijing: Renmin University Press, 1988.

Sargeson, Sally. *Reworking China's Proletariat*. New York: Macmillan/St. Martin's Press, 1999.

Sassen, Saskia. *The Mobility of Labor and Capital: A Study in International Investment and Labor Flow*. New York: Cambridge University Press, 1988.

SCESB (State Council Economic Studies Bureau). "Guangyu jiakuai xiao-chengzhen fazhan de duice yanjiu" (On the acceleration of the development of small towns), *Jingji yanjiu cankao* (Economic studies references), Beijing, no. 3 (2000).

Schmitter, Phillippe, and Guillermo O'Donnell, eds. *Transitions from Authoritarian Rule: Tentative Conclusions About Uncertain Democracies*. Baltimore: Johns Hopkins University Press, 1986.

Schultz, Theodore W. *Food for the World*. New York: Ayer, 1976.

———. *The Long View in Economic Policy: The Case of Agriculture and Food*. New York: Ayer, 1986.

Schurmann, Franz. *Ideology and Organization in Communist China*. Berkeley, CA: University of California Press, 1966.

Scott, James C. *The Moral Economy of the Peasants*. New Heaven: Yale University Press, 1976.

SDN (Superintendency for the Development of the Northeast). *Northeast: Citizenship and Development Outline of a Regional Policy*. Recife, PE, Brazil: SDN, 1995.

Segal, Ronald. *The Crisis of India*. New York: Penguin Books, 1971.

Seidman, Gay W. *Workers' Movements in Brazil and South Africa, 1970–1985*. Berkeley, CA: University of California Press, 1994.

Selden, Mark. *The Political Economy of Chinese Socialism*. Armonk, NY: M. E. Sharpe, 1993.

Selvam, Solomon. *Caste and Class in India in the Late Twentieth Century*. New York: Edwin Mellen, 2000.

Sen, Amarty. *Inequality Reexamined*. Cambridge, MA: Harvard University Press, 1995.

———. *Development As Freedom*. New York: Anchor Books, 2000.

SEPB (State Environment Protection Bureau). *Zhongguo 21 shiji yicheng: zhongguo 21 shiji renkou, huangjing yu fazhang baipishu* (China's agenda in the 21st century: White paper on China's population, environment, and development in the 21st century). Beijing: Zhongguo Huangjing Kexue Press, 1994.

Sernau, Scott. *Economies of Exclusion: Underclass Poverty and Labor Market Change in Mexico*. Westport, CT: Praeger, 1994.

Shang, Jude, et al., eds. *Zhongguo chuantong wenhua daolun* (Introduction to the traditional Chinese culture). Shijiazhuang: Hebei University Press, 1996.

Sharping, Thomas, ed. *Floating Population and Migration in China: The Impact of Economic Reform*. Hamburg: Institut für Asienkunde, (1997) 1998.

Shaw, Victor. *Social Control in China: A Study of Chinese Work Units*. New York: Praeger, 1996.

Sheleff, Leon S. *Social Cohesion and Legal Cohesion: A Critique of Weber, Durkheim, and Marx*. Amsterdam: Rodopi, 1997.

Shen, Laiyun. "Zhongdi shouru nongmin fudan renran chengzhong" (The burden is still heavy for the low-middle income peasants), *Zhongguo guoqing guoli* (China national conditions and strength), Beijing, no. 98 (Feb. 2001), 20–21.

Sheng, Xinli, and Feng Pinying. *Zhongguo xin—huaxia minzhu xinge de lishi xingcheng* (Chinese heart—the historical formation of the Chinese national character). Nanchang: Jiangxi Gaoxiao Press, 1995.

Shenzhen City Personnel Bureau, ed. *Putong gaodeng xuexiao biyeshen fengpei youguan wenjian ji ziliao huibian* (Documents and materials on the allocation of college graduates), internal publication. Shenzhen, 1992.

———. *Shenzhen shi renshi gongzuo wenjian huibian* (Document collection of Shenzhen city's personnel works), issues 1–4, Shenzhen, internal publication, 1994–97.

———. *Shenzhen renshi* (Shenzhen personnel), internal periodical, selected issues, 1993–99.

Shin, Gi-Wook, and Michael Robinson, eds. *Colonial Modernity in Korea*. Cambridge, MA: Harvard University Press, 1999.

Shue, Vivienne. *The Reach of the State: Sketches of the Chinese Body Politic*. Stanford, CA: Stanford University Press, 1988.

Sibley, David. *Geographies of Exclusion: Society and Difference in the West*. London: Routledge, 1995.

Siddle, David, ed. *Migration, Mobility and Modernization*. Liverpool: Liverpool University Press, 1998.

Simai, Mihály, ed. *Global Employment: An International Investigation into the Future of Work*. Tokyo: United Nations University Press, vol. 1, 1995, vol. 2, 1996.

Singh, Gurharpal. *Ethnic Conflict in India: A Case Study of the Punjab*. London: Macmillan, 2000.

Singh, Marjinder, ed. *Caste among Non-Hindus in India*. New Delhi: National, 1977.

Singh, Soran. *Schedule Castes of India: Dimensions of Social Change*. New Delhi: Gian Publishing, 1987.

Sjoberg, Orjan. "Rural Retention in Albania: Administrative Restriction on Urban-bound Migration," *East European Quarterly*, no. 2 (1994), 205–33.

Skeldon, Ronald. *Population Mobility in Developing Nations: A Reinterpretation*. New York: John Wiley, 1993.

Skidmore, Thomas E., and Peter H. Smith. *Modern Latin America*. New York: Oxford University Press, 1997.

Skinner, G. William. *The City in Late Imperial China*. Stanford, CA: Stanford University Press, 1977.

Smith, Adam. *The Wealth of Nations: An Inquiry into the Nature and Causes*. New York: Modern Library, (1776) 1994.

Smith, Anthony J. *National Identity: Ethnonationalism in Comparative Perspective*. Reno: University of Nevada Press, 1993.

Smith, Mark M. *Debating Slavery: Economy and Society in the Antebellum American South*. New York: Cambridge University Press, 1999.

Smith, Michael Peter, ed. *City and Nation: Rethinking Places and Identity*. New Brunswick, NJ: Transaction, 2001.

Smith, William C., and Roberto P. Korzeniewicz, eds. *Politics, Social Change and Economic Restructuring in Latin America*. Miami: North-South Center Press, 1997.

Sniderman, Paul M., et al. *The Outsider: Prejudice and Politics in Italy*. Princeton, NJ: Princeton University Press, 2000.

Solinger, Dorothy J. *Contesting Citizenship in Urban China: Peasant Migrants, the State, and the Logic of the Market.* Berkeley, CA: University of California Press, 1999.

———. "Why We Cannot Count the 'Unemployed,'" *The China Quarterly*, no. 167 (Sept. 2001), 671–88.

Soros, George. *George Soros on Globalization.* New York: Public Affairs, 2002.

Speare, Alden, et al. *Urbanization and Development: The Rural-Urban Transition in Taiwan.* Boulder, CO: Westview, 1988.

SSB (State Statistics Bureau). *Zhongguo tongji zhaiyao 1992* (A statistical survey of China 1992). Beijing: Zhongguo Tongji Press, 1992.

———. "Cong gini xishu kan pingfu chaju" (Gap between rich and poor based on the Gini index), *Zhongguo guoqing guoli* (China national conditions and strength), Beijing, no. 97 (Jan. 2001), 29–30.

———. *Zhongguo Tongji Nianjan* (China statistical yearbook) 2000, 2001, and 2002. Beijing: China Tongji Press, 2000, 2001, and 2002.

SSB-PB (State Statistics Bureau, Population Bureau), ed. *Zhongguo renkou tongji nianjian 1993* (China population statistics yearbook 1993). Beijing: Zhongguo Laodong Press, 1993.

SSRC (State System Reform Commission). *Gaige neichan* (Internal reference on economic reform). Beijing, internal publication, selected issues, 1996–99.

Stampp, Kenneth M. *The Peculiar Institution: Slavery in the Ante-Bellum South.* New York: Vintage Books, 1989.

State Council. *Changjiang sanxia gongcheng yimin tiaoli* (Regulation on the population relocation for the Chang River Three Gorges project). Decree # 299, Beijing, Feb. 21, 2001.

———. *Guangyu jingzhi zai shichang jingji hudong zhong shixing diqu fengsuo de guiding* (Regulation on prohibiting regional barriers in market economic activities), Decree 303, Beijing, Apr. 21, 2001.

State Council-LB (Legal Bureau). *Zhonghua renmin gongheguo xianxing fali xingzheng fagui mulu, 1949–1994* (Index of PRC current laws and administrative regulations, 1949–94). Beijing: Zhongguo Fazhi Press, 1995.

State Council-MLSS (Ministry of Labor and Social Security), eds. *Shehui baozhang changyong zhengce fagui* (Commonly used laws and regulations on social security). Beijing: Legal Press, 1999.

Studwell, Joe. *The China Dream: The Quest for the Last Great Untapped Market on Earth.* New York: Atlantic Monthly Press, 2002.

Su, Fubin, and Dali L. Yang. "Political Institutions, Provincial Interests, and Resource Allocation in Reformist China," *Journal of Contemporary China* 9.24 (July 2000), 215–30.

Su, Yang, and Guo Hongxin, eds. *Zhongguoren zhengmu kan zhongguoren* (How do Chinese view themselves). Beijing: Gaige Press, 1997.

Subramanian, Nerendra. *Ethnicity and Populist Mobilization: Political Parties, Citizens, and Democracy in South India.* Delhi: Oxford University Press, 1999.

Sun, Weibeng, ed. *Zhonghua Renmin Gongheguo xinzheng guangli dacidian* (Dictionary of public administration in the PRC). Beijing: Renmin Ribao Press, 1992.

Sun, Xiaofen. *Qingdai qianqi de yimin tian sichuan* (Moving people to fill up Sichuan in early Qing Dynasty). Chengdu: Sichuan University Press, 1997.

Sun, Yao. *Hukou guanlixue jiaocheng* (Textbook on *hukou* management). Beijing: Qunzhong Press, for MPS use only, 1994.

Supreme People's Court of the PRC, ed. *Xinzheng shengpang shouce* (Handbook of administrative trials), vols. 1–10. Beijing: Renmin Fayuang Press, 1989–99.

Tan, Shen. *Zhujiang sanjiaozhou wailai nugong yu waizi qiye, dangdi zhengfu he shehui zhijian de guangxi* (The relationship between the out-of-town female workers and foreign-invested enterprises, local governments and society in the Pearl River Delta region). Beijing: Tsinghua University Press, 2000.

Tan, Youlin. "Zhongguo laodongli jiegou de quyu chayi yanjiu" (A study on the regional difference of China's labor force), *Renkou yu jingji* (Population and economics), Beijing, no. 124 (Jan. 2001), 53–60.

Tang, Yijie, ed. *Zhongguo zongjiao: guoqu yu xiangzai* (Religion in China: past and present). Beijing: Beijing University Press, 1992.

Tardanico, Richard, and Rafael Menjivar Larin, eds. *Global Restructuring, Employment, and Social Inequality in Urban Latin America*. Miami: North-South Center Press, 1997.

Techernina, Natalia. *Economic Transition and Social Exclusion in Russia*. Geneva: ILO, 1998.

Telles, Edward. "Urban Labor Market Segmentation and Income in Brazil," *Economic Development and Cultural Change* 41 (Jan. 1993), 231–49.

Tian, Bingxin. *Zhongguo diyi zhengjian: zhongguo huji zhidu diaocha shougao* (The first ID of China: manuscript of investigation of China's *hukou* system). Guangzhou: Guangdong Renmin Press, 2003.

Tian, Fang, and Lin Fatang, eds. *Zhongguo renkou qianyi* (Internal migration in China). Beijing: Zhishi Press, 1986.

Tian, Xueyuan, ed. *1995 Zhongguo renkou nianjian* (1995 Yearbook of the Chinese population). Beijing: Jingji Guangli Press, 1995.

———. *Daguo zhinan: dangdai zhonguo de renkou wenti* (Hardship of a large nation: current population problems in China). Beijing: Jinri Zhongguo Press, 1997.

Todaro, Michael P. "A Model of Labor Migration and Urban Development in Less Developed Countries," *American Economic Review* 58.1 (1969), 138–48.

———. *Economic Development*. New York: Addison-Wesley, 1999.

Troyer, Ronald J., et al., eds. *Social Control in the People's Republic of China*. New York: Praeger, 1989.

Turner, Bryan S. *Citizenship and Capitalism: The Debate over Reformism*. London: Allen & Unwin, 1986.

———. *Citizenship and Social Theory*. London: Sage, 1993.

Turner, Karen G., et al., eds. *The Limits of the Rule of Law in China*. Seattle: University of Washington Press, 2000.

Turner, R. C. J. *A History of Vagrants and Vagrancy and Beggars and Begging*. London: Longman, 1887.

UNCTAD (United Nations Conference on Trade and Development). *African Development in a Comparative Perspective*. New York: UNCTAD, 1999.

UNDP (United Nations Development Programme). *Human Development Report.* New York: Oxford University Press 1990.

———. *Human Development Report 1999.* New York: Oxford University Press, 1999.

———. *Human Development Report 2001.* New York: Oxford University Press, 2001.

———. *Overcoming Human Poverty: UNDP Poverty Report 1998.* New York: UN 1998.

———. *The China Human Development Report,* New York: Oxford University Press, 1999.

UNDP (United Nations Development Programme) and World Bank. *World Resources 2000–2001.* Oxford: Elsevier Science, 2000.

UNFAO (United Nations Food and Agriculture Organization). *The State of Food Insecurity in the World.* Rome: UNFAO, 1999.

UNSD (United Nations Statistical Division). *Statistical Chart on World Families.* New York: UN, 1993.

U.S. Congress Joint Economic Committee. *China's Economic Future: Challenges to U.S. Policy.* Armonk, NY: M. E. Sharpe, 1997.

Van Ness, Peter, ed. *Debating Human Rights: Critical Essays from the United States and Asia.* London: Routledge, 1999.

Varshney, Ashutosh. "Ethnic Conflicts and Civil Society: India and Beyond," *World Politics* 53.3 (Apr. 2001), 362–98.

Vogel, Ezra. *One Step Ahead in China: Guangdong under Reform.* Cambridge, MA: Harvard University Press, 1989.

Wade, Robert. *Governing the Market: Economic Theory and the Role of Government in East Asian Industrialization.* Princeton, NJ: Princeton University Press, 1990.

Walder, Andrew G. *Communist Neo-Traditionalism—Work and Authority in Chinese Industry.* New Haven, CT: Yale University Press, 1986.

———, ed. *Zouping in Transition: The Process of Reform in Rural North China.* Cambridge, MA: Harvard University Press, 1998.

Wallerstein, Immanuel. *The Modern World-System: Capitalist Agriculture and the Origins of the European World-Economy in the Sixteenth Century.* New York: Academic Press, 1974.

Wan, Chuan. "Shangyang de huji gaige jiqi lishi yiyi" (Shang Yang *hukou* reform and its historical significance), *Gongan daxue xuebao* (Public security university journal), no. 1 (1998).

Wang, Chunguang. *Shehui liudong he shehui chongzhu* (Social mobility and social reorganization). Hangzhou: Zhejiang Renmin Press, 1995.

———. "Xinshengdai nongcun liudong renkou de shehui rentong yu chengxiang ronghe de guangxi" (Social identity of the new generation of rural migrants and merger of the urban and rural), *Shehui kexue yanjiu* (Sociological research), Beijing, 6.3 (May 2001), 63–74.

Wang, Deyi, et al., eds. *Xin hunyanfa beiti wenda* (One hundred Q & A's on the new marriage law). Beijing: Qunzhong Press, 2001.

Wang, Fang. "The Break of a Great Wall, Recent Changes in Household Registration System in China," in Thomas Sharping ed., *Floating Population and*

Migration in China: The Impact of Economic Reform. Hamburg: Institute of Asian Studies, 1998, 149–65.

Wang, Fei-Ling. "Reformed Migration Control and New List of the Targeted People: China's *Hukou* System in the 2000s," *The China Quarterly*, Mar. 2004, 115-132.

———. *From Family to Market: Labor Allocation in Contemporary China.* Lanham, MD: Rowman & Littlefield, 1998.

———. *Institutions and Institutional Change in China: Premodernity and Modernization,* London: Macmillan Press & St. Martin's Press, 1998.

Wang, Guangzhou, et al. "Beijiing liudong renkou zhiliu shijian ji yingxiang qiangdu fengxi" (Analysis of the duration and impact intensity of the migrant population in Beijing City), *Renkou yu jingji* (Population and economics), Beijing, no. 115 (Feb. 2000), 51–55.

Wang, Guichen, et al. *Zhongguo nongcun jingji xue* (Rural economics of China). Beijing: Renmin University Press, 1988.

Wang, Guixin. *Zhongguo renkou fenbu yu quyu jingji fazhan* (Population distribution and regional economic development in China). Shanghai: Huadong Normal University Press, 1997.

Wang, Gungwu. *The Chinese Overseas: From Earthbound China to the Quest for Autonomy.* Cambridge, MA: Harvard University Press, 2000.

Wang, Hongjun, ed. *Gongmin dao gongan jiguan banshi zhinan* (Guide to citizens' handling of various matters in the public security agencies). Beijing: Zhongguo Renmin Gongan Daxue Press, 1999.

Wang, Hong-Zen. "Ethnicized Social Mobility in Taiwan," *Modern China* 27.3 (July 2001), 328–58.

Wang, Huaian, et al., eds. *Zhonghua renmin gongheguo fali quanshu* (Complete collections of the laws of the People's Republic of China). Changchun: Jilin Renmin Press, 1989.

Wang, Jianmin, and Hu Qi. *Zhongguo liudong renkou* (Chinese migrant population). Shanghai: Shanghai Caijing University Press, 1996.

Wang, Ju, et al. "Beijing shi liudong renkou de zhuangkuan ji guanli" (The status and management of Beijing city's migrant population), *Renkou yu jingji* (Population and economics), Beijing, Mar. 1993, 38–42.

Wang, Jun. "Dushi lide cunzhuang" (Villages in the cities), *Tianya* (Frontier), Haikou, no. 1 (2001), 58–69.

Wang, Shaoguang. "The Construction of State Extractive Capacity: Wuhan, 1949–1953," *Modern China* 27.2 (Apr. 2001), 229–61.

Wang, Shida. "Jingdai zhongguo renkou de guji" (Estimate of China's population in the modern era), *Shehui kexue* (Social science), Beijing, 1.4 (1931) and 2.1 (1932).

Wang, Shihua. *Fujia yifang de huishang* (The super-rich merchants from Anhui). Hangzhou: Zhejiang Renmin Press, 1997.

Wang, Taiyuan. *Huzheng yu renkou guanli lilun yanjiu zhongshu* (Comprehensive summary of the theoretical study of the *hukou* system and population management). Beijing: Qunzhong Press, for law enforcement agencies only, 1997.

Wang, Tay-Sheng. *Legal Reform in Taiwan under Japanese Colonial Rule, 1895–1945: The Reception of Western Law*. Seattle: University of Washington Press, 2000.

Wang, Ya-Ping, and Alan Murie. *Housing Policy and Practice in China*. London: Macmillan, 1999.

Wang, Yongping. "Lun guangzhou chengjiao jiehebu de shehui zhian wenti" (On the public security issues in the near suburbs of Guangzhou), *Guangdong shehui kexue* (Guangdong social sciences), Guangzhou, no. 2 (1998), 139–44.

Wang, Yumin. *Zhongguo renkou shi* (Population history in China). Nanjing: Jiangsu Renmin Press, 1995.

Wang, Zhongfang, et al., eds. *1995 Zhongguo fali nianjian* (Legal yearbook of China, 1995). Beijing: Zhongguo Fali Nianjian Press, 1996.

Weber, Max: *Economy and Society*. Berkeley, CA: University of California Press, 1978.

Wei, Yehua. "Urban Policy, Economic Policy, and the Growth of Large Cities in China," *Habitat International* 18.4 (1994), 53–65.

Wen, Guanzhong. "Nianan de tudi zhidu" (The land system on the two sides of the straits) in Wen Guanzhong et al., *Taiwan Moshi* (Taiwan model). New York: Oriental News Corp., 1992.

Wen, Juntian. *Zhongguo baojia zhidu* (Chinese *baojia* system). Shanghai: Shangwu Press, 1935.

Wen, Tiejun. "Congxin jiedu woguo nongcun de zhidu bianqian" (Reunderstand the institutional changes in our country's countryside), *Tianya* (Frontier), no. 2 (2001), 18–25.

———. "Hukou zhidu gaige de lishi, xianzhuang yu weilai," in Ru Xin et al., eds. *Zhongguo shehui xingshi fenxi yu yuce* (Analysis and forecast of China's status quo and prospect). Beijing: Shehui Kexue Wenxian Press, 2003, 109–206.

Wertheimer, Richard F., II. *The Monetary Rewards of Migration within the U.S.* Washington, DC: Urban Institute, 1970.

West, Loriane A., and Yaohui Zhao, eds. *Rural Labor Flows in China*. Berkeley, CA: Institute of East Asian Studies, 2000.

Weyland, Kurt Gerhard. *Democracy without Equity: Failures of Reform in Brazil*. Pittsburgh: University of Pittsburgh Press, 1996.

White, Lynn T., III. *Careers in Shanghai*. Berkeley, CA: University of California Press, 1978.

———. *Policies of Chaos*. Princeton, NJ: Princeton University Press, 1989.

Whyte, Martin, and William Parish. *Urban Life in Contemporary China*. Chicago: University of Chicago Press, 1984.

Wilkinson, Thomas O. *The Urbanization of Japanese Labor: 1868–1955*. Amherst: University of Massachusetts Press, 1965.

Williamson, J. G. "Migration and Urbanization," in *Handbook of Development Economics*, vol. 1, ed. H. Chenery & T. N. Srinivasan. Amsterdam: North Holland, 1988, 425–65.

Williamson, Oliver E. *The Economic Institutions of Capitalism: Firms, Market, and Relational Contracting*. New York: Free Press, 1985.

———, and Scott E. Masten, eds. *The Economics of Transaction Costs*. New York: Elgar Publishing, 1999.

Wilson, Edward O. *On Human Nature*, Cambridge, MA: Harvard University Press, 1978.

Wittman, Donald. "The Size and Wealth of Nations," unpublished paper, Department of Economics, University of California, Santa Cruz, 2000.

Wohlmuth, Karl, et al., eds. *Good Governance and Economic Development*, vol. 2 of *African Development Perspectives Yearbook*. New Brunswick, NJ: Transaction Publishers, 1999.

Wong, Linda. "China's Urban Migration: The Public Policy Change," *Pacific Affairs* 67.3 (1994), 335–55.

Woodruff, A. M., and J. R. Brown, eds. *Land for Cities of Asia*. Hartford, CT: University of Hartford Press, 1971.

World Bank. *Country Data,* updated on the World Bank website at: www.worldbank.com/data/countrydata/countrydata.html, accessed 2001–4.

———. *Poverty and Human Development.* New York: Oxford University Press, 1982.

———. *World Development Report, 2000/2001.* Washington, DC: World Bank, 2000.

Wu, Caisheng, et al., eds. *Mianxian ershiyi shiji de xiao chengzhen jianshe* (Small town construction toward the twenty-first century). Beijing: Guojia Xingzheng College Press, 1999.

Wu, Changping, et al., eds. *Zhongguo jingji kaifaqu wailai renkou yanjiu* (Study on the nonnative population in the economic and technological development zones in China). Shanghai: Huadong Normal University Press, 1996.

Wu, Harry Xiaoying. "Rural to Urban Migration in the People's Republic of China," *The China Quarterly*, 1994, 668–96.

Wu, Li. "Zhongshi chengshihua guocheng zhong de renkou fengbu bianhua: yi shanghai weili" (Emphasize the changes in population distribution in the process of urbanization: the case of Shanghai), *Renkou yu jingji* (Population and economics), Beijing, no. 128 (May 2001), 39–42.

Wu, Pengsen. "Mingongchao dui zhongguo xibu diqu fazhan chaju de fumian yingxiang" (The negative impact of the tide of migrant peasant workers on the economic backwardness in the western regions), *Shehui* (Society), Shanghai, no. 7 (2001), 4–6.

Wu, Xiaoping. "Zaijing wailai renkou zinu jiaoyu wenti" (The issue of educating the children of outsiders in Beijing), *Beijing shehui kexue* (Social science of Beijing), no. 3 (2001), 146–49.

Wu, Yanrui. "Regional Disparities in Post-Reform China: Reviews and New Evidence," unpublished paper, East Asian Institute, Singapore, 1999.

Wu, Zhongmin, and Lin Juren. "Chengshi jumin de shehui liudong" (Social movement of urban residents), *Zhongguo shehui kexue* (Chinese social sciences), Beijing, no. 2 (1998), 71–81.

Xi, Guoguang, and Yu Lei, et al., eds. *Zhongguo renmin gongan shigao* (Draft history of the Chinese people's public security). Beijiing: Jingguan Jiaoyue Press, internal publication, 1997.

Xia, Jizhi, and Dang Xiaoji, eds. *Zhongguo de jiuye yu shiye* (Employment and unemployment in China). Beijing: Zhongguo Laodong Press, 1991.

Xia, Xueluan, et al. *Shequ zhaogu de lilun, zhengce yu shijian* (The theory, policy, and practice of community care). Beijing: Beijing University Press, 1996.

Xie, Ying. "Zhongguo xiangaishi xianxiang da toushi" (Perspectives on China's phenomenon of county-changed-to-cities), *Xinxi chuang* (Information window), Fuzhou, no. 1 (1996), 10–12.

Xu, Dong, and Ding Richang, eds. *Baojia shu jieyao* (Key selections of the books on the *baojia* system). Taipei: Chengwen Press, (1871) 1968.

Xu, Fongxian, and Wang Zhengzhong. "Jingti: Quyu fazhan chaju zhubu kuoda" (Warning: The regional gap of development is gradually enlarging), *Zhonghua gongshan shibao* (China business times), Beijing, Jan. 16 and 23, 1995.

Xu, Ming, ed. *Guanjian shike: dandai zhongguo jidai jieju de 27 ge wenti* (Crucial moment: the 27 issues that urgently need to be resolved). Beijing: Jingri Zhongguo Press, 1997.

Xu, Nailong. *Zanzhu renyuan xingwei zhinan* (Behavioral guide for temporary residents). Beijing: Qunzhong Press, 1992.

Xu, Yukun, et al. "Guangdong kongzhi liudong renkou jingyan" (Lessons from Guangdong's control of the migrant population), *Renmin gongan* (People's public security), Beijing, no. 10 (1995), 25–26.

Xue, Lan Rong, and Tainjian Shi. "Inequality in Chinese Education," *Journal of Contemporary China* 10.26 (Feb. 2001), 107–24.

Yan, Shanping. "Zhongguo jiushi niandai diqujian renkou qianyi de shitai jiqi jizhi" (Reality and mechanism of the cross-region migration in China in the 90s), *Shehuixue yanjiu* (Sociological research), Beijing, no. 2 (1998).

Yang, Dali L. *Beyond Beijing: Liberalization and the Regions in China*. London: Routledge, 1999.

Yang, Shoujian. *Zhongguo xueshu fuba pipan* (Critique of China's academic corruption). Tianjin: Tianjin Renmin Press, 2001.

Yang, Xiushi. "Household Registration, Economic Reform and Migration," *International Migration Review* 27 (Winter 1993), 796–820.

Yang, Ziwan. *Sannong wenti yu nongcun jingwu* (Three rural issues and rural policing). Beijing: Qunzhong Press, for MPS use only, 2003.

Yao, Weizhang, ed. *Gongan paichusuo zhifa xuzhi* (Rules on law enforcement by police stations). Beijing: Qunzhong Press, for MPS use only, 2003.

———. *Gongan zhifa zhong de gongmin quanli baohu* (Protection of citizen rights in law enforcement). Beijing: Zhongguo Renmin Gongan Daxue Press, for MPS use only, 2003.

Yao, Yang. "Shehui paiche he jingji qishi: dongbu nongcun diqu yimin de xian-zhuan diaocha" (Social exclusion and economic discrimination: an investigation of the situation of the migrants in the eastern rural areas), *Zhanlue yu guanli* (Strategy and management), no. 3 (2001), 32–42.

Yao, Yuan. "Zhongguo renkou de lishi bianqian ji pucha" (The historical changes and census of the Chinese population), *Beijing ribao* (Beijing daily), Nov. 13, 2000.

Ye, Wuji. "Woguo huzheng guanli zhidu gaige chutang" (Preliminary study of the reform of our nation's *hukou* management), *Gongan xuekan* (Journal on public security), Beijing, no. 6 (1996), 25–27.

Yin, Zhang. "Lun eryuan chengshi tixi ji chengxiang geju de quanmian gaige" (On the dual urban systems and overall reform of the urban-rural divide), *Shehuixue yanjiu* (Sociological studies), Beijing, no. 4 (1988), 92–100.

Ying, Songnian, ed. *Xinzhengfa yu xinzheng shusongfa cidian* (Dictionary of administrative laws and administrative lawsuits). Beijing: Zhongguo Zhengfa University Press, 1992.

Ying, Yong, and Zhou Changkang, eds. *Dangdai zhongguo xiaochengzheng shequ fanzui kongzhi* (Crime control in the communities of small cities and towns in contemporary China). Beijing: Zhongguo Fazhan Press, 1995.

Ying, Zhijing, and Yu Qihong. *Zhongguo huji zhidu gaige* (Reform of China's *hukou* system). Beijing: Zhongguo Zhengfa University Press, 1996.

Yu, Depeng. *Chengxiang shehui: cong geli zouxiang kaifang—zhongguo huji zhidu yu hujifa yanjiu* (Urban and rural societies: from separation to open—a study on China's *hukou* system and *hukou* laws). Jinan: Shangdong Renmin Press, 2002.

Yu, Depeng, et al. "Heli pinggu wailai renkou fanzui yingzhong chengdu ying zhuyi de jige wenti" (Several issues regarding a reasonable estimation of the crime rate among migrant people), *Zhejiang shehui kexue* (Zhejiang social sciences), Hangzhou, no. 1 (1998), 77–80.

Yu, Jing. "Qiantan hukou qianyi shengpi quanxian de xiafang" (Preliminary discussion on the delegation of the approving authority of *hukou* relocation), *Zhongguo renmin jingguan daxue xuebao* (Journal of the Chinese Police Officer University), Beijing, no. 1 (1991), 55–57.

Yu, Xiaoqiu, et al. *Beinian zhiguo fanglue* (Strategy of statecraft for one hundred years). Hangzhou: Zhejiang Renmin Press, 1994.

Zha, Ruichuan, et al., eds. *Zhonguo disici quanguo renkou pucha ziliao fengxi* (Analysis of the data from the fourth Chinese national census), 2 vols. Beijing: Higher Education Press, 1996.

———. *Zhongguo renkou dili* (Chinese demographic geography). Beijing: Shangwu Press, 1997.

Zhang, Jing. *Jicheng zhengquan: xiangcun zhidu zhu wenti* (Local governing: issues in the rural institutions). Hangzhou: Zhejiang Renmin Press, 2000.

Zhang, Kaiming, et al. *Shanghai liudong renkou* (Floating population in Shanghai). Shanghai: Zhongguo Tongji Press, 1989.

Zhang, Kevin Honglin, and Shunfeng Song. "Rural-Urban Migration and Urbanization in China: Evidence from Time-Series and Cross-Section Analyses," conference paper, Xiamen, 2001.

Zhang, Lutian. *Gaobie lixiang: renmin gongshe zhidu yanjiu* (Farewell to idealism: study of the people's commune system). Shanghai: Dongfang Press, 1998.

Zhang, Ping. "Shichang jingji de fazhan yu woguo huji zhidu de gaige" (The development of market economy and the reform of our nation's *hukou* system), *Renkou yu jingji* (Population and economics), Beijing, no. 118 (June 2000).

Zhang, Qingwu. *Huji guanli xue* (Study of *hukou* management). Beijing: Zhongguo Gongan Daxue Press, 1987.

———. *Hukou dengji changshi* (Common knowledge of *hukou* registration). Beijing: Fali Press, 1983. English edition, translated by Michael Dutton, *China's Household Registration System*. Armonk, NY: M. E. Sharpe, 1988.

———. "Lun nongye renkou yu feinongye renkou de xingcheng yu fazhan" (On the formation and development of agricultural and nonagricultural populations), *Zhongguo renkou kexue* (Chinese demographics), Beijing, no. 5 (1993).

———, and Yang Zihui. *Zhongguo lidai renkou yu huji* (China's population and *hukou* in past eras). Tianjin: Tianjin Jiaoyu Press, 1992.

Zhang, Shanyu, et al. *Renkou chuizhe fenbu guilu he zhongguo shanqu renkou heli zaifenbu yanjiu* (Study on vertical distribution of population and rational redistribution of population in mountainous areas). Shanghai: Huadong Normal University Press, 1996.

Zhang, Shenbin, et al., eds. *"Dayuejing" he sannian kunnan shiqi de zhongguo* (China during "Great Leap Forward" and three-year difficulty). Beijing: Zhongguo Shangye Press, 2001.

Zhang, Siqian, et al. *Zhongguo nongye fazhan zhanlue wenti yanjiu* (A study on the strategic issues in Chinese agricultural development). Beijing: Zhongguo Shehui Kexue Press, 1988.

Zhang, Tongji, et al. "Dui guyuanxian dazhanchang yimin diaozhuangxiang yimin ji huangjing yu fazhan wenti de kaocha bagao" (An investigative report on the wholesale relocation of Dazhanchang Township in Guyuan County and the related issue of environment and development), *Ningxia shehui kexue* (Ningxia social sciences), Yingchuan, no. 86 (Jan. 1998), 26–32.

Zhang, Xinbao. *Yingsi quan de fali baohu* (Legal protection of the right to privacy). Beijing: Qunzhong Press, 1998.

Zhang, Zhiliang, ed. *Kaifa fuping yu huanjing yimin* (Develop to relieve poverty and environmental relocation). Shanghai: Huadong Normal University Press, 1992.

Zhao, Wenlin, and Xie Shujun. *Zhongguo renkou shi* (Chinese population history). Beijing: Renmin Press, 1988.

Zhao, Yaohui. "Labor Migration and Returns to Rural Education in China," *American Journal of Agricultural Economics* 79.4 (1997), 1278–87.

———. "Labor Migration and Earnings Differences: The Case of Rural China," *Economic Development and Cultural Change* 47.4 (1999), 767–82.

Zheng, Hangsheng, and Li Qiang, et al. *Dandai zhongguo shehui jiegou he shehui guanxi yanjiu* (Study on the social structure and social relations in contemporary China). Beijing: Shoudu Normal University Press, 1997.

Zhong, Dajun. "Huji zhidu yu eryuan jiegou dui zhongguo nongcun de yingxiang" (*Hukou* system and dual structure and their impact on China's countryside), *Zhongguo guoqing guoli* (China's national conditions and strength), Beijing, no. 73 (Jan.), 1999.

———. "Huji zhidu shifou yi chengwei zhongguo shehui fazhan de zhuli" (Has the *hukou* system become the obstacle to China's social development?), *Zhongguo guoqing guoli* (China's national conditions and strength), Beijing, no. 98 (Feb.) 2001.

Zhonghua renmin gongheguo fali quanshu (Complete collection of laws and regulations of the PRC). Changchun: Jilin Renmin Press, multivolume, 1990–98.

Zhonghua renmin gongheguo gongan fali quanshu (Complete collection of laws and regulations on public security in the PRC), for public security agencies only, Changchun: Jilin Renmin Press, multivolume, 1990–98.

Zhonghua renmin gongheguo guowuyuan gongbao (PRC State Council Bulletin), Beijing, selected issues, 1995–2004.

Zhonghua renmin gongheguo quanguo renmin dabao dahui changwu weiyuanhui gongbao (PRC National People's Congress Standing Committee Bulletin), Beijing, selected issues, 1998–2004.

Zhonghua renmin gongheguo zuigao renmin fayuan gongbao (PRC Supreme People's Court Bulletin), Beijing, selected issues, 1995–2004.

Zhou, Daming, et al. "Chengxiang jihebu shequ de yanjiu" (Study on the urban-rural bordering areas), *Shehuixue Yanjiu* (Sociological studies), Beijing, no. 4 (2001), 99–108.

Zhou, Guoxiong, et al., eds. *Zhongxin chengqu jingwu lilun yu shijian* (Theory and practice of policing in urban centers). Beijing: Qunzhong Press, internal publication, 1995.

Zhou, Kate Xiao. *How the Farmers Changed China: Power of the People*. Boulder, CO: Westview, 1996.

Zhou, Liangtuo. "Shequ kongzhi yu nongcun shehui zhian" (Community control and public security in the countryside), *Zhongguo renmin jingguan daxue xuebao* (Journal of the Chinese Police Officer University), Beijing, no. 2 (1991), 46–49.

Zhou, Xiaohong. *Chuantong yu bianqian: Jiangzhe nongmin de shehui xinli* (Tradition and changes: social-psychology of the peasants in Jiangsu and Zhejiang). Beijing: Sanlian Press, 1998.

Zhou, Yi. "Zhongguo renkou liudong de xiangzhuan he duice" (The state and policy of China's population movement), *Shehuixue yanjiu* (Sociological research), Beijing, no. 3 (1998), 83–91.

Zhou, Yongliang. *Huaxia wenming yansheng zhimi* (The secrets of the longevity of Chinese civilization). Beijing: PLA Wenyi Press, 1995.

Zhou, Zhongyi. *Baojia yanjiu* (Study on the *baojia*). Shanghai: Duli Press, 1947.

Zhu, Baoshu. "Shanghai shi liuru renkou zhiliu taishi fengxi" (Analysis of the staying pattern of the migrant population in Shanghai City), *Renkou yu jingji* (Population and economics), Beijing, no. 102 (Mar. 1999), 38–45.

Zhu, Dexin. *Ershi shiji sansishi niandai henan jidong baojia zhidu yanjiu* (On the *baojia* system in North China in the 1930–40s). Beijing: Zhongguo Shehui Kexue Press, 1994.

Zhu, Jingde. "Zhongguo sanyuan laodongli shichang geju xia de xiang-cheng laodongli qianyi yanjiu" (A study on the rural-to-urban labor migration under China's three-dimensional labor market structure). Ph.D. diss., Nankai University, Tianjin, 1996.

Zhu, Nong. "Zhongguo siyuan jingji xiade renkou qianyi" (China's population movement under a four-dimensional economy), *Renkou yu jingji* (Population and economics), Beijing, no. 124 (Jan. 2001), 44–52.

Zhu, Nong, and Wang Bin, eds. *Changjiang diqu renkou wenti yu kechixu fazhan* (Changjiang region population problems and sustainable development). Wuhan: Wuhan Press, 1999.

Zhu, Qingfang. "Chengzheng pingkun renkou de tedian, pingkun yuanying he jiekun duice" (The characteristics, causes, and mitigating measure of urban poverty), *Shehui kexue yanjiu* (Social science studies), Chengdu, no. 1 (1998), 62–66.

Zweig, David. "China's Stalled 'Fifth Wave': Zhu Rongji's Reform Package of 1998–2000," *Asian* Survey 41, no. 2 (Mar.–Apr. 2001), 231–47.

———. *Freeing China's Farmers: Rural Restructuring in the Reform Era*. New York: M. E. Sharpe, 1997.

Index

In this index an "f" after a number indicates a separate reference on the next page, and an "ff" indicates separate references on the next two pages. A continuous discussion over two or more pages is indicated by a span of page numbers, e.g., "57–59." *Passim* is used for a cluster of references in close but not consecutive sequence.

academic corruption, 94, 230–31n35
Africa, 150, 157, 165, 169, 172, 236n13, 247n50
agrarian economy, 54–55, 119
Angola, 137
Anhui, 143f, 192, 213n91, 215n28, 222n26
Antivagrancy Laws of England, 152–53
Argentina, 18, 123, 237n37
Avarna, 164. *See also* untouchables

Bangalore, 166
baojia, 34–35, 39–43 *passim*, 86–87, 157, 214n9, 215nn33, 40, 216nn46, 47
baosongsheng (sure-admission student), 146
Barnet, Robert Warren, 213n98
Beijing city, 43f, 60, 66ff, 71, 79, 100–104 *passim*, 111, 223n1, 226n69; and *hukou* reform, 188–96 *passim*, 230n27; and migration quota/control, 81, 84, 90–95 *passim*; and regional gaps, 120–23, 128–32 *passim*, 137, 141–47 *passim*, 202, 222n26, 238n52, 242n110
Beijing University, 146, 222n26
Birth Planning Certificate, 75, 222n21
birth quota, 67, 71 222n21, 224n44
black kids (*hukou*-less children), 71, 224n44
blue-seal *hukou*, 50–51, 68–74 *passim*, 93,

99, 144, 190–93, 218n89, 224n46, 229nn23, 24, 230nn25, 28
Brahmans, 164–67 *passim*
Brazil, xiv, 18, 27f, 138, 151, 163, 168–78, 210n57, 238n38, 241n97, 244n1, 251–53; compared with India and China, 162, 169–71, 174–78
Campaign of Eliminating Counter-revolutionaries, 104
Campaign of Suppressing Counter-revolutionaries, 104
Cao Jinqing, 213n90
capital flight, 18, 122–23, 170
castes, 8, 12, 151, 164–69, 177, 249n85, 250; as a Type 1 institutional exclusion, 167–69, 177, 219n101; in other nations, 165, 250n91; scheduled, 165f, 250n95
Catholic Church, 169
CCP (Chinese Communist Party), 23, 27, 33, 41–46 *passim*, 50–65 *passim*, 84, 88, 95f, 99, 104ff, 112–15 *passim*, 148, 179–86 *passim*, 195–202 *passim*, 216n47, 255n30, 259n99; Central Committee, 116–17, 182; membership, 235n2
Central Military Commission, 66, 92
central planning economy, 33, 40, 56, 119, 161, 181f, 196, 212n85
cha hukou, see hukou verification/inspection